Errata for *Forms of Discovery*

p. 17, l. 10, huntsman

p. 22, l. 8, Commanded

p. 37, l. 4, see

p. 37, l. 13, *My lute, awake*

p. 42, l. 9, *They*

p. 52, l. 11, and

p. 52, l. 12, Geoffrey

p. 64, l. 29, Though

p. 69, l. 26, effectiveness

p. 70, l. 15, especially

p. 74, l. 8, given

p. 80, l. 7, deserts

p. 82, l. 14, beauties

p. 89, l. 1, *for* shall *read* will

p. 97, l. 16, Maker

p. 106, l. 20, *Salutation*

p. 116, l. 31, Dorset

p. 119, l. 35, though

p. 122, l. 29, centuries

p. 131, l. 28, unknown

p. 136, l. 7, *delete* are

p. 154, ll. 33-34, unconvinced

p. 167, l. 25, deserts

p. 172, l. 2, *for* gone *read* now

p. 172, l. 33, Byron

p. 177, l. 8, dost

p. 183, l. 22, mannerisms

p. 188, l. 8, matter

p. 212, l. 17, inanité

p. 239, l. 36, entitled

p. 255, l. 14, century

p. 255, l. 22, nineteenth

p. 257, ll. 16-17, remarkably

p. 258, l. 26, occasions

p. 263, l. 6, clusters

p. 263, l. 28, occurred

p. 264, l. 6, *for* columns *read* volumes

p. 276, l. 15, sink,

p. 276, l. 16, darkness,

p. 279, l. 2, intent.

p. 292, l. 9, *should be first line of final stanza*

p. 302, l. 1, is the projection of reason in which reason can only see its own

p. 302, l. 2, identity is such

p. 302, l. 6, alterations in its surface

p. 302, l. 14, This pool

p. 302, l. 17, On the unrippled

p. 302, l. 18, I see a willowed pool

p. 307, l. 29, These fools

p. 314, l. 15, entitled

p. 319, l. 25, but is not.[4]

p. 319, l. 32, for he did

p. 320, l. 30, successful

p. 333, l. 4, still."

p. 334, l. 32, Foster

p. 334, l. 32, professor of English

p. 347, l. 18, just as good

p. 354, l. 34, interest

p. 355, l. 9, well back in the nineteenth century. The translators were anthropologists, not poets; the anthologists culled the translations from the

p. 358, l. 24, volume

p. 358, l. 25, mannerism

p. 361, l. 17, Vol. VI, No. 4

p. 365, l. 14, *delete* Jr.

p. 371, ll. 1-5, *Three successive notes have been inadvertently numbered 4; they occur on pages 319, 320, and 327.*

p. 373, l. 34, account

p. 375, l. 33, 2nd col., Googe, Barnabe

p. 376, l. 5, 1st col., *delete* Jr.

Appreciation is extended to the following persons who helped compile this errata list: Philip Dacey, Kenneth Fields, Fred Robinson, Janet Winters.

FORMS OF DISCOVERY

*Critical and Historical Essays on the Forms
of the Short Poem in English*

BOOKS BY YVOR WINTERS

The Brink of Darkness
Collected Poems
The Early Poems of Yvor Winters
Forms of Discovery
In Defense of Reason
Uncollected Essays and Reviews, Francis Murphy, Editor

FORMS
OF
DISCOVERY

by
YVOR
WINTERS

Critical & Historical
Essays on the Forms
of the Short Poem
in English

THE **SWALLOW PRESS** INC.

CHICAGO

Published by
The Swallow Press Incorporated
811 West Junior Terrace
Chicago, Illinois 60613

This book is printed on recycled paper

LIBRARY OF CONGRESS CATALOG CARD NUMBER: 66-30433
ISBN 0-8040-0119-7

To D.L.W.

Prefatory Note

Somewhat more than a third of this book was written or put into its present form during the academic year of 1961-62 with the aid of a grant from the John Simon Guggenheim Memorial Foundation.

I am greatly indebted to Mr. Kenneth Fields, for his reading of my manuscript and for his suggestions, and for occasional help in research. He is one of the very few people whom I would have trusted to help me in this fashion; I was very fortunate to have him near at hand and willing to help.

When this book was set up in type, and while I was reading the galley proofs, Alan Swallow, my friend and publisher of twenty years, died suddenly; my debt to Mr. Swallow, and the debt of the best poets of this century whose work I know, is too great for brief acknowledgment. At my age one begins to be accustomed to the deaths of one's friends, but the shock of this death was very great.

Mr. Gus Blaisdell of the University of New Mexico Press and the New Mexico Quarterly, a friend of mine and of Mr. Swallow's of some years' standing, kindly offered to take up where Alan Swallow left off in seeing this book through the press.

Acknowledgments

The Introduction to this book and the essay on T. Sturge Moore in Chapter IV have appeared in The Southern Review, New Series. Large portions of the discussion of the poetry of the sixteenth century in Chapter I are repeated, more or less revised, from my old essay, *The 16th Century Lyric in England*, Poetry, 1939; the essays on Shakespeare's sonnets and the poems of Ben Jonson, which form a part of Chapter I, are reprinted unchanged from my essay *Poetic Styles, Old and New*, which appeared in *Four Poets on Poetry*, a volume edited by Don Cameron Allen (The Johns Hopkins University Press, 1959); a few paragraphs in my essay on Donne come from the same essay, and a paragraph or two from my essay on Stevens in Chapter V. The essay entitled *The Poetry of Charles Churchill* appeared originally in Poetry for April and May of 1961. The essay on Yeats in Chapter IV and the essay on Cunningham in Chapter VI appeared originally in Twentieth Century Literature and were later published as separate pamphlets by Alan Swallow: the essay on Yeats is slightly revised, the essay on Cunningham slightly revised and greatly shortened. The essay on Tuckerman in Chapter V appeared originally as a critical foreword to *The Complete Poems of Frederick Goddard Tuckerman*, edited by N. Scott Momaday (Oxford University Press, New York, 1965). This essay has been slightly revised and enlarged.

Contents

Introduction

LET ME BEGIN by saying that this book is not an attempt at a formal history of poetry in English. Any such attempt would be the work of a lifetime, and my life is nearly spent, and I have written other books. Nevertheless I have devoted my life to the study of poetry, mainly in English, rather extensively in French, and incidentally in a few other languages. I have taught English and American poetry for well over thirty years and have tried to understand what has happened, why it happened, and how to distinguish the better from the worse—have tried to understand this for my own improvement and for the improvement of my students.

This book will be a series of essays, essays both historical and critical, dealing with what seem to me the most important stages of our poetry considered as an art. The history of critical ideas, sometimes relevant to my business and sometimes not, has been treated by a fair number of able scholars such as Croll, Tuve, Cunningham, Abrams, and Trimpi, to mention only a few, and probably the best, of our century. I shall touch upon this material only as I am forced to do so. I shall have to confine myself as closely as possible to poetry as an art, a subject which is rarely treated and never at length.

I am not speaking of art for art's sake. My subject is the art of writing, or rather of a particular kind of writing, the art of saying something about something in verse. The term *art*, as I use it, signifies *method*. We speak of the "fine arts" and usually mean literature, painting, sculpture, and music, and sometimes architecture, and there are philosophers who believe that a comprehensive "aesthetic" philosophy can be discovered which will account for all of these in a single definition: the word to be defined is *Beauty*. These philosophers are deluded: the matter and the method of each of the arts are peculiar to that art itself. *Beauty* is merely a term denoting exceptional excellence of one kind or another, and it usually involves the idea of pleasing proportions. The proportions of a poem, like the proportions of musical composition, are rhythmical, for both compositions exist in time. I will let the musicologists speak for music; but if the proportions of a poem are "pleasing," they are pleasing because they further the intention of the poem: they contribute to the definition of the emotion to be conveyed, and this, in turn, is related to the matter with which the poem began. But more of this later.

The modern Catholic thinkers are the most stubbornly confused in this matter. Maritain is the worst sinner, but he has had many followers, and even Gilson has fallen into line in recent years. Some of them go so far as to say that such arts as poetry, painting, and the making of furniture are essentially similar. A moment's consideration of the idea of the *final cause*, the purpose for which an object is created, should be sufficient to disabuse them: a chair is created to provide repose for the human posterior, a poem to provide a certain kind of activity for the human mind; the two ends have nothing in common, in spite of the fact that we may employ both creations simultaneously. And what about the pleasing proportions of the chair? Pleasing to what? The aesthete will usually say to the eye, but there seems to be a problem here.

A poem says something in language about a human experience. The poet writes about human experience because there is no escape from it. And he writes in language because there is nothing else in which to write. And language is conceptual in nature. Most of the philosophers of this century have been nominalists of one kind or another; they have written extensively to prove that nothing can be said in words, because words are conceptual and do not correspond with reality. We are told also that our senses deceive us, and in some ways this is obviously true, for the physicists and the mathematicians have discovered realms of what appears to be reality beyond the apprehension of our senses. Yet they have employed language (even mathematics is a language) to approach this reality and they have employed their senses in reading their instruments. The realm which we perceive with our unaided senses, the realm which our ancestors took to be real, may be an illusion; but in that illusion we pass our daily lives, including our moral lives; the illusion is quite obviously governed by principles which it is dangerous, often fatal, to violate; this illusion is our reality. I will hereafter refer to it as reality.

But our perceptions of this reality are inseparable from our conceptions; I am not interested in which should be given priority, nor do I know—I am interested in the fact. I will illustrate with a vulgar example. For many years I bred and exhibited Airedale terriers, and for a period of perhaps eight years had some exceptionally beautiful[1] specimens. I prepared my own dogs for the ring and handled them in the ring, and in the course of this experience came to perceive Airedales with a precision which would surprise most of my readers. For the purposes of this discussion, I will assume that my reader has had no such experience. If he and I were to stand beside a ring where the Airedales were being judged, he would see merely a ring full of Airedales (if he were able to recognize the breed at all); I would see individual specimens, and after a reasonable time I would be able to discern the individuality of each. If the two of us were to repeat the experience a year later, and two or three of the same dogs were in the ring, I would be able to recognize them and he would not. In fact, I can call before my mind's eye clear images of fifteen or sixteen dogs that I have observed over the years and only in the ring, some of them more than fifty years ago, can recall most of their peculiar qualities of size, conformation, gait, temperament, and expression, and this ability is not uncommon among dog fanciers. In brief, my perceptions are sharper than my friend's; they are sharper because I know the relevant universals, those of the standard of the breed, and have used them professionally for many years to perfect my seeing. This kind of seeing involves no great effort on my part at the time; I merely see, my vision is clear instead of blurred. The breeders who devised the standard and created the breed, however, started with neither a perfect standard nor perfect specimens; they started with a general idea of what they wanted and with a multiplicity of variously crude specimens with which to begin their breeding. One improves one's understanding of the general by examining the particular; one improves the particular by referring it to the general. Precisely where or how this process began not even the most learned among us can say. This example will serve as a parable of our experience. The romantic lover of nature dislikes universals and can neither see nor describe nature; like Wordsworth, he sees nature in terms of clichés, which are the universals of the uneducated amateur; nature is a blur—he prefers to accept it with enthusiasm and *en masse*. To write about human experience with distinction, one must know the relevant universals; to manage poetic form with distinction or to perceive it clearly when managed by others, one must know the relevant universals.

Language, then, is essentially conceptual or denotative; and, since language was created by man in the course of his long effort to understand the reality of himself and his world, this fact regarding language would appear to indicate something of human nature and of general nature. If it indicates nothing else, it indicates the situation in which we live, from which there is no escape save self-destruction, and which we would do well to endeavor to understand. But conception and perception, denotation and connotation, are inseparable, for man is more than a merely rational animal; the signs for concepts acquire connotations, historical, emotional, or whatever; man lives and changes; but man has a memory, personal, historical, and racial, so that his changing is not absolute and should not be irresponsible. His changing may be growth, diminution, or disintegration, and the choice among these possibilities is his own.

The philosopher or the scientist endeavors as far as may be to employ only the denotative aspect of language; the poet employs the total content[2]. But language as a tool of denotation has had a history in the occident which has not, so far as I can discover, had a parallel elsewhere in the world. Plato and Aristotle undertook the exploration of language as a medium of precise thought; they had their Greek predecessors—Socrates and others earlier—but these two men appear to have given to western civilization its definitive character. Their work was continued with diminishing vigor in Athens until the closing of the philosophical schools in 529, and in Alexandria and elsewhere. But Rome had conquered the known world and Latin was becoming the universal language of the educated, and in fact had been the universal language in western Europe long before the closing of the schools. When Charlemagne established new schools throughout his empire in 787, Latin was naturally the language of the schools; the empire was extensive and it established Latin as the international language of the educated. From the ninth century to the end of the fourteenth, in particular, Latin was the language of theology, of logic, of rhetoric, and of metaphysics. Albert the Great was a German; Thomas Aquinas was an Italian; they met in Paris and conversed in Latin. This was a conjunction as momentous, perhaps, as the conjunction of Plato and Aristotle at an earlier date. But to say that the scholastics made Latin a tool for thought is imprecise: they made it rather a way of thinking, the life of the mind, each successive generation of heirs expanding and refining it a little further until it reached its finest form in the work of Aquinas. Much Greek thought had been known to the scholastics from an early date and was a major influence upon them. Nearly all of Aristotle became known to Albertus Magnus, the teacher of Aquinas.

With the rebirth of nationalistic ambitions in the Renaissance, there arose an interest in the vernaculars among men of letters; but men of letters had been educated in Latin, and some knew Greek, and they found their native tongues crude and inadequate. Then began the remaking of the modern languages. In the early sixteenth century in England, the problem was an obsession; Latinate terms were adopted by the hundreds, most of them to be dropped, many to remain; grammar and syntax were studied and refined; Latin was the rival and the teacher. Oddly enough, composition in verse became civilized far earlier than composition in prose. Chaucer was distinguished; after Chaucer there was a depression; but from Wyatt onward the style of poetry goes into one of its two greatest periods in English, a period which came to an end with the death of Dryden in 1700. Except for an occasional writer—Bacon, for example—prose is a crude instrument until near the end of the seventeenth century. The reasons for this discrepancy might be hard to assign. Metrical form, however, provided guidance to syntactic structure and variation; the more talented writers probably were ambitious to rival the great poets of antiquity; there may have been other reasons. Some of the best poets wrote prose, but most of them were no better in prose than were their unpoetical contemporaries. The poets of the Renaissance were the immediate heirs of what had been accomplished in the Middle Ages, not merely in the improvement of language itself but in the improvement of the knowledge of man—scholastic psychology was the guide to the understanding of experience, and even its technical terminology can be found everywhere in Renaissance poetry.

The mind of western man had been profoundly changed and enlarged by the Middle Ages. It seems unlikely that modern science would have been possible without these centuries of discipline in rigorous thinking; modern science, in any event, is an occidental creation. I am told, by those who should know, that the oriental languages have no such capacity for precise and complex abstraction; oriental philosophy is largely metaphorical and lends itself to multiple and somewhat vague interpretation; oriental poetry, so far as one can guess from the best translations, is simple in theme and associational in method. The creation of occidental language seems to me easily the greatest communal achievement in the history of man.

Two thousand years or so of expert work in the refinement of conceptual precision affected more than the merely conceptual. The concepts involved were those of metaphysics, psychology, ethics, and religion in all its aspects, that is, of the most profoundly human realms of our being. Since the concepts were of this nature, the words representing them, or many of these words, acquired connotations, emotional content, often of great intensity. That is, with increasing complexity and precision of our conceptual understanding, there came increasing complexity and precision in our emotions. This, of course, is most obviously true for those men with the greatest natural gift for apprehending and commanding language, but it is true to a large extent for most men. Western man has been profoundly altered by this experience.

I have been talking mainly about prose. Poetry is more complex than prose, but occidental poetry is composed in the language which I have described, by men whose lives are conducted in such language. A poem is a statement in language about a human experience; since language is conceptual in its nature, this statement will be more or less rational or at least apprehensible in rational terms, or else the medium will be violated and the poem weakened. But language has connotation as well as denotation, as I have said, for man is more than a merely rational animal. In so far as the rational statement is understandable and acceptable, and in so far as the feeling is properly motivated by the rational statement, the poem will be good. The rational and the emotional, denotation and connotation, exist simultaneously at every stage of the poem. But poetry is written in verse: verse is exceptionally rhythmical language and is usually metrical. Meter controls rhythm and renders rhythmical structure more precise, not merely in its general outlines but in its variations[a]. Rhythm is expressive of emotion, and the language of verse makes possible a more precise rendition of emotion, a more precise relationship of emotion to rational content, than would otherwise be possible. The use of versification introduces complexities into the management of grammar and syntax, and makes it possible to use them more emphatically or more subtly or both; and the new kinds of precision made possible (and therefore necessary) by versification enforce the need for greater precision of diction than one can hope to find in prose. When I speak of meter, rhythm, syntax, grammar, I am speaking of elements of language: these are not ornaments; they are not extraneous or imposed from without; they are as surely a part of language as words, and words have little value without them.

It would be false to say that the occidental mind created the languages of metaphysics, scholasticism, and modern science in order to express what it knew; it created these languages slowly, as ways of living and discovering. The languages were modes of being which were slowly enlarged to discover and embody an increasing extent of reality; they were forms of being and forms of discovery. It is in our language that we live the life of human beings, and only in our language; if you argue that the art of the painter or sculptor is free of language, you are wrong—a Phidias or a Rembrandt wholly unaware of linguistic culture is unimaginable—although the intellectual content of these arts is smaller and is somewhat vaguer in its nature than that of literature, a fact which probably accounts for the emergence and relatively high development of these arts in otherwise primitive civilizations.

The only important difference between a chimpanzee and a professor of English is that the professor has a greater command of language. The professor may think himself more handsome, but the chimp thinks otherwise, and the chimp is beyond argument the better athlete. The chimp, of course, would not admit the one kind of superiority which belongs to the professor, because he does not know what it is. The only important difference between the professor and a distinguished poet is that the poet has a greater command of language; but few professors will admit this difference, because almost none understand the nature of the difference—it is for this reason that nearly all are so feeble when they come to the defense of their profession. The scientist knows what he is doing; the professor of literature does not.

There is a feeling abroad at the present time that the complexity of poetic language hampers the poet; that he can free himself only by throwing away the language of civilization and writing "naturally." There is a question, however: "naturally" for whom? This dislike for the language of civilization might fairly be termed chimpism, or chimpolatry. The language of the chimp (he has one, of course) is natural to the chimp, and he likes it, but over the millenia he has accomplished very little with it. Let us leave him in peace; let us proceed with our own business.

The complexity of the poetic medium does not hamper the great poet. The great poet is like the great athlete in two respects: he must have a great natural talent, and the talent must be trained. The great poet resembles the great boxer in the ring. Joe Louis was trained by a great scholar, Jack Blackburn. He was taught every move and when to make it; he was born with the ability to make it instantaneously and with great precision. His knowledge did not bind him; it set him free—with the result that he seemed to move by instinct. So with the great poet.

I have compared the poet to the breeder of dogs and to the boxer, and the critic to the judge of both. The breeder of dogs and the boxer have very limited ends, however; the end, the purpose, of poetry is the understanding of the human condition, the understanding both rational and emotional, and this is the most important activity of the human mind. The talent of the great poet is far more rare than that of the dog-fancier or the boxer, and the training is far more arduous. But the great poet is not hampered by his medium; he is at home in it. It permits him to move more freely, more rapidly, and more precisely than he could without it.

Poetry is potentially (and actually, in certain poems) the most intellectual of the arts and the most difficult for the student. It is the finest medium that we have for the exploration and understanding of the complete human experience: the experience which we must understand if we are to survive individually or collectively. And the experience is not two-dimensional, is not the experience of a hypothetical immediate present; for we are the products of history, of our personal histories, of our family histories, of the history of our nation, and the history of the occident—and the anthropologists tell us that we are in some part the product of that which preceded history. Unless we understand the history which produced us, we are determined by that history; we may be determined in any event, but the understanding gives us a chance. The very subject matter of the poet calls for all of the intellectual equipment that the poet can muster; and language itself has a history and poetic forms have a history, and the poetic forms of language are the medium in which the poet lives and he had better know as much about them as possible.

I have now made clear, I hope, what I mean when I speak of poetry as an art. It has not always, however, been regarded or practiced as an art in this sense. The doctrine of associational psychology, as developed in the eighteenth century and as applied to literature in the eighteenth, nineteenth, and twentieth centuries, has led to versified revery and to versified confession (a form of revery), with the poet conceived as a more or less passive medium retreating farther and farther, from generation to generation, toward the unconscious mind. Wordsworth is an eminent example, about midway in a long and relaxing tradition toward chimpolatry; he was born with talent but was wholly without training, and he is notable mainly for a handful of fine lines and short passages and for his infinitely tedious pomposity and foolishness. Writers of this kind contribute little to the art of poetry, and I shall treat them very briefly. If my reader is offended by this neglect, let him write his own book. But let me suggest that he may be able to learn a good deal from mine.

When one writes a poem, one revises it; the practice is familiar to all of us. One revises the poem in order to make it better, to achieve in the poem a more nearly true understanding of what one is trying to say. The practice implies a belief in absolute truth; although many poets who write in this manner today would deny such a belief, there is no other justification for the practice. Many critics of my present book will disagree with my judgments of certain poems; they will believe that I am wrong and that they are right, and a good many will write bitterly on the subject. Some of these will be gentlemen who regard themselves as relativists, but a relativistic doctrine provides no justification for argument in these matters. Argument implies a belief that there is a basis for argument, a true judgment which both arguers are trying to reach.

But let us set my critics aside. The poet, for reasons which I have given, may be said to live most fully in his medium; it is his finest mode of thinking and perceiving, of being, of discovering reality and participating in reality. But when one speaks of discovering reality, one implies that the reality was there to be discovered, and I think that this implication is justified by our experience. In a sense, then, the mind is led. Not wholly, for this is not a matter of passive acceptance on the part of the poet. The poet must be born with ability and must train the ability; he must train every part of his mind. But the reality is there to be discovered at least in part; by reality, I mean the true nature of any subject with which the poet may deal. To participate in reality, even imperfectly, is to be to that extent alive.

The critic — that is, the intelligent reader — may enter this reality by way of the mind of the poet, in so far as his native talent and his training enable him to do so. If the poem in question is truly a fine poem, the critic may thus share for the time an intelligence which was on the occasion of writing the poem, in any event, greater than his own. And the human mind is so constituted that it is capable of growth; it can grow in this way. The poet, of course, is a critic, a reader of other poets, most of the time; it is through this activity that he improves his own art. Samuel Johnson once said that he did not care to converse with a man who had written more than he had read. Most of us will not care to read him. No man will write more than a small number of memorable poems; some of our finest specimens are single performances.

I trust that I have not given the impression that I believe the occidental mind to be progressing by way of poetry or even by way of language in general to some kind of universal perfection. I am pessimistic about the human race. Few men are born with sufficient intelligence to profit by more than a small part of the tradition available to them. The practical mind, the mind which conquers, rules, invents, manufactures, and sells, has dominated every civilization and ultimately has destroyed every state. The great philosopher, the great poet, the great painter or musician has almost always lived precariously on the fringe of the state, sometimes as the servant or dependent of the "great," sometimes in poverty, sometimes in the priesthood, in our times as one of the most contemned members of the academic profession. But he has created and preserved civilization, often while working in the rubble of a collapsing state. Alexander of Macedon conquered the known world, but any mark that he has left on later times would be hard to identify. Aristotle, his tutor and his father's servant, remains as one of the fundamental rocks on which our civilization is built.

This book is an effort to define what seem to me the most important forms that poetry has taken in modern English, that is, from about 1500 to our time. Five hundred years is a short period in the history of the world, but our poetry has been rich and much can be learned from it. I shall deal also, sometimes briefly and sometimes at length, with some of the most misguided efforts. I have dealt with certain poets at length elsewhere, and I will not repeat work already published but will refer to it in passing.

One final word of warning to the reader: this book is not a collection of unconnected essays; it is a coherent book and should be read from beginning to end — the reader who merely reads a chapter in the middle and a chapter at the end will not understand what he is reading.

If we can disengage ourselves sufficiently, then, from the pre-
conception that sixteenth-century poetry is essentially Petrarchist,
to sift the good poems, regardless of method, from the bad, we
shall see that the Petrarchist movement produced nothing worth
remembering before Sidney and Spenser, in spite of a large
amount of Petrarchan experimentation during the early period,
and that the pre-Sidneyan poetry which is worth remembering
belongs to a school which is in every respect antithetical to the
Petrarchist school. The early school, that of the native plain style,
received brilliant contributions from Wyatt, and Surrey is in
some measure a representative, but it flourished mainly between
Surrey and Sidney and in a few men who came to maturity somewhat later. It laid the groundwork for the greatest achievements
in the short poem in English, and it left us some of those achievements. It is largely neglected by the anthologists and historians
of the period[4].

The characteristics of the typical poem of the school are these:
a theme usually broad, simple, and obvious, even tending toward
the proverbial, but usually a theme of some importance, humanly
speaking; a feeling restrained to the minimum required by the
subject; a rhetoric restrained to a similar minimum, the poet being
interested in his rhetoric as a means of stating his matter as
economically as possible, and not, as are the Petrarchans, in the
pleasures of rhetoric for its own sake. There is also a strong
tendency toward aphoristic statement, many of the best poems
being composed wholly of aphorisms, or, if very short, being
composed as single aphorisms. The aphoristic lyric, like the
logical lyric, of which the aphoristic lyric is usually a sub-form, is
medieval in its origins, but certain poems by Wyatt, Gascoigne,
Raleigh, and Nashe probably represent the highest level to which
the mode has ever been brought. The aphoristic structure, however, is not invariable: *Gascoigne's Woodmanship*, for example,
is cast in the form of consecutive and elaborate exposition, and
so are many poems by Wyatt.

The wisdom of poetry of this kind lies not in the acceptance
of a truism, for anyone can accept a truism, at least formally, but
in the realization of the truth of the truism: the realization re-

sides in the feeling, the style. Only a master of style can deal in a plain manner with obvious matter: we are concerned with the kind of poetry which is perhaps the hardest to compose and the last to be recognized, a poetry not striking nor original as to subject, but merely true and universal, that is, in a sense, commonplace; not striking nor original in rhetorical procedure, but economical and efficient; a poetry which permits itself originality, that is, the breath of life, only in the most restrained subtleties of diction and of cadence, but which by virtue of those subtleties inspires its universals with their full value as experience.

The most obvious defect of the school is one which appears in varying degrees in the work of Gascoigne, Googe, and Turbervile, and in the work of many of their lesser contemporaries. It is a tone which appears to have in it almost an affectation of plainness, even of brusqueness. This tone is, however, or so I suspect, the result of the combination of certain traditional devices and limitations which were to be overcome in the last quarter of the century, and in the overcoming of which Sidney probably played a greater part than any other poet: the use of a heavily stopped line with a heavy cesura, the dependence upon heavily accented syllables in as many as possible of the accented positions, and, to clinch the whole effect, the excessive use of alliteration. This procedure is used with best effect by Gascoigne and Googe in some of their aphoristic pieces; it is often used as a pointless mannerism by Turbervile; Googe is less bound to it than Turbervile, and Gascoigne often departs from it widely.

II

WYATT'S POEMS FALL into four main groups: the early poems, many of them translations, in which his difficulty with the pentameter line is most evident; the main body of his work, of which I shall have the most to say; the three satires, written to John Poins and to Sir Francis Bryan; and the *Penitential Psalms*, with Wyatt's comments upon them. The first, third, and fourth groups are for the most part standard exercises. Wyatt never really overcame his difficulty with the pentameter line, although a few

4

short poems do not exhibit the difficulty and *They flee from me* appears to be an interesting experiment. I see no reason to believe that the rough pentameters in general were the result of any subtle theory of meter or rhythm. One can find the same difficulties, for example, in the early sonnets of Sidney and even in the *Holy Sonnets* of Donne. The difficulties are the result of ineptitude with a particular line, which at Wyatt's time had not really been mastered since Chaucer. Surrey discovered the principles of the line and handled the line correctly most of the time but somewhat obviously; Tottel revised some of Wyatt's poems in the light of Surrey's discoveries. Gascoigne, Googe, and Turbervile, a generation or so later, wrote the line correctly but heavily, as did Spenser. Sidney eventually learned how to write the line with distinguished rhythms.

Wyatt's worst meter can be seen in some of the early sonnets; for example, this line from Petrarch 109:

> And wills that my trust and lust's negligence.

The line has ten syllables, but no measure, no rhythm, and it does not improve when one puts it back in the context. The first and last lines of *Whoso list to hunt* are metrical curiosities, but are not impossible rhythmically. The first line appears to be a beheaded alexandrine in a pentameter poem. The last line appears to consist of an iamb, an anapest, an iamb, and two monosyllabic feet.

They flee from me is more complicated. Tottel revised it in accord with Surrey's metrics, and Quiller-Couch used Tottel's version in the first edition of the *Oxford Book of English Verse*. Wyatt's version appears to be that of the Egerton Manuscript; this is easily available, with modernized spelling, in the *Oxford Book of Sixteenth Century Verse*, and it is this version which I shall use. The second edition of the *Oxford Book of English Verse* gives us a compromise, and this I shall neglect.

> They flee from me, that sometime did me seek
> With naked foot, stalking in my chamber.
> I have seen them gentle, tame, and meek,
> That now are wild, and do not remember
> That sometime they put themselves in danger

To take bread at my hand; and now they range
Busily seeking with a continual change.

Thanked be fortune it hath been otherwise
Twenty times better; but once, in special,
In thin array, after a pleasant guise,
When her loose gown from her shoulders did fall,
And she me caught in her arms long and small,
Therewith all sweetly did me kiss
And softly said, 'Dear heart how like you this?'

It was no dream; I lay broad waking:
But all is turned, through my gentleness,
Into a strange fashion of forsaking;
And I have leave to go of her goodness,
And she also to use newfangleness.
But since that I so kindly am served,
I would fain know what she hath deserved.

Most of the problems of scansion in the poem can be solved if we recognize that the dissyllabic rime-words were regarded by Wyatt as trochees and not as words ending on extrametrical syllables, and furthermore that Wyatt sometimes employed a license practiced by Chaucer, that of omitting the unaccented syllable of an initial iamb. Let us consider the second line of the poem:

With ná/ked fóot/ stálking/ ín my/ chámber/.

Most of us today would mark the first syllable of *stalking* as a monosyllabic foot, the remainder of the line as iambic, and the last syllable as extrametrical, but Wyatt's practice in this poem is too consistent to permit this view: lines two, four, five, fifteen, seventeen, twenty, and twenty-one employ the final trochee in this fashion. In line three we have a monosyllabic foot in the first position, followed by iambs. We may have perfectly regular iambic lines, such as twelve and fourteen. Line five is trochaic throughout, and trochaic substitutions may occur in any position, not merely in the common first and third, but in the uncommon and emphatic second and fourth as well as in the fifth. Line thirteen is the only metrical departure from this procedure, for it contains only four feet, but the rhythm causes no trouble; the line is iambic. Line fifteen may seem to be another tetrameter, with an extrametrical ending, and it has the rhythmical effect of one, but it follows Wyatt's pattern:

It/ was nó/ dréam I/ láy broad/ wáking/.

Seventeen is less difficult but deserves marking:

Into/ a stránge/ fáshion/ óf for/sáking/.

The fourth line may seem difficult for some readers, but the difficulty is slight: the movement already established requires that the words *and do* be read as a light trochee; any other reading destroys the rhythm. There are only two lines in the poem which fail rhythmically, but the failure is miserable; they are the last two, and they follow the general rule but violate a principle which had been clearly indicated in the preceding lines: that the trochee in the last position must be immediately preceded by two other trochees.

But sínce/ that I/ so kínd/ly ám/ sérved/,
I would/ fain knów/ what shé/ háth de/sérved/.

Wyatt seems to have relied here on arithmetic alone, and without reliance on his ear. It is possible, of course, to read both of these lines as tetrameters, each with an anapest in the last position, and each with an extrametrical syllable, but this will not help the rhythm and seems little in agreement with what Wyatt has done before. I doubt that my scansion of this poem will throw much light on the other difficult passages in Wyatt.

The metrical variations are very sensitive in their relation to the subject. The first line is regularly iambic, and so are the first two feet of the second. The shift to trochees, beginning with *stalking*, however, gives us a pause and the feeling of hesitancy in the movement of the wild animals to which the women are now compared. The Chaucerian opening of the next line continues the effect of these trochees in spite of the fact that we have no trochees; the wavering trochee in the third position of the fourth line continues this effect, as does the unbroken series of trochees in the fifth line. The next line is slow, with a trochee in the second and emphatic position. The last line of this stanza is iambic

7

except for the trochee in the first and unemphatic position and the very light anapests in the fourth and fifth positions: the line gives us the effect of the light, quiet, rapid, and persistent movement of the animals. It seems unnecessary to analyze these effects further, but they appear perfectly successful until we arrive at the two final lines.

They flee from me and *Whoso list to hunt* are probably the most popular of Wyatt's poems in our time. The reason is obvious: both are nostalgic in tone, the first almost dream-like, and the meters are wavering; both are serious also, the first especially. *They flee from me*, in fact, is one of Wyatt's half-dozen best poems, and it deals with a very general version of a theme which is usually more particularized: the faithlessness of women. *My lute awake* deals with a somewhat more particularized version of the theme: the vanity and heartlessness of women. The theme is common, and most of the details are commonplace, but the sixth stanza exhibits extraordinary psychological insight:

> Perchance thee lie withered and old,
> The winter nights that are so cold,
>   Plaining in vain unto the moon;
> Thy wishes then dare not be told.
> Care then who list, for I have done.

The vigorous trochees in lines one and three of this stanza, each in the third position, are characteristic of Wyatt's use of the tetrameter line.

None of the poems which I have mentioned is really exemplary of Wyatt's major theme, however, and there are at least three poems which are better than any of them: *Blame not my lute, It was my choice,* and *Is it possible*. These, and many lesser poems, deal with Wyatt's dislike of the poetic style variously known as courtly, ornate, aureate, sugared, or Petrarchan, and with the corresponding form of making love—the courtly or affected way. Wyatt was a believer in the plain style in both activities. The relationship between these two activities is close and is not trivial. If poetry is, as I believe it to be, a form of moral judgment, then the poetic form, in regard to this matter, is merely a more refined and precise embodiment of the social form: poetry and morality

8

are one. Wyatt, if we may accept his explicit comments, believed in an honest and permanent love and in a style which would deal with such a love in an honest and plain way: he was a disciple of what was known in the sixteenth century as the plain style.

Blame not my lute is one of the finest examples of his central theme:

> Blame not my lute! for he must sound
>   Of these and that as liketh me;
> For lack of wit the lute is bound
>   To give such tunes as pleaseth me.
> Though my songs be somewhat strange
> And speaks such words as touch thy change,
>   Blame not my lute!
>
> My lute, alas! doth not offend,
>   Though that perforce he must agree
> To sound such tunes as I intend
>   To sing to them that heareth me;
> Then though my songs be somewhat plain,
> And toucheth some that use to feign,
>   Blame not my lute!
>
> My lute and strings may not deny,
>   But as I strike they must obey;
> Break not them then so wrongfully,
>   But wreak thyself some wiser way;
> And though the songs which I indite
> Do quit thy change with rightful spite,
>   Blame not my lute!
>
> Spite asketh spite, and changing change,
>   And falsed faith must needs be known;
> The fault so great, the case so strange,
>   Of right it must abroad be blown;
> Then since that by thine own desert
> My songs do tell how true thou art,
>   Blame not my lute!
>
> Blame but thyself that hast misdone
>   And well deserved to have blame;
> Change thou thy way, so evil begone,
>   And then my lute shall sound that same;

But if till then my fingers play
By thy desert their wonted way,
    Blame not my lute!

Farewell, unknown! for though thou break
  My strings in spite with great disdain,
Yet have I found out, for thy sake,
  Strings for to string my lute again.
And if, perchance, this silly rhyme
Do make thee blush at any time,
    Blame not my lute!

In the first stanza he says that his songs may be "somewhat strange" to the lady; in the second stanza we learn why—they are "somewhat plain." That is, they are in the plain or unaffected style which would be strange to the affected lady, and they also speak plain truths about herself which she may not like. There are no metrical problems here, or, I think, in any poems in the shorter lines. Line five of the first stanza has a monosyllabic foot in the first position; line three of the fifth stanza has a light and swift anapest in the last position; but these are effective and present no difficulty. There are a few trochees in the first position, but this is the commonest metrical variation in English verse. The rhythm of line, sentence and stanza is vigorous. The poem is devoid of imagery, and this fact is worth noting in the light of the prejudice of our time to the effect that a poem has imagery or nothing. The organization of the poem is closely rational, and the diction is distinguished and moving at every point. The subject is limited and the poem is not a great poem, but one finds little as well executed until one gets to Jonson and the later Greville.

I will quote one more poem for illustration of the characteristic method and theme:

It was my choice; it was no chance
That brought my heart in other's hold;
Whereby it hath had sufferance
Longer, perdie, than reason would.
Since I it bound where it was free
Methinks, y-wis, of right it should
    Accepted be.

Accepted be without refuse;
Unless that Fortune have the power
All right of love for to abuse.
For as they say one happy hour
May more prevail than right or might;
If Fortune then list for to lower,
        What 'vaileth right?

What 'vaileth right if this be true!
Then trust to chance, and go by guess;
Then who so loveth may well go sue
Uncertain hope for his redress.
Yet some would say assuredly
Thou mayst appeal for thy release
        To Fantasy.

To Fantasy pertains to choose.
All this I know: for Fantasy
First unto love did me induce;
But yet I know as steadfastly,
That if love have no faster knot,
So nice a choice slips suddenly;
        It lasteth not.

It lasteth not, that stands by change;
Fancy doth change; Fortune is frail;
Both these to please the way is strange.
Therefore methinks best to prevail,
There is no way that is so just
As truth to lead; the other fail
        And thereto trust.

The poem is curious and unreasonable in one respect: Wyatt
says in the first stanza that the lady ought rightly to accept him
because he chose her deliberately, but from her point of view
this argument might well seem arrogant. The early part of the
argument seems to have in it something of courtly ingenuity; but
once we are past this stage the moralizing is sound and impressive, and the writing is even more impressive than in the poem
previously quoted. The first line of the poem, for example, and
the second line of the third stanza have moral implications that
go beyond the limits of the theme; in fact the last three stanzas

have such implications. The meter shows Wyatt at his best: the strong trochees in the first and third positions of the first line and of the second line of the last stanza, in the third position of the sixth line of the second stanza and of the fourth line of the last stanza, and the anapest in the third position of the third line of the third stanza are all exceptionally effective.

I believe that I have mentioned or quoted the best of Wyatt's poems, but there is slighter work which is worth study, partly for the writing, partly for the understanding of Wyatt's central theme. I list the following: *I abide and abide, It may be good, Your looks so often cast, Disdain me not, Perdie I said it not, If thou wilt mighty be, I have sought long, And wilt thou leave me thus, Forget not yet, What should I say, Hate whom ye list, Sighs are my food, Madam withouten many words, Within my breast, It burneth yet alas, Speak thou and speed, Under this stone, All heavy minds, Comfort thyself, Tagus farewell, Lo what it is to love, Leave then to slander love,* and *Ah my heart what aileth thee.*

In connection with Wyatt one should mention his younger Scots contemporary, Alexander Scott (1520?-158-?). Scott often imitated Wyatt and sometimes translated him, but his most moving poem is neither an imitation nor a translation but an original work within the same tradition. It is called *The Lament of the Maister of Erskyn.* Of this poem, my editor, David Laing (1821) quotes as follows from Lord Hailes:

> It is probable that the person here meant was the Master of Erskine, killed at the battle of Pinkie-Cleugh. Knox says, p. 79: "In that same battle was slain the Master of Erskine, deirlie belovit of the Quein (Mary of Lorraine, Queen Dowager); for quhome sche maid gret lamentation, and bure his deythe mony dayis in mynd." This passage in Knox may lead us to conjecture what lady is here meant.[5]

Since the poem is not easily obtainable, I quote the whole of it:

> Departe, departe, depart / allace! I most departe
> Frome hir that hes my hart, / with hairt ful soir,

III

GEORGE GASCOIGNE (1542-1577) was born in the year of Wyatt's
death. A generation passes between the work of the two men, a
generation in which little happens in the development of poetry.
The pentameter line has become regular, sometimes to the point
of monotony. There is still a great deal of experimentation with
the Petrarchan forms. The old ornament of alliteration has been
recovered and exploited. But the plain style is the dominant
style so far as successful work is concerned. Gascoigne appears to
be the founder of a new school, although the influence of Wyatt
is still evident. Gascoigne is, I believe, one of the great masters
of the short poem in the century[7]. I base this opinion on the following poems: *The Lullaby of a Lover* (sometimes known as
Gascoigne's Lullaby)[8], *Gascoigne's De Profundis*, the second and
third of *Gascoigne's Memories*, *The Constancy of a Lover*, *Dan
Bartholmew's Dolorous Discourses* (from *Dan Bartholmew of
Bath*), *Gascoigne's Woodmanship*, and *In Praise of a Gentlewoman Who though She Was not Very Fair Yet Was She as Hard-
Favored as Might Be*. I am not sure that I have not overlooked
other valuable poems.

The third of the *Memories*, a poem on the subject of the
spendthrift, one which bears superficial resemblances to Wyatt's
poem addressed to Sir Francis Bryan but which is more pointed,
compact, and moving, is among the finest and displays on a large
scale the mastered hardness, the aphoristic analysis, to which I
have alluded. The tone is set in the opening and never falters:

> The common speech is, spend and God will send,
> But what sends he? a bottle and a bag,
> A staff, a wallet, and a woeful end,
> For such as list in bravery so to brag.
> Then, if thou covet coin enough to spend,
> Learn first to spare thy budget at the brink,
> So shall the bottom be the faster bound:
> But he that list with lavish hand to link,
> In like expense, a penny with a pound,
> May chance at last to sit aside and shrink
> His hare-brained head without Dame Dainty's door.

The most striking lines are probably those embodying the colloquial personification toward the middle:

> Yet he that yerks old angels out apace,
> And hath no new to purchase dignity,
> When orders fall, may chance to lack his grace,
> For haggard hawks mislike an empty hand:
> So stiffly some stick to the mercer's stall,
> Till suits of silk have sweat out all their land.
> So oft thy neighbors banquet in thy hall,
> Till Davy Debet in thy parlor stand,
> And bids thee welcome to thine own decay.

In Gascoigne's society the destruction of the patrimony was a major disaster and might well be irreparable; it was almost as serious as death or moral disintegration, both of which it might easily involve. Considered in this light, the poem becomes something more than practical didacticism; it becomes a piece of moral analysis. Davy Debet is not only debt, he is the bailiff, the new host, decay itself, and the moral judgment.

The Constancy of a Lover is an honest love poem and stands in contrast to most of the sonnets of the century. The first two lines of the sestet are remarkably fine:

> That happy hand which hardily did touch
> Thy tender body to my deep delight . . . .

In Praise of a Gentlewoman, although it is far too long, contains lines of a similar quality but of greater power. Of Cleopatra he says:

> And she, to quite his love, in spite of dreadful death,
> Enshrined with snakes within his tomb, did yield her parting breath.

And of his own lady, whom he compares to Cleopatra:

> If fortune favored him, then may that man rejoice,
> And think himself a happy man by hap of happy choice.
> Who loves and is beloved of one as good, as true,
> As kind as Cleopatra was, and yet more bright of hue,
> Her eyes as grey as glass, her teeth as white as milk,
> A ruddy lip, a dimpled chin, a skin as smooth as silk,
> A wight what could you more, that may content man's mind,
> And hath supplies for ev'ry want that any man can find,

> And may himself assure, when hence his life shall pass,
> She will be stung to death with snakes, as Cleopatra was.

Some of the mannerisms of the school are here, no doubt; above all, the irritating alliteration and playing on words, for example *a happy man by hap of happy choice.* But I cannot see that these are worse than Shakespeare's *when first your eye I eyed,* and the seriousness, passion, and power should be obvious.

Gascoigne's greatest poem is *Gascoigne's Woodmanship.* It is addressed to Lord Grey of Wilton, and the allegory takes the form of an apology for the author's bad marksmanship as a hunstman: it appears that he usually misses his deer or else kills by accident a doe carrying or nursing young and so unfit for food.

> My worthy Lord, I pray you wonder not,
> To see your woodman shoot so oft awry,
> Nor that he stands amazed like a sot,
> And lets the harmless deer unhurt go by.
> Or if he strike a doe which is but carrion,
> Laugh not, good Lord, but favor such a fault,
> Take will in worth, he fain would hit the barren,
> But though his heart be good, his hap is naught.

He explains this weakness as one aspect, merely, of his fatal tendency to failure; he has likewise shot at law, philosophy, and success as a courtier, and each time he has failed—he admits his own weakness as the sole cause of his failure in philosophy:

> For proof he bears the note of folly now
> Who shot sometimes to hit philosophy . . . .

With regard to the law and the court, he complains of his incapacity in the baser arts of succeeding, and his complaints have remarkable force. Then follows the sombre and moving passage in which he describes his next failure:

> But now behold what mark the man doth find,
> He shoots to be a soldier in his age,
> Mistrusting all the virtues of the mind,
> He trusts the power of his personage.

But he finds that he cannot free himself into the exercise of

17

unalloyed physical strength; he has no taste for injuring the innocent villager:

> He cannot spoil the simple sakeless man
> Which is content to feed him with his bread;

and neither has he a taste for the kind of corruption within the army by which officers are able to acquire wealth. There follows a general meditation upon all of his failures; it concludes with a brilliant passage in which the poem is returned to the allegory:

> Now when my mind doth mumble upon this,
> No wonder then although I pine for pain:
> And whiles mine eyes behold this mirror thus,
> The herd goeth by, and farewell gentle does.

Then follows the conclusion, the greatest passage in the poem, in which the subject is rehearsed and explained in terms of the allegory; in which the subject is explained in terms of Christian morality; in which the author is justified in so far as it comports with Christian humility that he should justify himself:

> But since my Muse can to my Lord rehearse
> What makes me miss, and why I do not shoot,
> Let me imagine in this worthless verse,
> If right before me at my standing's foot,
> There stood a doe, and I should strike her dead,
> And then she prove a carrion carcase too,
> What figure might I find within my head,
> To scuse the rage which ruled me so to do?
> Some might interpret by plain paraphrase
> That lack of skill or fortune led the chance,
> But I must otherwise expound the case.
> I say Jehovah did this doe advance,
> And made her bold to stand before me so,
> Till I had thrust mine arrow to her heart,
> That by the sudden of her overthrow,
> I might endeavor to amend my part,
> And turn my eyes that they no more behold
> Such guileful marks as seem more than they be:
> And though they glister outwardly like gold,
> Are inwardly but brass, as men may see:
> And when I see the milk hang in her teat,
> Methinks it saith, old babe now learn to suck,

Who in thy youth could never learn the feat
To hit the whites which live with all good luck.
Thus have I told my Lord (God grant in season)
A tedious tale in rime, but little reason.

The poem is one of a number of poems written in the century which deal with Christian pessimism, or disillusionment with the world, and is one of the best of them.

The best poems of Barnabe Googe (1540-1594) are the following: *Of Nicholas Grimald, To Dr. Balle, To Mistress A., To the Translation of Pallingenius, Of Mistress D.S., Of Money,* and *Coming Homeward out of Spain.* These are all very minor but very good, and they illustrate the qualities of the school which I have been trying to describe. The only collection by Googe which we have was published in 1563, early in the reign of Elizabeth, when Gascoigne was about twenty-one years old, and when Googe was about twenty-three. The poems are obviously exercises based on the rhetoric books, but some of them bring their subjects to life. *Of Money* is the most interesting in regard to its structure and in regard to later work:

Give money me, take friendship whoso list,
For friends are gone come once adversity,
When money yet remaineth safe in chest,
That quickly can thee bring from misery.
Fair face show friends, when riches do abound;
Come time of proof, farewell they must away.
Believe me well, they are not to be found
If God but send thee once a lowring day.
Gold never starts aside, but in distress,
Finds ways enough to ease thine heaviness.

The poem exhibits the even iambic pattern of the period, with heavy accents in the accented positions, light accents in the light positions, and heavy cesuras. But there is one form of variation: the use of the spondee. In the fifth line we have spondees in the first and second positions, in the sixth line a spondee in the first position, and in the ninth line a spondee in the first position. The first foot of the last line can be read as a spondee or as an iamb.

19

Googe employs spondees in this way in no other poem that I can recollect, but the spondees provide a vigorous variation on what would otherwise be a monotonous movement. Later in the century spondees are sometimes used with great skill. Without such variation the rhythm employed by Googe is effective only in very short pieces. One of the most charming is *Coming Homeward out of Spain*:

> O raging seas, and mighty Neptune's reign
> In monstrous hills that throwest thyself so high,
> That with thy floods dost beat the shores of Spain
> And break the cliffs that dare thy force envy,
> Cease now thy rage and lay thine ire aside,
> And thou that hast the governance of all,
> O mighty God, grant weather, wind, and tide,
> Till on my Country coast our anchor fall.

This poem and its very inferior companion-piece, *Going Toward Spain*, were obviously inspired by Wyatt's far better *Tagus Farewell*, but Googe at his best writes poems which are touching and honest exercises in a period of poetic depression.

George Turbervile (1540-1598) is one of the most minute of the stylists of the century: perhaps only Thomas Morley, the madrigalist, is more nearly infinitesimal, as he is likewise more polished. Among the best poems by Turbervile are these: *To the Roving Pirate, To One That Had Little Wit, To an Old Gentlewoman Who Painted Her Face*, and *That all Things Are as They Are Used. To One That Had Little Wit* raises pertness to artistry:

> I thee advise
> If thou be wise
> To keep thy wit
> Though it be small.
> 'Tis rare to get
> And far to fet —
> 'Twas ever yit
> Dear'st ware of all.

To an Old Gentlewoman combines a good deal of the same quality with pathos:

Leave off, good Beroe, now
   To sleek thy shrivelled skin,
For Hecube's face will never be
   As Helen's hue hath been.

Let Beauty go with youth,
   Renounce the glozing glass,
Take book in hand: that seemly rose
   Is woxen withred grass.

Remove thy Peacock's plumes
   Thou crank and curious dame:
To other trulls of tender years
   Resign the flag of fame.

Sir Walter Raleigh (1552-1618) may fairly be considered a later member of the School of Gascoigne. The first poem in *The Poems of Sir Walter Raleigh*, edited by Agnes M. C. Latham[6], is a poem in praise of *The Steele Glasse* by George Gascoigne. This poem appears also as one of the commendatory poems which introduce Gascoigne's poem, published in 1576; Raleigh would appear to have been acquainted with Gascoigne, who at this date was the most eminent English poet living. The two shared certain attitudes toward the world, attitudes of bitter disillusionment, which, though by no means limited to these two, are strikingly similar in both. The commendatory poem is in Gascoigne's manner, as are many later poems in the pentameter line. I quote the second stanza:

> Though sundry minds in sundry sort do deem,
> Yet worthiest wights yield praise for every pain,
> But envious brains do nought (or light) esteem
> Such stately steps as they cannot attain.
> For whoso reaps renown above the rest,
> With heaps of hate shall surely be oppressed.

His best poems are *The Lie, What is our life, Even such is time, The Passionate Man's Pilgrimage,* and *Walsinghame (As you came from the Holy Land),* if this last be indeed by Raleigh.

The Lie, apparently fairly early, is the best of these. Like *Gascoigne's Woodmanship* and like other poems of the period, it

21

is a catalog of the corruptions of the world; the subject was one to which Raleigh's mind and temperament made him acutely sensitive, and his personal experience did nothing to diminish the sensitivity. I have seen it argued in print that the poem was an ironic parody on the author himself, and that the word *blabbing* in the last stanza is conclusive evidence to this effect:

> So when thou hast, as I
> Comamnded thee, done blabbing,
> Although to give the lie
> Deserves no less than stabbing,
> Stab at thee he that will,
> No stab the soul can kill.

No theory could be farther from the truth. The poem is typical of the period and of Raleigh. Of the verb *blab* the *Shorter Oxford English Dictionary* gives these meanings among others: "To open one's mouth about; to reveal indiscreetly, 1583. To talk indiscreetly, to betray secrets, 1601." We have in these definitions the theme of the poem, and the theme is intended seriously. The poem is a defiant attack on corruption.

The Passionate Man's Pilgrimage appears to have been written while Raleigh was awaiting execution. The first four stanzas are excited, decorative, irregular in meter, and somewhat out of control; the fifth and sixth stanzas are a prayer for grace and an accusation of the world. The final stanza continues the prayer, and the fourth and fifth lines are among the most extraordinary of the century:

> And this is my eternal plea
> To him that made heaven, earth, and sea:
> Seeing my flesh must die so soon,
> And want a head to dine next noon,
> Just at the stroke when my veins start and spread,
> Set on my soul an everlasting head.
> Then am I ready, like a palmer fit,
> To tread those blest paths which before I writ.

"Just at the stroke when my veins start and spread!" It would be better at this moment not to think of Sidney and Spenser.

What is our life deals with a commonplace of the period, but the fifth, sixth, and last lines are works of genius, and the whole is well executed:

> What is our life? A play of passion,
> Our mirth the music of division.
> Our mothers' wombs the tiring-houses be,
> Where we are dressed for this short comedy.
> Heaven the judicious sharp spectator is,
> That sits and marks still who doth act amiss.
> Our graves that hide us from the searching sun
> Are like drawn curtains when the play is done.
> Thus march we, playing, to our latest rest,
> Only we die in earnest, that's no jest.

Raleigh's poems, in so far as we have them, all deal with commonplace themes of the period, but with themes that are important in terms of human life. His methods of writing are standard methods, but in the best poems and passages the writing is honest and sometimes brilliant. He is not a great poet, but he sometimes is close to greatness. He is a far more serious poet than Sidney or Spenser. He is less expert than Wyatt and has a more limited range. He is no more expert than Gascoigne, whose range and profundity are greater than his and probably greater than Wyatt's.

There are two memorable poems by Thomas Nashe (1567-1601): *Adieu, farewell earth's bliss* and *Autumn hath all the summer's fruitful treasure*. The first of these appears in every anthology of the period and has been often discussed; the second appears in *The Oxford Book of Sixteenth Century Verse* and doubtless elsewhere. The best discussion of the first of these with which I am acquainted is by J. V. Cunningham[10]. Cunningham demonstrates the logical structure of the poem, with the principle of repetition within each stanza. The poem deals with a standard theme, that of the vanity and transitoriness of human life; but the theme is intensified by the immediate presence of the plague. Each stanza save the next to the last employs familiar stereotypes but employs them brilliantly. The next to the last introduces the personal experience of Nashe and his dissolute but brilliant generation, and this stanza raises the poem above the talented commonplace of so many of the poems of the century:

> Wit with his wantonness
> Tasteth death's bitterness;
> Hell's executioner
> Hath no ears for to hear
> What vain art can reply.
> I am sick, I must die.
>   Lord, have mercy on us!

We have here plain and bitter truth in the plain style at its best.

The meter and the rhythm of the poem, however, contribute a great deal to its general effect; in fact as an exhibition of pure virtuosity the poem is one of the most remarkable performances of the century. The last line of each stanza is written in trochaic trimeter. The other lines are in iambic trimeter, with the substitution of trochees and spondees. There is no question about the trochees: they are obvious. Some of the feet which I am inclined to read as spondees may appear to be iambs or trochees:

> Bríghtness/fálls fróm/ the áir,
> Quéens have/ díed yóung/ and fáir . . . .

I have marked the second foot in each of these lines as a spondee. The first spondee can be read as a trochee without much wrenching; the second can be read as an iamb, but I think only with a good deal of wrenching. The next to the last line of each stanza contains an unmistakable spondee in the second position:

> Í am/ síck, Í/ must díe.

The following line contains an unmistakable spondee in the first position:

> Cóme! cóme! / the bélls/ do cry.

Any attempt to force this foot into a trochee or an iamb will merely render the line comical. Many of the doubtful lines are improved if read with spondees, and the use of the spondee in reading provides a very beautiful shifting between kinds of rhythm throughout the poem.

24

I will quote the second poem complete, since it is the less known:

Autumn hath all the summer's fruitful treasure;
Gone is our sport, fled is poor Croydon's pleasure.
Short days, sharp days, long nights come on apace,
Ah! who shall hide us from the winter's face?
Cold doth increase, the sickness will not cease,
And here we lie, God knows, with little ease.
From winter, plague, and pestilence, good Lord, deliver us!

London doth mourn, Lambeth is quite forlorn;
Trades cry, woe worth that ever they were born.
The want of term is town and city's harm;
Close chambers we do want, to keep us warm.
Long banished must we live from our friends;
This low-built house will bring us to our ends.
From winter, plague, and pestilence, good Lord, deliver us!

The poem is immediately a song from *Summer's Last Will and Testament* and has a bearing on the situation in the play, but the poem refers also to the situation of the law students who had apparently been removed from London to Croydon during the Michaelmas term ("The want of term") to avoid the pestilence. According to McKerrow and Wilson[11] "This low-built house" refers to the palace of the Archbishop of Canterbury at Croydon, which was built in a low and unwholesome spot. It seems to me at least possible, however, that Nashe may also have had in mind the inferior housing in London with which he was familiar: houses which were drafty, damp, and close to the ground, and infested with vermin. It was such housing that caused recurrences of the pestilence. We have here a poem in the plain style, dealing with the plain facts of life as Nashe knew them. Realistic detail of this kind is very rare in the century and is nowhere else so striking and effective.

The meter again is important in the history of the poetry of the century. The first line is simple and rapid, with a trochee in the first position, and then a series of iambs. The second line has a heavy trochee in the first position and another in the third, with a strong cesura. This prepares us for the three spondees and cesuras which open the third line. The fourth line is again rapid except for the slow trochee in the first position. The internal rime in the next line, and the heavy cesura render the line violent. The violence is abated somewhat in the sixth line, although the two cesuras in mid-line echo it. The second stanza contains similar effects: internal rimes in lines one and three, spondees in the first two positions of line two, in the first position of four and in the second position of six. Line five of this stanza is the most curious in the poem; I would scan it as follows:

> Long bán/ ishéd/ múst we/ líve from/ our fríends.

An alternative scansion would be the following, but I see no need for it; it indicates the rhythm more closely, but not the meter from which the rhythm is a departure:

> Long bán/ ished múst/ we líve/ fróm / our fríends.

Either way the line is a strange one, and either way we have a heavier stress on *from* than we would expect, but what has preceded prepares us for what occurs, and the line appears to be successful.

One should mention John Heywood (1535-1598), who contributed a few poems to *The Paradise of Dainty Devices*. He was a Jesuit and for much of his life an exile. His poetry is competent in execution; his moral ideas are commonplace but sometimes show penetration. He suffers from the fact that his morality is purely a morality of expediency—he expresses grief that the best laid plans go wrong; though a priest, he is worldly. His best poem, so far as I know him, is that beginning, *My friend if thou wilt credit me in ought*, an analytical poem strongly suggesting Gascoigne, but looser in texture.

IV

WYATT WAS AN isolated figure. In his command of language, meter, and matter, he far surpassed any of his contemporaries and any predecessor since Chaucer. His influence on Googe and Gascoigne is easily observable in a few poems, but it was an influence more of subject than of method, and it was not great. Nevertheless, Wyatt, Googe, Gascoigne, Raleigh and others were all practitioners of the plain style in most of their poems, and in a fairly pure form. The personal influence of Wyatt on such contemporaries as Vaux and Scott does not seem to have been great, in spite of the fact that Scott imitated and translated Wyatt on a few occasions. These men seem rather to have been mild precursors of Gascoigne. Gascoigne was the dominant figure of his time, and he influenced Raleigh as well as lesser men. He was a less finished stylist than Wyatt and was perhaps a shade less finished than was Raleigh in one or two poems, but he had a greater scope than either, and when the score is balanced he seems to me a somewhat more impressive figure than either. Nashe in his two memorable poems is far more complex in method than any poet whom I have discussed since Wyatt, but he remains essentially a brilliant exemplar of the early plain style, in spite of his dates.

The technical range of this school is narrow, but this is not in itself a defect; the defect, when it shows, is in a certain harshness and monotony. The defect appears in varying degrees in Gascoigne, Googe and Turbervile, and in their lesser contemporaries, and one can see a trace of it in much of Wyatt, even when he is not being troubled by the pentameter line. It does not appear strongly enough in the best poems to damage them seriously, however; Raleigh in his best work does not show it, and Nashe has gone far beyond it.

Morally these poets display a respectable range and acute perceptions. A limited technique, if it is mastered, may be capable of perception as fine and as varied as a more elaborate one in many hands. In fact, the elaboration of technique may be carried considerably beyond the point at which the elaboration has any immediate usefulness, and that is more or less the service which Spenser, and especially Sidney, performed for English letters and the disservice which they performed for themselves. They are concerned largely with the pleasures of rhetoric for its own sake. As a result Sidney and his colleagues communicate the joy of purely rhetorical invention, but they spin out small themes

27

to tenuity, for their sensitivity to language is greatly in excess of their moral intelligence. Spenser worked at the outlines of an elaborately decorative rhetoric, and so taught something to the dramatists and to Milton. Sidney perfected most of the lyrical graces, and worked out in detail the relationships between elaborate syntax (that is, the forms of reason) and a variety of beautiful stanzaic and linear structures: he thus became the schoolmaster of more than a century of poets, and his teachings can be seen in a degraded form as late as Swinburne. He introduced a mode of perception too complex for his own powers, and was often forced to seek matter in the precious and the trivial—a mode of perception too complex, indeed, for any save the greatest masters of the Renaissance, and which was not incapable of leading some of these masters frequently astray. In such poems as Ben Jonson's *To Heaven*, George Herbert's *Church Monuments*, or Edward Herbert's *Elegy over a Tomb*, we have the best qualities of the plain style combined with all that is valuable in the teachings of Sidney and perhaps in classical sources.

Throughout the last decade of the sixteenth century and throughout most of the seventeenth century—that is, until poetry begins to deteriorate for other reasons—we have the taint of decadence, of decoration, of means in excess of matter, frequently beguiling, sometimes appropriating most of the poem, sometimes scarcely discernible, but likely always to appear a little trivial if confronted with one of the tougher products of Wyatt, Gascoigne, or Raleigh. But during a hundred years, or nearly that, we find a few poets who are aware in some measure of the implications of all of this, both for good and for ill, and who in their best work profit to the utmost from their knowledge. The poems in which this intelligence appears represent the highest achievement in the history of the short poem in English until we reach great poetry of a very different kind in the late nineteenth century and in the twentieth. Sidney and Spenser, then, are poets of transition who modified a well-established tradition and who enabled their successors to improve that tradition. They are not the originators of English lyric poetry, as they have often been thought to be; they are inferior to their predecessors and to their successors equally.

V

THE PRINCIPAL MASTERS of the Petrarchan movement of the close of the century, if we exclude for a moment the poets of the song-books, are Sir Philip Sidney, Edmund Spenser, Samuel Daniel, Michael Drayton, Sir Fulke Greville (with regard mainly to his early work), and William Shakespeare. Greene, Peele, Lodge, Lily, and other lesser figures show the same influence, and there are many bad Petrarchan sonneteers who are of historical rather than of critical interest and who need not be mentioned.

The Petrarchan movement gained its first great impetus in the eighties with Sidney and Spenser, and it continued in part unaltered, in part somewhat altered, beyond the end of the century. In saying this, I am not thinking of the "Petrarchan sonnet," which represents a certain number of rime-patterns; I am thinking of a concept of poetic style. The Petrarchan movement, so conceived, and in so far as it may be said to exist in a fairly pure form, reaches its highest development in its first two masters, Spenser and (especially) Sidney. Spenser's greatest contribution to the movement is his *Epithalamion*, a poem too familiar to need quoting: the poem is long to the point of being diffuse, but the diffuseness is fresh, enthusiastic, and lovely; the poem is ornate, but the ornament sometimes has splendor; the poem lacks weight and intellectual concentration, and it has little of the moral grandeur, the grandeur of intellectual substance and of personal character to be found in Gascoigne and Raleigh. In this poem, however, Spenser handles the pentameter line with greater skill than elsewhere in his work; there is a better balance than elsewhere between subject and treatment. It is the only one of his poems that appears in any measure to justify his reputation.

The form that we commonly regard as most characteristic of the school is the sonnet. In style, Spenser's sonnets resemble *The Faerie Queene:* they are ornate, yet the metaphors are not realized in themselves with any vigor; and if there is much intellectual

29

significance it is offered in language so insipid that it cannot be said to live in the text. In metrical procedure, Spenser is midway between Gascoigne and Googe on the one hand, and Sidney on the other, and he lacks the virtues of either. His accents are less heavily stressed than are those of the earlier poets, and so lack a kind of hard vigor; they are less subtly varied than those of Sidney, and so lack perceptivity. He does not stress the cesura as heavily as do the early poets, yet it falls mostly after the fourth syllable, occasionally after the sixth, and more rarely elsewhere. His rhythm has a pedestrian—really, a pedantic—regularity, which lacks energy on the one hand and sophistication on the other.

The following sonnet by Sidney illustrates a good deal of the common Petrarchan quality:

> Highway, since you my chief Parnassus be,
> And that my Muse, to some ears not unsweet,
> Tempers her words to trampling horses' feet
> More oft than to a chamber melody,
> Now blessed you, bear onward blessed me
> To her, where I my heart, safe left, shall meet;
> My Muse and I must you of duty greet
> With thanks and wishes, wishing thankfully.
> Be you still fair, honored by public heed;
> By no encroachment wronged, nor time forgot;
> Nor blamed for blood, nor shamed for sinful deed;
> And that you know I envy you no lot
> Of highest wish, I wish you so much bliss,
> Hundreds of years you Stella's feet may kiss.

Sidney's rhythm is more skillful in a few other sonnets than here, yet even here it is very skillful. The cesuras fall as follows: in line one after a first and inverted foot (heavy cesura); in line two after the second foot (heavy); in line three after the second foot, but the cesura is light here, and the effect is further varied by the inversion of the first foot; in line four after the first foot (extremely light); in line five after the second foot (heavy) and in the middle of the fourth foot (light); in line six after the first, third, and fourth feet (all heavy); in line seven after the fourth foot (light); in line eight in the middle of the third foot (heavy); in line nine after the second foot (heavy), and the inversion of the third foot (if it was really so pronounced) results in a light cesura subsequent to it; in line ten after the third foot (heavy); in line eleven after the second foot (heavy) and after the third foot (light); in line twelve after the second foot (light); in line thirteen after the second foot (heavy); in line fourteen after the second foot (heavy) and after the fourth foot (light). The terms *heavy* and *light* are merely descriptive in a loose way and do not indicate the many degrees of variation. The management of the cesura alone constitutes something of a revolution.

In its substance, however, the poem is less admirable. The opening quatrain is not only graceful but is direct and forceful; but the second quatrain becomes progressively more whimsical, till it culminates in a trivial and stereotyped play upon words, introduced no doubt in the interests of elegance and perhaps in part for lack of something better to say. The quatrain of the sestet is a slightly precious prayer on behalf of the highway, the assumption that the highway is an interested listener and actor being purely decorative, and the couplet with which the sestet ends, a continuation of the prayer, enabling the poet to pay to his lady the formulary compliment of so many Petrarchan conclusions.

The poem might be paraphrased thus: Highway, since I write most often under your influence, I beg you to bear me to my lady; and, since you appear to be doing so, my Muse and I will thank you. May you never suffer infamy, and—as a final proof of my sincerity—may you kiss Stella's feet for hundreds of years. I do not offer this paraphrase as an equivalent of the poem (in this respect I am far more hesitant than that modern master of paraphrase, Mr. Cleanth Brooks); nor do I offer it in levity. The rational framework of a poem should bear inspection, and the framework of this poem is trivial and inconsecutive. The feeling achieves dignity mainly in the first quatrain, which, although it states a falsehood regarding Sidney's poetry, implies a truth regarding his life, but a truth which is irrelevant to the poem as a whole. The incoherence of thought and feeling is smoothed over by conventional technical methods.

Some of Sidney's sonnets are better than this. Yet this is generally and fairly regarded as one of the best, and in spite of gross faults it has vitality and is still charming to most of us. It should be observed, however, that Sidney is concerned here primarily with what he regards as a graceful manner, a polished surface; that his theme is trivial; and that his best poetry is irrelevant to his theme and a casual accident. Furthermore, in spite of what Sidney accomplished toward the sophistication of poetic style, many of the early sonnets, and a few later, are mechanically faulty to an extent that might have surprised even Wyatt. For example, there are obvious blunders in XVI, XXXVI, XXXVIII, XLIII, LXIII, and CII, blunders in the mere arithmetic of scansion. In general these faults diminish after the first forty-five or fifty sonnets.

The best sonnets in *Astrophel and Stella* are probably the following: *With how sad steps* (XXXI), *Come, Sleep! O Sleep!* (XXXIX), *Having this day my love, my hand, my lance* (XLI), *I never drank of Aganippe well* (LXXIV), *Highway, since you* (LXXXIV), *O Fate or Fault* (XCIII), *Ah bed! the field* (XCVIII), *When far spent night* (XCIX), and *Unhappy sight* (CV). Surpassing any of these are three sonnets which have the semblance of postscripts to *Astrophel and Stella* and which are sometimes attached to the sequence in popular collections; *Oft have I mused, Thou blind man's mark*, and *Leave me, O Love*. In the first of these three, as in some of Shakespeare's sonnets, the play upon words, superficially as trivial as in the sonnet from Sidney which I have quoted, is used more seriously: it is not the most dignified or efficient of methods, but the word *part* in each of its forms and compounds defines an aspect of the theme, and the repetition of the syllable emphasizes the definitions and distinctions. *Thou blind man's mark* and *Leave me O love* are on essentially the same theme, although the second poem carries it a little farther. They deal with the renunciation of worldly love in favor of heavenly love. They are the most serious of his sonnets, as we now employ the term sonnet (his songs, which he classed as sonnets, I shall discuss later and separately). They exhibit his mastery of rhythm and his command of the sentence in relation to line and stanza. But they also exhibit his incurable tendency to softness of diction.

I will consider the second and more famous:

> Leave me, O Love which reachest but to dust,
> And thou my mind aspire to higher things.
> Grow rich in that which never taketh rust:
> What ever fades, but fading pleasure brings.
>
> Draw in thy beams, and humble all thy might
> To that sweet yoke where lasting freedoms be,
> Which breaks the clouds and opens forth the light
> That doth both shine and give us sight to see.
>
> O take fast hold, let that light be thy guide
> In this small course which birth draws out to death,
> And think how evil becometh him to slide,
> Who seeketh heaven and comes of heavenly breath.
>
> Then farewell world, thy uttermost I see.
> Eternal Love, maintain thy life in me.

This is a rejection of the love which reaches but to dust in favor of divine love. The first stanza is composed mainly of the clichés of devotional literature—*reachest but to dust, aspire to higher things,* the entire third line and the fourth—but they are not obtrusive and are handled gracefully. *Draw in thy beams:* the reference here seems to be to the beams of light which are shot from the lady's eyes, or from Cupid's, in so many sonnets, and which are often compared to Cupid's arrows. Here the contrast is between these beams—the light of earthly love—and the light of heavenly love mentioned in line three of the second quatrain. It is a routine contrast, and gets whatever effectiveness it has from the technical grace of the quatrain. In the second line of the quatrain we have the yoke which gives freedom. "Humble all thy might to that sweet yoke": this seems to refer to the yoke of servitude, in other words to the Christian notion of surrendering life to gain life. But according to the *Shorter Oxford Dictionary* a yoke may be "a board or bar fixed transversely to the head of the rudder, and having two ropes attached for steering." One

33

would humble one's might to the first kind of yoke, but not to the second; on the other hand, one would take fast hold of the second and while doing so be guided by a light. Either way it is a dead metaphor, a metaphor which indicates a physical object purely for its abstract significance, but one does not know which dead metaphor, and the bare abstraction with no figurative vehicle would be preferable to either. *Breaks* and *opens* may be the singular forms which are now standard; but in this case *yoke* (the steering apparatus, presumably) is the antecedent of *which*. They may be examples of the common Renaissance plural, in which case *freedoms* is the antecedent of *which:* this reading seems to make more sense. *O take fast hold:* but of what? Of the steering gear? Of the yoke of servitude? And what does either mean? Presumably of your life, of truth, or of both, but we have another metaphor both dead and ambiguous. The remainder of the poem is stereotyped, but the rhythm of the third line of the third quatrain is fine: the anapest in the third position, a very light one, followed by the very lightly accented syllable of the subsequent iamb, makes the sliding perceptible, however subtly. The couplet is commonplace but honest. The subject is serious; the language is the small-change of Christian moralizing, but it is sincerely felt and gracefully arranged; the rhythm is beautiful. The poem is moving but essentially second-rate.

Michael Drayton is a Petrarchist who does not take naturally to the method. His rhythms, as compared to the best of Sidney, are, though correct, stiff and plain. In his search for decoration he often becomes grotesque, for he lacks Sidney's talent for charming triviality. In estimating these qualities we should remember that Drayton wrote, in his two fine patriotic odes, poetry as forthright as any of Gascoigne's, though on simpler subjects, and that nearly all of his best lines are in the plain style, in spite of the fact that they often appear in ornate settings. The three following passages will illustrate what I have said: in fact the first two of these are so similar to the lines which I have already quoted from Surrey that they might easily have come from the same hand:

34

> How happy are all other living things,
> Which though the day disjoin by several flight,
> The quiet evening yet together brings,
> And each returns unto his love at night.
> . . . .
> Since there's no help, come let us kiss and part.
> Nay, I have done; you get no more of me.
> . . . .
> Three sorts of serpents do resemble thee.

On the other hand, the conflict between the two qualities in Drayton sometimes produces a new quality. The laborious effort which Drayton expended to achieve the ornate sometimes resulted in great magnificence: one has not only splendor of language but heroic feeling, a feeling of great difficulties overcome; and, within certain passages, one has the economy which is born of difficulty. Consider two lines from the sonnet beginning *Cupid, dumb idol, peevish saint of love,* a poem in dispraise of Cupid and in its main outlines perfectly formulary:

> Thy bow, half-broke, is pieced with old desire;
> Her bow is Beauty with ten thousand strings . . . .

Having achieved such lines, however, Drayton characteristically mars them, for the sentence continues to the end of the quatrain:

> Of purest gold, tempered with virtue's fire,
> The least able to kill an host of kings.

The third and fourth lines are not bad in themselves, but, following the first and second are unnecessary and are comparatively weak. The concluding couplet may well be the greatest final couplet to be found in the Elizabethan sonnets, and its virtues are those of the plain style:

> With these she steals men's hearts for her relief;
> Yet happy he that's robbed of such a thief.

This is perhaps the best single poem by Drayton, but it is imperfect. His genius—a remarkable genius—shows itself in great lines and passages.

Drayton's best poems I take to be the following: the sonnets beginning *The glorious sun went blushing to his bed, Cupid dumb idol, Three sorts of serpent, Sweet, sleep so armed, To nothing fitter, You not alone, Dear why should you command me to my rest, How many paltry, foolish, painted things, Since there's no help, Stay, speedy time, Calling to mind since first my love began;* the two patriotic odes, on the Virginia voyage and on the battle of Agincourt; and *The Shepherd's Sirena.*

Of Samuel Daniel little need be said. His best poem is the sonnet beginning *Beauty, sweet love;* his best poems are all available in the standard anthologies and are well known. Like Sidney, he aims primarily at grace of expression; his tone is less exuberant than that of Sidney; his style is more consistently pure; he has less talent. His tone is one of polished melancholy.

VI

A FORM NEARLY as popular with the Petrarchan poets as the sonnet was the song—that is, the lyric written expressly to be set to music, written as if intended to be set, or capable of being set. England possessed fine musical composers before the age of Elizabeth, but most of the great English music was written during the twenty-five years or so that saw the rise and decline of Petrarchan poetry in England, and it is not surprising that most of the lyrics set to music in this period should be the products of the Petrarchan movement. Most of the songs of Sir Philip Sidney are written as if they were meant to be sung, and a fair number were actually set; but I am told that his songs are imperfectly adjusted to setting in two respects—they are too long to be sung and they are too closely organized to be cut. Of those composers who appear in the main to have set the lyrics of other men, John Dowland the lutanist is perhaps the most valuable collector of poems, as he is one of the greatest of composers, but many beautiful poems, most of them of unknown authorship, are to be found in the collections of other men. Of the composers who regularly wrote or appear to have written their own lyrics, the best poets are Campion and Morley. Of the poets, not composers, who wrote lyrics to be set, the best are Sidney and Shakespeare.

Thomas Morley, the gayest and one of the finest composers of madrigal music, and the most minute of all the masters of the English lyric, may be used to illustrate the song:

> Ladies, you seee time flieth,
> And beauty, too, it dieth.
> Then take your pleasure,
> While you have leisure.
> Nor be so dainty
> Of that which you have plenty.

This is a very concise and very graceful statement of well-established stereotypes; but the grace is extraordinary. The following poem from Morley is a comparable statement of a theme which one will find in Wyatt's *Awake my lute* and from there on through the seventeenth century. Morley is aware of the stereotypes: his grace provides an almost imperceptibly subtle and witty comment upon them:

> No, no, Nigella!
> Let who list prove thee,
> I cannot love thee.
> Have I deserved
> Thus to be served?
> Well then, content thee
> If thou repent thee.
>
> No, no, Nigella!
> In sign I spite thee,
> Lo, I requite thee.
> Henceforth complaining
> Thy love's disdaining,
> Sit, thy hands wringing,
> Whilst I go singing.

The poem is almost nothing, but it is very amusing.

The songs of Campion are at least equally fine in execution and are far more serious. The finest are probably *Now winter nights enlarge, Follow your saint*, and *When thou must home to shades of underground*, and of these the first is the best, as it is the most nearly in the tradition of the plain style:

37

Now winter nights enlarge
    The number of their hours,
And clouds their storms discharge
    Upon the airy towers.
Let now the chimneys blaze
    And cups o'erflow with wine;
Let well-tuned words amaze
    With harmony divine.
Now yellow waxen lights
    Shall wait on honey love,
While youthful revels, masques, and courtly sights
    Sleep's leaden spells remove.

This time doth well dispense
    With lovers' long discourse;
Much speech hath some defense,
    Though beauty no remorse.
All do not all things well;
    Some measures comely tread,
Some knotted riddles tell,
    Some poems smoothly read.
The summer hath his joys,
    And winter his delights;
Though love and all his pleasures are but toys,
    They shorten tedious nights.

The first two lines, if considered literally, make a simple statement about the increased length of the winter nights; but the firm stop at the end of the first line gives us the momentary illusion of a spatial image, as if the nights were expanding visibly. This may have been unintentional, but the next two lines appear so obviously to depend upon it and to reinforce it, that I am inclined to believe that Campion knew what he was doing. One should note the fusion, in images of light, of the fire, wine, and wax, the continuation of this in the word *honey* (although it is used metaphorically), and the way in which the spirits of the convivialists leap in the line subsequent to that in which the cups overflow. The word *amaze*, in relationship to its immediate context, means to fill with wonder, but in connection with the wine and the images of blurred light suggests a secondary meaning, to bewilder or confuse, and both seem intended. The second stanza moralizes the situation previously described, and ends with a gentle but convincing statement of disillusionment. The poem is so unpretentious as to be easily overlooked, but the subject is serious and the language is consistently brilliant[12].

The songs of Shakespeare are roughly similar to those already discussed: they show the combination of gaiety and pathos common to Elizabethan song; they often combine realistic detail, of more or less popular antecedents, with Petrarchan ornament and elaborate meter; they display, in fact, greater metrical virtuosity even than the songs of Campion. But in spite of their remarkable beauty, and in spite of the reflection of Shakespeare's reputation, it would be unjust to say that they are better than the best of Campion.

Sidney's best songs are probably the following: *Only joy, now here you are, O you that hear this voice, Who is it that this dark night, The Nightingale as soon as April bringeth, Who hath his fancy pleasëd, Ring out your bells, Doubt you to whom my Muse these notes intendeth, In a grove most rich of shade.* Sidney's best work was done in the form of song, and this list does not exhaust the fine poems. The songs almost always approach perfection of execution; the slighter songs display extraordinary wit and polish, and some of the more ambitious have considerable force both of feeling and of thought. But whereas the songs of Campion and of Shakespeare and of the lesser writers tend to be simple in structure (I am alluding now to the general plan, not to the meter), Sidney, like Wyatt before him, often employs elaborate expository frames, and he makes no discernible sacrifice in doing so. These frames are often expended on very slight subjects, but sometimes are dignified by serious subjects: he thus combines the graces of song with the close argument of the main tradition. Ben Jonson's debt to Sidney is very great; so is that of Donne; so is that of most of the seventeenth century. As late as the nineteenth century, we find Swinburne trying to imitate Sidney's methods of riming and Browning apparently modeling his best poem — *Serenade at the Villa* — upon Sidney's lyric *Who is it that this dark night.*

The innumerable anonymous songs of the period likewise

played an important part in refining English style, more than one song being notable for a single phrase or cadence, but so notable for that alone as to be unforgettable. No one will understand much of Jonson, Herrick, and Crashaw, for examples, who is not thoroughly familiar with the song-books and miscellanies. I would like to quote an anonymous piece from Dowland's second book of airs and from *England's Helicon*. Fellowes deduced an incorrect lineation from Dowland's musical setting. I offer the version in the miscellany:

Come away, come, sweet love,
The golden morning breaks;
All the earth, all the air,
Of love and pleasure speaks.
Teach thine arms then to embrace,
And sweet rosy lips to kiss:
And mix our souls in mutual bliss.
Eyes were made for beauty's grace,
Viewing, ruing, love's long pain:
Procured by beauty's rude disdain.

Come away, come, sweet love,
The golden morning wastes:
While the sun from his sphere
His fiery arrows casts,
Making all the shadows fly,
Playing, staying, in the grove;
To entertain the stealth of love.
Thither, sweet love, let us hie
Flying, dying, in desire:
Winged with sweet hope and heavenly fire.

Come away, come, sweet love,
Do not in vain adorn
Beauty's grace that should rise
Like to the naked morn.
Lilies on the river's side,
And fair Cyprian flowers new blown,
Desire no beauties but their own.
Ornament is nurse of pride,
Pleasure, measure, love's delight:
Haste, then, sweet love, our wished flight.

The subject of the poem is trivial. The poem lacks wholly the virtues of Gascoigne and Raleigh. But there is an elaboration of technical grace in this poem which is wanting in the early poets. One could get along with less elaboration in a serious poem, but the knowledge of the elaboration is valuable and leads to refinement of style.

I will quote two other poems from Dowland, poems which are more complex and more interesting. The first is famous, and can be found in Dowland's second book:

> Fine knacks for ladies, cheap, choice, brave and new!
>   Good pennyworths! but money cannot move.
> I keep a fair but for the fair to view;
>   A beggar may be liberal of love.
> Though all my wares be trash, the heart is true.
>
> Great gifts are guiles and look for gifts again;
>   My trifles come as treasures from the mind.
> It is a precious jewel to be plain;
>   Sometimes in shell the Orient's pearl we find.
> Of others take a sheaf, of me a grain.
>
> Within this pack, pins, points, laces, and gloves,
>   And divers toys fitting a country fair.
> But my heart lives where duty serves and loves,
>   Turtles and twins, court's brood, a heavenly pair.
> Happy the heart that thinks of no removes.

The meter is very brilliant. There are spondees in the first, second, sixth, seventh, eleventh, thirteenth, and fourteenth lines. The setting of the spondees is sometimes new and original. The first foot of the first line is a spondee, the second iambic, and the third is also iambic, but the cesura, reinforced by the comma, in the middle of the third foot, throws the accent onto *cheap* with unusual force, and *cheap* is then followed by a spondee consisting of two syllables which are likewise set off by commas, so that we have the illusion of a foot consisting of three accented syllables, or an English molossus. In the eleventh line, the heavily iambic foot is followed by the heavy spondee *pins, points*, which in turn is followed by the heavily inverted foot *laces*, with the result that we have four strong accents in sequence, though only one spondee.

The subject is also of interest: we have again a poem dealing with the relationship between the plain style in poetry and the plain style in love. The theme is summarized in the third line of the second stanza, but the whole poem deals explicitly with this theme. Intellectually the poem is simpler than the best of Wyatt; metrically and rhythmically it is more complex than any of Wyatt save *Thy flee from me,* and it is more successful than that.

My next poem may be found in Dowland's third book:

> Flow not so fast, ye fountains;
>   What needeth all this haste?
> Swell not above your mountains,
>   Nor spend your time in waste.
> Gentle springs, freshly your salt tears
> Must still fall dropping from their spheres.
>
> Weep they apace whom Reason
>   Or lingering Time can ease.
> My sorrow can no Season,
>   Nor aught besides, appease.
> Gentle springs freshly your salt tears
> Must still fall dropping from their spheres.
>
> Time can abate the terror
>   Of every common pain;
> But common grief is error,
>   True grief will still remain.
> Gentle springs freshly your salt tears
> Must still fall dropping from their spheres.

The elements of the poem are interesting. The first quatrain is pure ornament, and so is the refrain, which has the excuse, however, of being there for the musical setting. The second and third quatrains, although they are not great poetry, are very moving minor poetry written purely in the plain style.

I will quote one more song and comment upon it. This is xxvii-xxviii from *Songs and Psalmes,* by John Mundy, 1594:

In midst of woods or pleasant grove
  Where all sweet birds do sing,
Methought I heard so rare a sound
  Which made the heavens to ring.
The charm was good, the noise full sweet,
  Each bird did play his part;
And I admired to hear the same;
  Joy sprung into my heart.

The blackbird made the sweetest sound,
  Whose tunes did far excel,
Full pleasantly and most profound
  Was all things placed well.
Thy pretty tunes, mine own sweet bird,
  Done with so good a grace,
Extols thy name, prefers the same
  Abroad in every place.

Thy music grave, bedecked well
  With sundry points of skill,
Bewrays thy knowledge excellent
  Engrafted in thy will.
My tongue shall speak, my pen shall write,
  In praise of thee to tell.
The sweetest bird that ever was,
  In friendly sort, farewell.

This is in some respects a naïve performance as compared to the
songs from Dowland. In this connection, however, some readers
may need to be warned that the author of this poem is not ignorant of his verb-forms: in stanza two, *was, extols,* and *prefers* are
plural forms correctly used and common in the Renaissance. I
am interested mainly in what is said here. The poem comes from
a song-book and was originally published with its muscial setting.
Elizabethan music was complex; yet the ladies and gentlemen
present at any social gathering were expected to be proficient in
this music, to be able to sing a part if the books were passed out.
In brief, the birds in this poem are really ladies and gentlemen
exhibiting their skill in music and their love for it. An entire
theory of propriety in the arts is condensed into such phrases as
"the charm was *good*" (not marvelous or magical), "Each bird

did play his part," "full *pleasantly*," "placed *well*," "bedecked *well* with sundry points of *skill*," and "knowledge *excellent*." And in "thy knowledge excellent engrafted in thy will" we have the classical, medieval, and Renaissance theory of habit, a theory relevant to matters artistic and moral about equally, and still as sound a theory as it ever was. The poem is obviously a brief theoretical treatise on madrigal music, but it will serve just as well as an Elizabethan *ars poetica*. Shelley's *To a Skylark* is an *ars poetica* for a later period. Each poem gives an unmistakable account of the ideas of its period. The Elizabethan period, whatever its limitations (and it had real limitations), produced a fair amount of poetry which was great both in conception and in execution and produced a large body of beautifully executed minor poetry; the nineteenth century in England, until we approach its end, was a period in which major talents were shattered to fragments (a few of them interesting) and in which minor talents had no opportunity to show themselves.

VII

FULKE GREVILLE, Lord Brooke (1554-1628), the friend and biographer of Sidney, is a man whose early work in some ways resembles Drayton's, although it is far better. Furthermore, in his later work he became a greater poet in every way than any of the associates of his youth. It is my opinion that he should be ranked with Jonson as one of the two great masters of the short poem in the Renaissance. In addition, he is the main connection between the School of Gascoigne and the School of Sidney; and then again he is the main connection between the School of Sidney and the Schools of Donne and Jonson. He is thus a figure of considerable interest to the student of the history of method.

His epitaph on Sidney[13] is written in a measure common to the early school, and in a style very much like that of Gascoigne. Here are the final lines:

> Farewell to you, my hopes, my wonted waking dreams,
> Farewell, sometimes enjoyed joy; eclipsed are thy beams.
> Farewell, self-pleasing thoughts, which quietness brings forth:
> And farewell, friendship's sacred league, uniting minds of worth.

And farewell, merry heart, the gift of guiltless minds,
And all sports which for life's restore variety assigns;
Let all that sweet is void; in me no mirth may dwell.
Philip, the cause of all this woe, my life's content, farewell!

Now rhyme, the son of rage, which art no kin to skill,
And endless grief, which deads my life, yet knows not how to kill,
Go, seek that hapless tomb, which if ye hap to find,
Salute the stones, that keep the limbs, that held so good a mind.

In other early poems Greville is able to combine the Petrarchan
polish and bucolic wit of his friend with the realism of the earlier
Elizabethans:

> I, with whose colors Myra dressed her head,
> I, that ware posies of her own hand-making,
> I, that mine own name in the chimneys read
> By Myra finely wrought ere I was waking,
>   Must I look on, in hope time coming may
>   With change bring back my turn again to play?
>
> I, that on Sunday at the church-style found
> A garland sweet, with true-love knots in flowers,
> Which I to wear about my arm was bound,
> That each of us might know that all was ours;
>   Must I now lead an idle life in wishes,
>   And follow Cupid for his loaves and fishes?

The traces of Petrarchism are most obvious in Greville's love
poems, especially in the earlier love poems. These traces, moreover, are largely in the way of incidental decoration: Greville
does not construct his poems from pseudo-reasoning, for example,
as Sidney sometimes does. Like Sidney, but almost more consistently, Greville is preoccupied with the bearings on his love of
the Aristotelian faculties: reason, will, fancy, and sense. Among
the best of the early love poems are the following: *Love, the delight of all well-thinking minds, The world that all containes,
Love, of man's wandering thoughts, Cupid, thou naughtie boy,
I, with whose colors, Absence the noble truce,* and *Away with
these self-loving lads.* From this point, or near it, the poems tend
to become more sombre and to prepare the reader for the great
devotional, moral, and theological poems which close the series.

One can observe the beginnings of the change in the fine short poem *Cynthia, because your horns look divers ways,* and more obviously in the poem which follows it. This poem states that love is physical and no more and that he who is distracted by spiritual concerns is a fool:

All my senses, like Beacons flame,
Gave *Alarum* to desire
To take arms in *Cynthia's* name,
And set all my thoughts on fire:
Furies wit persuaded me,
Happy love was hazards heir,
Cupid did best shoot and see
In the night where smooth is fair;
Up I start believing well
To see if *Cynthia* were awake;
Wonders I saw, who can tell?
And thus unto my self I spake:
Sweet God *Cupid* where am I,
That by pale *Diana's* light:
Such rich beauties do espy,
As harm our senses with delight?
Am I borne up to the skies?
See where *Jove* and *Venus* shine,
Showing in her heavenly eyes
That desire is divine:
Look where lies the Milken way,
Way unto that dainty throne,
Where while all the Gods would play,
Vulcan thinks to dwell alone.
I gave reins to this conceit,
Hope went on the wheel of lust:
Thoughts take thought that go of trust,
Phansies scales are false of weight,
I stept forth to touch the sky,
I a God by *Cupid* dreams,
Cynthia who did naked lie
Runs away like silver streams;
Leaving hollow banks behind,
Who can neither forward move,
Nor if rivers be unkind,
Turn away or leave to love.
There stand I, like *Artick* pole,

46

Where *Sol* passeth o'er the *line,*
Mourning my benighted soul,
Which so loseth light divine.
There stand I like Men that preach
From their Execution place,
At their death content to teach
All the world with their disgrace:
He that lets his *Cynthia* lie,
Naked on a bed of play,
To say prayers ere she die,
Teacheth time to run away:
Let no love-desiring heart,
In the stars go seek his fate,
Love is only Nature's art,
Wonder hinders Love and Hate.
  None can well behold with eyes,
  But what underneath him lies.

The poem is, among other things, an attack on the courtly
concept of love and of love poetry; in the first thirty lines he employs the mythological ornament of the concept, but only to discredit it. The next lines give us the startling image of Cynthia (a
river) deserting her lover (the river-bed). Then the lover is the
arctic pole deserted by the divine light of the sun (that is, by
Cynthia). Then the lover is a convicted criminal confessing his
sins before execution. Are these figures ornamental? Perhaps they
are, in a measure, but if so they are among the best ornamental
figures in the period, and they certainly are not courtly. The last
ten lines are among the plainest in the plain tradition. The word
die in this last passage has the meaning which it often has in the
Renaissance: it refers to the orgasm; and the meaning of the
final couplet is double. It is curious that this poem has never
been picked up by the admirers of Donne's poems of disillusionment with love, for few — probably none — of Donne's love poems
equal it in power, and none are more disillusioned. The explanation probably lies in the fact that Donne's poems are more dramatic, as the current jargon goes: the disillusionment seems more
an outburst of momentary feeling, sometimes even for the sake
of the rhetorical effect. There is no such impression in this piece:
though the imagery is elaborate and even violent, the feeling is

cold, convinced, and even brutal; this is a poem in praise of the soulless body, and it means what it says. Once Greville had made this Calvinistic separation of the soul and the body, it is not remarkable that he should have revolted against his allegiance to the body and announced his allegiance to the soul.

After this there is less of love and more of the soul:

> You that seek what Life is in Death,
> Now find it air that once was breath.
> New names unknown, old names gone:
> Till time end bodies, but souls none.
>   *Reader!* then make time, while you be,
> But steps to your Eternity.

The meter of this poem is interesting. The form is iambic tetrameter, yet in the first line the first three feet are trochees; the second line is regular, but the accents and the cesura are heavy, and this fact, combined with the influence of the first line, results in an unusually slow and heavy movement; this movement is reëmphasized in the third line, in which the first and third feet are trochees and the fourth foot is monosyllabic. The fourth line is iambic until the last foot, which, if not a spondee, is very nearly one.

Following the poem which I have just quoted is a poem in poulter's measure which recalls Gascoigne:

> The Ship of Greece, the Streams and she be not the same
> They were, although Ship, Streams and she still bear
>   their antique name.
> The Wood which was, is worn, those waves are run away,
> Yet still a Ship, and still a Stream, still running to a Sea.
> She lov'd, and still she loves, but doth not still love me,
> To all except myself still is, as she was wont to be.

And following this is the farewell to Cupid, which marks the transition to the final group, a group composed mainly of poems devotional or moralistic:

> Farewell, sweet Boy, complain not of my truth;
> Thy Mother lov'd thee not with more devotion;
> For to thy Boy's play I gave all my youth,
> Young Master, I did hope for your promotion.

48

While some sought Honors, Princes' thoughts observing,
Many woo'd Fame, the child of pain and anguish,
Others judged inward good a chief deserving,
I in thy wanton Visions joy'd to languish.

I bow'd not to thy image for succession,
Nor bound thy bow to shoot reformed kindness,
Thy plays of hope and fear were my confession,
The spectacles to my life was thy blindness;
    But Cupid now farewell, I will go play me,
    With thoughts that please me less, and less betray me[14].

This poem is far more effective than Sidney's *Leave me, O Love*. On a casual reading, Sidney appears to be more serious, but he is spiritually indolent and his language is not controlled. The language in this poem is precise (and disillusioned).

Of the last poems, the best appear to be the following: *The Earth with thunder torn, Man, dream no more of curious mysteries, The Manichaeans did no idols make, Eternal Truth, almighty, infinite, Wrapt up, O Lord, in man's degeneration, Down in the depth of mine iniquity, In Night when colors all to black are cast, Man's youth, it is a field of large desires, O false and treacherous probability,* and *Syon lies waste.* These lines from *Man's youth* will give a fair idea of the power which Greville can obtain through concentrated generalization:

But States grow old, when Princes turn away
From Honor, to take pleasure for their ends;
For that a large is, this a narrow way,
That wins a world, and this a few dark friends . . .

The greatest single poem in Greville is this:

Down in the depth of mine iniquity,
That ugly center of infernal spirits;
Where each sin feels her own deformity,
In these peculiar torments she inherits,
    Depriv'd of human graces, and divine,
    Even there appears this *saving God* of mine.

And in this fatal mirror of transgression,
Shows man as fruit of his degeneration
The error's ugly infinite impression,

Which bears the faithless down to desperation;
  Depriv'd of human graces, and divine,
  Even there appears this *saving God* of mine.

In power and truth, Almighty and eternal,
Which on the sin reflects strange desolation,
With glory scourging all the Sprites infernal,
And uncreated hell with unprivation;
  Depriv'd of human graces, not divine,
  Even there appears this *saving God* of mine.

For on this sp'ritual Cross condemned lying
To pains infernal by eternal doom,
I see my Savior for the same sins dying,
And from that hell I fear'd, to free me, come;
  Depriv'd of human graces, not divine,
  Thus hath his death rais'd up this soul of mine.

The word *depriv'd*, by modern standards, is a dangling participle, for it modifies the understood pronoun *I*, which does not appear until we reach the last stanza, and then in a position which does not justify the modification. This construction, however, was common among learned writers well into the eighteenth century, and among novelists in the nineteenth century and perhaps later. "This fatal mirror of transgression" is God (see *Syon lies waste*); the subject of *shows* is *impression*. The remarkable inversion of construction in the first four lines of the second stanza is not due to awkwardness; rather, it enables Greville to place the details in the order of increasing importance.

The poem is theological in its inspiration and language. It gives us a Calvinistic version of the dark night of the soul, in which the poet sees himself in his own personal hell, which resembles the Hell to come unless the protagonist is rescued by Grace. The theme is as follows: God is perfect being, and all creatures are in one way or another imperfect — that is, they suffer from privation; privation is damnation; punishment consists in part in the realization of one's own imperfection, and punishment is thus in each case peculiar to the sin; Hell is a condition, not a place, and, since the condition consists of privation or non-being, it is uncreated; and damnation in the fullest sense consists in the realization on the part of the damned of their removal from God (that is, from perfect being or "unprivation"). The poem is Calvinistic in its exclusive emphasis on Divine Grace as a means to salvation.

The modern reader may be inclined to regard these theological concepts as obsolete, as having become through the passage of time merely meaningless abstractions. But they are founded in observable reality; they are psychological as well as theological. Sin and evil, so conceived, are real in purely psychological terms, and the punishment is as terrible as it is inevitable:

> Where each sin feels her own deformity
> In these peculiar torments she inherits.

The precise grasp of the abstractions enables the poet to state his theme with economy; and the grandeur of the language is wholly the product of the grandeur of the theme, and is not imposed from without, as it sometimes appears to be in Milton and in Crashaw.

Greville's later poems are written with a polish equal in its way to that of Sidney's best songs and superior to that of his sonnets. They are replete with thought; they are profound in feeling; and there is almost never any graceful exhibitionism. His weakness is a tendency to use the hendecasyllabic line, with a heavy cesura, too consistently, so that one feels a certain monotony in proceeding from poem to poem; yet within any given poem the medium is used with subtlety and power. Greville was one of the first poets to endeavor with some consistency to employ the Petrarchan refinements, or such of them as he needed, on matter worthy of them. His *Caelica* is a remarkable collection in another respect: in spite of the fact that he appears to have set out in emulation of Sidney, to have discovered more or less by the way that his talent was of a different and more serious kind, and to have changed his interests from the theme of love to more serious themes, nevertheless his collection covers an unusually wide range of human experience and has the effect more of a book than of a casual collection. Some of the poems are faulty, but almost none are trivial or otherwise bad; most of the poems are impressive; many are magnificent. He gives us a great mind in a book which is compact, profound, and comprehensive.

Of himself Greville wrote in his life of Sidney: "For my own part I found my creeping genius more fixed upon the images of life, than the images of wit, and therefore chose not to write to them on whose foot the black ox had not already trod, as the proverb is, but to those only that are weather-beaten in the sea of this world, such as having lost sight of their gardens and groves, study to sail on a right course among rocks and quicksands." M. W. Croll, in quoting this passage[15] points to the difference between Sidney nad Greville, although neither Croll nor Greville's recent editor, Geoffry Bullough, seems to understand how great a poet Greville is. Among other things Croll says: "By trying to make his words tally exactly with actual experience he succeeded in giving to single lines, and sometimes to longer passages, in absolutely simple words, a peculiar power which is unlike anything in the poets with whom he was personally associated. It is different in kind rather than in degree from the fanciful eloquence of Sidney . . . . The best parallel . . . is to be found in the works of John Donne." He might have added the more striking parallel of Gascoigne and the still more striking parallel of Ben Jonson. And one can object to this passage on another count. Greville's words are frequently far from simple: there is a greater density of intellectual content in his work than in the work of any other poet of the Renaissance; but the words are chosen for their accuracy, and so may give the illusion of simplicity. It is in this concern for his matter and in the corresponding indifference to his own personality that he differs equally from Sidney and from Donne.

VIII

THERE ARE FEW of the sonnets of Shakespeare (1564-1616) which do not show traces of genius of an unusually beguiling kind; and in a fair number we have more than traces. Yet in the past ten years or so I have found them more and more disappointing[16]. In the first place there is in a large number of the poems an attitude of servile weakness on the part of the poet in the face of the person addressed; this attitude is commonly so marked as to render a sympathetic approach to the subject all but impossible, in spite of any fragmentary brilliance which may be exhibited. It will not do to reply that this is a convention of the courtly style and should not be taken seriously. If it is a convention of the courtly style, then it is a weakness in that style. But it is not an invariable quality of the courtly poets, it occurs very seldom in poets of the plain style, and Shakespeare seems to mean it seriously. In the second place, Shakespeare seldom takes the sonnet form with any real seriousness. The sonnets are almost invariably conceived in very simple terms and are developed through simple repetition or antithesis, so that they never achieve the closely organized treatment of the subject which we find in the best of Jonson and Donne. This weakness is often aggravated by the fact that Shakespeare frequently poses his problem and then solves it by an evasion or an irrelevant cliché: this is more or less the method of the courtly style at its weakest, but the element of genius which goes into many of these sonnets raises one's expectations to the point that one cannot take this sort of triviality with good grace. In the third place, Shakespeare often allows his sensitivity to the connotative power of language to blind him to the necessity for sharp denotation, with the result that a line or passage or even a whole poem may disappear behind a veil of uncertainty: in this last weakness he is even farther from his major contemporaries than in any of the others. I shall endeavor to illustrate these weaknesses as they occur in poems which I shall discuss.

I will begin with LXVI:

> Tir'd with all these, for restful death I cry
> As to behold desert a beggar born,
> And needy nothing trimm'd in jollity,
> And purest faith unhappily forsworn,
> And gilded honor shamefully misplac'd,
> And maiden virtue rudely strumpeted,
> And right perfection wrongfully disgrac'd,
> And strength by limping sway disabled,
> And art made tongue-tied by authority,

53

And folly — doctor-like — controlling skill,
And simple truth miscalled simplicity,
And captive good attending captain ill:
    Tir'd with all these, from these I would be gone,
    Save that, to die, I leave my love alone.

This is one of a number of Elizabethan poems dealing with dis-illusionment with the world. Others are *Gascoigne's Woodman-ship, The Lie* by Raleigh, and *False world, goodnight,* by Ben Jonson. But whereas Gascoigne, Raleigh, and Jonson offer the best solution that they can, Raleigh with righteous defiance, Gascoigne and Jonson with a combination of scorn for corruption and Christian acceptance of the individual fate, Shakespeare (like Arnold after him in *Dover Beach*) turns aside from the issues he has raised to a kind of despairing sentimentality, and the effect is one of weakness, poetic and personal. The same thing occurs in many sonnets: for examples XXIX *(When in disgrace with for-tune and men's eyes)* and XXX *(When to the sessions of sweet silent thought).* I do not wish to deny the many felicities in these poems, for they are real; but the poems do not rise to the occa-sions which they invoke. The poem which I have just quoted would be a fine example of the plain style, except for the couplet, which represents sentimental degeneration of the courtly rhe-toric.

It would be easy to make a list of inept phrases from the son-nets. The clichés, for example, are numerous and well-known, and so are the bad plays on words ("When first your eye I eyed"). But most poets sin in this fashion much of the time, or in some comparable fashion. There is another kind of weak phrasing in Shakespeare, however, which is prevalent in his work and more serious than the cliché or the bad pun; it is characteristic of later ages rather than his own, and it sets him apart from his great con-temporaries. This is his use of words for some vague connotative value, with little regard for exact denotation. An interesting ex-ample occurs in CXVI:

    Let me not to the marriage of true minds
    Admit impediments. Love is not love
    Which alters when it alteration finds,

Or bends with the remover to remove:
O no! it is an ever-fixed mark,
That looks on tempests and is never shaken;
It is the star to every wandering bark,
Whose worth's unknown, although his height be taken.
Love's not Time's fool, though rosy lips and cheeks
Within his bending sickle's compass come;
Love alters not with his brief hours and weeks,
But bears it out even to the edge of doom.
   If this be error, and upon me proved,
. I never writ, nor no man ever loved.

The difficulty here resides in the word *worth*. The fixed star, which guides the mariner, is compared to true love, which guides the lover. The mariner, by taking the height of the star, can estimate his position at sea, despite the fact that he knows nothing of the star's "worth." Worth, with reference to the star, probably means astrological influence, though it might mean something else. The lover, by fixing his mind on the concept of true love, similarly can guide himself in his personal life. But what does *worth*, as distinct from *height*, mean in this second connection? For the lover can scarcely guide himself by a concept of true love, he can scarcely indeed have a concept of true love, unless he has some idea of the worth of true love. The comparison blurs at this point, and with it the meaning. One may perhaps push the astrological influence here and say that the lover, although he has a general knowledge of the nature and virtue (if virtue can be separated from worth) of true love, yet does not know precisely the effect upon him that true love will have. But this will not do: he obviously knows something of the effect, for the rest of the poem says that he does. There is simply no such separation between the two functions of true love as there is between the two functions of the star, yet the comparison is made in such a way as to indicate a separation.

This kind of thing does not occur in Greville or Donne or Jonson. Even in the more ornate Sidney — for example in the clumsy figurative language of *Leave me, O love* — it is usually possible to follow the thought even though the figure may be mishandled. But here one loses the thought. Greville, in *Down*

55

in the depth, employs the language of theology; Donne employs the language of astrology (and other technical language) in the *Valediction of my Name in a Window.* Nothing is lost by this precision, but on the contrary there is a gain, for the emotion cannot have force when its nature and origin are obscure. Shakespeare contents himself here with a vague feeling of the mysterious and the supernatural, and the feeling is very vague indeed.

The sonnet is characteristic in other respects. The successive quatrains do not really develop the theme; each restates it. This makes, perhaps, for easy absorption on the part of the more or less quiescent reader, but it makes also for a somewhat simple and uninteresting poetry. The sonnet form is short, and the great poet should endeavor to use it more efficiently, to say as much as can be said of his subject within its limits; such efficiency is never characteristic of Shakespeare. Lines nine and ten are clichés, which are barely rescued by an habitual grace, and the concluding couplet is a mere tag, which has no dignity or purpose in relationship to the sonnet or within itself. Yet the first four lines have precision, dignity, and simplicity, which are very moving, and the twelfth line has subdued grandeur, due in part to the heavy inversion of the third foot and to the heavy anapest and iamb following. The high reputation of the sonnet is due about equally, I suspect, to its virtues and its faults.

One of the most perplexing of the sonnets is CVIII:

> Not mine own fears, nor the prophetic soul
> Of the wide world, dreaming on things to come,
> Can yet the lease of my true love control,
> Suppos'd as forfeit to a confin'd doom.
> The mortal moon hath her eclipse endur'd,
> And the sad augurs mock their own presage;
> Incertainties now crown themselves assur'd,
> And peace proclaims olives of endless age.
> Now with the drops of this most balmy time
> My love looks fresh, and death to me subscribes,
> Since, spite of him, I'll live in this poor rime,
> While he insults o'er dull and speechless tribes:
>   And thou in this shalt find thy monument
>   When tyrants' crests and tombs of brass are spent.

The sonnet has given rise to a great deal of scholarly speculation, most of which the reader can find summarized in Rollins's variorum edition of the sonnets. One of the commonest interpretations is that which identifies the mortal moon with Elizabeth and the eclipse with her death. The friend, then, is Southhampton, who was released from prison upon the accession of James, and lines six, seven, eight, nine, and ten refer to the general fears that there would be civil disorder upon the death of Elizabeth and to the fact that James was nevertheless crowned with no disorder. The interpretation is fairly plausible, though by no means certain; but it involves two difficulties which, I think, have never been met. The tone of the poem is scarcely explained by this interpretation: the tone is sombre and mysterious, as if supernatural forces were under consideration — this tone is most obvious in the first quatrain, but it persists throughout. Furthermore, in line eleven we have a monstrous non-sequitur, for there is not the remotest connection between Southhampton's release from prison or the events leading up to it and Shakespeare's making himself and Southhampton immortal in verse. To this objection the reader may reply that the concluding lines are merely in a Petrarchan convention and should not be taken too seriously. They may represent such a convention, but they have to be taken seriously, for the tone of seriousness and mystery, the magnificence of the language, are such that we are not prepared for triviality at this point. If this interpretation (or I think any other in the variorum editions) is accepted, then the poem stands as one of the most striking examples of Shakespeare's inability to control his language, of his tendency to indulge vague emotion with no respect for meaning. And the poem may, in fact, be such an example.

Leslie Hotson, however, has come forward with another theory[17]. He believes that the mortal moon (mortal: deadly, death-dealing) is the Spanish Armada, of which the line of battle was moon-shaped, and which attacked England and was defeated in 1588, a year of which there had been dire predictions for generations, some of the prophets having thought it the year in which the world would end. Hotson is an irritating writer, as everybody who has read him carefully must know. But whatever objections one may have to Hotson's theory, there is no denying the fact that he documents it fully and impressively. Furthermore—and this is a point which Hotson fails to mention—this interpretation explains the mysterious tone of the poem (for in these terms we are dealing literally with supernatural forces, as well as with the most terrifying of natural forces), and it eliminates the non-sequitur (for the lives of both the poet and the friend had been threatened, and both have survived). Hotson's theory clarifies the poem at every point, in spite of the conventional elements in the poem and the obscurely allusive manner of writing.

One can make certain obvious objections to Hotson's theory. For example, Hotson claims that the entire sequence was done by 1588; this in spite of the facts that Shakespeare repeatedly refers to himself as an aging man and that there are many parallels in phrasing between the sonnets and the later plays. Furthermore, Hotson bases this claim on the explication of only one sonnet other than the sonnet just discussed. But in favor of Hotson's view would be the very weaknesses which I have been describing—weaknesses which might well be those of a young man —although Hotson appears to be unaware of them. However, these weaknesses might easily be those of an older man, more at home in the dramatic form, writing carelessly for a private audience, and working in a style which in the course of his mature life became obsolete. Even with Hotson's explanation, however, or with another as good, the poem is faulty. No poem is wholly self-contained, but most poems work within frames of reference which are widely understood. This poem appears to have a very particular frame of reference, about which it will always be impossible to be sure. The poem is almost all connotation, with almost no denotation; it is almost purely vehicle, with almost no tenor; it is almost wholly ornament, with almost nothing to which the ornament can be attached. It would be easy to say that such a poem is a kind of forerunner of some of the deliberately obscure work of the past hundred years; but this work is all based on closely related theories—those of Mallarmé or of Pound, for examples—and Shakespeare had no such theories. Shakespeare's ideas about the nature of poetry were those of his age, but he was often unable to write in accordance with them. Such a poem as this must have been the result of inadvertence.

Whatever the faults of the sonnets as wholes, their incidental beauties are numerous. These beauties are often of the most elusive kind, and they are probably felt by many readers without ever being identified. Consider, for example, line six of Sonnet **XIX:**

> And do whate'er thou wilt, swift-footed Time.

There is a plaintive desperation in the line which it is impossible to describe but which any sensitive reader can feel. In what is being said there is a stereotyped but real and timeless fear, and this is expressed in part by the helplessness of the imperative and in part by the archaic cliché *swift-footed*. It is expressed also in the emphases of the rhythmical pattern: the first three feet are all heavily accented, but each succeeding foot more heavily than the one preceding, so that we reach a climax on *wilt*, followed by the long pause of the comma, the pause in turn followed by a foot lighter and more evenly stressed, and this by a very heavily stressed foot. This is not an original line nor a great one; it is derivative and minor—but it is moving.

More obvious are the moral perceptions in the second quatrain of XXIX:

> When in disgrace with fortune and men's eyes
> I all alone beweep my outcast state,
> And trouble deaf heaven with my bootless cries,
> And look upon myself, and curse my fate,
> Wishing me like to one more rich in hope,
> Featur'd like him, like him with friends possess'd,
> Desiring this man's art, and that man's scope,
> With what I most enjoy contented least;
> Yet in these thoughts myself almost despising,
> Haply I think on thee, — and then my state,
> Like to the lark at break of day arising
> From sullen earth, sings hymns at heaven's gate;
>   For thy sweet love remember'd such wealth brings
>   That then I scorn to change my state with kings.

The first quatrain of this sonnet is a passable example of what the French would call *la poésie larmoyante;* it is facile melancholy at its worst. And yet the next four lines are precise and admirable; they are a fine example of the plain style. In the third quatrain we have the lark which has made the sonnet famous. The lark is an ornament, in the same way as Donne's compasses. In the last six lines we are told, of course, that the poet's state of mind has changed; and we are told why—he has thought of the friend or lady, whichever it may be. But this is a sentimental, an almost automatic, change, and it is hard to understand after the four lines preceding. It is what I have previously called an evasion of the issue posed. And the lark is a sentimental lark: at the descriptive level, *sullen, sings hymns,* and *heaven's gate* are all inaccurate. The lark is burdened with the unexplained emotions of the poet. But the lark is not representative of any explanatory idea. The lark suffers in these ways from comparison with the pigeons of Wallace Stevens, of which I shall write briefly later in this book. We have more lark than understanding in these lines, and more easy sentiment than lark.

One of the most fascinating passages is the description of the imperceptible but continuous action of Time in CIV:

> Ah! yet doth beauty, like a dial hand,
> Steal from his figure, and no pace perceived;
> So your sweet hue, which methinks still doth stand,
> Hath motion, and mine eye may be deceived.

And yet even here we are in grammatical difficulty, for it is the dial hand (or its shadow) which should steal from the figure; it is not beauty. Or if we take *figure* to mean the human form or face, then the dial hand is left with no reference, and there is no basis for the second half of the comparison. We understand the passage, of course, but the statement is careless.

One can find good poems among the sonnets which do not achieve at any point the greatness of certain lines from sonnets which fail. Such, for examples, are XXIII, CXXIX, and CXLVI. The first of these is correct but minor; the second (*The expense of spirit*) is powerful in phrasing, but repetitious in structure—as

Douglas Peterson has shown (Shakespeare Quarterly V-4), it derives its structure and much of its matter from a passage in Wilson's *Art of Rhetorique*—and appears to be a forceful exercise on a limited topic; the third is somewhat commonplace when compared with the best of Donne's *Holy Sonnets*.

The most impressive sonnet of all, I suspect, is LXXVII, in which the peculiarly Shakespearian qualities are put to good use, in which the peculiar faults are somehow transformed into virtues. Jonson, Donne, and Greville—indeed most of the great poets of the Renaissance—tend to deal with the experiential import of explicit definitions and sometimes to offer explicit and figurative excursions from definitions. In the plain style at its plainest, the passion with which the human significance of the definitions is felt is communicated by the emotional content of the language in which they are stated: that is, we do not have definition here and emotion there, but meaning and emotion coexist at every moment; in the relatively ornate style, the excursions are controlled in a general but clear way by the definitions. But Shakespeare's approach to his subject is indirect and evasive. In LXXVII the explicit subject is not very important: it provides the occasion for the entry into the poem of certain perceptions which appear to be almost accidental but which are really Shakespeare's obsessive themes.

LXXVII apears to have been written to accompany the gift of a blank book:

> Thy glass will show thee how thy beauties wear;
> Thy dial how thy precious minutes waste;
> The vacant leaves thy mind's imprint will bear,
> And of this book this learning may'st thou taste.
> The wrinkles which thy glass will truly show
> Of mouthed graves will give thee memory;
> Thou by thy dial's shady stealth mayst know
> Time's thievish progress to eternity.
> Look! what thy memory cannot contain
> Commit to these waste blanks, and thou shalt find
> Those children nursed, delivered from thy brain
> To take a new acquaintance of thy mind.
>   These offices, so oft as thou wilt look,
>   Shall profit thee and much enrich thy book.

The first quatrain states the ostensible theme of the poem: time passes and we age, yet by writing down our thoughts, we take a new acquaintance of our mind, acquire a new learning. The second quatrain enlarges upon the passage of time; the last six lines revert to the moralizing.

But something very strange occurs along the way. The imperceptible coming of wrinkles displays the physical invasion of the enemy, just as the imperceptible movement of the dial's shadow displays the constant movement of the enemy. In the ninth line, however, the enemy invades the mind, the center of being; it was the figure of the book which enabled the poet to extend the poem to this brilliant and terrifying suggestion, yet so far as the development of the theme is concerned, the extension occurs almost by the way, as if it were a casual and merely incidental feeling.

> Look! What thy memory cannot contain
> Commit to these waste blanks. . . .

This command, in isolation, is merely a command to make good use of the book, and the remainder of the passage deals wholly with the advantages of doing so; yet the command follows the lines in which we have observed the destruction of the physical being by time, and in this position it suggests the destruction of the mind itself. This terrifying subject, the loss of identity before the uncontrollable invasion of the impersonal, is no sooner suggested than it is dropped.

There is a related but more curious employment of pure suggestion in the word *waste* in the same passage. The word is obviously a pun, with the emphasis on the secondary meaning. It means not only *unused* or *blank* (this is the primary meaning, and it gives us a tautology), but it means *desert* or *uninhabited* or *uninhabitable,* a sense reinforced by the verb *waste* in the second line; but rationally considered, the pages are not waste in this second sense, but are instruments offered for actually checking the invasion of the waste. A feeling, in other words, is carried over from its proper motive to something irrelevant to it, and the dominant feeling is thus reinforced at the expense of the lesser; this dominant feeling, one should add, arises not from the ostensible theme of the poem—the book and its use—but from the incidental theme which has slipped into the poem. In order to express the invasion of confusion, the poem for a moment actually enters the realm of confusion instead of describing it. The poem, I think, succeeds; but after having examined the unsuccessful confusion of other sonnets, I cannot decide whether the success is due to skill or to accident.

IX

THE STYLE OF Ben Jonson (1573-1637) is plain, but it is also urbane and polished. It has the solid structure of the styles of Gascoigne and Raleigh, with evidence of a knowledge of the flexibility of Sidney. Jonson is no such enraptured rhetorician as Sidney, but on the other hand his understanding of Sidneyan rhetoric prevents his indulging in any such affectation of roughness as we find to some extent in Gascoigne; he is freer from mannerism and a purer stylist than either, and, since he operates from a central position, he is more sensitive and more skillful than either, for he can employ the tones of both without committing himself wholly to one direction. Shakespeare, in comparison, succumbed to excessive and uncontrolled sensitivity; Donne shows the vices of both Gascoigne and Sidney, the affectation of harshness on the one hand and of sophisticated ingenuity on the other. Greville alone of the group rivals Jonson in control of his style; yet Jonson's style is more varied than Greville's and places him as the first master stylist of the plain tradition: that is to say, of the great tradition of the Renaissance.

Jonson is a classicist in the best sense, and though his classicism is no doubt in part the result of his study of the Greek and Latin poets, critics, and rhetoricians, as it was probably in greater part the result of his natural bent, it is reasonable to see in his work a resolution of the qualities to be found in Sidney and the poets of the plain style. One does not learn to write English verse from studying Latin verse, though one may thus acquire applicable theories. Jonson must have been familiar with the poets whom I have mentioned; and these and a few others *were the English language,* so far as poetic style was concerned, at the time when Jonson was mastering the language, and there was little to distract the attention from them.

Like most of the lyrics of the period, Jonson's are expository in structure; but, unlike many, they engage in very little figurative excursion (such as one gets in Donne) and very little illustrative repetition (such as one gets in Nashe's *In Time of Pestilence*). They are very closely written arguments, or at least a good many of them are, and they have to be read very closely if one is not to lose the continuity of the arguments. He wrote a little devotional poetry of a high order, but his subject matter is chiefly ethical in the narrowest sense: that is, he deals with problems of conduct arising between one human being and another, or between one human being and the social group, or between one human being and other serious problems; indeed, his devotional poetry concerns itself explicitly with man's moral relationship with God. The language is accurate and concise with regard to both idea and feeling; there is an exact correlation between motive and feeling that may easily be mistaken for coldness and mechanical indifference by the reader accustomed to more florid enticements, but which impresses the present reader rather as integrity and nobility. Among the greatest poems illustrating these qualities are the following: *Though beauty be the mark of praise, Where dost thou careless lie, High-spirited friend, From death and dark oblivion near the same, False world, good night, Good and great God, can I not think of Thee, Let it not your wonder move,* and *To draw no envy, Shakespeare, on thy name.*

I will begin with *An Elegy:*

> Through beauty be the mark of praise,
>   And yours of whom I sing be such
>   As not the world can praise too much,
> Yet is't your virtue now I raise.
>
> A virtue like allay, so gone
>   Throughout your form, as though that move,
>   And draw and conquer all men's love,
> This subjects you to love of one.

64

Wherein you triumph yet: because
   'Tis of yourself, and that you use
   The noblest freedom, not to choose
Against or faith, or honor's laws.

But who should less expect from you,
   In whom alone love lives again?
   By whom he is restored to men,
And kept, and bred, and brought up true?

His falling temples you have reared,
   The withered garlands tane away;
   His altars kept from the decay
That envy wished, and nature feared.

And on them burn so chaste a flame
   With so much loyalty's expense,
   As love, t'acquit such excellence,
Is gone himself into your name.

And you are he: the Deity
   To whom all lovers are designed,
   That would their better objects find:
Among which faithful troop am I.

Who as an off'ring at your shrine,
   Have sung this hymn, and here entreat
   One spark of your diviner heat
To light upon a love of mine.

Which if it kindle not, but scant
   Appear, and that to shortest view,
   Yet give me leave t'adore in you
What I, in her, am grieved to want.

This is a poem in praise of a woman who is a friend, not the beloved; she is praised for her virtue and her constancy in love, at the expense of the woman whom the poet loves; and because of these qualities she is identified with the god of love. The theme is serious, and it is worked out in greater detail than my summary would suggest. On the other hand, the theme is in no wise difficult to understand, either in part or in detail, in spite of the compactness of the writing.

The poem is far from simple, however, and much of it may escape the reader who has read it for its paraphrasable content alone. It is a fusion of two kinds of poetry: the song and the didactic poem. It is a poem in praise of virtue in love; and, in connection with love, the machinery of the old Religion of Love (in which virtue as here conceived was scarcely an element) is employed discreetly. The stanza frequently suggests a song stanza as it opens, and then seems to stop the song with a didactic close, as if strings had been plucked and then muted; and this effect, more or less inherent in the form of the stanza itself, is sometimes stressed and sometimes softened. In the first stanza, for example, the effect of the single-hearted love-song is suggested in the first three lines, but qualified by *though* and by the harsh rimes *such* and *much;* and in the fourth line the tone is brought down firmly to the didactic. The second stanza suggests a song-movement throughout, and the subject of love in the second and third lines reinforces the movement; but the treatment of the subject is moralistic, and the song-quality is softened by this fact. The third stanza is one of the most explicitly moralistic, yet the first clause suggests another tone, that of the triumphant love-song; and this tone dominates the first three lines of the fourth stanza and is only partly muted in the fourth line. The fifth stanza resembles the fourth, but here the Religion of Love, which has been introduced quietly in the fourth, emerges strongly; and, in the first two lines especially, the accented syllables are heavy and long, and the unaccented are light, in such a way as to suggest a triumphal chant. In the remainder of the poem the didactic tone dominates, but it has already been so qualified by the other that the echo of the song is present most of the time, most plainly, perhaps, in the eighth stanza and most muted in the last.

It is all but impossible to describe the nuances of feeling which I have been trying to describe. The reader who comes to this poem must have a reasonably full acquaintance with the Elizabethan songs and with the tradition of the plain style; he must understand metrical structure and the various methods of rhythmic variation; and he must read carefully. There is nothing wasted in this poem. Every word is necessary to the argument;

every cadence, every suggestion of literary tradition, whether that suggestion occur in the cadence or in the explicit meaning of the words, contributes to the feeling which the argument endeavors to convey; and the theme, though not the greatest conceivable, is a great one.

The language of the poem is essentially abstract, but it is worth our trouble to examine briefly the few references to concrete details. In the first stanza, *mark*, as I understand it, is a target, but we are not expected to visualize a target or shooting at a target or the raising of a target. The terms have receded into almost pure abstraction. In the second stanza, *allay* is, if this is possible, even closer to pure abstraction. The third and fourth stanzas are purely abstract. In the remainder of the poem, *temples, garlands, altars, flame, shrine, spark,* and *kindle* come a little closer to visibility, but the degree of visibility is small and the degree of abstraction is great. If these details were visualized more sharply, they would obstruct the argument, and the poem would be weakened further by the fact that these images, merely as images, would be stereotyped. The argument, however, is not stereotyped, but· is original and moving, and these details do not obstruct: rather, they contribute to the feeling communicated by the argument by way of their connotations.

To Heaven is a greater poem. For one thing, the subject is greater. For another, the poem depends less heavily upon an antecedent body of poetry; and, although it depends upon an understanding of the Christian religious experience, this is more generally understood, and the poem moves more rapidly and with greater weight of meaning line by line. In other words, the poem is more nearly self-contained.

> Good and great God, can I not think of Thee,
> But it must, straight, my melancholy be?
> Is it interpreted in me disease,
> That, laden with my sins, I seek for ease?
> O be Thou witness, that the reins dost know
> And hearts of all, if I be sad for show;
> And judge me after: if I dare pretend
> To aught but grace, or aim at other end.
> As Thou art all, so be Thou all to me,

First, midst, and last, converted One and Three!
My faith, my hope, my love; and in this state,
My judge, my witness, and my advocate.
Where have I been this while exiled from Thee,
And whither rap'd, now Thou but stoop'st to me?
Dwell, dwell here still! O, being everywhere,
How can I doubt to find Thee ever here?
I know my state, both full of shame and scorn,
Conceived in sin, and unto labor born,
Standing with fear, and must with horror fall,
And destined unto judgment after all.
I feel my griefs too, and there scarce is ground
Upon my flesh t'inflict another wound:
Yet dare I not complain or wish for death,
With holy Paul, lest it be thought the breath
Of discontent; or that these prayers be
For weariness of life, not love of Thee.

This poem deals with a major theme, and there are no crude flaws; yet this could be true and the poem still fall short of mastery. The reasons for the success of the poem are hard to describe, for there is no imagery, no decoration, and the metrical and stanzaic forms employed are the simplest in English. The poem has no faults that I can discover, and faults are always easier to discuss than virtues. The surface is tight and smooth; there is almost no opening.

Yet one can note certain facts, at the risk, perhaps, of seeming pedantic. The rhythmic structure of the line is of the post-Sidneyan variety: that is, the accented syllables (and the unaccented also) vary widely in degree of accentuation, so that the line is flexible and subtle, rather than heavy and emphatic. The cesuras are managed with great skill: they fall most often after the second foot or the third, or in the middle of the third, but in line twenty the cesura falls in the middle of the fourth foot; and in many lines the secondary pauses complicate the cesural structure greatly, for examples, in ten, eleven, and twelve, and there are other less obvious examples. The heroic couplet is used in these respects with a skill that one can seldom find equalled within similar limits by Dryden or Pope. The relationship of sentence-structure to linear and stanzaic structure is similarly brilliant: the closed couplet is the norm, and the first, second, seventh, and eighth couplets are complete units, the last of these containing two closely related sentences, the others one each; the third and fourth couplets, the fifth and sixth, the ninth and tenth, the eleventh and twelfth and thirteenth, are longer units; and within these sentences there is considerable variety of structure regardless of length, this variety affecting not merely the sentence but the rhythm of the line and of the group of lines.

Jonson employs two other common devices in this poem: the play upon words in the eighth couplet (*everywhere* and *ever here*), and the play upon an idea (that of the Trinity) in the fifth and sixth couplets. This kind of ingenuity resulted in some of the best and some of the worst passages in the Renaissance; the ingenuity here seems not only justifiable but inescapable: it is an essential part of the argument.

The series of triads resulting from the concept of the Trinity is especially impressive: it occurs in brief space and rapidly; it is not forced but seems a natural series of comparisons; it speeds the rhythm for a few lines (at a moment when the increased speed is a proper expression of passion); and it varies the rhythm of the whole poem, providing a fine preparation for the slower and more sombre movement of the later lines. It prepares us likewise for the final series of theological statements, which, however, are not arranged in triads—those in couplets nine and ten.

The devices which I have described are simple, when considered in general; their effectiveness, like the effectivenes of that other simple device, good diction, depends upon the fine shades in which they appear in the particular context—these fine shades are among the principal marks of genius. These fine shades of statement, however, could not exist were it not for the clear organization of the substance. In connection with this clarity—which may appear to some to be simplicity—there is one point which I think it worthwhile to bring surely to light: the theme of this poem is somewhat less simple than it may appear at first glance. The poem deals with love for God and the desire for death. God is perfect being, and therefore good; life, as the poet knows it, is being, however imperfect, and therefore good as a matter of theory. But the poet, in middle age, does not fear death, as Shakespeare professes to fear it and as Donne apparently fears it in fact: his temptation is "weariness of life"; his duty, which he accepts with a semi-suppressed despair, is to overcome this weariness. There is a recognition of reality here, distinct from a literary convention (as in Shakespeare) and from a gift for personal drama, or perhaps melodrama (as in Donne), which is very impressive. Much of the power of the poem resides in one of the elementary facts of life: the fact that a middle-aged man of intelligence is often readier to die than to live if he merely indulges his feelings. Jonson deals with the real problem, not with a spurious problem.

These two poems illustrate the qualities which I have been trying to describe; they illustrate a plainness more akin to Gascoigne or Wyatt, or especialy to Greville, than to any obvious quality in Sidney; Jonson, like Greville, is one on whom the black ox has trod. But these poems illustrate especially that fine control of nuances of feeling which are possible only to the stylist who deliberately abandons, yet remembers, the obvious graces; such writing is not only more weighty than that of Sidney, but it is more sensitive, more skillful.

Jonson's major poems have been neglected in favor of his minor poems, masterly performances in themselves, but less illustrative both of Jonson's genius and the age. The minor poems carry something over from the old courtly tradition to the new: the courtly element is offered playfully in Jonson and in his disciples of the seventeenth century; it is not offered with the benumbing pretense of seriousness which we find in Sidney and Spenser and others. The minor lyrics, however, with the aid of his plays, other writings, and legendary personality, have been able to keep him in some measure before the student's eye as a lyrical poet; he has never, in this capacity, lapsed into the obscurity in which Raleigh was long permitted to rest and in which Gascoigne and Greville rest to this day. If the reader with fixed habits could wrench his attention to the major poems long enough to appreciate them, this act would not only put him in possession of one of the two greatest bodies of short poems composed in the English

70

Renaissance but would aid him to understand a number of other great poets as well.

Among the lesser poems which should be read with especial care are these: the epitaphs on his children, especially that on his son, the epitaph on Salathiel (or Salomon) Pavy, *This morning timely rapt with holy fire* (to the Countess of Bedford), *A Hymn to God the Father*, the second poem to Charis, *The Hour Glass, My Picture Left in Scotland*, and the song in *Love's Triumph through Callipolis* beginning: *Joy, joy to mortals the rejoicing fires*. There are in addition the justly famous minor masterpieces such as *Drink to me only with thine eyes*, and *Queen and huntress chaste and fair*, poems which discipline the heritage of the song-books and bequeath it to the seventeenth century.

X

BEFORE I BEGIN to discuss John Donne (1573-1631), I would like to rehearse a few facts which I have already mentioned.

The short poem of the late middle ages, of the sixteenth century, and of the early seventeenth century was usually rational in structure and was often logical. This structure began to break down toward the middle of the seventeenth century: the signs are most obvious in *Lycidas*, but one can find them in Marvell and Vaughan and elsewhere. The rational structure was often used for irrational ends, as in much of Sidney and Donne, but the structure is almost always there. These facts are well known to scholars by now, and they may seem unworthy of mention; but they appear to be unknown to many of our critics. Within this rational frame, however, there were two main schools of poetry in the sixteenth century and earlier: on the one hand there were the poets of the plain style, and on the other hand the style which has been called courtly, ornate, aureate, sugared, or Petrarchan. Some poets employed both methods, but most poets worked mainly in one or the other, for the difference was a difference of principle, and the principles were commonly understood. Wyatt, Gascoigne, Raleigh, Greville, and Jonson wrote for the most part in the plain style. Sidney and Spenser can serve as examples of the courtly.

71

Donne can hardly be described as courtly or sugared, but he is ornate, and to this extent Petrarchan. Donne is only superficially a rebel against the tradition of Sidney; essentially he is a continuator, at least in a large number of his poems. His mind is more complex than that of Sidney, and more profound; his temperament is more violent and more perverse; his virtues and his vices are more striking; but in most of his famous poems he is working in the same tradition.

I would like to begin with a brief discussion of *A Valediction Forbidding Mourning*. The entire poem, like most of Donne's poems, is hyperbolic: he overstates his case violently, in a manner which, in our time, is called dramatic. The theme of the poem, though fairly serious, is also simple: that is, the lovers are united by their rational souls rather than by their sensible souls, and their love is therefore stable, and they can endure a parting more easily than can those lovers who are united merely by sense. This idea in itself is an overstatement, and Donne, of all people, must have been aware of the fact: this overstatement is a part of the hyperbole. But there is more than this in the hyperbole: there are the metaphors and similes. The figures in the first twelve lines are both trite and ridiculous. Mr. Cleanth Brooks says that some of the same figures in *The Canonization* are offered as parody; I doubt this, but they are not offered as parody here. They are offered here in absolute seriousness, and they are bad. But this is not the main point, so far as I am concerned. The main point is that they are ornament, decoration. They say very little about the subject, say it loosely, and say it with a kind of naïve violence. Jonson could have said more in two lines than Donne says in twelve.

The decoration in the opening lines is bad decoration, but later the decoration is good. The gold and the compasses are brilliant, and they have made the poem famous; nevertheless, the gold and the compasses are decoration. The gold and the compasses tell us nothing about the lovers, really, except that the lovers are inseparable in terms of the rational soul, yet the gold and the compasses are sensory details. There is much reference to sensory—usually to visual—detail in Renaissance poetry which is not meant to be visualized. But the gold and the compasses are meant to be visualized, or, if they are not so meant, Donne out-did himself. Yet we do not visualize the lovers either as gold or as compasses: if we did so, the poem would become preposterous. We visualize the gold and the compasses, and between these and the lovers there is a very general, an almost uncertain, intellectual correspondence. It is the gold and the compasses which save these passages, and very nearly in their own right. The passages are ornament, or very nearly so. They are very quotable, and they have often been quoted. They are quotable because they are detachable; they are detachable because they are attached. It is foolish to say, with Mr. Eliot, that Donne thinks with his sense (that is, with his sensible soul); he thinks with his rational soul, and he often ornaments his thought with his sensory perception, sometimes well and sometimes badly. The formula is Horatian: profit and pleasure — profit from reason, pleasure from sensory perception or from other decoration. The formula is common in the Renaissance, but it is not the only formula possible in the Renaissance or at other times. The formula of our own time which corresponds in part to the Horatian formula is that of tenor and vehicle, although the modern formula has a wider applicability. In Donne's poems the constancy of the lovers is the tenor; the gold and the compasses are the vehicles; the vehicles are more interesting than the tenor: therefore they are ornaments, and the tenor—the essential theme—suffers. In our time the most famous Renaissance vehicle, as far as I know, has been Marvell's chariot. It functions in much the same way as Donne's gold and compasses.

The rhythm of the poem is undistinguished. There is a fairly regular alternation of very light and very heavy syllables and the relation of sentence to line and stanza shows little variation: the result is a kind of mechanical repetition, which, though it has a certain effectiveness in the last three stanzas in relationship to the movement of the compasses, is not very effective in relationship to the serious theme embodied by the compasses. The poem is near enough to Jonson's *Elegy* ("Though beauty be the mark of praise") in subject, form, and length for comparison to be possible. Both are impressive poems, but Jonson's appears to me the better poem at every point. Jonson examines his subject more fully, he never falsifies it by emotional exaggeration, and he exhibits far greater command of the resources of his medium.

Before proceeding further, I will give a brief list of Donne's more obvious faults, some of which I have already indicated; after that I can proceed to his virtues. Donne is a man of harsh and often of imperceptive temperament. He is give to over-dramatizing himself, even to the point of dismal melodrama. He is over-sexed, neurotically so; and he never copes with the problem of sexual relations in a mature fashion, as Jonson does, for example, or Greville. And as Ben Jonson remarked, he should have been hanged for his misplacing of accents. As to his frequent misuse of metaphor and simile, the causes are in part the weaknesses which I have mentioned and in part the bad side of the traditions which formed him: if one will consider the Petrarchan fascination with ingenious figures, the Gascoignian passion for harsh realism, and the complications of Donne's own character, one will not find it hard to understand how Donne came to commit the sins to which Samuel Johnson objected. There were European influences as well, but they were scarcely necessary. Understanding, however, should not involve forgiveness. The sins were real, and they vitiate most of Donne's poetry.

The matter of accents can best be illustrated separately, the other matters as they come up in separate poems. In the second of the main group of the *Holy Sonnets* ("As due by many titles I resign"), we have this

> Thy servant, whose pains thou hast still repaid . . .

If this line is given the accentuation demanded by the sense and by the inherent mechanics of the language, we get an iamb, a clumsy anapest, another clumsy anapest, and an iamb, and this gives us four feet where we should have five. The anapests are clumsy for this reason: when a trisyllabic substitution is made in iambic verse, the unaccented syllables should be as light as possible and as short as possible, to avoid slowing the foot and the line, whereas here both principles are violated. If we wish, as we must, to get this line somehow into a pentameter pattern, we shall have to revise our accentuation as follows:

Thy sérvant whóse pains thóu hast stíll repáid . . .

and this revision involves a brutal deformation of the natural language in the second and third feet. In the third sonnet we have a similar but milder difficulty in the line:

Háve the remémbrance of pást jóys for relíef . . .

in which we have a trochee, an iamb, an anapest, a trochee (in a difficult position), and an iamb, and no skill or perceptivity in any of them. This kind of roughness is sometimes supposed to be defensible on the grounds that it is expressive of passion; but passion is expressed in the arts through the mastery of form, not through the violation of form. The number of such lines is large, but the real trouble with them is the defect in Donne which they seem to emphasize, a relative unawareness of the nature and importance of sound. Even in the poems in which there are no mechanical blunders, the meter has the effect of a convention observed or of an obstacle overcome rather than of an instrument employed. One of the best of the *Holy Sonnets* is the one beginning *Thou hast made me;* fine though it is, it is less great than Jonson's *To Heaven,* and the difference resides not merely in the relatively stereotyped language of Donne but even more in Donne's simple and mechanical use of syntax and rhythm. The greatest of Donne's love poems is probably *A Valediction of My Name in the Window;* yet here also the matter seems to have been forced into the stanza rather than to have been written by means of the stanza—the one obvious exception to this statement, perhaps, occurring in the eighth stanza, especially in the opening lines.

One of the most popular of the love poems is *The Canonization,* and its second half has a good deal of power. Mr. Cleanth Brooks has given us an excellent paraphrase of this poem[18] and has demonstrated beyond doubt the solid rationality of its structure. Yet the first half of the poem is badly written and exhibits characteristic weaknesses. The "dramatic" opening—"For Godsake

75

hold your tongue, and let me love"— is affected, is an example of a somewhat low grade of cleverness, and is in no sense a concentrated or important statement. The rest of the first two stanzas are in much the same tone. Brooks defends the use of stereotyped figures in the second stanza as follows:

> The second stanza, he fills with the conventionalized figures of the Petrarchan tradition: the wind of lovers' sighs, the floods of lovers' tears, etc. — extravagant figures with which the contemptuous secular friend might be expected to tease the lover. The implication is that the poet himself recognizes the absurdity of the Petrarchan love metaphors. But what of it? The very absurdity of the jargon which lovers are expected to talk makes for his argument: their love, however absurd it may appear to the world, does no harm to the world.

Whether Donne realized the absurdity of the figures employed here is a fine question, for he used all of them, or nearly all, in deadly seriousness in other poems; but let us assume that he realized it. The figures are still bad, and the passage, line by line, is a bore. If the poet is forced to write badly in order to develop his theme, then there is something wrong with his theme or with his method[19]. I am not interested in the petulant conversation of Donne or of any other man, and I see no reason why Donne should have to inflict his on me in order to prove his sincerity.

The Extasie shows Donne's virtues fragmentarily and his faults at length. I believe that nothing intelligent can be said in defense of the first twelve lines: they are as bad as Donne's worst detractors have ever claimed. Lines thirteen to forty-four inclusive form another unit, that in which the souls of the two lovers are united to form a third soul. The passage begins with the comparison of the two souls to armies, a false comparison, for the two souls are not in conflict but are about to unite. Near the end of this passage we have the figure of the violet, which I find incomprehensible: we are reading about the union of two souls in one, and then, without explanation, we are told that if a single violet is transplanted it redoubles and multiplies. The remainder of the poem, which is the best of it, deals mainly with the Aristotelian concept of the soul: the idea that the rational soul is able to function—and hence, really, to exist—only through working upon the materials provided by the sensory soul. These lines have force and dignity, in spite of the formulary nature of the final quatrain. The poem as a whole is in Donne's characteristically mechanical meter, and one line is difficult to read: "They are ours, though they are not we. We are." The line opens with two heavy and protracted anapests which almost stifle the movement.

The greatest of the love poems is *A Valediction of my Name, in the Window*. The poet is taking leave of a mistress whom he believes to be capable of infidelity during his absence, and he imagines the progress of this infidelity. As a charm against it, he has cut his name in her window-pane, with a diamond, and the poem consists of a series of comparisons in which the engraved name is an invariable element. In this respect the poem resembles *The Weeper*, by Crashaw, in which the eyes of the Magdalen are compared to a great many things indeed; but in Crashaw's poem there is no principle of coherence save the very general notion of the Magdalen's piety, whereas in Donne's poem the comparisons are used to warn the mistress and to give details of the imagined infidelity, so that the poem is very closely organized. There is a little of the neurotic intensity that mars so many of the poems, although here it is relatively under control, and I confess that for my own taste the details exhibit a somewhat excessive straining for mere ingenuity, and ingenuity which is in the tradition of the ornate style. But whatever these objections may be worth, the poem has, nevertheless, unusual power. In the first seven stanzas, we get the lover's warnings and advice, and with these is communicated the lover's desire to possess his mistress completely. Then, with no explicit preparation, the eighth stanza introduces the theme of overt infidelity, in the finest lines of the poem:

> When thy inconsiderate hand
> Flings ope this casement, with my trembling name,
> To look on one whose wit or land,
> New battry to thy heart may frame,
> Then think this name alive, and that thou thus
> In it offendst my Genius.

77

The previous stanzas, in the course of the poet's intense efforts to hold the lady by his warnings, have identified the poet with his name, the identification culminating in images drawn from the doctrine of the resurrection of the body and from astrology. We are thus prepared to watch the suffering of the "trembling name"; this stanza is the climax of the poem. In the three final stanzas the poem is brought to a quiet but embittered close.

This poem exhibits more fully than any other Donne's desire for a stable love, his fear of betrayal, and a kind of sublimation of his excessive sexuality. He gives us the feeling that he is endeavoring to master his problem through an enormous act of the will operating through an equally enormous act of the intellect. The engraved name, the possession of the lady in his absence, become real, in part because of the effort made before our eyes to make them real, though we, like the poet, are aware that the effort is toward something transcending human power and cannot wholly succeed. The immensity of the effort, the illusion that it can exert real power, the awareness that it cannot exert enough power or cannot exert power which is quite real, these in combination result in moving poetry.

Donne's greatest poetry and some of his worst meter can be found in the *Holy Sonnets*. The best of these appear to be the first *(Thou hast made me)*, the seventh *(At the round earth's imagined corners)*, the thirteenth *(What if this present were the world's last night)*, and perhaps the fourteenth *(Batter my heart)*, though not a great deal can be said for the last. None of the four contains any serious blunder in meter, although there are a few slightly awkward lines and there is in general more of rhythmic violence than of subtlety. Of the four named, the best are the first and the seventh. The first has a simplicity uncommon in Donne, atlhough it is a simplicity slightly marred by clichés. It is free of his usual exaggeration, and it moves firmly to the magnificent pun in the final couplet. The seventh sonnet has comparable virtues; in fact the last seven and a half lines may well surpass anything else in Donne. The first line has always bothered me, however: unless I have missed something here, Donne is endeavoring to exhibit his scientific knowledge to the effect that the world is really round and has no corners, and the occasion hardly seems appropriate; or he may have in mind a flat map, with trumpeting cherubs at the corners, but this would seem excessively allusive. The series of disasters in lines six and seven strikes me as somewhat obviously violent. Nevertheless, the poem is one of the great devotional poems in our language. It is worth noting that the long sentence is brilliantly managed in this sonnet; we shall see further developments in the long sentence later. The first eight lines of the thirteenth sonnet are again among the greatest in Donne; but the comparison of Christ in the sestet to the profane mistresses is a serious flaw, for the beauty, pity, foulness, and rigor are not of the same order in the two instances and indeed have little if any relationship to each other. The fourteenth sonnet is the weakest of the four: in this sonnet we have the mannerism of strong feeling with little real perception to support it; we have again a confusion of the devout and the erotic, although here it is less noticeable (and less likely to be found moving) because it occurs in a traditional cliché of second-rate devotional poetry.

Donne differs from Jonson in ways that are obvious. As I have said, his meters are sometimes grossly incorrect and are almost never distinguished. Though Donne owes much to Sidney, his debt differs from that of Jonson: Donne utilizes the ornate method of Sidney, whereas Jonson learned a good deal from Sidney's refinement of meter and skill in grammar and syntax. Donne appears to be less a disciple of Sidney than a serious parodist. When I say *parodist*, I do not mean that I think Donne is ridiculing Sidney, but he adds to Sidney's procedure a touch of the grotesque and the violent, and for Sidney's remarkable skill he substitutes his own awkwardness, and it is hard to be sure whether the parody in question is intentional or merely inevitable. Donne, of course, had the better mind of the two men; it is a pity that he did not make better use of it. If there is an affectation of directness in Gascoigne, there is a greater affectation of directness in most of Donne. Jonson's employment of abstraction shows the easiness that comes of use; Donne, though capable of profundity, affects profundity, often with grotesque results. These defects sometimes override Donne's genius wholly and produce bad poetry. On the other hand, they are sometimes restrained sufficiently for the corresponding virtues to emerge, and we then have one of the great English poets, although it is only fair to add that the defects are never wholly absent.

Donne's present reputation seems to me to be somewhat in excess of his desserts. The excess is due in part, I suspect, to his defects, for roughness and uncontrolled feeling are widely regarded as signs of genius in our time; it is due in part, also, to the wide range of subjects which he attempted and which he handled with at least fragmentary brilliance. This matter of range is no mean virtue, and had the writing not been so consistently damaged by Donne's weaknesses, the range might well have justified his being considered the greatest master of the short poem in English. He missed this position, however, and missed it unmistakably; great as he is, one can find greater poems than any of Donne's in Greville, Jonson, and the two Herberts, and one can find more great poems in the first two of these.

XI

IT SHOULD BE possible in the remainder of this essay to proceed somewhat more rapidly, for by now, I believe, I have explained the critical and historical principles which are guiding me. I shall endeavor first of all to deal with certain Metaphysical poets following Donne; then I shall go back and deal briefly with a few poets, definitely minor, who are not of the Metaphysical School; then I shall have a little to say of Milton. I shall neglect a large amount of excellent minor poetry of the seventeenth century, and this may seem unreasonable, for I have devoted some space to the minor poetry of the sixteenth century—that of the song-books, for example—and the minor poetry of the seventeenth century is in many ways better. But the earlier body of minor poetry prepared the way in some measure for major poetry, whereas the later body of minor poetry is merely the debris of a major tradition. I do not hold the later poetry in contempt for this reason: it should be read and remembered; but it is available, some of it in the standard anthologies, much of it elsewhere. The intelligent reader should be able to find it. My aims in this book are limited.

One other thing: in any period in which one finds a large body of expert minor poetry, one finds a sign of communal health; that is, a large number of people understand the art and are working at it intelligently, and these people presumably understand the work of their betters. In the eighteenth and nineteenth centuries there is very little minor poetry which is readable today. There are the poets with major ambitions, and they are still remembered, but for the most part they think and write badly and will be remembered before long merely as curiosities in the history of culture. The reader might compare Dowland's *Fine Knacks* with Thomas Moore's *Believe me, if all those endearing young charms* —compare both words and music. Both songs were widely known in their respective periods and were commonly sung by ladies and gentlemen. The comparison will indicate the complete collapse of a culture.

XII

EDWARD, LORD HERBERT of Cherbury (1583-1648), and his brother George Herbert (1593-1633) are almost symbolic figures. Edward was a vain and worldly man and an amateur philospher who did much to prepare the way for the decay of Renaissance poetry and for the curious philosophizing of the subsequent century. George was the first of the great poets who retreated, in fact and in subject matter, from the concerns of the world into a kind of isolated pietism—a pietism which in some of his successors was to move into mysticism and sometimes into mysticism of no very orthodox varieties. The two brothers mark the break in the poetic mind, or the beginning of the break: on the one hand a worldliness which is beginning to leave religion behind, and on the other a pietism which is beginning to forget the world. There is no such cleavage in either Jonson or Greville, or even in Sidney or Spenser. Yet both of the Herberts are at their best great poets; and although much great poetry is written later in the seventeenth century, there is never again the firm command of the art which these two exhibit in their best work.

81

I agree with G. C. Moore Smith, the editor of the Oxford edition of Lord Herbert's poems, that the greatest of the poems is *Elegy over a Tomb,* which I shall quote:

Must I then see, alas! eternal night
    Sitting upon those fairest eyes,
And closing all those beams, which once did rise
    So radiant and bright,
That light and heat in them to us did prove
    Knowledge and love?

Oh, if you did delight no more to stay
    Upon this low and earthly stage,
But rather chose an endless heritage,
    Tell us, at least, we pray,
Where all the beauty that those ashes ow'd
    Are now bestowed?

Doth the Sun now his light with yours renew?
    Have waves the curling of your hair?
Did you restore unto the sky and air,
    The red, and white, and blue?
Have you vouchsafed to flowers since your death
    That sweetest breath?

Had not Heaven's lights else in their houses slept,
    Or to some private life retired?
Must not the sky and air have else conspired,
    And in their regions wept?
Must not each flower else the earth could breed
    Have been a weed?

But thus enriched may we not yield some cause
    Why they themselves lament no more?
That must have changed the course they held before,
    And broke their proper laws,
Had not your beauties given this second birth
    To Heaven and Earth?

Tell us, for Oracles must still ascend,
    For those that crave them at your tomb:
Tell us, where are those beauties now become,
    And what they now intend:
Tell us, alas, that cannot tell our grief,
    Or hope relief.

The poem is inferior to George Herbert's *Church Monuments,*
which I shall discuss presently, in this: the third, fourth, and
fifth stanzas are primarily preparations for the last. In these
stanzas Lord Herbert employs more or less standard hyperboles,
somewhat Petrarchan in their rhetorical origin, somewhat pantheistic in their philosophical content, but employs them with a
kind of melancholy irony, in order to discredit the semi-pantheis-
tic and sentimental solace which the figures imply. My defense of
these stanzas, in so far as it is a defense, may seem to resemble
the defense offered by Mr. Cleanth Brooks of the opening lines of
The Canonization. In fact there is a resemblance, but there is a
measure of difference. There is no imitation, here, of petulant
conversation; the style is formal throughout. There are clichés,
but they are not as over-worked nor as violent as the clichés of
Donne; in fact the pantheistic element in these figures is relatively
new at the time, although that fact does not help them much now.
The tone of the stanzas is quiet and distinguished and is in keeping with the tone of the whole poem; the irony is so restrained
that many readers may not recognize it. The stanzas, however,
are repetitious, and thus eighteen lines are employed to say what
might have been said in six. When one considers Lord Herbert's
explorations of the long sentence, of the quiet tone, and of elaborate ornament in other poems, the fact is not surprising, and the
devices are beautifully managed. The final stanza, in the simplicity and accuracy of its diction, and in its refusal of all sentimental
evasion, is a statement of extraordinary power; it is a masterly
stanza in the plain style. The poem is the last word in the sophistication of the ornamental style in combination with the plain style.

I will now quote *Church Monuments,* by George Herbert:

> While that my soul repairs to her devotion,
> Here I entomb my flesh, that it betimes
> May take acquaintance of this heap of dust,
> To which the blast of death's incessant motion,
> Fed with the exhalation of our crimes,
> Drives all at last. Therefore I gladly trust
>
> My body to this school, that it may learn
> To spell his elements, and find his birth

Written in dusty heraldry and lines;
Which dissolution sure doth best discern,
Comparing dust with dust, and earth with earth.
These laugh at jet and marble, put for signs,

To sever the good fellowship of dust,
And spoil the meeting: what shall point out them,
When they shall bow, and kneel, and fall down flat
To kiss those heaps which now they have in trust?
Dear flesh, while I do pray, learn here thy stem
And true descent, that, when thou shalt grow fat,

And wanton in thy cravings, thou mayst know
That flesh is but the glass which holds the dust
That measures all our time; which also shall
Be crumbled into dust. Mark here below
How tame these ashes are, how free from lust,—
That thou mayst fit thyself against thy fall.

This poem might be described as the last word in the sophistication of the plain style; there is nothing of the ornamental style
left in it; but the sophistication, as in the best work of Jonson, is
doubtless in part the result of the ornamental poets. The poem,
nevertheless, contains a large amount of figurative language, of
which I shall presently speak in some detail: the quality of this
language verges on what I shall endeavor later in this book to
describe as post-Symbolist. The figures are not ornament; neither
are they intended to be wholly unvisualized; they are not symbols
in the medieval sense, nor is the poem allegorical. The thought
is wholly and clearly embodied in the figures, phrase by phrase,
and it could not have been as well expressed in any other way.
The method is uncommon in the Renaissance, but it appears
fairly often in the French and American poetry of the nineteenth
and twentieth centuries, frequently in a more obvious form. It
is always rash to give extremely high praise, and most critics
avoid doing so; yet in the matter of importance of theme and
mastery of execution, this poem and Jonson's *To Heaven* appear
to me the most impressive short poems in the English Renaissance.
There are poems by Greville which are quite as serious as either
and which are nearly as well executed; Greville is very great; yet

whenever I turn for an example in English of what the short poem should be at its best, these are the first two poems which come to mind.

I will consider first the relationship between syntax and line and between syntax and stanza[20]. The employment of enjambement and the avoidance of enjambement are instructive in themselves, but they assume meaning only in relationship to sentence-structure and rhythmic structure, and, beyond these, in relationship to the total intention of the poem. Of the twenty-four lines fourteen end in punctuation marks, and each of these marks indicates a real structural break in the sentences. The ten lines remaining should be examined individually.

The second line of the poem ends with an adverb which modifies the verb at the beginning of the next line; but it is an adverb which, if the sentence were less heavily punctuated, would be set off by commas, and the effect of the commas is there, so that the enjambement is of the slightest. Line six ends on a verb, of which the object follows at the beginning of the next line, a stronger break, but one justified by the length of the sentence and the solidity of the following sentence elements. Line seven again ends on a verb, but the verb is followed by two parallel infinitive phrases, so that the break is less abrupt. Line eight ends in a noun serving as direct object, so that the unit here is fairly self-contained and the subsequent line functions as a single adjectival unit modifying the noun in question and again we have a contained unit. Line fifteen could almost as easily end on a comma, for the three verbal units are parallel, and, although the infinitive phrase of the next line modifies the last of these directly, it likewise modifies the entire line. Line seventeen ends on the first of two direct objects, and, since the second reinforces the first, the line-ending provides a means of emphasis. Line nineteen ends on a verb, of which the object is the long noun-clause following, a clause which continues to the period, so that the suggestion of enjambement here is again a means of emphasis, of indicating the importance of what is to follow. Line twenty-one ends with an enjambement which in itself would be violent: the verb *shall be* is split by the line-ending. But there has been very careful preparation for this break: the tentative approaches to enjambement, the long sentences, the quiet tone; and *shall* is a crucial word here and deserves the controlled emphasis which it gets—the emphasis comes down quietly and firmly on the word which indicates the certain end of man.

The length of sentence varies a good deal. Each period ends a sentence, as does the question mark at the end of line sixteen, and (in effect) the colon in line fourteen. This in itself gives great variety of length, yet the first two sentences are so closely related as very nearly to form one—and from line twelve to the period in line twenty-two we have a series of three closely related units. The points within the line and within the stanza at which the sentences end are varied. The sentences are complex but firmly constructed. The total effect of the relationship of sentence to line and to stanza is one of a slow, subtle, and intricate, but controlled, rhythm. This rhythm is further complicated by cesuras which are marked by minor punctuation and by light pauses which are not punctuated; these cesuras vary greatly in position.

In its theme the poem stands somewhat aside from most of the devotional poetry of the Renaissance and certainly aside from most of the poetry of George Herbert: that is, although we know that Herbert was a devout Christian, there is nothing explicitly Christian in the poem, no reference to any exclusively Christian doctrine or attitude. The poem deals with the vanity of life and the necessity of preparing for death. The first sentence states the general theme; the second, by way of metaphor, introduces two of the most seductive aspects of the world, scholarship and family greatness; the third introduces conviviality; the next to the last sentence begins the summary by introducing the appetites of the flesh in general; and the short final sentence provides the ultimate moral.

As to the diction, I shall content myself with two examples in order to illustrate what seems to me the obvious. First a fragment from the comparison to scholarship:

> Which dissolution sure doth best discern,
> Comparing dust with dust, and earth with earth.

86

The language here is that of the scholarly man in search of the most careful scholar specializing in his interest, and who finds his scholar in dissolution. The action is that of scholarly investigation. The tone is ironic, if I may be forgiven for using an unfortunate term, and yet the irony, here as elsewhere in the poem, is so grim and so quiet that one scarcely thinks of it as irony. There is the same quality in the lines involving conviviality:

> To sever the good fellowship of dust
> And spoil the meeting . . .

And one could illustrate a comparable mastery of diction throughout, though not all of the illustrations would involve this particular form of irony. There is no attempt in this poem to gain an effect through mere repetition, however skillful, as in the *Elegy over a Tomb;* but every detail has weight in and for itself, as well as in and for the poem. The diction and all of the elements of rhythm which I have mentioned contribute to the quiet profundity of the poem and to its all but impeccable organization.

The lesser poems of the Herberts are disappointing. Both Herberts display syntactic and rhythmic skill. Edward Herbert is more consistently interested in the possibilities of the unusually long sentence than is his brother. After the *Elegy over a Tomb,* the two best poems by Edward Herbert are probably *To Her Hair* and *An Ode upon a Question Moved, Whether Love Should Continue For Ever.* The first of these, in its explicit theme, is conventional: it is in praise of a lady's black hair. The first three stanzas are composed of statements partly ingenious and partly stereotyped: the ideas are commonplaces of the earlier poetry. The stanzas are notable mainly for the quiet suavity of sentence, line, and stanza, in interrelation with each other. The remaining half of the poem goes into a discussion of blackness and the implications of blackness; it is very fine in its way, and yet the structure of the whole poem is conceited and tenuous. This poem, like most by Lord Herbert, shows the influence of Donne in a decorative use of the elaborate conceit, and perhaps the influence of Jonson in grace and decorum. But these poems lack the compactnes and vigor of Jonson and of the best of Donne. The *Ode,* for example, though it is an interesting poem and in many ways more civilized than anything comparable in Donne, nevertheless dissipates itself in suave gentility and constantly verges on the sentimental. I admire the poem for some of its qualities, but I have to force myself to read it to the end.

Of George Herbert's poems, the best, after *Church Monuments*, is certainly *The Pulley*, and after this a few other anthology favorites: *Throw away Thy Rod, Sweet Day*, and *I got me flowers*. These poems have grace, but they exhibit a cloying and almost infantile pietism. This pietism is the characteristic mark of almost all of the poet's work, and in most of his poems it leads him into abject clichés. For the reader who shares Herbert's faith, or for the reader who is merely in search of easy emotion of any kind, these poems are likely to seem better than they seem to me. For this reason *Church Monuments* is not characteristic of Herbert's work; and because it is not characteristic, or so I suspect, it has been neglected by critics and anthologists. *Content* contains a few lines toward the end which are among Herbert's best.

XIII

HENRY KING, BISHOP of Chichester (1592-1669), is famous primarily for *The Exequy*, but he wrote one other, though less valuable, poem which is worth remembering, *The Dirge*. *The Exequy*, like much of the most brilliant poetry of the seventeenth century, is weak in execution. One does not encounter the same difficulty here that one encounters in Milton and Marvell and in most of Crashaw, of uncertainty with regard to the theme or the proper procedure: the theme is sound and clear; the procedure in general is sound; but the writing is careless. Quiller-Couch, in his edited version of the poem in *The Oxford Book of English Verse*, improves it a good deal by simple cutting, but it could have been improved still further by the author had he cut and rewritten, especially in the first half of the poem. Poe quotes a couplet from this poem as an epigraph to his story *The Assignation:*

> Stay for me there; I shall not fail
> To meet thee in that hollow Vale.

Lawrence Mason, editor of the Yale and Oxford edition of King, believes that *hollow* is merely a casual spelling of *hallow*, or *hallowed*, and I believe that he is right. *Hollow* is romantic and in a mild way frightening. *Hallow* is something else. T.S. Eliot, in quoting these lines and others, remarks: ". . . there is that effect of terror which is several times attained by one of Bishop King's admirers, Edgar Poe." I am doubtless imperceptive, but I find no effect of terror and no resemblance to Poe. The poem is a love poem, and, in spite of its faults, one of the most deeply moving love poems in English. The grave is no longer a place of terror, but is the home toward which the poet is moving:

> So close the ground, and 'bout her shade
> Black curtains draw, my *Bride* is laid.
>
> Sleep on, my *Love*, in thy cold bed
> Never to be disquieted!
> My last good night! Thou wilt not wake
> Till I thy fate shall overtake:
> Till age, or grief, or sickness must
> Marry my body to that dust
> It so much loves; and fill the room
> My heart keeps empty in thy tomb.
> Stay for me there; I will not fail
> To meet thee in that hallow Vale.
> And think not much of my delay;
> I am already on the way,
> And follow thee with all the speed
> Desire can make, or sorrows breed.
> Each minute is a short degree,
> And every hour a step towards thee . . . .
>
> But heark! My pulse like a soft drum
> Beats my approach, tells *Thee* I come;
> And slow howere my marches be,
> I shall at last sit down by *Thee*.

Poe found an effect of terror in these lines and in a few others, and he tried to bring it out more clearly in his unfortunate effort entitled *The Sleeper*. The result was inadvertently ridiculous: it was bad poetry and bad criticism. Longfellow borrowed the soft drum:

> Art is long, and Time is fleeting,
>   And our hearts, though stout and brave,
> Still, like muffled drums, are beating
>   Funeral marches to the grave.

Baudelaire, strangely enough, was a reader of Longfellow (he put the opening lines of *Hiawatha* into French Alexandrines), and the muffled drums became quite correctly *tambours voilés* in one of his poems, only to reappear in English as *veiled drums*, whatever those may be, in a well-known translation. These remarks illustrate the way in which the history of poetry may distract one from the poetry.

I would like to return briefly to the poetry. The first thirty-eight lines are mainly an exercise in the ingenious style of the period which was later to be known as Clevelandizing. Two and a half lines stand out from this passage, however, with a force belonging to the archaic tradition of Gascoigne and Raleigh:

> And I remember must in tears
> Thou scarce had'st seen so many years
> As Day tells hours.

And the last four lines of the passage are moving and serve to introduce what follows. It is in line thirty-nine that the poem begins to live, and it is in line seventy-nine that it begins to be great. And yet the last passage is not without errors: the passage gains its strength from the firm development of the figure of the walk, which at the end becomes a military march, to the grave, where the bride is waiting; yet this passage is interrupted by a comparison, eight lines in length, of the poet's progress to the sailing of a ship, a comparison which contributes nothing but additional ingenuity and which is omitted by Quiller-Couch. The last six lines are too long for the occasion, and they contain three very awkward details: the parenthetical interruption and the two overflows from the third to the fourth and from the fourth to the fifth.

90

The Dirge is a kind of anthology of the clichés of the period which had been used to illustrate the brevity of life. The life of man is compared to a war, to a storm, to a flower, to a dream, to a sun-dial, and to a dramatic interlude. The poets of the Renaissance, however, sometimes showed a remarkable gift for realizing the possibilities of the commonplace comparison: Nashe did so in *Adieu, farewell*, for example, and Shakespeare did so in many of his sonnets. King does so in the third, fourth, and fifth of his stanzas, and Poe and Eliot might have found a little more of terror in these than in the *Exequy*, had they taken the trouble to look. For example:

> It is a dream, whose seeming truth
> Is moraliz'd in age and youth:
> Where all the comforts he can share
> As wandring as his fancies are;
> Till in a mist of dark decay
> The dreamer vanish quite away.

XIV

IN THE TWO BEST POEMS by the Herberts, the great period is still at its greatest. In their weaker poems, the rhetorical skill of the period, or certain aspects of it, are still evident, but the sources of the later decay begin to appear. King seems to have been a minor poet, ingenious and at the same time lacking in judgment, who succeeded in writing two memorable poems. In Richard Crashaw (1613?-1649), the evidence of both genius and decay is almost everywhere. I shall have to confine myself largely to a discussion of a few of his best poems. But I shall have to speak of his worst qualities.

Crashaw is, first of all, fascinated with the mystical experience, or at least with the theory of it. This experience, the mystics tell us, is supra-rational, is intuitive in the theological sense of the term, and is essentially unrelated to human experience; and since human language is the tool of discursive reason and functions in time rather than in eternity, the mystical experience cannot really be discussed. Its nature can be suggested by analogies with hu-

91

man experience, and the analogical experiences can be described. In the older Christian tradition, the common analogy is that of sexual union, and this is the analogy employed by Crashaw. It seems to me obvious, however, that the mystical experience is either real or a psychological delusion. If it is real, it is quite as distinct from sexual union as from any other human experience; if it is a delusion, it should be treated as a delusion or else not treated. I cannot see any way to defend poetry which purports to deal with the mystical experience in itself, for by definition one cannot deal with the experience and the poetry is bound to be fraudulent. One can write of a longing for the experience, or of the discipline which prepares one for the experience, but hardly of the experience. And the poet who insists on dealing with the experience and who becomes involved emotionally in the sexual analogy runs the risks of corrupting his devotional poetry generally with sexual imagery. It is not that sexual experience is "immoral"; but it is irrelevant to the religious experience, and, in so far as it is introduced into the religious experience, can result in nothing but confusion. If one wishes to see this confusion in an obvious form, one may turn to one of the Latin poems, *In sanguinem circumcisionis Dominicae;* and if one wants a milder example in English, one may read *Suppose he had been tabled at thy Teates.* These poems deal directly, of course, with the Jewish ceremony of the circumcision, and indirectly with the Christian ceremony of the Eucharist, but in imagery and tone they go a good deal beyond these ceremonies.

What interests me, however, is the effect of this confusion upon Crashaw's more ambitious works. The most famous of these is *A Hymn to salute the Name and Honor of the Admirable Sainte Teresa.* The poem is greatly over-estimated. If George Herbert's lesser poems exhibit a kind of childish pietism, one may say that this poem is a fairy-tale of childish pietism. One knows the story of Teresa, of course, and it may be largely true—that portion, at any rate, which took place in this world; but as given here it is not credible and certainly is far from interesting. The best writing occurs in the portion which is least sound intellectually, the portion which deals with mystical communion in

terms of the orgasm. That is, a very rich sensuality is substituted
for intellectual understanding, and it will not serve. One should
compare the poem to Ben Jonson's *To Heaven* and to George
Herbert's *Church Monuments*. The comparison will indicate the
extraordinary nature of the decay of poetic intelligence within a
very few years.

*In the Holy Nativity of Our Lord God a Hymn Sung as by the
Shepherds* is a better poem but shows similar weaknesses. Consider these lines:

> We saw thee in thy balmy Nest
> Young dawn of our eternal Day!
> We saw thine eyes break from thine East
> And chase the trembling shades away.

The image here comes from the *albas* or *aubes*, the poems in
which the lover takes leave of the lady at dawn, poems which, in
the European tradition, go back at least to the tenth century.
The image had long been familiar in English; there are, for
example, these lines from Donne, lines which had been set by
Gibbons:

> Stay, O sweet, and do not rise!
> The light that shines comes from thine eyes . . .

This image could easily be transferred from the one subject to
the other, in spite of its accretions of connotation, but it occurs
more than once, and another from the same erotic tradition appears repeatedly: the contrast (or likeness) of whiteness and
coldness. Quiller-Couch, in his capacity as editor of *The Oxford
Book of English Verse,* has the irritating habit of cutting and
rearranging poems without giving the reader any real notice of
what he is doing; yet it is only fair to say that he often improves
poems in this manner, and he improves this one by simplifica-
tion of arrangement. He includes a stanza which is omitted by
Waller , in the Cambridge edition of 1904:

> She sings Thy tears asleep, and dips
> Her kisses in Thy weeping eye;
> She spreads the red leaves of Thy lips,
> That in their buds yet blushing lie.

93

> She 'gainst those mother diamonds tries
> The points of her young eagle's eyes.

Now whether this stanza should be included or omitted is a question, but it is in keeping with much else in the poem, and the language is erotic rather than maternal or devotional. Some of the same elements appear in the *Full Chorus* at the end, then the references to April and Maia, and then the gifts. As to the gifts, the dove is sacred not merely to Venus but to the Virgin, and the lamb, of course, is symbolic of Christ as well as of the fertility rites; but the total effect of the chorus is ambiguous—it is hard to be sure whether we have been reading of the infant Jesus or of the infant Eros.

Yet many of the details to which I have been objecting are excellent in themselves, in spite of their effecting a measure of distraction from what one takes to be the subject of the poem, and there are other details which involve no distraction and which are very impressive in terms of the subject and in themselves—for example:

> Proud world, said I, cease your contest
>   And let the Mighty Babe alone.
> The Phoenix builds the Phoenix' nest.
>   Love's architecture is his own.
> The Babe whose birth embraves this morn
> Made his own bed ere he was born.

But the poem as a whole tends to disintegrate, the more carefully one inspects it.

The paraphrase of Psalm 23 is more nearly successful, though less ambitious. The paraphrase is not as impressive as the prose version in the King James Bible, but it has its own qualities, some admirable, some not. The following lines exhibit a pert uncharitableness which is not in the King James version and which I find unpleasant in a Christian (and would find unpleasant in anyone else):

> At the whisper of thy word
> Crown'd abundance spreads my board:
> While I feast, my foes do feed

> Their rank malice, not their need,
> So that with the self-same bread
> They are starv'd and I am fed.

The next couplet profits by a fleeting allusion to the poetry of conviviality:

> How my head in ointment swims!
> How my cup o'erlooks her brims!

The head is swimming *in ointment*, not *with drink;* we have an implicit but not an explicit metaphor. It is very effective, but *o'erlooks* is a stroke of genius: the cup does not overflow, although it is about to overflow, and the animation of the contents of the cup reinforces the delirium, or the ecstasy, or both of the preceding line. From here on the poem moves very expertly to its close, and in fact much of what precedes is beautifully done, but erotic irrelevance occurs in the early part of the poem:

> When my wayward breath is flying,
> He calls home my soul from dying,
> Strokes and tames my rabid grief,
> And does woo me into life.

If there had been no antecedent body of erotic poetry, if we did not know what the verb *to die* means in erotic poetry, this passage could be taken literally at the devotional level; the suggestion and the evasion of the suggestion are about equally skillful. But the suggestion is there, and Crashaw knew it and expected us to know it, and the suggestion is irrelevant. The following lines are the final stanza of a love poem which Crashaw translated from the Italian and which he obviously echoed in the paraphrase of the psalm:

> When my dying
> Life is flying,
> Those sweet airs that often slew me
> Shall revive me,
> Or reprive me,
> And to many deaths renew me.

There are many brilliant passages scattered through Crashaw's work. The following is stanza 23 from *Sospetto d'Herode:*

That he whom the Sun serves, should faintly peep
Through clouds of Infant flesh; that he the old
Eternal Word should be a Child and weep;
That he who made the fire should fear the cold;
That Heaven's high Majesty his court should keep
In a clay cottage, by each blast control'd;
    That Glory's self should serve our Griefs and fears;
    And free Eternity submit to years.

His worst poems, such as *The Weeper* and *Wishes to His Supposed Mistress,* are, like their faults, so well known that they hardly seem worthy of discussion: they exemplify the faults of the Metaphysical poets at their extreme. His most successful poems are minor in intention and in fact. Perhaps the best are *The Recommendation,* an ingenious but compact and moving statement of a devotional commonplace, and the more striking piece on a text from *Mark,* "Why are ye afraid, O ye of little faith?" The latter has something of the hard clarity of the shorter pieces by Wyatt and Raleigh.

XV

THE BEST POEMS by Henry Vaughan (1622-1695) are almost certainly *The Lamp* and *To His Books.* There are other excellent poems of less force, such as *Departed Friends, The Retreat, Regeneration, The Night, Resolve,* and *Cock-Crowing,* and there are many poems with impressive lines and passages, such as *The World, Man,* and *The Timber.* Vaughan was an orthodox Anglican and was thus familiar with the doctrines of the Church of England; but he was also a Welshman, and was doubtless familiar with Celtic folklore; and he was a physician (of the Hermetic variety); and his twin brother was a student of magic, alchemy, and related subjects; and Henry Vaughan spent his mature life in relative isolation in the company mainly of his own restless curiosity. In temperament he tended strongly toward the mystical and even the obscurantistic. It seems fairly clear that one cannot always use, in reading Vaughan, the same intellectual tools which would serve to clarify Donne or Greville.

Let me cite a few passages which I am by no means sure that

I or others can clarify. *In Departed Friends* ("They are all gone")
we find this:

> He that hath found some fledg'd bird's nest may know
>   At first sight if the bird be flown;
> But what fair well or grove he sings in now,
>   That is to him unknown.

One editor believes that *well* is a misprint for *dell*. But in Celtic
folklore one has to cross water to reach the Other World: one
crosses a river, one proceeds to an island, or one dives down a
well (that is, a spring). On reaching the Other World one encounters trees and bushes full of singing birds, which are the
souls of the dead. In the poem called *Man*, we find these lines:

> He knocks at all doors, strays and roams;
> Nay hath not so much wit as some stones have,
> Which in the darkest nights point to their homes
> By some hid sense their Marker gave . . .

For years my students have assured me that the stones in question are lodestones, and they may well be such, but I am not convinced. There is a theory of ancient and medieval physics to the
effect that

> The "natural" place of a body is the place toward which it tends in
> virtue of its own nature, and wherein, once it is there it naturally rests.
> (Gilson, *History of Christian Philosophy in the Middle Ages*, p. 194)

The modifier *some* in the lines from Vaughan would seem to
exclude the physics in question (in this passage, the physics of
Avicenna), which presumably would include *all* stones. But
grammar in Vaughan is very loose, and his treatment of natural
details, especially stones, is curious. This whole matter, with
especial reference to stones, is discussed at some length, though
without much clarification, by F. E. Hutchinson in *Henry
Vaughan: A Life and Interpretation* (Oxford: 1947). Hutchinson
is aware of Vaughan's unorthodox interests and of the possible
effects of Vaughan's Welsh heritage, and he sees in the stones
and related matters the possibility of a kind of pre-Christian
animism. He may be more nearly right than am I or my students.
Hutchinson points out further that English was a second lan-

guage for Vaughan, and that this fact may account for some of his curious rhythms and for his unreliable grammar. As an example of another problem, let us consider the opening lines of *The Lamp:*

> 'Tis dead night round about: Horror doth creep
> And move on with the shades; stars nod and sleep
> And through the dark air spin a fiery thread,
> Such as doth gild the lazy glow-worm's bed.

The third line is strange: it gives one the impression that Vaughan had seen a time-exposure photograph of the stars, in which the stars appear as threads instead of as points; but of course he had not, and the stars as one regards them at any moment with the eyes appear as points. However, the French expression for *shooting star* is *étoile filante,* or thread-spinning star. The verb is *filer,* which means primarily to spin thread, or to flow (as of a liquid) without division into drops. I know nothing of Vaughan's French, but he may have acquired at least a little and have encountered this expression, or he may have been struck independantly by the resemblance which inspired the French expression. But if we accept this interpretation, we are in the same difficulty in which we have found ourselves with *some stones,* for Vaughan writes: "stars nod and sleep . . . . *and* spin," as if all stars were shooting stars, and there is the additional difficulty that what they do is slow and sleepy, and the trail is compared to the slow and relatively permanent trail left by a glow-worm. If he had meant to describe shooting stars, he should have written *or* in place of *and,* but, as I have said, his grammar is unreliable. The trail of the glow-worm appears to be there partly for its own sake and partly because it belongs to the night, but it serves only to confuse the image of the star. In brief, we are involved in a heavily sensuous description of details for their own sake, with little reference to their relationships to each other and (as we shall presently see) with little concern for their effect in the total poem. This is a minor example of the breakdown of the great Renaissance style, but it is a real example. There are other examples more obvious in Vaughan—and there is a good deal of the great style left.

I quote *The Lamp* complete:

'Tis dead night round about: Horror doth creep
And move on with the shades; stars nod and sleep,
And through the dark air spin a fiery thread,
Such as doth gild the lazy glow-worm's bed.
    Yet burns't thou here a full day, while I spend
My rest in cares, and to the dark world lend
These flames, as thou dost thine to me; I watch
That hour which must thy life and mine dispatch,
But still thou dost out-go me: I can see
Met in thy flames all acts of piety;
Thy light is Charity; thy heat is Zeal;
And thy aspiring active fires reveal
Devotion still on wing; then thou dost weep
Still as thou burn'st, and the warm droppings creep
To measure out thy length, as if thou'dst know
What stock and how much time were left thee now;
Nor dost thou spend one tear in vain, for still
As thou dissolv'st to them, and they distill,
They're stored up in the socket, where they lie,
When all is spent, thy last and sure supply:
And such is true repentance; ev'ry breath
We spend in sighs is treasure after death.
Only one point escapes thee; that thy oil
Is still out with thy flame, and so both fail;
But whensoe're I'm out, both shall be in,
And where thou mad'st an end, there I'll begin.

The first four lines, even if we are not troubled by the difficulties which I have mentioned, are faulty with regard to the whole poem. They give the setting, but the setting is too detailed and too long; since these lines are purely descriptive and since the remainder of the poem is didactic, the two sections tend to fall apart. The poet should have moved on to the lamp immediately after the colon in the first line.

This fault in *The Lamp* is slight, but the same fault appears elsewhere in Vaughan on a larger scale: for examples, in *The Timber* and in *The World*. In each of these poems we have a brief descriptive opening, followed by a long didactic passage which is scarcely related in tone. The short openings, printed as separate poems, are among the favorites of the anthologists. In these two poems, moreover, the short openings are the best parts of the poems; in the long didactic passages following, the organization is bad and the diction is worse. In these poems Vaughan seems to have lost control—completely—of the abstract language of his tradition: the language of theology, of ethics, of religious moralizing. He writes like a poetizing country curate of the early nineteenth century; he is thus one of the most striking examples of the decay of the great tradition to be found in his period, for after all he is a great poet, not a small one, and he ought to have done much better.

But in *The Lamp* the situation is reversed: it is the didactic portion of the poem which rises to mastery. The influence of George Herbert upon Vaughan is well known. Vaughan acknowledged the influence, and scholars have noted many echoes in theme and in phrasing. But in this poem Vaughan may have learned something from Herbert regarding the relationship of sentences and smaller syntactic units to the line and stanza. The stanza here is the pentameter couplet, not the longer stanza of *Church Monuments;* but the variety of length among the sentences and the parts of sentences, the variety of the positions in the line in which these units end, and the use of enjambement are almost equally skillful. The reader might object that we have something approaching the pathetic fallacy of the romantics, that Vaughan is attributing a human experience to the lamp. But the objection, I think, has only a very limited validity. The comparison is ingenious and deliberate rather than naïve, and the concentration throughout is on the experience of the speaker. We have a speaker who is confronting death, alone, in a remote countryside, and laboring, with the tools of his religion, to adjust himself. The labor, in general and in detail, is evident in the diction and in the structure at every point. The poem is not as great as a few poems by earlier poets, but it is one of the great poems of the tradition.

Even finer is the poem *To His Books,* which, since it is almost never cited, I shall quote entire:

> Bright books! the perspectives to our weak sights,
> The clear projections of discerning lights,

Burning and shining thoughts, man's posthume day,
The track of fled souls and their milky way,
The dead alive and busy, the still voice
Of enlarged spirits, kind Heaven's white decoys!
Who lives with you lives like those knowing flowers,
Which in commerce with light spend all their hours;
Which shut to clouds, and shadows nicely shun,
But with glad haste unveil to kiss the Sun.
Beneath you all is dark and a dead night,
Which whoso lives in wants both health and sight.
   By sucking you the wise, like bees, do grow
Healing and rich, though this they do most slow,
Because most choicely; for as great a store
Have we of Books as bees of herbs, or more:
And the great task to try, then know, the good,
To discern weeds, and judge of wholesome food,
Is a rare scant performance. For man dies
Oft ere 'tis done, while the bee feeds and flies.
But you were all choice flowers; all set and drest
By old, sage florists, who well knew the best:
And I amidst you all am turned a weed!
Not wanting knowledge, but for want of heed.
Then thank thyself, wild fool, that would'st not be
Content to know—what was too much for thee!

In this poem we have the same concern which we find in *The Lamp* with self-improvement, and the same feeling of labor and anxiety. But in this poem we do not have the explicitly Christian context, which the modern and non-Christian reader may be able to share only by an act of the historical imagination; we have, rather, the more nearly universal context of the struggle toward the intellectual life, and, at the end, the desperate awareness of one's own limitations, an awareness which was Christian in Vaughan's view of the matter, but which is not given in explictly Christian terms.

The poem is not without its weaknesses, but these are not serious. The first six lines depend for their total effect on repetition, which is primarily emotional. Nothing in these lines is really bad, but some details are better than others and not all are necessary. One of the greatest strokes of Vaughan's genius, however, is in the phrase "the dead alive and busy." The flowers and

101

the bees are employed in a manner common to the Renaissance: that is, we are not expected to visualize them or to feel any great interest in them as flowers and bees, but rather we are expected to understand their relationship to the total theme of the poem as mere concepts, and if we do this they contribute extraordinary force to the poem, especially in the last eleven and a half lines, which are certainly among the greatest in our poetry. The faults, I think, are real but slight. The poem is great.

Departed Friends is the best-known of Vaughan's poems, and it is unquestionably moving, but it seems to me less impressive than the two poems I have just quoted. The best passages in the poem give us images more or less similar to each other, which are characteristic of Vaughan's fascination with night, obscure splendor, and obscure experience:

> It glows and glitters in my cloudy breast
> Like stars upon some gloomy grove . . . .

and:

> Dear, beauteous death; the Jewel of the Just!
> Shining no where but in the dark . . . .

The remaining lines communicate the subject with emotional conviction but with intellectual and perceptual vagueness; what we have is the Renaissance style, moving through a kind of obscure mysticism in the direction of eighteenth and nineteenth century hymnography. The chief force of the poem comes by way of its rhythm.

The Retreat deals with a more or less Platonic concept of pre-natal beatitude, purity (or relative purity) in infancy, corruption through maturity, and the desire to return to beatitude by a reversal of one's course. If one takes the theme in these bare and theoretic terms, it appears to have little relationship to reality; but it is true that sensitive children may often have a kind of ecstatic vision of the world around them and that this vision may be remembered at maturity with nostalgia. Yet if this is what we are dealing with, the explicit theme and the matter perceived are not at one with each other, and the poem, in spite of its beauties of detail, remains a kind of sentimental fantasy. The poem may well have had a great influence on Thomas Traherne, who deals almost exclusively with this subject, and it may have influenced Wordsworth's *Ode on the Intimations of Immortality*, a poem far inferior to Vaughan's poem and to the best of Traherne.

XVI

THE BEST POEMS by Andrew Marvell (1621-1678) are *To His Coy Mistress, The Garden,* and *An Horatian Ode upon Cromwell's Return from Ireland.* There are others which are important in connection with his thought, and there are others which contain passages of interesting poetry, but these three are the best, just as they are the most famous. The *Horatian Ode* is on the most serious subject of the three, but it is perhaps the least successful in execution. The first twenty-six lines are stereotyped and of no interest in themselves; they may be the sort of dead rhetoric which is expected in this kind of ode, but if this is so, then this kind of ode is intrinsically defective. There is a great deal of the same kind of language in the remainder of the poem, but there are good passages: lines twenty-seven through thirty-six, and fifty-seven through sixty in particular. Fifty-seven, however, introduces a mild structural weakness: up to this point the pronoun *he* has referred to Cromwell; in fifty-seven it refers to Charles. There is no transition, and we have to remember the historical fact of the beheading after we have read two or three lines in order to understand the new reference. The poem may well have the structure which is expected of this kind of ode[21] but the virtue of any structural principle lies in the results produced: the general effect of the ode is that of a kind of newsletter for the year. Here as in *Lycidas* and as in much of Vaughan the close organization of Renaissance poetry can be seen in the initial stages of its disintegration.

To His Coy Mistress is an elaborate treatment of a trivial and stereotyped subject. The best discussion of the poem with which I am acquainted is that of J.V. Cunningham[22]. The structure is that of close rational argument: Had we but time . . . But we have not time . . . Therefore let me seduce you now. Each stage of the argument is expanded by a great deal of ingenious detail. The poem might fairly be described as an exceptionally brilliant academic exercise on a set theme, but it is no more than that.

The best poem is *The Garden*. The poem is famous and has often been explained. The best discussion—a very fine discussion —is by Frank Kermode.[23] The essay is too long to summarize; it deals with the poem partly in terms of the philosophical ideas involved, mainly in terms of the literary tradition which had used these ideas and from which Marvell's poem emerges. The poem deals with a longing which at times appears almost mystical, although it is probably literary for the most part, for a return to Eden, an Eden in which man had not yet been corrupted by women or civilization. Instead of sexual love we have a "pure" love for the vegetation of the garden. Yet the sources of Marvell's ideas and tradition are also remote sources of Romanticism, and the poem seems to be a precursor as well as a result. The love for the vegetation is "pure," yet in the fifth stanza it is very sensual, and the last lines suggest—no doubt remotely—Whitman's illicit love-affair with Mother Nature early in the *Song of Myself*. Whitman is gross and grotesque, and Marvell is extremely civilized, but the suggestion is there. As Kermode tells us, the sixth stanza is Platonic, yet it verges on pantheism. Green, Kermode tells us, signifies innocence, and this, I suppose, should eliminate all traces of pantheism from the last couplet, but it does not:

> Annihilating all that's made
> To an innocent thought in an innocent shade.

If anything, this reading is more pantheistic than the lines in the poem. For the pantheist this would be satisfactory, but I cannot understand pantheism and consequently I cannot grasp the idea by which I am supposed to be moved. For most scholars, it is sufficient merely to understand the poet's intention, but this understanding brings us only to the brink of the poem, to the brink of the critical judgment. Unless we go beyond the scholar's mere elucidation, we have not even tried to experience the poem; the poem is an interesting puzzle, no more. In the seventh stanza,

104

the soul becomes a bird and sings in the branches; it is a charming bird, but it casts little light on the experience of the soul. That is, we have ornament at the expense of meaning, a great deal of vehicle and very little tenor. Kermode provides us with a good deal of the literary background of Marvell's bird-soul, but the background does not help us. The writing of the poem is beautiful throughout if we can be satisfied with a meaning which seems to escape us at the crucial moments. The theme is not profoundly serious; the poem is witty in the sense in which Marvell would have used this term, and it is charming, but it is far from great.

XVII

THOMAS TRAHERNE (1637-1674) represents in much of his work an extreme of esoteric mysticism, and in all of his work there is a kind of ecstatic and child-like pietism. His principal theme is that of the beatitude of infancy. His style is consistently distinguished and is often brilliant, but the themes are limited and to the present writer appear naïve, and through the endless repetition of his themes he dulls our appreciation of his style. His best poem was entitled *On News* by himself and was entitled *News* by his brother Philip in his revision of the poem. Philip appears to have been a devoted and untalented servant to his brother's talent: he deadened almost everything that he touched. So far as this particular poem is concerned, Philip (or some one) made only one change, but that change is brutal. The poet's version appears in *Centuries of Meditation*, edited by Bertram Dobell. The other version appears in the Dobell Folio Manuscript as reissued in *The Poetical Works of Thomas Traherne* by Gladys I. Wade (on page 112) and appears also in Traherne's *Poems of Felicity*, edited by H. I. Bell. Miss Wade gives what I take to be the poet's version on page 212 of her volume. Quiller-Couch uses this version, with modernized spelling, in *The Oxford Book of English Verse*, and I quote the second stanza from his text:

> As if the tidings were the things,
> My very joys themselves, my foreign treasure—
> Or else did bear them on their wings—
> With so much joy they came, with so much pleasure.

> My Soul stood at that gate
> To recreate
> Itself with bliss, and to
> Be pleased with speed. A fuller view
> It fain would take,
> Yet journeys back would make
> Unto my heart; as if 'twould fain
> Go out to meet, yet stay within
> To fit a place to entertain
> And bring the tidings in.

The effect of ecstasy, of disembodied activity is extraordinary. This effect is thoroughly deadened in the revised version, and the effect of the deadening pervades the poem. Instead of

> and to
> Be pleased with speed,

the revision gives us

> and woo
> Its speedier approach.

The next best poems on this theme, and probably in Traherne, are *The Salutation* and *Wonder,* and they are memorable poems. Both are available in *The Oxford Book of Seventeenth Century Verse.* Many other poems—*The Preparative* is an example—contain brilliant moments. The command of rhythm, syntax, and precise diction is beyond praise.

Traherne's poems, of course, were first discovered by Bertram Dobell late in the nineteenth century, and Dobell published the first collection in 1903. It is a pity that the poems were not published at least a century earlier. Had they been, the influence of Traherne upon Blake and Wordsworth would have provided careers for a great many scholars, and the same influence might have improved the styles of those poets, especially Wordsworth. Wordsworth's *Intimations* ode deals in some measure with Traherne's favorite subject, but a comparison of the style of this poem with the style of Traherne is depressing:

> There was a time when meadow, grove, and stream
> The earth, and every common sight,
> To me did seem

106

> Apparell'd in celestial light,
> The glory and the freshness of a dream.
> It is not now as it hath been of yore;—
> Turn wheresoe'er I may,
> By night or day,
> The things which I have seen I now can see no more.

As to the diction of the poem, it continues in this mode of rural pomposity and deadly commonplace to the very end, whereas the poems of Traherne are distinguished in diction throughout. Wordsworth's rhythms are heavy and obvious, whereas those of Traherne are almost electrically perceptive. Wordsworth's poem is loosely put together, on the basis of association, for the most part, from section to section, and on the basis of repetition of illustration, for the most part, within each section, whereas Traherne's poems are closely organized. Wordsworth's poem depends heavily upon natural description, for which he showed no talent, except in a few short passages, throughout his work.

XVIII

I WOULD LIKE to mention briefly two more poets in the metaphysical tradition, Philip Pain (dates unknown) and Edward Taylor (1642?-1729)[24]. Of Pain nothing is known beyond what we learn from his *Daily Meditations*. It was begun in July of 1666 and was published in Massachusetts in 1668, and was written "By Philip Pain: Who, lately suffering Shipwrack, was drowned." He was probably a very young man, perhaps little over twenty. Since the book was published in New England and was widely read there, he was probably a New Englander. But there is no real evidence regarding these matters. He was obviously influenced by George Herbert, and there are traces of other metaphysical influences. The poems are very devout and are fairly well executed, but only one is really memorable; since this one (naturally enough) has never found its way into an anthology, I will quote it:

> Scarce do I pass a day, but that I hear
> Some one or other's dead; and to my ear
> Me thinks it is no news; but Oh! did I

> Think deeply on it, what it is to dye,
> My Pulses all would beat, I should not be
> Drown'd in this Deluge of Security.

The poem conveys a profound insight into the human predicament, whether Christian or other, and it should be retained in our literature.

Edward Taylor came to New England in 1668 and entered Harvard, apparently with advanced standing, to study for the ministry. He eventually became a clergyman at Westfield, Massachusetts, and spent the rest of his life there. His poetry is clearly in the metaphysical tradition, although it is difficult to be sure of particular influences. His poems fall into two main groups: *Preparatory Meditations before my Approach to the Lord's Supper. Chiefly upon the Doctrin preached upon the Day of administration;* and *God's Determinations touching his Elect: and the Elects Combat in their Conversion, and Coming up to God in Christ together with the Comfortable Effects thereof.* There are a few miscellaneous poems. The poems are written in conformity with the Westminster Confession, and *God's Determinations* is a didactic piece dealing with this doctrine, and resembling in some respects the morality play and the miracle play. The best poems are to be found among the *Meditations.* The best single poem is *Meditation 112* of the Second Series. The poem is a very orderly exposition of a theological doctrine: Christ, the second head of mankind, died, not for mankind, but for the saints, the predestined elect of the Calvinistic churches; in doing this, he slew death. The whole concept is stereotyped, and so are the subdivisions of the concept; and for most modern readers (at least for this one) the concept, although it can be understood in its historical context, cannot be taken very seriously. But Taylor took it seriously, and a good deal of passion went into the poem:

> Infinities fierce firy arrow red
> Shot from the Splendid Bow of Justice Bright
> Did Smite thee down, for thine. Thou art their head.
> They di'de in thee. Their death did on thee light.
> They di'de their Death in thee, thy Death in theirs.
> Hence thine is mine, thy death my trespass clears.

How sweet is this: my Death lies buried
   Within thy Grave, my Lord, deep under ground,
It is unskin'd, as Carrion rotten Dead.
      For Grace's hand gave Death its deadly wound.
      Deaths no such terror on th' Saints blesst Coast.
      Its but a harmless Shade: No walking Ghost.

The Painter lies: the Bellfrey Pillars weare
   A false Effigies now of Death, alas!
With empty Eyeholes, Butter teeth, bones bare
   And spraggling arms, having an Hour Glass
   In one grim paw. Th'other a Spade doth hold
   To shew deaths frightful region under mould.

    Whereas its Sting is gone . . . . . .

And so on.

One should notice first of all the vigorous syntax and rhythm. The relationship of sentence to line and stanza is varied and the variations are powerful. We do not know much about Taylor's reading in poetry, but these qualities are characteristic of the high Renaissance. The diction is equally vigorous. The treatment of death is of interest historically. Bryant, in *Thanatopsis* (a remarkable poem for its period), treats death from a genteel distance; Poe, in poems and stories alike, treats it melodramatically but as a form of hallucination. Taylor is realistic, and, one might say, practical. He does not fear death, because he is sure that he is one of the Saints; but he deals with a familiar reality. The mortality figures in early New England, especially among women and children, were appalling. Death was everywhere.

The next best poem is probably *Meditation 20* of the First Series. It is an unsatisfactory poem, but it contains some of Taylor's most brilliant lines. The poem deals with the ascension of Christ into Heaven. In the first two stanzas Christ is going up in a chariot; in the third stanza he is *not* going up in a chariot but is climbing up on a ladder; in the fourth and thereafter he is in a chariot. This is curious, for Taylor's work is almost invariably orderly and rational, in the manner of the Renaissance; I can only suppose that there was some error in transcription on an occasion when Taylor was tired, but this is merely a supposition. The two final stanzas offer one of the commonest stereotypes of the devotional poetry of the Renaissance: the poet will be provided with the quills and feathers of an angel's wings by Faith and Grace. But the fourth and fifth stanzas are brilliant, and I quote them:

> Methinks I see Heavens sparkling Courtiers fly,
> In flakes of Glory down him to attend:
> And heare Heart Cramping notes of Melody,
> Surround his Charriot as it did ascend
> Mixing their Musick making e'ry string
> More to inravish as they this tune sing.

> God is Gone up with a triumphant Shout
> The Lord with sounding Trumpets melodies.
> Sing Praise, sing Praise, sing Praise, sing Praises out,
> Unto our King sing praise seraphick wise.
> Lift up your Heads ye lasting Doore they sing
> And let the King of Glory Enter in.

The entire passage is brilliantly written. The descending angels in the first two lines are splendid. The second stanza might appear violent, especially the third line, if the preceding stanzas had not prepared us. And yet we find ourselves here, as in the other poem from which I have quoted, in a special and narrowly constricted world, which no longer has much reality for us. Fulke Greville was also a Calvinist. He did not always write on Calvinistic themes, but, even when he did write on such themes, he was aware of the psychological and moral implications of his themes: he shows a richness of intelligence which is simply not present in Taylor. In Taylor we are in a realm of pure myth; in Greville we are in a realm of profound human understanding. In Traherne we are for the most part in the realm of the extremely sensitive and entranced child, and the realm is limited, but in a way it is more human than Taylor's realm. Traherne and Greville both are abler stylists than Taylor. In Taylor we have an impressive remnant of the great Renaissance style, but very little of the informing intellect which gave that style its authority. He is the end of a great tradition.

XIX

IN WRITING OF the metaphysical poets, I have passed over a good many other poets, most of them minor, and I will now revert to earlier dates.

In the seventeenth century there are a good many continuators (more or less) of the Elizabethan song tradition: one can mention, among others, Barnefield, Dekker, Thomas Heywood, John Fletcher, Webster, Phineas Fletcher, Giles Fletcher, Francis Beaumont, Shirley, Davenant, Waller, Fanshawe, Cartwright, and Dryden. Many of the poems in question come from plays; most of the best will be found in the standard anthologies. The best single poems by the men I have mentioned are probably these: *Hark! Now everything is still* by John Webster (1580?-1625?), from *The Duchess of Malfi;* and *No, no, poor suffering Heart* by John Dryden (1631-1700), from *Cleomenes.* There are other fine songs by Dryden. The poems in question require no exegesis, and their virtues are obvious.

Ben Jonson left his mark on a good many of the poets who are commonly classed as members of the School of Donne—on the Herberts and on Vaughan assuredly. But there are other and simpler poets who are usually regarded as disciples of Jonson, and, in so far as they may be, they appear to have been influenced primarily by his smaller poems. As to Sir Robert Ayton (1570-1638) he is a trifle older than Jonson, but they are almost exactly contemporary. Ayton may or may not have been influenced by Jonson, but both men were working in the same tradition. Ayton was a Scot, who began writing verse before he came to London, and who did a few crude poems in the poulter's measure, perhaps under the influence of Gascoigne, Googe, and Turbervile[25]. His mature work is small in quantity, but distinguished. His best single poem is the one beginning *I lov'd thee once, I'll love no more.* It can be found in the *Oxford Book of English Verse,* along with his next best poem; both can be found in the *Oxford Book of Seventeenth Century Verse,* along with three other poems; and there is not much else that is worth reading. The poem in question is one of many denunciations of the fickle mistress. In the management of the theme and in the style the poem resembles Wyatt's *Blame not my Lute* so closely that one is inclined to suspect an influence, especially as Ayton seems to have been reading the early poets before the later, but the resemblance may be accidental. Ayton's poem is better than Wyatt's: the analysis of the moral situation is more acute and complex, the poem is more succinct, and there is less involvement in conventional stereotypes. The poem rises well above the level of the conventional poetry of the period and deserves far more attention than it has received.

Robert Herrick (1591-1674) is by his own account and obviously in fact a disciple of Ben Jonson, but essentially of Jonson's lesser poems. Herrick learned the art of writing from Jonson but he lacked Jonson's intelligence. Here and there in Herrick one finds lines which indicate moral insight, for example these lines from the *Litany to the Holy Spirit:*

> When the Tempter me pursu'th
> With the sins of all my youth,
> And half damns me with untruth;
> Sweet Spirit comfort me!

Most of Herrick's best poems are available in the standard anthologies: the elegies on the flowers, the *Night-Piece to Julia,* and some of the little epitaphs in the tradition of Jonson. Some of his more ambitious poems on the mortality of man and the immortality of art are impressive: the best are *Now is the time for mirth* and *Only a little more.* They are in a classical tradition which has continued almost into our own time: the finest poem on the subject within the past century and a half is *L'Art,* by Théophile Gautier. This poem has far greater intellectual content than the poems by Herrick, and is at least as well written. The treatment of the subject is noble; Herrick's treatment is conventional. We tend to think of Gautier as a minor poet, and perhaps he was, but perhaps we should reread him. If he was a minor poet, he was a minor poet in one of the greatest periods of occidental literature, the French period from Gautier through Valéry. I have wandered from my subject, but an occasional wandering may prevent one from being unduly provincial.

112

The best of Herrick's epitaphs is the following:

*Epitaph on the Tomb of Sir Edward Giles and his Wife
in the South Aisle of Dean Prior Church, Devon.*

No trust to metals nor to marbles, when
These have their fate and wear away as men;
Times, titles, trophies may be lost and spent,
But virtue rears the eternal monument.
What more than these can tombs or tombstones pay?
But here's the sunset of a tedious day:
These two asleep are: I'll but be undress'd
And so to bed: pray wish us all good rest.

The poem resembles George Herbert's *Church Monuments* in a
very general way. Both are fine poems, but the intellectual content of Herbert's poem is great; the first four lines of Herrick's
poem are strictly conventional, and the last four, though moving,
are domestic and somewhat simple. There is no real intellectual
activity anywhere in Herrick. Occasionally, when the style is
stripped to an absolute minimum, the bare mortuary theme ac-
quires a remarkable and ominous impressiveness:

Upon His Departure Hence

Thus I
Pass by,
And die:
As one
Unknown
And gone:
I'm made
A shade
And laid
I' th' grave:
There have
My cave,
Where tell
I dwell.
Farewell.

The poem has a certain technical interest, merely as a curiosity:
so far as I can recollect, it is the only poem in English in iambic
monometer. This is a trivial consideration, but the poem is a

good one, however small. The following is similar, but perhaps better:

To the Yew and Cypress to Grace His Funeral

Both you two have
Relation to the grave:
 And where
The funeral-trump sounds, you are there.

I shall be made,
Ere long, a fleeting shade:
 Pray, come
And do some honour to my tomb.

Do not deny
My last request; for I
 Will be
Thankful to you, or friends, for me.

In a way, these poems are very small stylistic games, like some of the songs of Morley, but the poems are, at the same time, serious. It is possible that some of the anthology favorites are better, but they are certainly not much better, and these have been neglected. Herrick's best poems—and there are many of them —are written with extraordinary finish, but their content is very small.

Let me quote one of Jonson's smaller poems, the *Hymn to Diana*, from *Cynthia's Revels*. The poem is in praise of Queen Elizabeth, who liked to be called the Virgin Queen, and who was, as a result, identified by most of the poets of the time with the Virgin Goddess. She liked also to be considered as a great beauty who commanded love wherever she moved.

Queen, and Huntress, chaste and fair,
Now the Sun is laid to sleep,
Seated in thy silver chair,
State in wonted manner keep:
 Hesperus intreats thy light,
 Goddess, excellently bright.

Earth, let not thy envious shade
Dare itself to interpose;
Cynthia's shining orb was made
Heaven to clear, when day did close:
  Bless us then with wished sight,
  Goddess, excellently bright.

Lay thy bow of pearl apart,
And thy crystal-shining quiver;
Give unto the flying hart
Space to breathe, how short soever:
  Thou that mak'st a day of night,
  Goddess, excellently bright.

"Excellently bright": the goddess is not bewilderingly bright or excessively bright; she is excellently bright—that is, she provides the proper illumination. She keeps state in wonted manner—that is, in the accustomed and proper manner; she is the ruler and provides the necessary dignity for her realm. Hesperus, the evening star, asks for her light, and the Earth is warned not to interpose its darkness. In the last stanza, we have, I suspect, a pun on *hart*: in the light of Elizabethan spelling (or perhaps in the darkness) this does not seem impossible. Diana was the huntress who used the bow and arrow; Elizabeth was, or fancied herself to be, a beautiful woman, who controlled men's hearts, even in her old age, when this poem was written. Elizabethan ladies, as we encounter them in the love-poetry of the period, shot little arrows from their eyes, arrows which struck down the male victims. Sometimes Cupid did the shooting from behind the eyes, but Cupid was not always necessary. Elizabeth-Diana appears to be in the final stanza the goddess of love and of hunting; she is entreated to show mercy to her victims; and, since she has already been established as the goddess of intellectual order (that is, for the duration of her reign), it is to be supposed that she will grant the entreaty.

The poem is not a great poem, but it is probably the best of Jonson's lesser poems. The poem is very ingenious, but the ingenuity is so carefully controlled that most of it has been overlooked. It has in it traces of the ornate style, and yet it tends in the direction of what I shall later call the post-Symbolist style: we do not have theoretic statement followed by ornamental sensory detail, but intellectual and sensory material are so intimately related that they exist as one and the same, simultaneously.

It would be brutal to compare even the best of Herrick with one of Jonson's great poems. Herrick modeled himself on Jonson's lesser poems and probably lacked the understanding to deal with the greater. But there is nothing in Herrick to compare with this poem, either in execution or in intellectual scope.

John Wilmot, Earl of Rochester (1648-1680), is one of the few minor poets of the seventeenth century who still seem to have much vitality. He was a rake and a foolish young man, who seems to have died as a result of his excesses, but he was also a brilliant stylist who wrote a few memorable poems. His best poem, and a very moving one, is *Absent from thee*. It can be found in the *Oxford Book of English Verse* and in the *Oxford Book of Seventeenth Century Verse*. *Upon Drinking in a Bowl* and *Upon Nothing* are perhaps more characteristic, and can be found in the second volume mentioned. The first of these two is frivolous, but graceful and witty; the second begins as a serious metaphysical poem and ends as routine Restoration satire. There are other poems in Rochester which are well executed: he was the heir of a long and sophisticated tradition in style, and he wrote on the common subjects of his time; occasionally his native talent adds something to what he was given by his predecessors and contemporaries[26].

There are other little poets in the seventeenth century who inherit a good deal from Jonson and sometimes a little from Donne: among them, Browne, Carew, Habington, Suckling, Graham of Montrose, Cotton, Dorest, and Sedley. The best poem by any of these is probably Browne's epitaph on the Countess Dowager of Pembroke: *Underneath this sable hearse*. It has often been attributed to Jonson.

XX

THIS LEAVES ME with John Milton (1608-1674). I have set Milton
aside until this point, in spite of his dates, because he is less representative of the Renaissance than any other poet whom I have
discussed, and because he provides the most obvious link between the Renaissance and the sentimental-romantic tradition of
the eighteenth and nineteenth centuries. As to *Lycidas*, I shall
say what little I have to say of it in my next chapter. I would
like to say a few words about *An Epitaph on the Marchioness of
Winchester, L'Allegro, Il Penseroso,* and the sonnets.

Milton has certain great and pervasive defects: first, a pompous redundancy, a tendency to expand every subject which he
touches beyond the justification of the subject in the interests of
an elaborate rhetoric which sometimes loses all connection with
comprehensible syntax[27]; second, a dependence on literary stereotypes which becomes extremely tedious. *An Epitaph on the
Marchioness of Winchester,* an early poem, is a fair introduction.
Like many elegies, it is also a eulogy: one of the consecrated procedures in the eulogy is an opening which praises the ancestry
of the subject; Milton's sonnet in praise of the Lady Margaret Ley,
for example, is devoted almost wholly to her father; Browne's
famous epitaph on the Countess Dowager of Pembroke names
her as Sidney's sister, Pembroke's mother. Milton begins:

> This rich Marble doth enter
> The honored Wife of Winchester,
> A Viscount's daughter, an Earl's heir. . . . .

He uses a form of versification common in the elegiac tradition,
the same form used by Thomas Carew (1595?-1639?) in his
epitaph on the Lady Mary Villiers:

> The Lady Mary Villiers lies
> Under this stone; with weeping eyes
> The parents that first gave her birth,
> And their sad friends, laid her in earth.
> If any of them, Reader, were
> Known unto thee, shed a tear;
> Or if thyself possess a gem
> As dear to thee, as this to them,

117

> Though a stranger to this place,
> Bewail in theirs thine own hard case;
> For thou, perhaps, at thy return
> May'st find thy Darling in an urn.

Carew's poem does not employ the formulae of eulogy, but it is a formulary epitaph, one of many. Nevertheless, it has the brevity appropriate to the epitaph, and it is very moving. Milton's epitaph is long and is weighted with decorative commonplace. The lady appears to have died in childbirth, and we have lines such as these:

> Gentle Lady may thy grave
> Peace and quiet ever have;
> After this thy travail sore
> Sweet rest sease thee evermore,
> That to give the world encrease,
> Shortened hast thy own lives lease;
> Here besides the sorrowing
> That thy noble House doth bring,
> Here be tears of perfect moan
> Weept for thee in *Helicon*,
> And some Flowers, and some Bays,
> For thy Hearse to strew the ways,
> Sent thee from the banks of *Came*,
> Devoted to thy Vertuous name. . . .

The poem is early, but it indicates clearly a weakness which remained with Milton to the end. We have here the soft dust of Renaissance rhetoric, which a good house-keeper would have swept into a dust-pan and thrown away.

L'Allegro is more charming in its details, but it is overexpanded, devoid of any real content, and essentially an exercise by a talented university student. There are pretty details:

> While the Cock with lively din,
> Scatters the rear of darkness thin. . .

There are inept details:

> Russet Lawns, and Fallows Gray,
> Where the nibling flocks do stray,
> Mountains on whose barren brest
> The laboring clouds do often rest:

118

> Meadows trim with Daisies pide,
> Shallow Brooks, and Rivers wide.

These are platitudes of the worst sort. The mere reference to rustic details is supposed to be poetic; we find the same procedure in Walt Whitman when he merely mentions birds, trees, or rivers in North America. And we find the same procedure in Milton when he merely mentions mythological figures. We find the same procedure in popular songs which merely mention love and moonlight, or home and mother. There is the expectation of an automatic response. Milton, of course, is more scholarly and literate than Whitman and the writers of popular songs, but essentially he is no more serious. This is lazy associationism; the method is the same. *Il Penseroso* is similar, but weaker. The "pensive Nun" for example, is unimpressive at the descriptive level and does nothing to clarify the nature of melancholy. She is an example of the unrealized figure of speech: this kind of figure can be found occasionally in any period, but it is common in Milton and becomes more common in the eighteenth and nineteenth centuries and in our own time. We have a situation in which the tenor, the essential theme, is not clear in the poet's mind, and in which, therefore, the vehicle cannot be given precision.

The best of Milton is in the later sonnets, and these are often impressive. The pomposity is there, however, in nearly all of them, though in varying degrees. The *Tetrachordon* sonnets are magnificent invective in a good cause. The sonnet *To the Lady Margaret Ley* is one of the best, but has characteristic faults. It consists of a single sentence, an interesting fact but not a fault or a virtue in itself. Milton's use of the long sentence in the short poem may have been a development in part from the work of the Herberts, perhaps from Jonson, perhaps from a few of Donne's poems; it seems more likely that it derived from his classical studies. In the ninth line the syntax gets out of control: the line seems to modify "that old man eloquent" (Isocrates), but, as one examines the context, it is evident that the line has to modify the lady herself. And, as in most of the sonnets, the language, through noble in a way, is primarily that of oratory; it lacks the swift perceptiveness, the profundity, of the best of the earlier poets. The

119

language of the sonnet *On the Late Massacre in Piemont* is similar in quality, although here, of course, there is no occasion for the genealogical introduction. The sonnet is one of the best, but the bones, groans, stones, and moans almost get out of hand. The sonnet *To Mr. Lawrence* and one of the sonnets *To Cyriack Skinner* (Cyriack, whose grandsire) are on much the same theme, and both employ the genealogical opening. Both are imitations of Horace; the sonnet to Skinner is much the better. There is something almost comical about the spectacle of John Milton's inviting Cyriack Skinner to gather rosebuds while they may, especially when the invitation is couched in the familiar Miltonic rhetoric; but the poem is indubitably impressive and may be the best of the sonnets. Lines seven through ten are among the best in Milton; the harsh rimes are beautifully managed.

The greatest defect of Renaissance poetry as a body is the narrow limitation of subjects and methods. In the later sonnets, Milton extended the subject matter into the realm of public (united with personal) morality, and the public aspect of this morality may have been responsible for the oratorical style, or, on the other hand, the oratorical style may have made the union possible. But the style, even of these sonnets, is symptomatic of Milton's great weakness. The weakness was continued and extended in the two centuries following, centuries in which new subjects as well as new methods were explored, but most often with disastrous results. The ultimate results of such exploration has been an enrichment of poetry as regards both subject and method; but this enrichment comes late and appears for the most part in American poetry. The enrichment is not Miltonic in aim or in quality; it results, rather, from a breakdown in traditional procedure which Milton inaugurated and which proceeded rapidly in the eighteenth and nineteenth centuries, and from the recovery from this breakdown.

2

The Poetry of Charles Churchill

CHARLES CHURCHILL was born in Westminster, then a suburb of London, in 1731, and died at Boulogne, France, in 1764. At the time of his death he was a few months under thirty-four years of age, and was the most famous English poet of his time, in England and abroad. He was ordained a deacon in 1754 and a priest in 1756. As a clergyman he seems to have disappointed himself and his parishioners about equally. After the publication of *The Rosciad*, a satire on the actors of the day, in 1761, he relied upon his poetry for a livelihood and did fairly well; previously he had had great difficulty. *The Rosciad* is the first poem which he preserved; his work, as we know it, was composed in a little over three years. His life, even before he was ordained, had been irregular; after he abandoned his cure he became notoriously dissolute. This was a period in English history when debauchery on the part of the noble and the wealthy and many of the literary men was more brutal, if possible, than it had been under Charles the Second. It is not too surprising that Churchill was drawn into this kind of life in London. For a time he associated with the members of the so-called Hell-Fire Club, of which the Earl of Sandwich, Sir Francis Dashwood, and George Bubb-Doddington were the leaders; but the brutality of this group was too much for him, and he left them and later attacked them savagely.

He shortly became acquainted with John Wilkes, whose political principles he shared, and he joined with Wilkes in writing and publishing *The North Briton*, a Whig periodical. This paper attacked Tory principles in general and the Bute government in particular. As we look back on this political war from a later date, especially if we do not look into it, we may decide that Churchill and Wilkes were mere brawlers, for most of the famous

121

men of the period were Tories — Samuel Johnson and Hogarth, for examples—whereas Churchill and Wilkes were the only men of their own group worth remembering. But the matter is not so simple. Wilkes had the support of the common people of London, for they believed that he was defending them against the arbitrary power of the wealthy. He was six times elected to Parliament and finally became Lord Mayor of London. His influence in the American colonies was very great; his principles, generally, were those which we accept today as the civilized principles of constitutional governments, and the principles of his enemies almost any of us would find harsh, primitive, corrupt, and intolerable.

Until recently it has been almost impossible to obtain much reliable information about Churchill. In 1953 Wallace Cable Brown published a biography through the University of Kansas Press. The book is badly written, but it contains a good deal of information, although not all that one could desire. In 1956 Douglas Grant published *The Poetical Works of Charles Churchill* (Oxford, at the Clarendon Press). This is, I imagine, as nearly definitive as anything we are likely to have. The notes contain nearly everything that one needs in order to understand the poems, and nearly all of the facts of biography and political history to which I refer in this essay.

Before examining Churchill's poems, one should recall briefly the main outlines of English poetry for the preceding two and a half centuries, with especial reference to the poetry nearest in time to Churchill.

The short poem of the sixteenth century develops more or less obviously from the tradition of the two preceding cenuturies. It is, or tries to be, rational in structure and as often as not logical. Within this rational frame one has two main lines of style: the ornate (as in Sidney) and the plain (as in most of Wyatt and Raleigh). The rational frame (as in much of Sidney and Donne) is often perverted to irrational ends, but the method is clearly there. This rational procedure, at its most effective in the plain style or something close to it, reaches its highest development in Fulke Greville and Ben Jonson and in one poem by George Herbert *(Church Monuments)*. From there on the tradition begins to deteriorate. In the seventeenth century the poets begin to divide into two fairly obvious kinds, and the division can be seen in the work of the two Herberts. We have naïvely pietistic verse, such as one finds in most of George Herbert, this running into various kinds of mysticism, some Christian, as in Crashaw, some in part esoteric, as in Vaughan, Marvell, and Traherne; and we have worldly poetry, such as that of Edward Herbert, Ayton, Sedley, and Rochester. The lines sometimes cross, as in Marvell and Herrick, but on the whole they are perceptibly distinct. For the greater part the worldly poets continue the plain style and the pietistic the ornate, but this generalization does not always hold: Edward Herbert, for example, is predominantly ornate. One can make another passably sound generalization: the ornate style had been the courtly style of the sixteenth century; the plain style became the courtly style of the seventeenth.

Milton continues the ornate style, but in Milton the rational structure is decaying toward association. At the time when Milton was writing *Lycidas*, the doctrines of English associationism were not yet current, but he had his models in another decadent tradition: that of Vergil and his Sicilian and Alexandrian predecessors. *Lycidas* is a poem of which the scheme is held together by a loose pun: that on the word *pastor*. King was a divinity student and thus would have been a pastor in the ecclesiastical sense; but he was also a poet, and in pastoral poems shepherds were addicted to poetry. In Milton's opinion, of course, a poet had a moral responsibility, and there was a general relationship between the two kinds of shepherd. But Milton does not even indicate this relationship in the poem. Ben Jonson or Fulke Greville would have defined it. The poem falls apart here, or at best depends upon loose association; and much of the rest of the poem is a matter of loose association; — partly in the progression of the poem, partly in the pseudo-descriptive details, the numerous flowers, fauns, satyrs, and so on which are named but not seen or understood and are named purely for the connotations of the names. Milton does this kind of thing with more skill than anyone else who has ever attempted it in English — with more skill even

123

than Ezra Pound — but the poetry is of a decadent kind and is not great. *Lycidas* gets what unity it has from Milton's magnificent gift for sound and for rhetorical tone. Milton provides a kind of link between the ornate-pietistic tradition of the seventeenth century and the ornate-sentimental and associationistic tradition of the eighteenth. It is no accident, for example, that Dyer's *Grongar Hill* is an imitation of *L'Allegro* and *Il Penseroso*, nor that the word *contemplation* in the opening lines of Dyer's poem means sentimental revery over the landscape. Dyer's use of this word indicates a revolution in the history of thought. It is no accident that Gray echoes Milton in the *Elegy* nor that Collins echoes him in the *Ode to Evening*. Both of these poems have proceeded farther than Milton toward disintegration, that of Collins the farther of the two. Their method is the dominant method of English poetry nearly to the end of the nineteenth century, and it is often with us still, in both England and the United States.

The sources of the modern theory of this kind of poetry are to be found in two anti-intellectual traditions which support and supplement each other: the sentimentalism of Shaftesbury, in which impulse is treated with respect and reason with suspicion, a sentimentalism succinctly summarized by Pope in the *Essay on Man*, especially in the third and fourth epistles; and the doctrine of association, derived from Hobbes and Locke, and developed by Addison, Hartley, Alison, and others in the course of the eighteenth century. According to the first of these doctrines, we do not need to study ourselves in order to understand ourselves: we need merely to entrust ourselves to our feelings, and all will be well. As Pope puts it, equal is common sense and common ease. This doctrine may or may not be sound morally (I personally think it unsound), but it deprives the poet at a stroke of his proper subject matter, which is the understanding of human nature. It generates the eighteenth-century cliché, the formulary generalization, almost automatically. More than two thousand years of ethical and psychological study were thrown away, in favor of a few easy phrases, and the precise evaluation of human experience which had marked the best poetry of the Renaissance was rapidly lost. According to Hobbes and Locke, all ideas arise from sense-perceptions and the complex association of sense-perceptions. Little by little this came to mean, in literary theory, that ideas can be expressed in sense-perceptions: this theory was pretty well established by the end of the eighteenth century, and even Addison treated poetry largely in terms of visual perception. In our time the theory is axiomatic folk-wisdom: Pound, for example, tells us to go in fear of abstractions, that the natural object is always the *adequate* symbol. Associationism also affected the structure of the poem: it justified the neglect of the traditional structure, that of reason or logic, in favor of the structure of revery. One can observe both aspects of the associative method in the *Ode to Evening* and in Pound's *Cantos*.

These two aspects of associative writing, however, do not invariably coincide. One can scarcely depend wholly on imagery without employing the structure of revery; but one can employ associative structure, loose or controlled, without much in the way of imagery: the work of Charles Churchill is an example. Furthermore, these methods may be employed to enrich both the structure and the content of poetry if their possibilities and limitations are understood and the methods controlled. I have tried to describe such procedure elsewhere in writing of Valéry.

The immediate background of Churchill's early poems, however, is the satiric poetry of Dryden and Pope, and it was only gradually that he worked away from these into a different style. He professed great admiration for Dryden and much less for Pope, but he obviously learned something from both. He is inferior to both of them when he is writing in their manner, but this is the manner which is expected of the satiric poet of the eighteenth century, and consequently it is Churchill's inferior work for which he is known today — in so far as he is known.

In Dryden and his followers there is not much left of the older English traditions: the models are mainly Latin, and to some extent Greek and French, but in a general way the poets of this line have styles which correspond to the older ornate and plain styles. We might say, at least figuratively, that the heroic style corresponds to the old ornate style and the directly didactic or satiric to the plain: I use the adverb *directly* with the explicit intention of excluding the mock-heroic, which is something else. We can see the heroic style in a fairly distinguished form in Dryden's Vergil, and it is not without minor virtues in Pope's Homer. We can see it, or something very like it, in the "great odes," more or less Pindaric in intention, which obsessed so many poets from Dryden until late in the nineteenth century. *Alexander's Feast,* by Dryden, will serve as an example. It is, I suppose, the most coldly misbegotten monster in the history of English verse, yet Dryden considered it his greatest work. The best single poem by Dryden is certainly *MacFlecknoe,* and the best by Pope *The Rape of the Lock.* Yet these are mock-heroic poems; their principal virtues arise from the fact that they exploit the ridiculous aspects of the style that both poets held in the highest esteem. This is a sad commentary on the main preoccupations of the period; and parody is a dangerous style, because it depends upon clichés for its effectiveness, and clichés are still clichés even when used in the interest of wit. Even poems as remarkable as these two are essentially a kind of light verse. Churchill employs the mock-heroic method, but in most poems occasionally, and in his last work with great discretion. He never employs the heroic.

The directly satiric and didactic are not invariably combined with each other, but we find them together in the most memorable poems. I will take *Absalom and Achitophel* and the *Epistle to Arbuthnot* as examples. Most readers — myself among them — remember these poems fragmentarily: the portraits of Zimri, Achitophel, and Atticus, and a handful of Pope's epigrams stay in the mind, but the poems do not. The reason for this is simple: neither poem has any really unifying principle. Dryden employs a dull narrative, which elaborately and clumsily parallels the biblical narrative, and he does this in order to praise a monarch who was a corrupt fool. One cannot take the whole poem seriously, but one can find interest in the brilliant details. Pope's poem is more honest, and for that reason more obviously fragmentary: nothing holds it together except Pope's exasperation with people who have exasperated him. They were doubtless exasperating, but so are most people; so is life. The form of each poem is an excuse for satirical portraits and epigrams, rather than a unifying principle. The models for this kind of thing are Roman; Dryden's translations provide a good introduction to the topic. The form is similar to that of many pastorals.

Churchill's earliest poems belong to what I have called the directly satiric and didactic tradition, and they employ a versification much like that of Dryden. *The Rosciad* is the first of his poems which we have and one of his weakest. It appears in all of the anthologies of eighteenth-century poetry and is required reading in most universities. His other work is almost never studied (except, occasionally, for passages from *The Ghost*), and few scholars or critics have read it. *The Rosciad* is a satire on the actors of the day: it is composed of a factitious frame and a great many portraits. Some of the portraits are amusing; most are not. The poem is tedious. The poem satirizes people whom we have forgotten and who were unimportant at the time. In fact, actors are always unimportant and their qualities are unimportant, and it seems foolish to devote so much attention to them. *The Author*, which follows *The Rosciad*, and which was written as an attack on the critics of *The Rosciad*, is a little better unified, but not much. It is better than *The Rosciad*, however, in two ways: it contains some remarks on the morality of reviewers which are well-put and are valid even today, and it is very much shorter. The next poem, *Night*, is by far the best of these three, but it is what one might call a classic example of the type. It is addressed to Churchill's friend, Robert Lloyd. We gather that Churchill and Lloyd prefer to sleep by day and wake by night. The reason for this preference is simple: they can converse (when together) or think (when separate) without interruption from the persons whom they dislike. This notion provides an excuse for descriptions of the persons whom they dislike: most of these are types rather than individuals. Much of the satire is excellent, though not great; one feels that one has read much of the same kind of thing before, and in fact one has. Dryden's translation of the *Third Satire of Juvenal*, for example, might have served as a model, both in structure and in general method, although it is only fair to add that Churchill's poem is better than Dryden's.

The next poem is *The Ghost*. This deals nominally with the

127

investigation of the Cock Lane ghost, but the plot provides merely a frail excuse for satirical portraits. The portraits of Dr. Johnson are the most famous, mainly because Dr. Johnson is the most famous person portrayed, and in some university courses these portraits are assigned reading. The poem is interminably tedious, but it is interesting in connection with Churchill's development. The first part, or draft, seems to have been written early, on another topic. Then, when the story of the ghost appeared, Churchill revised and expanded the piece in order to include more and more people. This expansion doubtless accounts in part for the disorderly progression of the poem, but not wholly. The Roman satire, as we find it in Pope's *Epistle to Arbuthnot* or in Churchill's *Night*, is capable of a good deal of expansion so long as the poet merely inserts more details of the same kind; but here we have what purports to be a narrative, and the narrative is lost in confusion. The confusion might merely be an accident resulting from rapid expansion and uncertain intentions, but there seems to be more reason than that. Lines ninety-nine to one hundred and twenty-two of Book II offer a brief defense of associative progression, and lines one hundred and seventy-one to one hundred and seventy-four offer an admiring comment on Sterne. Lines nine hundred and sixty-six through nine hundred and eighty-two of Book III give us both in combination, and it becomes evident that a theory of composition is at work:

> Could I, whilst *Humour* held the Quill,
> Could I *digress* with half that skill,
> Could I with half that skill return
> Which we so much admire in Sterne,
> Where each *Digression*, seeming vain,
> And only fit to entertain,
> Is found, on better recollection,
> To have a just and nice Connection,
> To help the whole with wond'rous art,
> Whence it seems idly to depart;
> Then should our readers ne'er accuse
> These wild excursions of the Muse,
> Ne'er backward turn dull pages o'er
> To recollect what went before;

> Deeply impress'd, and ever new,
> Each image past should start to view. . . . .

The doctrine of inspired digression, which Sterne practiced or endeavored to practice, and the doctrine of associationism which he held, are here described, and Churchill says that he is imitating Sterne. Churchill's account of the method makes it appear more respectable than, I think, it is in this poem or in *Tristram Shandy*, but it gives an idea of the kind of controlled association to which Churchill was later to return in his best work. The poem is interesting in another respect which may be related to this. Although it is written in tetrameter couplets instead of the pentameter at which Churchill was far more expert, it introduces for the first time the consistent use of the long sentence and the parenthetical interruption, with which Churchill was to accomplish so much later. The effect in this poem is one of looseness, even of carelessness, but later these devices were polished into an effective instrument.

Following *The Ghost* we have a series of poems which I shall mention briefly: *The Prophecy of Famine, An Epistle to William Hogarth, The Conference, The Author, The Duellist,* and *Gotham.* The best of these is the poem to Hogarth, which was written in retaliation for Hogarth's caricature of Wilkes, and for which Hogarth retaliated by doing his caricature of Churchill. The poem is too long, but it gains unity from concentrating on the analysis of the character of a single man, and in this way is a fore-runner of the *Dedication.* It deals with Hogarth's personal vices, mostly of jealousy and vanity, separates the vices from the art, and attacks the man for putting the art to the service of a corrupt cause. The concluding portions of the poem, which are the best, attribute Hogarth's fall to senility and express a kind of contemptuous pity for him. In *The Conference* we have the beginnings of the long sentence and the parenthetical interruption in the pentameter line. We have likewise certain rhetorical formulae which are to be picked up later and used with better effect: beginning with line three hundred and one, for example we have a kind of *'Tis not* sequence (*'Tis not the Title, 'Tis not the Star*) which appears later in the *Dedication.* Churchill had a way of improving on previous lines: a complete account of such improvements would make an interesting paper for one of our learned journals. These poems are not, on the whole, exciting reading, except perhaps for the scholarly specialist in the period; but there is one objection to neglecting them: one never knows when one will encounter one of the great moments in English satire, such as the following:

> Grown old in villainy, and dead to grace,
> Hell in his heart, and Tyburne in his face;
> Behold, a Parson at thy Elbow stands,
> Low'ring damnation, and with open hands
> Ripe to betray his Saviour for reward;
> The Atheist Chaplain of an Atheist Lord.

Following *Gotham* comes *The Candidate*. The major poems remaining are *The Farewell, The Times, Independence,* and *The Journey*. All four of these display the complicated sentence-structure which I shall discuss in connection with the *Dedication*, and the poems are all worth reading, at least a few times.

The Candidate appears to me now a less successful poem than it did thirty years ago, but it is one of the eight or ten best and indicates most clearly Churchill's transition from the style of Augustan satire to the style of the *Dedication*. The poem opens with machinery too elaborate for the occasion. Churchill is now discarding all of his previous themes: Enough of Actors, Enough of Authors, Enough of Critics, Enough of Scotland, Enough of States, Enough of Patriots, Enough of Wilkes, Enough of Self, and Enough of Satire. Each of these phrases introduces a fairly long passage. Then: Come Panegyric, and with this we have the theory, at least, of the new method. Churchill will employ what seems on the surface to be panegyric but will employ it ironically. He tells us that he has seen his errors, has changed political sides, and will now write in praise of Sandwich, who, at this time, was a candidate for the high stewardship at Cambridge.

The method of this poem is on the whole more confusing than subtle. The opening address in praise of Sandwich sometimes appears to be satire, sometimes praise. This is followed by a por-

130

trait of Lothario, the perfect rake. At the end of the portrait we are told that Nature,

> having brought Lothario forth to view,
> To save her credit, brought forth Sandwich too.

The meaning of this couplet dawns on us gradually: Lothario and Sandwich are the same man; but the opening of the second passage on Sandwich is uncertain in the same manner as the first, and the passage moves gradually into an outright attack. The poem is awkward for these reasons and because of the heavy machinery of the opening, but we have at least the beginning of the method employed in the *Dedication,* and we have also the long sentence and the parenthetical interruption employed with a good deal of skill.

The Dedication is addressed to William Warburton, Bishop of Gloucester, who was a member of Bute's party. Of Warburton, *The Oxford Companion to English Literature* says: "He was a bad scholar, a literary bully, and a man of untrustworthy character." I am aware of no good reason to dispute this verdict. *The Dedication* was intended to precede an edition of Churchill's sermons, which actually was published posthumously by Churchill's brother John. There is little certainty that Churchill was the author of the sermons. He seems to have regarded the volume as an interesting joke which might on the one hand make money and which would on the other provide an excuse for the *Dedication.*

I will quote the entire poem, but in short passages, and will comment on the passages as I proceed:

> Health to great Gloster — from a man unkown,
> Who holds thy health as dearly as his own,
> Accept this greeting — nor let modest fear
> Call up one maiden blush — I mean not here
> To wound with flatt'ry — 'tis a Villain's art   5
> And suits not with the frankness of my heart.
> Truth best becomes an *Orthodox* Divine,
> And, spite of Hell, that Character is mine;
> To speak e'en bitter truths I cannot fear;
> But truth, *my Lord,* is panegyric here.   10

The first paragraph seems to be simple panegyric, but already the double meanings are at work. Churchill refers to himself as a man unknown, but at this time he was the most famous living English writer, not only in England but on the continent. When he had come to London a little more than three years earlier, he was wholly unknown, and Warburton had snubbed him, and he doubtless has this in mind. He may have in mind also the fact that he had attacked Warburton earlier and that Warburton would prefer not to know him, and the fact that Warburton was a bishop and Churchill an ordained clergyman who had left his cure in order to engage in politics and literature and lead a dissolute life and who had thus become "unknown" officially in the Church. In the second line the irony is similar, for at this time Churchill had ruined his health and was suffering from syphilis, gonorrhea, and the results of heavy drinking, and the fact was generally known. Had it not been for the present state of Churchill's health, he might possibly have survived the obscure infection which he picked up in France a few months later, and of which he died. In the next four lines, when he says that he does not intend to wound Warburton with flattery, he is speaking the literal truth, but the sentence disguises his intention; and the reference to the frankness of his heart is likewise misleading. In line eight, the phrase "spite of hell" refers quite simply and bitterly to his own personal sins; line nine is a direct statement of his intention in the poem, but the intention is disguised by the form of the tenth line. The tenth line may seem at first glance to be a downright lie, but in the context of the poem and of Churchill's previous literary method it is not quite that. Churchill had used the form of panegyric for satirical and ironical purposes with a good deal of skill: what he is saying, in effect, is that truth will emerge here through the ostensible form of panegyric.

> *Health* to great Gloster — nor, thro' love of ease,
> Which all Priests love, let this address displease.
> I ask no favor, not one note I crave,
> And, when this busy brain rests in the grave,
> (For till that time it never can have rest)
> I will not trouble you with one bequest.

15

Some humbler friend, my mortal journey done,
More near in blood, a Nephew or a Son,
In that dread hour Executor I'll leave;
For I, alas! have many to receive,   20
To give but little — To great Glo'ster *Health;*
Nor let thy true and proper love of wealth
Here take a false alarm — in purse though poor,
In spirit I'm right proud, nor can endure
The mention of a bribe — thy pocket's free,   25
I, tho' a Dedicator, scorn a fee.
Let thy own offspring all thy fortunes share;
I would not Allen rob, nor Allen's heir.

The references to Churchill's poverty here are a little perplexing. Churchill's poems had sold very well. We are told by Professor Brown that at Churchill's death his copyrights were valued at three thousand pounds, a large sum at the time, but Churchill, of course, did not have this sum in hand and may never have estimated it. What he had earned, he had earned in a precarious way — by writing — and he spent heavily. He was poor as compared to Warburton; and only a few years before he had nearly been imprisoned for debt. Had he lived longer, he might have left a smaller estate.

The word *note* in line thirteen is a pun. Superficially it refers to a bank-note; secondarily to a foot-note. Grant explains the reference as follows: "Warburton published his edition of Shakespeare in 1747, and his manner and method were satirized by Thomas Edwards (1699-1757), barrister and minor poet, in a very successful pamphlet, *The Canons of Criticism.* Warburton revenged himself by unscrupulously introducing Edwards into an additional note to *The Dunciad Variorum,* lv, 567-8." However, Churchill may have had something more in mind. Wilkes, probably with the aid of Churchill and Thomas Potter (who was reputed to be the real father of Warburton's son), had published an obscene poem called *An Essay on Woman.* To this poem they attached footnotes quite as obscene as the poem, attributing them to Warburton. This device of footnoting was, of course, a familiar method of ridicule in the period, and no one really believed that Warburton had composed the notes; nevertheless, he saw fit to proclaim his innocence in the House of Lords, and made himself ridiculous to friends and enemies alike. Ralph Allen, mentioned in the last line of this passage, was the uncle of Warburton's wife, and Warburton inherited his estate. Whether *Allen's heir* is a reference to Warburton or to his son and the rumor that the son was not really Warburton's, it would be hard to say.

We should consider briefly the style of the first twenty-eight lines; such consideration will shorten and simplify remarks about style later. Churchill is given, in this poem, to the use of the long sentence; yet Pope's portrait of Atticus consists of a single sentence of twenty-two lines, and there is not a single sentence in this poem of equal length. But Pope's sentence is composed of parallel constructions, balanced lines, and closed couplets, which give the effect of shorter sentences, and it occurs in a poem in which the sentences are mostly short. Pope's passage is composed of discrete epigrams. Even in Dryden the effect is commonly similar to that in Pope, and few of Dryden's sentences are as long as this by Pope.

In Churchill's first ten lines, the last two couplets are closed, and the construction of the lines is of a kind that one might encounter in either Dryden or Pope, though one is normally looking for lines more clipped and balanced in both poets, especially in Pope. As my eye falls at random on the *Epistle to Arbuthnot*, I observe these lines, which seem characteristic:

> But why then publish? Granville the polite,
> And knowing Walsh, would tell me I could write...

We have, of course, the balanced line and the closed couplet, but this is not all. The accented syllables, except one, are heavily accented, the unaccented lightly; the movement is obvious and rapid. Even in Churchill's two closed couplets, the rhythm is less closely controlled by the arithmetic of the meter; the movement is slow. Yet the movement is properly controlled: it is a different kind of movement. The first couplet in the first passage is similar in quality, but is not a complete grammatical unit: the first main verb is in the third line; a new independent clause starts in the middle of the third line, and its verb is in the fourth line; an inter-

134

jected independent clause begins in the fourth line and ends in the fifth; a new clause begins in the fifth and concludes at the end of the sixth. The end of the fifth line and the whole of the sixth give an incomplete echo of the standard eighteenth-century couplet. The entire passage, then, contains marks of the eighteenth-century couplet, with definite variations. Churchill's use of the dash as a punctuation mark is curious: sometimes it is the equivalent of a dash; sometimes of a semi-colon or period; sometimes a pair of dashes may be the equivalent of parentheses.

In the second passage there is no trace of epigrammatic structure, but we have closed lines and a few balanced lines. The first couplet is a complete sentence. The next two couplets have no runover lines, but they are far from standard eighteenth-century productions. Lines thirteen and fourteen are not a unit of thought, but are parts of a larger unit. Line thirteen is the introduction, lines fourteen and sixteen are the major unit, and line fifteen is a parenthetical interruption. The method here is not in the least epigrammatical: it is continuous in structure, and ironic rather than satirical. Churchill sees himself as obsessed by work and death; such lines are closer to Baudelaire than to Pope.

The next sentence begins with line seventeen and ends in the middle of twenty-one: the dash, here, is, in effect, a period. This sentence continues the embittered comment on Churchill's own condition, and the falling-off of this comment in mid-line emphasizes the melancholy.

To great Gloster, *Health*. We have had the other form of this invocation twice, each time at the beginning of a line and a passage. Here it is inverted, and comes at the end of a line and in mid-passage, though it introduces a sentence. The procedure has been that of controlled association: at the beginning of the second passage Churchill is still with Gloster, but the subject reminds him of his own misfortunes, and he speaks of them, and then suddenly in mid-line remembers that he is dealing with Gloster and returns to him. The inverted invocation, coming from his meditation on himself, and in the midst of the slow movement, has the effect of a kind of gloomy heraldic cry in a large hall.

Think not, a Thought unworthy thy great soul,
Which pomps of this world never could controul,   30
Which never offer'd up at Pow'r's vain shrine,
Think not that Pomp and Pow'r can work on mine.
'Tis not thy Name, though that indeed is great,
'Tis not the tinsel trumpery of state,
'Tis not thy Title, Doctor tho' thou are art,   35
'Tis not thy Mitre, which hath won my heart.
State is a farce, Names are but empty Things,
Degrees are bought, and, by mistaken kings,
Titles are oft misplac'd; Mitres, which shine
So bright in others eyes, are dull in mine,   40
Unless set off by Virtue; who deceives
Under the sacred sanction of *Lawn-Sleeves*,
Enhances guilt, commits a double sin;
So fair without, and yet so foul within.

This passage — the first part of the third paragraph — deals with a theme familiar in the sixteenth century and earlier: the corruption of the world and the hollowness of its shows. One will find the same subject, for examples, in *Gascoigne's Woodmanship*, Raleigh's *The Lie*, and Ben Jonson's *A Farewell to the World*. But the subject is more complex here and is handled with greater finish: we have not merely an account of the corruptions of the world but an account of the corruption of a man. Churchill says that Warburton is innocent of the sins in question, but by this time the indirection should be evident: Warburton is guilty, and the panegyric is a slow, careful, and ironic account of his guilt. This is not satire in the eighteenth-century tradition: it is not epigrammatic and it does not endeavor to make stupidity ridiculous. Stupidity is the result of privation of being; privation is evil; and when a stupid man rises to power he becomes pompous, hypocritical, and dangerous. The phenomenon is a common one: I have seen it a good many times in the academic world, but here the evil man is operating on a national scene and becomes a major representative of evil. At the end of *The Dunciad* Pope describes stupidity as evil, but he describes stupidity in general, not the psychological involutions of a stupid and powerful man; and in his portraits of individuals he is very remote from Churchill. The subtlety of the portrait depends very largely on the slow and intricate movement of the lines. I have already discussed this movement as we find it in the earlier paragraphs, but I will note a detail here. Lines thirty-seven to forty inclusive are all balanced and closed. Or could be closed: but the last line runs on into the phrase "Unless set off by Virtue," the ironic after-thought. And the passage ends with a line which recalls Pope and Dryden in its construction but which by this time has acquired an ominous power from the whole context, which one will ·seldom find equalled in either of them. I will quote the remainder of the third paragraph:

'Tis not thy outward form, thy easy mien,   45
Thy sweet complacency, thy brow serene,
Thy open front, thy Love-commanding eye,
Where fifty Cupids, as in ambush, lie,
Which can from sixty to sixteen impart
The force of Love, and point his blunted dart;   50
'Tis not thy Face, tho' that by Nature's made
An index to thy soul, tho' there display'd
We see thy mind at large, and thro' thy skin
Peeps out that Courtesy which dwells within;
Tis not thy birth — for that is low as mine,   55
Around our heads no lineal glories shine —
But what is Birth, when, to delight mankind,
Heralds can make those arms they cannot find;
When Thou art to Thyself, thy Sire unknown,
A Whole, Welch Genealogy *alone?*   60
No, 'tis thy inward Man, thy proper Worth,
Thy right just estimation here on earth,
Thy Life and Doctrine uniformly join'd,
And flowing from that wholsome source thy mind,
Thy known contempt of Persecution's rod,   65
Thy Charity for Man, thy Love of God,
Thy Faith in Christ, so well approv'd 'mongst men,
Which now give life and utt'rance to my pen.
Thy Virtue, not thy Rank, demands my lays;
'Tis not the Bishop, but the Saint I praise.   70
'Rais'd by that Theme, I soar on wings more strong,
And burst forth into praise with-held too long.

These lines continue the methods which I have already described, and they need no comment, except for two points. First, Churchill's remark about Warburton's contempt for persecution is a preparation for his later remarks about Warburton's persecution of Wilkes. Second, the passage closes with a cliché belonging to the tradition of the "great ode" of the eighteenth century, but the cliché is used ironically, is mock-heroic. Professor Brown finds this cliché "lyrical," but I cannot agree with him.

The fourth paragraph deals with Churchill's own sins, and introduces the long comparison between Churchill and Wilkes on the one hand and Warburton on the other. Churchill did not try to conceal his private sins — in fact the effort, had it been made, would have been fruitless. But repeatedly in his poems — sometimes to the point of tedium — he endeavors to distinguish between his own sins, which are those of private life and damage himself primarily, and the sins of his enemies, which are those of public life and damage the state. The distinction is a sound one. And although one grows a little tired of it in reading the whole body of his work, it is handled with discretion and justice in this poem.

> Much did I wish, e'en whilst I kept those sheep,
> Which, for my curse, I was ordain'd to keep;
> Ordain'd, alas! to keep thro' need, not choice, 75
> Those sheep which never heard their shepherd's voice,
> Which did not know, yet would not learn their way,
> Which stray'd themselves, yet griev'd that I should stray
> Those sheep, which my good Father (on his bier
> Let filial duty drop the pious tear) 80
> Kept well, yet starv'd himself, e'en at that time,
> Whilst I was pure, and innocent of rime,
> Whilst, sacred Dullness ever in my view,
> Sleep at my bidding crept from pew to pew,
> Much did I wish, tho' little I could hope, 85
> A Friend in him, who was the Friend of Pope.

But this passage is the weakest in the poem. *Ordain'd* is a pun, but a pun to little purpose. Line eighty is a sentimental cliché which seems to be offered in all seriousness.

The fifth paragraph is overtly ridicule, and the handling of the couplets comes much closer to that of Pope and Dryden. But even here the ridicule is subdued and bitter in tone:

His hand, said I, my youthful steps shall guide,
And lead me safe where thousands fall beside;
His Temper, his Experience shall controul
And hush to peace the tempest of my soul;   90
His Judgment teach me, from the Critic school,
How not to err, and how to err by rule;
Instruct me, mingling profit with delight,
Where Pope was wrong, where Shakespeare was not right;
Where they are justly prais'd, and where thro' whim,   95
How little's due to them, how much to him.
Rais'd 'bove the slavery of common rules,
Of Common-sense, of modern, antient schools,
Those feelings banish'd, which mislead us all,
Fools as we are, and which we Nature call,   100
He, by his great example, might impart
A better something, and baptize it Art;
He, all the feelings of my youth forgot,
Might shew me what is Taste, by what is not;
By him supported, with a proper pride,   105
I might hold all mankind as fools beside;
He (should a World, perverse and peevish grown,
Explode his maxims, and assert their own)
Might teach me, like himself, to be content,
And let their folly be their punishment;   110
Might, like himself, teach his adopted Son,
'Gainst all the World, to quote a Warburton.

The first four lines of this paragraph are what one might call
mock-sentimental, just as the last two lines of the third paragraph
are mock-heroic; after the introductory lines the paragraph settles
down to its real business.

Perhaps I should offer a summary of the poem as far as we
have proceeded. The first two paragraphs constitute a formal invocation; the third deals with Warburton's personal qualities; the
fourth deals with Churchill as the fallen clergyman who came to
London as an admirer of the great bishop and was snubbed by
him; then in the fifth we have an account of Warburton as the
great critic who might have taught Churchill. The sixth paragraph
continues the account of the personal relationship for which
Churchill had hoped, but it leaves the topic of Warburton's literary qualities and reverts to his personal qualities; it thus serves

as an introduction to the two paragraphs which follow it. I will quote the sixth paragraph:

> Fool that I was, could I so much deceive
> My soul with lying hopes; could I believe
> That He, the servant of his Maker sworn,   115
> The servant of his Saviour, would be torn
> From their embrace, and leave their dear employ,
> The cure of souls, his duty and his joy,
> For toys like mine, and waste his precious time,
> On which so much depended, for a rime?   120
> Should He forsake the task he undertook,
> Desert his flock, and break his past'ral crook?
> Should He (forbid it Heav'n) so high in place,
> So rich in knowledge, quit the work of Grace,
> And, idly wand'ring o'er the Muses' hill,   125
> Let the salvation of Mankind stand still?

There is something in this paragraph, although it is carefully controlled, of the mock-pastoral. Churchill has returned to his usual sentence and linear structure. The irony of the passage is obvious, for Warburton had devoted a good deal of time to literary study, though without distinguishing himself, and was vain of his accomplishments. The seventh passage follows easily from this, and describes the scene in the House of Lords when Warburton swore — to the amusement of all — that he was not the author of the notes in *An Essay on Woman:*

> Far, far be that from Thee — yes, far from Thee
> Be such revolt from Grace, and far from me
> The Will to think it — Guilt is in the Thought —
> Not so, Not so, hath Warburton been taught,   130
> Not so learn'd Christ — Recall that day, well-known,
> When (to maintain God's honour — and his own)
> He call'd Blasphemers forth — Methinks I now
> See stern Rebuke enthroned on his brow,
> And arm'd with tenfold terrours — from his tongue.   135
> Where fiery zeal, and Christian fury hung,
> Methinks I hear the deep-ton'd thunders roll,
> And chill with horrour ev'ry sinner's soul —
> In vain They strive to fly — flight cannot save,
> And Potter trembles even in his grave —   140
> With all the conscious pride of innocence,

> Methinks I hear him, in his own defence,
> Bear witness to himself, whilst all Men knew,
> By Gospel-rules, his witness to be true.

The language of this paragraph is largely that of the mock-heroic tradition; there have been only a few suggestions of this previously. The versification, however, is not of the mock-heroic tradition, but is Churchill's own. In lines eighty-seven through one hundred and twelve, Churchill came closer than usual to the familiar construction of the couplet, but maintained the coherence of tone in his poem by the use of irony instead of epigram. In this passage, in which he approaches a kind of language employed by Pope and Dryden (without the use of epigram, however), he maintains his unity by preserving his own rhythmic structure. He is thus able to draw upon the earlier tradition without submitting to it. Submission at any point would have destroyed the unity of the poem.

It was because of *An Essay on Woman* and *No. 45* of the *North Briton* that Wilkes was tried for libel under Lord Mansfield, who was Lord Chief Justice. As a result of the trial, Wilkes was expelled from the House of Commons, was outlawed, and fled to Paris. The next paragraph is merely the completion of the paragraph which I have just quoted:

> O Glorious Man, thy zeal I must commend,   145
> Tho' it depriv'd me of my dearest friend.
> The real motives of thy anger known,
> Wilkes must the justice of that anger own;
> And, could thy bosom have been bar'd to view,
> Pitied himself, in turn had pitied you.

This paragraph is so elaborate that it almost defeats itself. Superficially Churchill is saying that Wilkes, had he understood Warburton, would have pitied him for the suffering that Warburton underwent in pitying the misguided Wilkes. Actually, Churchill is saying that Wilkes would have felt the pity which is a form of contempt for a man such as Warburton who had the arrogance to pity his betters.

Lines seventy-three through one hundred and twenty-six have dealt with the relationship, real or hypothetical, between Churchill and Warburton, but this leads by a kind of inevitable association to Wilkes, who has not previously been mentioned. It is Wilkes who justifies the mention of Mansfield at the end of the next paragraph: Churchill is angry at Mansfield not merely because he tried Wilkes, nor even because he was a member of Bute's party, but mainly because of Mansfield's interpretation of the laws of libel, an interpretation which in the opinion of both Churchill and Wilkes gave the judge too much power and the jury too little and so made for tyranny. The paragraph, however, is largely devoted to a final comparison of Churchill and Warburton and thus draws this long portion of the poem to a close:

> Bred to the law, You wisely took the gown,
> Which I, like *Demas*, foolishly laid down.
> Hence double strength our *Holy Mother* drew;
> Me she got rid of, and made prize of you.
> I, like an idle Truant, fond of play,   155
> Doting on toys, and throwing gems away,
> Grasping at shadows, let the substance slip;
> But you, *my Lord*, renounc'd Attorneyship
> With better purpose, and more noble aim,
> And wisely played a more substantial game.   160
> Nor did *Law* mourn, bless'd in her younger son,
> For Mansfield does what Glo'ster would have done.

Churchill's comments on himself are meant seriously, I am sure: "Me she got rid of" is not ironic praise of himself; it is a moving confession. However, the next expression, "made prize of you" is bitter irony directed at Warburton and the Church about equally. The sentence beginning with line 155 and ending with 160 exhibits Churchill's style at its most brilliant. The sentence comes to a major break in the middle of the second couplet: "Grasping at shadows, let the substance slip" is unrimed momentarily and comes in like a melancholy afterthought. But then the other half of the sentence begins, and the comparison is harsh and realistic. Churchill had renounced the Church for dissipation, Warburton attorneyship for the Church, and this renunciation indicated a better purpose and more noble aim than Churchill's; but the final line, though quiet, is devastating. The play on *substantial* is the heart of it: *substance*, above, has the consecrated and theo-

142

logical meaning, *substantial* the debased modern meaning. The final passage summarizes the poem and intensifies the method. We have a single sentence of eighteen lines in which Churchill's virtuosity in managing complicated syntax and relating it to linear structure is at its greatest:

> *Doctor, Dean, Bishop, Gloster,* and *My Lord,*
> If haply these high Titles may accord
> With thy meek Spirit, if the barren sound   165
> Of pride delights Thee, to the topmost round
> Of Fortune's ladder got, despise not One,
> For want of smooth hypocrisy undone,
> Who, far below, turns up his wond'ring eye,
> And, without envy, sees Thee plac'd so high,   170
> Let not thy Brain (as Brains less potent might)
> Dizzy, confounded, giddy with the height,
> Turn round, and lose distinction, lose her skill
> And wonted pow'rs of knowing good from ill,
> Of sifting Truth from falshood, friends from foes;   175
> Let Gloster well remember, how he rose,
> Nor turn his back on men who made him great;
> Let Him not, gorg'd with pow'r, and drunk with state,
> Forget what once he was, tho' now so high;
> How low, how mean, and full as poor as I.   180

At this point, in all the editions which I have seen, the poem ends with a triple row of asterisks and the words *cetera desunt*. I suppose that the authority is Churchill's brother John, who published the first edition. I have not seen his edition, and I am aware of no explanation of this opinion. The poem appears to be complete, however, and I do not see how Churchill could have carried it further without damaging it. The combination of "wondering" and "without envy" exhibits Churchill's genius at its best.

I hope that I have made my points, but I would like to summarize.

The poem makes use of most of the best elements in preceding traditions and avoids nearly all of the worst. It does not, in its general plan, employ the strictly rational method of the Renaissance, but often moves from point to point by association. The association, however, is carefully controlled by a plan which is rationally apprehensible, and the transitions are never obscure;

and in fact many large segments of the poem proceed in the form of rational argument. The method makes for flexibility and complexity, without any loss of coherence. This poem, like Ben Jonson's *A Farewell to the World*, deals with social corruption, but whereas Jonson's poem deals purely with the theory of such corruption, Churchill's poem deals not only with the theory but with the psychological effect upon a particular man and is thus the more complete and, I think, the greater poem. The psychological complexity could not be rendered without the irony, and neither would be possible without the involved style. There is nothing of Renaissance ornament in this poem, and nothing of the sensory detail that one finds in contemporary associationists such as Gray and Collins, detail which too often is there for its own sake and has no real meaning.

The English-Augustan satire has its models in Roman satire, but it resembles the purely associational poems of the same period in one respect: it seldom exhibits any truly cohesive principle and is thus a mere conglomeration of details. Churchill's poem, however, is coherent primarily because it is an analysis of one man and his actions. Furthermore, the couplets of the English-Augustan satire tend to break even the best passages into epigrammatic fragments; Churchill's long sentences, his avoidance of clipped couplets, his use of ironic analysis, result in a unified exhibition of the psychology of evil. The method is a new one in the eighteenth century and in fact in English verse.

The poem is not without its faults, but few poems are without faults, especially poems of comparable length. Furthermore, the faults are faults of detail, and are not inherent in the method or in the conception; they do not damage the total structure. And they are few in number. I have objected to the mock-heroic style, not because it is bad but because it is a form of parody, which is an inferior kind, but Churchill employs this style only briefly and on a few occasions. In a few lines he employs the mock-sentimental style, and in a few the mock-pastoral, which involve the same dangers. The few truly sentimental lines about his father are a serious defect. Like the satires of Pope and Dryden, this poem deals with contemporary persons and events and needs annota-

144

tion. But the annotation is not bulky as compared to that required by his predecessors.

There remains another question: is the poem a mock panegyric, that is, a parody in the same sense in which the mock-heroic poem is a parody? I think not, but my reasons may not satisfy all readers. I would prefer to call the poem a pseudo-panegyric. It does not really parody the panegyric style; rather it employs this style ironically: ironically not with reference to the style, but with reference to the subject of the poem. The poem is not comical, in the manner of *MacFlecknoe*. It is a horrifying judgment of moral ugliness. In my opinion, it is the greatest English poem of the eighteenth century and one of the greatest in our language.

3

The Sentimental-Romantic Decadence of the 18th & 19th Centuries

I

THE POETS WITH whom I shall deal in this essay are the products of a rebellion against the authority of the rational mind, as that authority had been understood in the middle ages and the Renaissance. The rebellion was formulated in two closely related doctrines: the sentimentalism of the third Earl of Shaftesbury (later summarized by Pope, along with other ideas, in the *Essay on Man*), and the doctrine of the association of ideas, a psychological doctrine having its beginnings in Hobbes and formulated by Locke, a doctrine translated into literary theory by Addison and discussed interminably in the eighteenth century[1]. By the time we are well into the nineteenth century, both these doctrines have become folk wisdom, and their efficacy is questioned only here and there today.

Shaftesbury's view of the universe and of human nature is optimistic. As expounded by Shaftesbury and his followers, it teaches that whatever is, is right; that our impulses are good and can lead us only to virtue; that human reason is the principal source of error and of evil; that study and the effort to improve ourselves are unnecessary and in fact dangerous; and that whoever sees any contradictions among these ideas or between these ideas and experience is unworthy of refutation. Pope tells us that equal is common sense and common ease (*Essay on Man*, Epistle IV, section II, line 34); Emerson, that no man, no matter how ignorant of books, need be perplexed in his speculations (*Spiritual Laws*). The work of more than two thousand years of painstaking effort to understand human nature, the conclusions of some of the

147

greatest minds in the history of man, were discarded in favor of a few simple and irresponsible formulas. We were told that it is unnecessary to understand human nature, that in fact it is dangerous to try. But poets have always written about human nature, *faute de mieux,* and one can write well only if one understands one's subject, only if one has a vocabulary which is relevant to the matter in hand. The new doctrines eliminated precise understanding and generated the eighteenth-century cliché, and later the nineteenth-century cliché.

The doctrine of the association of ideas provided a psychological implementation of the Shaftesburian doctrines: it was said that all ideas arise from sensory perceptions and then from associations among these; by the end of the eighteenth century it was often held that all ideas could be expressed in terms of sensory impressions, and this notion is still with us: Pound tells us that the natural object is always the *adequate* symbol *(Pavannes and Divisions,* the essay called "A Retrospect," the subheading "Language"). But no matter how ideas may have arisen originally, they can no longer be expressed in terms of sensory impressions— their history has been too long and they have become too complex. The associationists taught (and still teach) that the natural (and therefore proper) mode of movement from one thought to another is by way of suggestion, or association. The philosophers of the doctrine cannot proceed thus in their philosophizing, although some have tried; but they have encouraged the poets to do so. Poetry became revery over remembered sensory impressions, sometimes abandoning even grammatical order.

In the Graeco-Medieval psychology, fancy (or imagination) was the faculty which linked the sensible soul to the rational soul. The sensible soul alone provides the materials upon which the rational soul may work; the fancy is a combination of memory and the power to recombine the elements of memory; the fancy thus frees the rational soul from bondage to that which is immediately before it. But the fancy (or imagination) so conceived is not the poetical faculty. That is, if I wish to write a poem about a murder, I may obtain my materials by committing a murder or by imagining a murder. But when I have done either, I do not have a poem;

148

I have the materials for a poem. The poetic faculty must then be brought to bear upon these materials. The poetic faculty is a particular activity of the mind which takes place in language, an activity which I have described in the *Introduction* to this volume and elsewhere. In the course of the eighteenth century, however, imagination and the poetic faculty gradually came to be identified, in ways which remain obscure, and imagination and revery became indistinguishable. The nature and function of language disappeared from critical theory, and the quality of the language employed in poetry deteriorated. The diction of Milton, especially early Milton, became a model; a degraded Miltonic blank verse and Miltonic sonnet became common.

In this essay I shall endeavor to illustrate the deterioration which I have mentioned. The essay must be brief, yet I must deal with a good many poets — the undertaking is difficult. One can make any poet appear ridiculous by citing his worst lines, and this practice is common. As far as my judgment permits, I will deal with the best poems and will cite the best passages; but I shall have to cite bad passages, for the good are few and I shall be trying to show what is wrong with the poets. Fortunately for me, the poems which I find the best by these poets are the common favorites; my reader and I can thus begin on familiar ground. All of these poems are easily available, most in standard anthologies.

I shall be able to devote only a few paragraphs to each poet; that is, I shall be writing about a period and illustrating the characteristics of the period by dealing briefly with the most famous poems. In spite of my brevity, this essay will be monotonous, for the characteristics repeat themselves, and the poets are bad.

II

NEARLY ALL OF THE best poems of the Restoration and of the early eighteenth century belong to the satirical tradition, although there are a few fine minor lyrics in the period of the Restoration. The deterioration in the style of the short poem at the beginning of the eighteenth century is shocking. One need only compare the best of Dryden's songs or even the best of Rochester to the work of Matthew Prior; it is not necessary to go to the comic figures like Isaac Watts. There are a few interesting poets, however. Anne Finch, Countess of Winchelsea (1661-1720), is a very minor poet indeed; her best single poem is *The Tree*, and there are charming passages elsewhere. Jonathan Swift (1667-1745) is not, I suppose, a perfect representative of the sentimental tradition, but the mark of the tradition is on his work. He is usually a writer of light verse often bearing some resemblance to that of Prior, and this is true even in the more satirical poems and in many of the most obscene. His lightness and his wit are so laborious that I, for one, find him somewhat dull reading. John Gay (1685-1732) is far more readable. *The Beggar's Opera* is outside my present scope. If one goes to Gay hoping for satire similar to that of Pope, however, one will be disappointed; Gay was a satirist whose satirical intentions were frustrated by his sentimental affection for his victims. The best works are *The Shepherd's Week, in Six Pastorals* (for Gay's shepherds were at church on Sunday) and *The Birth of the Squire*. These poems illustrate perfectly the sentimental tradition, yet they are so expert that they avoid the most embarrassing aspects of the tradition. The most amusing portions of *The Shepherd's Week* are *The Proem to the Courteous Reader* (in prose) and the *Prologue to the Right Honorable the Lord Viscount Bolingbroke* (in verse). The first of these is an elaborate parody of Spenser's *The Generall Argument of the Whole Booke*, which precedes *The Shepheardes Calendar*; and *The Shepherd's Week* is a gentle mockery of *The Shepheardes Calendar* and of pastorals in general. The entire performance is admirable but not great, and it has no real bearing on later poetry. Samuel Johnson (1709-1784) was one of our most eminent critics and one of the greatest masters of English prose; but poetry appears to have been an acquired language in which he was never entirely at home. He felt contempt for the deists of the Shaftesburian school, but he came late enough to inherit the poetic style which their ideas had generated — a style which consists of a kind of coagulation of clichés — without, so far as one can judge, suspecting the origins of the style. The force of the great character comes through some of the poems, especially through a few remarkable lines, but with labor. The most moving poems are the prologues for *Comus* ("Ye patriot Crouds") and for *A Word to the Wise* ("This night presents a play"). The language in each is the stereotyped language of the period; the structure is that of the Renaissance. The theme, in each case, is praise of an aristocratic and essentially contemptible audience for bestowing belated justice. Johnson's contempt for the audience is unmistakable, but one suspects that the audience could not discern it; he praises the audience as one might praise small children for behaving well on a rare occasion. The feeling is akin to that in his famous letter to Chesterfield; it is the bitterness of a great man who himself has been slighted. Another occasional piece, "At sight of sparkling bowls," expresses common sense throughout and arrives at a fine couplet. Still another, "As learn'd Eliza," might pass for one of the best poems in Landor. "When Stella strikes the tuneful strings" is a poem of a good deal of charm, but I fear that the charm depends in a large measure on an effect which is unintentionally comical. The theme is a common one of the late Elizabethan period, that of the relationship of art to morality, and the structure of the poem is Elizabethan; but the diction is that of a genteel sentimentalism of Johnson's period. The incongruity is noticeable. His two most famous poems, the two imitations of Juvenal, are, in my opinion, very dull reading.

III

THREE POEMS illustrate better than any others the formation of the sentimental and associationistic tradition in the eighteenth century: *Grongar Hill* by John Dyer (1700-1758), *Ode to Evening* by William Collins (1721-1759), and *Elegy Written in a Country Churchyard* by Thomas Gray (1716-1771). I name these poems because of the ways in which they embody the principles; they do not discuss the principles. Many other and duller poems discuss the principles; they also are well known.

Dyer's poem is the earliest of the three and the weakest. Little can be said for it except that it illustrates attitudes and methods which are shortly to become dominant; and it is obviously an imitation of Milton and thus one of many links between Milton and the decadence. I will quote lines thirteen through twenty-six:

> *Grongar Hill* invites my Song.
> Draw the Landskip bright and strong;
> *Grongar,* in whose mossy Cells
> Sweetly-musing Quiet dwells;
> *Grongar,* in whose silent Shade,
> For the modest Muses made,
> So oft I have, the Even still,
> At the Fountain of a Rill,
> Sate upon a flow'ry Bed,
> With my hand beneath my head;
> And stray'd my Eyes o'er *Towy's* Flood,
> Over Mead, and over Wood,
> From House to House, from Hill to Hill,
> 'Til Contemplation had her fill.

In its way, this is one of the most important passages in the history of English poetry. The imitation of *L'Allegro* and *Il Penseroso* is obvious; this is not merely in the use of meter and couplet — we have the same abject associationism. We are supposed to be moved by the mere mention of rural details, and not only in these lines but throughout the poem. In the fifth couplet quoted, we find the poet in the correct poetical situation and posture, although in later poems we are likely to find him prone while supporting his head in this fashion. And in the last line quoted, *contemplation* signifies revery over a landscape; this signification would have baffled the poets of the high Renaissance or even Dryden. The intellectual life is dead; in its place we have details of landscape which are not really visualized, automatic sentiment, and stereotyped language.

In the *Ode to Evening*, by Collins, we have a similar use of visual detail, and a similarly associative procedure, but with these differences: the visual detail is occasionally better, and the movement from line to line is far more irresponsible. The grammar is debatable in the first sentence; the syntax is unpardonable. The poem opens with an *if*-clause:

> If ought of oaten stop, or pastoral song,
> May hope, Chaste Eve, to soothe thy modest ear . . .

Such a clause calls for a conclusion introduced by *then*, either stated or implied: "If he is hungry, (then) he will eat." Collins' sentence goes: "If any song can please thee, (then) teach me now. . ." He does not employ *then; now* introduces the main clause. This would be acceptable, but we have been looking for the main clause for a long time before we encounter it in line thirteen, and line nine has been introduced by a *now* which is a careless equivalent of *now that* or *now when*. The first sentence consists of twenty lines; the following paraphrase gives us its substance and structure: "If any song may please thee, Evening, then teach me now to breathe a song in the evening which shall be appropriate to the evening, as I hail thy return, Evening." My sentence is firmer in structure than that of Collins; his sentence wanders loosely. The reader will say that I have destroyed the details, and so I have, but what are they? The bat is charming, if a bit mad and somewhat mysteriously so; the beetle is merely Milton's gray-fly; there is not another real detail, we have nothing but soft clichés. The details do not support each other; they distract from each other and confuse the form of the sentence. And finally — and this is really important — nothing is said.

There are two common versions of this poem: that of Dodsley's *Collection* (1748) and that of *Odes on Several Subjects* (1747). Dodsley's version is available in the *Oxford Book of English Verse* and in the *Oxford Book of Eighteenth Century Verse,* and may have been chosen by the editors because it was published later; if there is any reason to believe that Collins preferred either version, I have not found it, nor do I think the question important. The other version occurs in the edition which I have at hand of *Gray and Collins, Poetical Works,* edited by Austin Lane Poole (Oxford, 1926). In the Dodsley version, the eighth stanza reads as follows:

> Then lead, calm Vot'ress, where some sheety lake
> Cheers the lone heath, or some time-hallowed pile,
>   Or upland fallows grey
>   Reflect it's last cool gleam.

The grammar is impenetrable. Does the lake cheer either the heath or the pile? If so we would expect no comma after *heath*. Or is the gleam reflected either by the pile or by the fallows? If so we would expect a comma after grey, except for the fact that the change from singular to plural makes this impossible. And why do we have alternative choices in this simple landscape? But in any event, the fallows reflect the lake, and perhaps the pile reflects the lake. It would seem probable that Collins intended the lake to reflect both; if the pile were properly placed, the lake might reflect it, but it would be difficult to place the fallows conveniently. I have been assuming that *reflect* means *mirrors*; it may mean only *throws back*. If the ancient building (in this poem it seems a bit gothic) had glass windows, there might be such a reflection if the angle of light were right; but it is hard to conceive of fallows reflecting in this way or any other. And how are we to know that the light in the windows does not come directly from the sunset sky? We have problems of optics as well as of grammar. The other version of the poem gives us the following stanza instead of the one quoted above:

> Then let me rove some wild and heathy Scene,
> Or find some Ruin 'midst its dreary Dells,
> Whose walls more awful nod
> By thy religious Gleams.

There is little to trouble us here except gothic stereotypes. The poem suggests melancholy throughout except where the melancholy verges on madness in the line about the bat and in the line about winter near the end; the emotions, in so far as they are conveyed, are conveyed by descriptions of a scenery scarcely sufficient to have generated them. We know, of course, that Collins was a melancholiac and doubtless found cause for his favorite emotions in everything. In the last lines, however, the poem states explicitly that Evening governs "*Fancy, Friendship, Science, smiling Peace*"; I find myself unprepared for this moral and unconvinved by it. In its procedure from part to part the poem is associational to such an extent that even grammar is forgotten; we have also the associational use of visual details, for these are supposed to convey emotion without other aid — but even the

154

visual details, with few and imperfect exceptions, are not visualized but are merely catalogued in dead language.

Gray's *Elegy* is better than Collins' *Ode*, but it is a weak poem and for many of the same reasons. Collins' beetle appears in Gray's poem; it is interesting to observe the three versions:

What time the Gray-fly winds her sultry horn   (Milton);

Or where the beetle winds
His small but sullen horn   (Collins);

Save where the beetle wheels his droning flight   (Gray).

Gray is farther from Milton than is Collins, and his line is better, but the family relationship is there. The beetle provides an objective link with Milton, if one needs one; the important fact, however, is the similar degeneration of style in all three poets, a degeneration at its worst in Collins. There are lines in Gray which stay in the mind with a force uncommon in the poetry of the century: the last two lines of the third stanza, the last two of the fourth, and "the short and simple annals of the poor"; but these are not great lines. The epigram of the earlier part of the century is simplified to the epithet, "some mute inglorious Milton," for example; such epithets are frequent and most are commonplace, and they seem to float in associational melancholy. Almost every sentence or independent clause is contained in one line or at most in two. There is little variation in degree of accent; there is little metrical variation and only the simplest; the movement of the poem is almost as monotonous as possible, and the poem is much too long to support such monotony.

The first four stanzas describe the churchyard and the surrounding countryside at evening. The next three stanzas recall details of the daily lives of those now dead. The next four stanzas deal with the equality in death of great and small alike. Thus far the subject presents no difficulties. In the next three stanzas we are told that there may be potentially great men among these dead, men whose genius was repressed by penury; on the face of it, this seems sentimental rather than plausible, for many great men had risen from poverty or something near it up to this time in England — many of the greatest writers, certainly, had emerged from the lower classes. The next stanza gives us examples of great men: Hampden, a leader of the rebellion against Charles I; Milton, a poet; and Cromwell, the great master of the rebellion, who, unlike Hampden, it would seem, was guilty of his country's blood. In the eighteenth stanza the poet appears in an unpleasant role. Generally, stanzas twelve through eighteen appear uncertain of the moral. Stanzas nineteen through twenty-three revert to simple elegy; nineteen and twenty are the best stanzas in the poem.

In stanza twenty-four there is a shift in the point of view:

> For thee, who mindful of th'unhonour'd Dead
> Dost in these lines their artless tale relate;
> If chance, by lonely contemplation led,
> Some kindred Spirit shall inquire thy fate,
>
> Haply some hoary-headed Swain may say. . . . etc.

Thee, in spite of opinions to the contrary, must refer to Thomas Gray; he is addressing himself. For it is Thomas Gray who is relating the artless tale in these lines. He looks into the future, to find himself buried in the same churchyard, and to find some "kindred spirit" enquiring after him. The hoary-headed swain describes Gray in the worst clichés of the period, as the stereotyped poet of the period. Like Dyer, Gray is contemplating a stream, but he has got closer to earth than Dyer, and to the sentimental concept of the poet, for he seems to be prone. The worst thing about the passage, however, is this: Gray has no business in the poem at all; we have been reading a poem about the lives and the death of the poor and ignorant, and any force which the poem has derives from this fact. The sentimental and conceited poet, the affected dandy, is an intrusion; he must have entered by way of some personal "association," but for the innocent bystander it would appear that even "associationism" has been violated.

Then follows *The Epitaph,* in three stanzas. Many critics have objected to the obviously bad writing in these lines; Mr. Cleanth Brooks justifies the bad writing by saying that this is what one would expect in a country churchyard. Perhaps one would expect it in a country churchyard, but one does not expect it as the conclusion of a poem which has often been called a great one — it is

156

bad writing in either place. The language is stereotyped, but there are other defects. To what extent was Gray unknown to Fortune and to Fame? He was certainly not comparable in these respects to the local rustics, and the implied comparison is dishonest. "Fair Science frown'd not on his humble birth." *Science* at this period is merely *knowledge* or *learning (sciens)*. But what does *frowned* signify? Gray himself was a man of learning, so we may assume that Science smiled upon him in the sense that he was granted knowledge. But then we have the next line: "And Melancholy marked him for her own." *And* seems to imply that melancholy follows naturally from knowledge. But this is an unreasonable implication: some kinds of knowledge might cause melancholy, others might not. Gray, however, like Collins, was a melancholiac, and it would seem that everything moved him to melancholy, and, besides, melancholy was fashionable. In the last stanza, the parenthetical line intervenes between *abode* and *bosom*, which are in apposition; it is impossible to read this stanza aloud, even to a reader familiar with it, in such a way as to make it intelligible or other than ridiculous.

If we try to rescue the youth to Fortune and to Fame unknown by saying with Professor R. S. Crane that the poem is a dramatic monologue spoken by an imagined youth of the place and period, we shall have to imagine a local rustic who could have written a long poem in this language, or we shall have to imagine a youth all but undistinguishable from Thomas Gray, who (with very bad taste) inserted himself into the conclusion of a poem about people very different from himself.

IV

A SONG TO DAVID by Christopher Smart (1722-1771) runs to eighty-six stanzas (if I have counted correctly) of six lines each. If one examines the complete version with attention, one discovers that it is not without a plan: Quiller-Couch, in his shortened version, destroys the plan. In spite of its plan, however, the poem is more ecstatic than orderly, more violently assertive than precise in its language. Smart often suggests Blake, and his lion somewhat re-

157

sembles Blake's tiger, especially as we meet the tiger in the discarded lines. The tiger:

> In what clay and in what mould
> Were thy eyes of fury roll'd?

The lion:

> Strong is the lion — like a coal
> His eyeball — like a bastion's mole
> His chest against the foes.

Blake may or may not have known Smart's poem. The similarity in style, however, here and elsewhere, would seem to be due primarily to a violently religious temperament in both, operating in the decadent language of the eighteenth century. Smart's religious ideas were merely those of the "enthusiastic" Christianity of the period; Blake's were something else. Blake had the greater talent for poetry.

One might compare Smart's poem with Donne's *At the round earth's imagined corners*, with Jonson's *To Heaven*, with George Herbert's *Church Monuments*, to see what has happened to religious poetry and the religious experience. The early poems are intellectual, subtle, and compact; the later poem is violently emotional, obvious, and diffuse. Yet Smart is not without talent, and this fact makes him interesting; in him we can see real talent corrupted by historical forces.

There is another interesting fact about Smart: he alternated between periods of sanity, in which his life was debauched and lewd and his poetry inferior, and periods of madness, in which his religious enthusiasm was intense, and in one of which he wrote our poem. From the eighteenth century onward, and not, so far as I can recollect, before, we have a high incidence of madness among poets of more or less recognized talent: Collins, Gray, Chatterton, Smart, Blake, and others later; the same thing happens in other languages. A psychological theory which justifies the freeing of the emotions and which holds rational understanding in contempt appears to be sufficient to break the minds of a good many men with sufficient talent to take the theory seriously. Conversely, such a theory tends to equate irresponsible behavior and

158

even madness with genius, with the result that a good many men with no talent at all come to regard themselves and to be regarded as great poets. In the Renaissance the bad poets were merely dull; in our time they are exceptionally dull.

V

I WOULD LIKE to mention three poets who have little in common except that their best work is somewhat different from most of the work of the century. They differ not only from their contemporaries in general but from each other. They are all minor poets but all are distinguished in their best work: George Crabbe (1754-1832), Joel Barlow (1754-1812), and Robert Burns (1759-1796).

Crabbe is technically outside the scope of this study, for he is notable mainly for narrative poems of considerable length. But poets employing very different forms may be related to each other in certain ways, and I would like to mention Crabbe in passing. Crabbe is a moralist who endeavored to give a true picture of village life in all its rustic filth and ugliness; *The Village* satirizes *The Deserted Village* by Goldsmith in particular and the sentimental view of bucolic life in general. Crabbe's satire is often heavy and verges on sentimental melodrama of his own variety; sometimes it is effective. The best passages, however, are descriptive; for these he has been praised by Pound and others. If the reader will turn to *Letter I: General Description* of *The Borough* and run his eye down the left-hand side of each column until he comes to the indented line beginning "Turn to the watery world!" he will find a description of the sea which is a fairly complete poem in itself. The passage is uneven; there are solid sections of eighteenth-century stereotype and there are passages which are remarkably fine. The twelve lines beginning "Be it the summer noon" have been justly praised; the porpoise a few lines farther on is very fine; the last eight or ten lines may be the most impressive. Some of his best description is in Letter XXII, which gives us the melancholy story of Peter Grimes, a fisherman who had the lamentable habit of obtaining boys from the poor-house to help him and then murdering them. The passage beginning "Alas

159

for Peter!" gives an account of Peter sitting in his boat in the salt-marshes and contemplating the dismal scene. The best passages give us very fine descriptions of the tides and the mudbanks; the worst, very comical examples of the pathetic fallacy. Crabbe's faults will no longer make him popular, but his good passages still deserve study.

Joel Barlow was an American who lived abroad, mostly in France, for many years; he served as U.S. consul at Algiers and later as minister to France. He wrote some bad heroic poetry and a fine mock-didactic and mock-heroic poem *The Hasty Pudding*. The poem deals with the historical origins of Indian corn, with its cultivation, harvesting, and husking, with the grinding and cooking of the meal and with the proper way in which to eat the result. The poem resembles Gay in such pieces as *The Birth of the Squire*, but is better. The mock-heroic style is handled with extraordinary grace and wit; the description of rural life in New England is vivid; the poet's home-sickness is real and moving but never escapes the control of his wit. *The Hasty-Pudding* can be found in a good many anthologies of American literature or poetry; it may be hard to find elsewhere. It should not be forgotten.

Robert Burns, when he writes in English, is a typical sentimental poet of the period and he is not much better in his popular songs in Scots. But in his more or less satirical pieces in Scots, he is a better poet: the subjects, though small, are real; the poems are comprehensible; the language is vigorous. The best, I believe, is *Holy Willie's Prayer;* the subject of the poem (the speaker) is merely a village hypocrite, and the poem is comical rather than serious, but one is grateful for anything so well executed in the second half of the eighteenth century. *To a Louse* is quite as amusing as it is said to be.

VI

WILLIAM BLAKE (1757-1827) believed that the God of this universe was the spirit of evil and that the true God was chained in Hell. The God of this Universe is the God of matter, reason, law, organized society, the church, marriage, schools, and everything in any way related to any of these, with one exception — Blake believed that the artist should be trained in the techniques of his art. The true God, on the other hand, is the God of immaterial spirit and pure anarchy. Blake is a thoroughly didactic poet: that is, in every poem he tries to convince us of the rightness of his beliefs, and he expects us to be moved by his statement of his beliefs. I find his beliefs so foolish that I could not be moved by any statement of them. On the other hand, Blake's talent for poetic language, as we encounter it in a few short poems, is greater than that of almost any other poet in the romantic tradition. Yet his language in his best poems is marred by obscurity, an obscurity which turns out to be an awkward kind of virtue, for it almost saves him from self-destruction. I find it impossible either to accept Blake as a serious poet or to discard him outright. I will try to explain.

The Tyger is a good place to begin. The tense of dare has troubled certain critics, and if it were in the present tense it might well trouble them; but it is certainly preterite[2]. There is another grammatical problem, however; this is well known but must be mentioned. In an early version of the poem, which we have in Miscellaneous Poems and Fragments, we find this passage:

> And what shoulder and what art
> Could twist the sinews of thy heart?
> And when thy heart began to beat
> What dread hand and what dread feet
>
> Could fetch it from the furnace deep. . . etc.

In Songs of Experience the last line quoted above and the lines following are omitted, and the fourth line above reads merely:

> What dread hand? and what dread feet?

The hand and feet had a function and a predicate in the early version; in the later version they have neither, but are suspended, appalling objects (it would seem), in the void. Blake was more interested here in emotion than in understanding of the emotion; and this, in fact, is the trouble with the entire poem, in spite of the fact that the poem is otherwise grammatical. The Tyger is the

161

God of this Universe, the antithesis of the Lamb (somehow Christ is on Blake's side in this struggle); he is the spirit of evil. But we are told nothing of the nature of evil; in fact we cannot discover so much as an indication of Blake's ideas on the subject from this poem, but have to turn to others. The Tyger is obviously savage and powerful beyond anything in our experience, but with these characteristics he could easily represent the Christian notion of evil instead of Blake's — or he could represent something else. We have, in brief, a great deal of tiger, with no explanation of why he is there. Furthermore, if Blake had made his meaning clear, the poem would have been weakened or worse: An evil, raging, and supernatural tiger who is evil because he is the defender of law, marriage, churches, and the like would strike many of us as improbable. The best way to take the tiger, then, is with no explanation, in all of his vagueness, in spite of the fact that our doing so would have made Blake indignant. The poem is the best in Blake; it is a remarkable fusion of genius and foolishness; it is astonishing but is not great.

Erdman[3], however, like other scholars, believes that the Tyger represents Energy, presumably the revolutionary energy which Blake approves and which will overthrow the evil of the universe. If this is true, then we have the same problem which we find in the previous interpretation. There is nothing in the poem to prove that the Tyger is Energy or that the Energy is good; it certainly does not look good to me. We have an extremely energetic tiger, but that is another matter. Erdman says: "On the level of practice, it is clear that 'The stars threw down their spears' means: the armies of the counter-revolution were defeated." Furthermore, he cites other passages in Blake which seem to support this statement. I have assumed that:

> When the stars threw down their spears
> And water'd Heaven with their tears

referred to the battle between the opposing hosts of angels, in which Lucifer, the morning star and Blake's deity, was defeated by the Tyger, the God of this Universe. This interpretation is supported by Blake's general cosmology, which inverts the Christian myth, by the tragic tone of the lines, and by what seems to me their immediate import. I am quite aware that my argument really *proves* nothing. There is a difference of opinion on this poem and on others among Blake scholars, and this brings up another difficulty. Blake believed in the genuine antiquity of MacPherson's *Ossian*, admired the work, and was influenced by it. The style of the long prophetic poems is Ossianic but worse; it is bad poetry, but it is the most confused style possible for the exposition of ideas — one can derive many diverse interpretations of symbols from these poems. The style of these poems seems to me the clearest evidence that Blake was mad. His visions, whether real, imagined, or imputed, I can accept with greater equanimity than the style. Blake scholarship has become a kind of bramble-patch of divergent opinions. I began by saying that we cannot adjust our feelings to a poem which preaches obvious nonsense; but what are we to do if the poem's meaning cannot be determined? And whatever the meaning, we do not have an adequate account of it in the poem. The same problems arise in other poems.

The *Introduction* to the *Songs of Experience* exhibits the same difficulty. The language is less vigorous than that of *The Tyger* but it is remarkable. The scene which emerges is supernatural, vague but controlled in its vagueness, dewy, remote; the diction and rhythms are haunting (my adjective is overworked but seems proper here); the poem is insistently but discreetly hortatory, and in this fact lies much of its effect; the poem is like a hymn heard in a dream. I would not be surprised to learn that this poem was the greatest single influence on the early Yeats, the Yeats of the Celtic Twilight, but it clearly surpasses any of the poems which it may have influenced. But as I have said, the poem is hortatory, and what does it tell us to do? It tells us to turn from evil to good, and we cannot object to this advice in itself, but what are good and evil? If we pursue the question into Blake, we find Blake's doctrine. We must be deeply moved, as Blake intends, by an exhortation to what for most of us is vicious nonsense; or we must take the poem as a simple exhortation to turn from evil, an exhortation of which the meaning is so vague as hardly to exist. To understand Blake's meaning, we must read the subsequent poem, *Earth's Answer*.

London is one of the more vigorous poems, and in this the doctrine is explicit. I will quote the poem, italicizing the doctrinal phrases:

> I wander through each *charter'd* street
> Near where the *charter'd* Thames does flow,
> And mark in every face I meet,
> Marks of weakness, marks of woe.
>
> In every cry of every Man,
> In every Infant's cry of fear,
> In every voice, in every *ban*,
> The *mind forg'd manacles* I hear.
>
> How the Chimney-sweeper's cry
> Every *black'ning Church* appals,
> How the hapless soldier's cry
> *Runs in blood down Palace Walls.*
>
> But most through midnight streets I hear
> How the youthful Harlot's curse
> Blasts the new born Infant's tear
> And blights with plagues the *Marriage hearse.*

Law (charters, bans, mind-forged manacles), the Palace (which is the symbol of government), the Church (which institutionalizes the worship of the Devil), and the marriage hearse (instead of a marriage coach). The idea in the last stanza seems to be that marriage makes love legal and thus restrains what ought to be free; that if love were free there would be no harlots and consequently no venereal disease. Most people, I suppose, read the poem with no thought of Blake's precise meaning; the poem thus becomes merely an account of the ugly side of city life.

Erdman documents my italicized phrases as references to particular evils of the time, and so they were. But the general meaning remains: Reason, law, government, church, and marriage are evil in general; impulse, anarchy, Lucifer, and free love are good. Erdman's thesis is that Blake wrote in opposition to real evils in the social order; the evils were indeed real and were far greater than the same or comparable evils in our time, and Erdman makes his point. But Erdman seems to think that Blake's general doctrine was justified by this intention, and such an idea is nonsense. One does not cure a riot by starting a counter-riot. One does not remedy a bad social system by preaching a doctrine which, if practiced, would put an end to society. British (and other) society has been improved in many ways since Blake's day by criticism and elimination or diminution of particular evils; much remains to be done. The method is slow, but it is better than total destruction. The method, moreover, is that which was advocated by Churchill and Wilkes, both of them far more intelligent men than Blake, whatever their faults. In his identification of social justice and perfection (social or personal) with the rightness of impulse, in his justification of what we now call democracy in terms of romantic ethics, Blake was typical of his century. The French and American Revolutions were commonly justified in these terms in France, England, and America. But this justification is a betrayal, for the ends desired, ends which in some measure were achieved, cannot be achieved or perpetuated by moral or social anarchy. Blake did his cause no good, in so far as the cause was local in time and place; now that the particular evils are past, we find ourselves dealing with poems which, in themselves, are foolish in spite of his talent.

In the short rimed poem which serves as an introduction to the long poem *Milton*, we have these lines:

> And did the Countenance Divine
> Shine forth upon our clouded hills?
> And was Jerusalem builded here
> Among these dark Satanic Mills?

The Satanic Mills are usually taken to be the mills of the Industrial Revolution, and Erdman so treats them, with other passages from Blake to support him. Erdman does not mention F. W. Bateson, whose *English Poetry, A Critical Introduction*[4] precedes his own book by four years. Bateson's book is one of the most valuable books on English poetry which I know. Bateson proves to a certainty that the Satanic Mills are the English churches, and he also cites supporting passages from elsewhere in Blake. He says:

165

Blake's poem is now a popular hymn and is in process of becoming a sort of unofficial national anthem. No doubt it owes its popularity primarily to Parry's vigorous setting but the adoption by the Churches and women's organizations of this anti-clerical paean of free love is amusing evidence of the carelessness with which poetry is read today.

This situation illustrates the problem which I have been discussing: this poem, like others, is easily read in a way contrary to the author's intentions; the tone is that of protestant hymnography, of distinguished vagueness. But when we understand the poem are we still capable of feeling the same emotion, or any emotion? This is a serious critical problem.

Tirzah, in Blake's system, or at least in the poem which I shall quote, is the spirit of generation, who traps us into matter and thus subjugates us to the God of this Universe.

To Tirzah

Whate'er is born of Mortal Birth
Must be consumed with the Earth,
To rise from Generation free:
Then what have I to do with thee?

The Sexes sprung from Shame and Pride,
Blow'd in the morn; in evening died;
But Mercy chang'd Death into Sleep;
The Sexes rose to work and weep.

Thou, Mother of my Mortal part,
With cruelty didst mould my Heart,
And with false self-deceiving tears
Didst bind my Nostrils, Eyes, and Ears;

Didst close my Tongue in senseless clay,
And me to Mortal Life betray.
The death of Jesus set me free:
Then what have I to do with thee?

This also reads like a hymn, and, in spite of the obscure references in the second stanza, might be more or less acceptable to the Christian. It is moving but hardly great. Erdman, incidentally, tells us that Tirzah is the spirit of sexual repression.

Let me assure the reader that in citing Erdman and Bateson,

I do not believe that I have given a review of Blake scholarship. Such a review would be pointless in a book of this kind; in fact it might well fill another book. I have tried merely to indicate the nature of the problems in the understanding of Blake and the effect that these problems have on our evaluation of his work. The poems that can be taken seriously as poetry are few, short, and very faulty; I have referred to most of them. *The Tyger* is the only poem in which the style is in any sense vigorous. In general, the style is a refinement of the kind of poeticism that we find in the *Ode to Evening;* the emotional tone is that of the protestant hymn. Let the reader compare *The Tyger,* or any other poems by Blake, with two poems from other periods which treat of evil: *Down in the depth* by Fulke Greville and *Low Barometer* by Robert Bridges. In these poems the nature of evil is understood and is treated with power and precision; the poems are great in conception and in every detail. To read them after Blake is like returning to sanity, the human condition at its most rich, after experiencing a vague and confused dream. It is foolish to speak of Blake as a great poet; he is a talented poet who wasted his talent on his delusions of grandeur. Cocteau is said to have remarked of Victor Hugo, that Hugo was a madman who thought that he was Victor Hugo. The epigram can easily be adjusted to Blake.

VIII

WILLIAM WORDSWORTH (1770-1850) has a reputation far in excess of his desserts. He wrote a great deal and expounded the associational doctrines in heavily didactic and confessional verses, and has thus provided a livelihood for many scholars, who, being greatly in his debt, will defend him. He considered himself a very great man. But he is a very bad poet who nevertheless wrote a few good lines.

Most of the poems to which I shall refer can be found in the *Oxford Book of English Verse* or in other standard anthologies. Let us consider *Composed upon Westminster Bridge*. The opening line is an example of one of the worst formulae of amateur writing:

Earth has not anything to show more fair.

The line says nothing about the scene. "She is the most beautiful woman I have ever seen." "What a glorious day!" This is the ultimate in stylistic indolence. The next three and two-thirds lines proceed in much the same way. Then to the end of the octet we have simple but excellent description. The next three lines revert to the formula of the opening, and the twelfth line states a ridiculous falsehood in the interests of romantic pomposity: the river does not glide at its own sweet will, and this is very fortunate for London; the river glides according to the law of gravitation, and a much better line could have been made of this fact. Of the last two lines, the houses are good, the two exclamations are mere noise.

"It is a beauteous evening, calm and free" opens with the same cliché which we found in the first sonnet. We then meet the poetical nun who appears figuratively in so many poems from Milton onwards; but the evening is not like a nun; and neither evening nor nun is rendered with any clarity, nor is Wordsworth's emotion, which appears (inaccurately, I am sure) to be one of pompous pseudo-piety. The diction in the second quatrain is not much better except for the rhythm: here and in a few other places Wordsworth suggests the movement of the ocean. In his address to the little girl in the sestet, he says, in effect: "My dear, it is immaterial that you seem rather foolish, for your lack of thought brings you closer to my pantheistic God, you are more nearly one with Him." Emily Dickinson said the same thing, but with disapprobation, in a poem which is otherwise of no interest, *What mystery pervades a well*:

> But nature is a stranger yet;
>   The ones that cite her most
> Have never passed her haunted house
>   Nor simplified her ghost.
>
> To pity those that know her not
>   Is helped by the regret
> That those who know her, know her less
>   The nearer her they get.

168

The passage expresses cynical common sense with regard to a foolish delusion. In Wordsworth as in Blake, we are supposed to be moved by an idea that is patently wrong, but Wordsworth's style is bad in almost every detail, and Blake's style is sometimes interesting.

In "Great men have been among us" Wordsworth names some Englishmen whom he considers great; what he says of their greatness is so general as to be merely oratorical. Then he tells us in pseudo-Miltonic rhetoric that France has produced no great men, no code, no great books. He is obviously moved by his assertion, but how can we be moved to anything but contempt?

Mutability (Number 34 of Part III of the *Ecclesiastical Sonnets*) contains a few fine lines but exhibits his general illiteracy:

> From low to high doth dissolution climb,
>   And sink from high to low, along a scale
>   Of awful notes, whose concord shall not fail;
> A musical but melancholy chime,
> Which they can hear who meddle not with crime,
>   Nor avarice, nor over anxious care.
>   Truth fails not; but her outward forms that bear
> The longest date do melt like frosty rime,
> That in the morning whiten'd hill and plain
> And is no more; drop like the tower sublime
>   Of yesterday, which royally did wear
> Her crown of weeds, but could not even sustain
>   Some casual shout that broke the silent air,
> Or the unimaginable touch of Time.

Let us examine the poem point by point. Dissolution does not climb and sink; it is going on everywhere at every moment. Dissolution does not resemble a musical scale; this comparison gives us no aid in hearing, seeing, understanding, or imagining either dissolution or a musical scale. Only the most violent of dissolution is audible; the dissolution proceeding as I write, in my body and in the books on my shelves, is inaudible and bears no resemblance to music. The opening lines and those following are filled with words which seem to import a great deal but which are too vague to import anything: *high, low, awful, concord, melancholy,* and so on; this is the crudest kind of pseudo-poeticism. How does one "meddle" with crime? or avarice? What is "over-anxious" care? Does he mean that all care is "over-anxious" and that we should, in the proper romantic fashion, refrain from bothering our heads about anything? Or does he mean that there are degrees of anxiety and somewhere a proper degree? And if he means the latter, where is the proper degree? And why should *care* be made parallel with *crime* and with *avarice?* These are not trivial matters; if the poem means anything through line six the meaning is arrant nonsense, and the language is insufferably pretentious. "Truth fails not." Does he mean that the truth is always there or that we always know about it? The second meaning would be foolish, the first hardly worth stating in so empty a fashion — some things can be taken for granted. His meaning, I imagine, is about the same as that in the best line in XXXIV *(After-Thought)* of the sonnets to the river Duddon: "The Form remains, the Function never dies." The universal survives, the particulars vanish (it is an odd thought for Wordsworth, but never mind that). But the sentence "Truth fails not" is so general as to be both undefinitive and pompous. The illustration of transience by the melting of frost is trite, and the passage is redundant and otherwise dull. "Do melt" is a form which had been in bad repute for well over a century when the poem was written. It is bad for two reasons: it had long been obsolete except in pretentiously poetical language; it wastes a syllable, and this kind of inefficiency in poetry is a sin. The inversion "tower sublime" would be justified only if sublime were immediately modified, and, since it occurs at the end of a line, with a fairly long modifier, as if we were to say: "the tower sublime with pseudo-Miltonic ornaments." There is much else: "Did wear" follows; the weeds are a necesary detail, but "crown" is an unnecessary word, and "royally" compounds the cliché. The last two and a half lines are the best in Wordsworth and are among the few great lines to be discussed in this essay. These lines make us realize the true nature of dissolution, or an aspect of the true nature, as that which works continuously and so subtly as to be imperceptible until the indeterminable moment when the object can no longer sustain its own weight. This one perception was the occasion for the poem; the poem has nothing else to offer.

I have mentioned the best line from *After-Thought*, the last sonnet to the river Duddon; this line, and the line preceding it, which form something like a unit, are all that can be rescued from this popular poem — the rest is pure Wordsworth. One could proceed in the same fashion, but with less to praise, through other sonnets. *The Solitary Reaper* is sentimental in conception; the second and third stanzas give a graceful charm to a romantic commonplace; at no point in the poem is the writing distinguished. *To the Cuckoo* is similar; the charm resides mainly in the second and last stanzas; nearly all of the language is lazy. *Ode to Duty* undertakes a serious subject; the fourth and fifth stanzas are impressive — or, to be more precise, the first half of each stanza is very well written except for the second line of the fourth.

Ode: Intimations of Immortality is loosely associational in method: that is, the structure of the entire poem and of nearly every stanza, if one can speak of structure here, approaches that of revery. One thing suggests another. The poet endeavors to evoke emotion by the mere mention of natural details, a method which we have found to be common from early in the eighteenth century. Wordsworth is said to be the poet of nature, but his description of nature is almost invariably pompous and stereotyped; he *sees* almost nothing. He calls our attention to nature in oratorical terms which would disgrace the average political candidate:

> There was a time when meadow, grove, and stream,
> The earth, and every common sight,
>   To me did seem
> Apparell'd in celestial light,
> The glory and the freshness of a dream.
> It is not now as it hath been of yore;—
>   Turn wheresoe'er I may,
>   By night or day,
> The things which I have seen I now can see no more.
>   ● ● ● ● ● ●
> Now while the birds thus sing a joyous song.
>   And while the young lambs bound
>   As to the tabor's sound,
> To me alone there came a thought of grief. . . .

171

> Whither is fled the visionary gleam?
> Where is it gone, the glory and the dream?

I could quote more for the reader's delectation, but there is no reason to do so — the whole poem is available in all of the standard anthologies. There are a very few lines better than these, but they are very little better. This is the poetry of the country newspaper.

In discussing Traherne in an earlier essay, I suggested that the style of this poem be compared to the style of Traherne's *News from a foreign country came*. I repeat the suggestion:

> My Soul stood at that gate
> To recreate
> Itself with bliss, and to
> Be pleased with speed. A fuller view
> It fain would take,
> Yet journeys back would make
> Unto my heart; as if 'twould fain
> Go out to meet, yet stay within
> To fit a place to entertain
> And bring the tidings in.

Traherne seems to give us the life, the movements, of the soul. Wordsworth gives us bad oratory about his own clumsy emotions and a landscape that he has never really perceived. Yet Traherne is a minor poet, almost lost in his century, and we have been told that Wordsworth is one of the great poets of our language. Wordsworth would be a comical figure except for the appalling fact that he has been preserved in amber (or something) by (and with) a good many scholars and critics for more than a century.

VIII

I WILL DISCUSS more briefly four poets who, like Wordsworth, emerged in what used to be called the Romantic Period (1798-1832): S. T. Coleridge (1772-1834), W. S. Landor (1775-1864), Percy Bysshe Shelley (1792-1822), and John Keats (1795-1821). Lord Bryon (1788-1824) seems to have died a natural death, and I am willing to let him rest: his satirical work is amusing but

shallow — it is popular journalism — and the length of most of
it removes it from my present business; his lyrics are only a shade
better than those of Thomas Moore, and I doubt that many readers think otherwise.

S. T. Coleridge is famous primarily for *The Rime of the Ancient Mariner* (1798), and any real reputation that he may in the
long run retain will have to derive from this poem. *Christabel*
(1797-1800) and *Kubla Khan* (1797) are well known and have
had their admirers. There is no point, I think, in trying to find
any intellectual profundity in the *Mariner* nor in trying to import
such profundity from outside of the text; the poem is quite as
simple as it seems. It is a story for children with a Sunday-School
moral attached. Coleridge is quite as naïve intellectually as any
other poet discussed in this chapter; unlike most of these poets,
he has a charming command of style, but only, I think, in this
poem. He is at his best, as he intends to be, in his realistic description of preternatural or miraculous details:

> With sloping masts and dipping prow,
> As who pursued with yell and blow
> Still treads the shadow of his foe,
> And forward bends his head,
> The ship drove fast, loud roar'd the blast,
> And southward aye we fled.
> ••••••
> All in a hot and copper sky
> The bloody Sun, at noon,
> Right up above the mast did stand,
> No bigger than the Moon.

These lines and a few others (the account of the ghost-ship, for
example) exhibit a precision which we seldom find in the decadence. But it is a precision of description only, and the tone of
excitement is unconvincing and does not move the adult. Or not
this adult. It is the tone of refined elocution in the nursery. The
style nowhere collapses; the tone which the poet sought he
achieved and maintained; the poem is a relief after Wordsworth.
But there we are.

Christabel attempts a similar effect but fails. *Kubla Khan* appears to be a figurative account of the character of the poet and

the nature of poetry. The story of how the poem was composed and interrupted may or may not be true but matters very little; the poem as we have it says all that Coleridge had to say on the subject; had he continued, he could have given us nothing but more of the same. The poem is associational in its movement and in its use of sensory detail; the sensory detail is never realized as it is in the *Mariner*. Opium is not necessary to this kind of composition, nor is mental disorder; the wrong theories combined with spiritual indolence will suffice. The idea of the poet as an inspired madman is no creation of this author's; we can trace its course through the eighteenth century. And it is a foolish idea: if poets have any value, it is because of their superior intelligence, not because of their flashing eyes and floating hair. So much for the subject. What of the detail? We have the commonplace details of mysterious landscape in commonplace language: "gardens bright with sinuous rills," "many an incense-bearing tree," "forests ancient as the hills," "sunny spots of greenery," "that deep romantic chasm," "beneath a waning moon was haunted," "woman wailing for her demon lover," "chasms measureless to man," and much more of the same. Such phrases are equally empty of descriptive or intellectual content.

I will quote a passage from another poet which deals with romantic nostalgia, the nostalgia in this case functioning effectively as a part of a more comprehensive and very serious theme:

> She says: "I am content when wakened birds
> Before they fly, test the reality
> Of misty fields, by their sweet questionings;
> But when the birds are gone, and their warm fields
> Return no more, where, then, is paradise?"
> There is not any haunt of prophecy,
> Nor any old chimera of the grave,
> Neither the golden underground, nor isle
> Melodious, where spirits gat them home,
> Nor visionary south, nor cloudy palm
> Remote on heaven's hill, that has endured
> As April's green endures; or will endure
> Like her remembrance of awakened birds
> Or her desire for June and evening, tipped
> By the consummation of the swallow's wings.

174

I have known these lines by heart for almost fifty years, and they have seldom been far from my mind. The opportunities offered in these materials for sentimental cliché and for undistinguished emotionalism were very great, but Stevens touched none of them. The language is precise; the tone, though deeply moving, is quiet and controlled; the poetry is adult. If one desires the poetry of hallucination, let him turn to Rimbaud — to *Larme*, let us say. The subject is limited but serious; the diction and the rhythm, like those of Stevens, are beyond praise.

The scholars who are interested in the critical and philosophical ideas of Coleridge often turn to what they regard as his more serious poems. The favorite, perhaps, is *Dejection: an Ode*. If the scholar finds ideas to his purpose, he usually regards the poem as an important one, but in *Dejection*. and in everything else but the *Mariner*, Coleridge is merely one of the indistinguishably bad poets of an unfortunate period:

> A grief without a pang, void, dark, and drear,
>   A stifled, drowsy, unimpassioned grief,
>   Which finds no natural outlet, no relief
>   In word or sigh or tear,
>   O Lady! in this wan and heartless mood,
>   To other thoughts by yonder throstle woo'd,
>   All this long eve, so balmy and serene,
>   Have I been gazing on the western sky. . . .

Walter Savage Landor offers a real, if minor, relief. His best poems, and the best known, are very short pieces — poems which look like epigrams on the page but are seldom true epigrams: *Rose Aylmer* is probably the most famous:

> Ah, what avails the sceptered race,
>   Ah, what the form divine!
> What every virtue, every grace!
>   Rose Aylmer, all were thine.
> Rose Aylmer, whom these wakeful eyes
>   May weep but never see,
> A night of memories and of sighs
>   I consecrate to thee.

The poem is composed wholly of clichés, yet the tone of the clichés is controlled; they are all at about the same distance from

175

reality, so that there is unity of feeling, unity enforced by the firm and quiet rhythm. And the poem has another virtue, a virtue unusual in this period: it is brief — it seems unlikely that any skill could sustain a poem of fifty lines, or even of twenty, in language of this kind. The poem gives classical form, or something that looks like classical form in this period, to romantic sentiment. Its faults and limitations are serious, but it is distinguished. When we come to this poem and a few others by Landor from Wordsworth and Coleridge, we feel that we are meeting a man who has had at least some slight encounter with civilization. *Child of a Day* resembles *Rose Aylmer* and is at least as good. *Past ruin'd Ilion* is worth remembering. Better than any of these is *Dirce:* the concept is commonplace, but the language is less stereotyped. The best thing in Landor is the epigram *On Seeing a Hair of Lucretia Borgia*, or, to be more precise, the second couplet of the epigram:

> Borgia, thou once were almost too august
> And high for adoration; now thou'rt dust.
> All that remains of thee these plaits unfold,
> Calm hair, meandering in pellucid gold.

We have the living language for once, and there are few lines to equal these in the British nineteenth century until we reach Hardy and Bridges.

It would be possible to name a few more poems of the kind which I have mentioned, although none, I think, so good, and one could name a few of the *Hellenics* for their mild virtues; and Landor's experiments in longer forms are sometimes of technical interest. But Landor is not a great poet, nor is he the equal of many minor poets of the sixteenth, seventeenth, and twentieth centuries. Let the reader compare his best work to the poems by J. V. Cunningham which I quote in a later essay. Cunningham has a profound and original mind; that is, his subjects are real and his own. His style defines these subjects precisely; the best of his poems are great. Landor's matter had been commonplace for so long that people had lost the habit of thinking about it; it had become a trifle vague. Or to put the matter another way, his language had been commonplace for so long that people had lost

176

the habit of thinking about it; it had become a trifle vague. He was so immersed in a decadent tradition that he had lost the sense (and the understanding) of reality.

Percy Bysshe Shelley is at his best in a few lines from *To a Skylark:*

> The blue deep thou wingest,
> And singing still dost soar, and soaring ever singest.
> ••••••
> Thou doust float and run
> Like an unbodied joy whose race is just begun. . . .

The bird is there, alive and unforgettable; but the poem is unfortunate. The bird is a symbol of the extemporizing romantic poet:

> That from heaven or near it
> Pourest thy full heart
> In profuse strains of unpremeditated art.

Unpremeditated art is usually bad, and this poem is no exception. The bird is compared to a great many things, one after another in a great hurry. Only one of these comparisons is in any measure successful:

> All the earth and air
> With thy voice is loud,
> As, when night is bare,
> From one lonely cloud
> The moon rains out her beams, and heaven is overflow'd.

These lines are not as good as the first two passages which I have quoted, but they are better than anything else in the poem. Often the poem is comical:

> Chorus hymeneal
> Or triumpal chant,
> Match'd with thine would be all
> But an empty vaunt —
> A thing wherein we feel there is some hidden want.

The rimes *hymeneal* and *be all* and the semi-concealed rime *feel* are bad enough, but the flatness of the final line is worthy of Dryden's admirer and victim Flecknoe. The following stanza is, if possible, worse:

> Yet, if we could scorn
>   Hate and pride and fear,
> If we were things born
>   Not to shed a tear,
> I know not how thy joy we ever should come near.

To Night ("Swiftly walk oe'r the western wave") is too familiar to require quotation; it is in most anthologies. The poem is a prayer to Night to come quickly, but we are not told why. I have heard it said that Shelley wished to hasten an assignation with a lady, and this is possible; for one thing, Shelley is the author, and, for another, the imagery is erotic. But it may be merely an expression of the common romantic love of night, the home of mystery and the stars. There is one interesting detail: in the second stanza the sex of Day is female, in the third stanza male. Shelley seems to have overlooked this oddity while extemporizing, but Quiller-Couch, in his perceptive and silent way, corrected the blunder without mentioning it, so that the reader of the *Oxford Book of English Verse* is deprived of a moment of wonder. *Hymn of Pan* is one of the pleasanter poems; it employs a long and varied stanza with rhythms which are varied but not brilliant. The poem is not serious; at its best it is pretty, at its worst it is bad:

> Gods and men, we are all deluded thus;
>   It breaks in our bosom and then we bleed.

Shelley had a special weakness for this kind of writing:

> I fall upon the thorns of life! I bleed!

The Indian Serenade is Shelley at his worst, but most of Shelley is as bad or almost as bad.

To summarize: One can find a few lines; one can find no single poem that is not weak or worse in conception and predominantly bad in execution.

John Keats offers melancholy for the most part unexplained, melancholy for its own sake, combined with detail which is sensuous as regards intention but which is seldom perceived with real clarity. There is almost no intellect in or behind the poems; the poems are adolescent in every respect. Most readers of our time and for some generations have encountered Keats when they were young, have been touched by his unfortunate history, and have formed their taste on his poetry at a time when they knew little other poetry for comparison, and their feeling about him is immovable; they cannot imagine that he might be a bad poet. Our immediate forebears, especially among professors of English, were so taken by him that they evaluated the poets of the Renaissance in terms of his poems and personal taste: this, I am sure, is a major reason for the excessive esteem in which Sidney and Spenser are held today.

The *Ode to a Nightingale* is a mediocre poem with a very few good lines and some of the worst lines of the century. The fourth stanza contains neither the best nor the worst but is characteristic:

> Away! Away! for I will fly with thee,
> Not charioted by Bacchus and his pards,
> But on the viewless wings of Poesy,
> Though the dull brain perplexes and retards:
> Already with thee! tender is the night,
> And haply the Queen-Moon is on her throne,
> Cluster'd around by all her starry Fays;
>   But here there is no light,
> Save what from heaven is with the breezes blown
> Through verdurous glooms and winding mossy ways.

The stanza contains no idea except the romantic commonplace to the effect that Poesy is winged and the brain dull and ineffective. The imagery is pretty but not remarkable; in fact prettiness seems to be the aim of most of the poets treated in this chapter. The imagery is imagery for the adolescent, and perhaps for the adolescent of an age now gone. The third stanza contains the worst lines in the poem:

> Here where men sit and hear each other groan;
> Where palsy shakes a few sad last gray hairs,
> Where youth grows pale, and spectre-thin, and dies. . . .

He succeeds in making human misery the matter of unintentional comedy. The fifth stanza opens with two very perceptive lines but then relapses into the norm:

> I cannot see what flowers are at my feet,
>   Nor what soft incense hangs upon the boughs,
> But in the embalmed darkness guess each sweet
>   Wherewith the seasonable month endows... etc.

Here, as throughout the odes and indeed throughout much of Keats, the remarkable command of sound is the most beguiling aspect of the poetry.

The *Ode on a Grecian Urn* contains the best poetry in Keats but fails as a whole. The first two stanzas are good; the third becomes a trifle foolish in the first half and distinctly foolish toward the end; this, like so much of the poetry of Keats, and indeed of the period, is not for adults. The fourth stanza is excellently written, but the notion of the villagers who left their town and can never see it again because they were trapped on the urn is ultimately preposterous in spite of the suave rhetoric. One can argue that the real villagers can never return because they are dead and that Keats is addressing them through their representation, but one has to argue. The first six and a half lines of the last stanza seem to be moving toward great poetry—but then we encounter the famous passage. It will not do to examine Keats's reading in the hope of finding definitions of Truth and Beauty which will make sense here, and besides there are none. Beauty is one of the undefined myteries of our language, unless we restrict it to practical limits of which Keats would not have approved: Keats's concept of it is obviously romantic, if we can call it a concept. *Truth,* like *history,* is a very inclusive term. Crime and disease are true, but we do not often think of them as beautiful; a particular crime or a particular specimen of cancer might be described as *beautiful,* in the sense of *excellently representative,* by a specialist in crime or cancer, but this is too specialized a meaning for the occasion. Furthermore, even if the statement were true, that would not be all that we would need to know. The poem ends in magniloquent nonsense.

To Autumn is the most nearly successful of Keats's poems. It has no grave flaws and is charmingly written. But it is not very

serious, and the style, although controlled, is excessively melli-
fluous. Of all the unintentionally comical poems in the language,
the *Ode on Melancholy* is possibly the most amusing:

> Then glut thy sorrow on a morning rose,
>   Or on a rainbow of the salt sand-wave,
>   Or on the wealth of globed peonies;
> Or if thy mistress some rich anger shows,
>   Emprison her soft hand and let her rave,
>   And feed deep, deep upon her peerless eyes.

Gray's youth to fortune and to fame unknown appears to have
evaded all restraints.

IX

I WILL NOW write of the chief Victorians: Alfred Tennyson (1809-
1892), Robert Browning (1812-1889), Matthew Arnold (1822-
1888), Christina Rossetti (1830-1886), and A. C. Swinburne
(1837-1909).

Alfred Tennyson deserves the neglect into which he is obviously falling. His talent was a mild one; he gradually perfected his
style, in the sense of smoothing the surface, of controlling a particular tone; but the tone is one of imperceptive sweetness. *The
Idylls of the King* provide us with the Tennysonian norm, a norm
which he almost never surpasses. The best lines in Tennyson are
the last thirteen lines of *Tithonus*. The poem deals with the man
who loves the goddess of the Dawn and who was inadvertently
granted eternal life without eternal youth; he is the speaker in
the poem, and the final lines deal with his longing for death. The
lines are moving but are too heavily diluted with the sweet Tennysonian diction. *Tiresias* contains a passage which should be
mentioned: the passage in which Tiresias sees the naked Athena,
the living Truth, who then strikes him blind and puts a curse upon
him. In general, however, Tennyson has nothing to say, and his
style is insipid.

Robert Browning, more than any other poet in my present
collection, escaped from the pseudo-poetical clichés which make
most of these poets so abominable, but he did not really solve his
problem. He does not achieve the precise concentration that we

find in any of the great poems, such as *Down in the depth* by Greville or *The Astronomers* by Bowers. He approaches the quality of these poems, without really achieving it, in one poem, *Serenade at the Villa,* and perhaps in an occasional line or two elsewhere. In general, the language is fresh, brisk, shallow, and journalistic, as in these lines from *The Last Ride Together:*

> My mistress bent that brow of hers;
> Those deep dark eyes, where pride demurs
> When pity would be softening through,
> Fixed me a breathing while or two
>   With life or death in the balance: right!
> The blood replenished me again;
> My last thought was at least not vain:
> I and my mistress, side by side
> Shall be together, breathe and ride,
> So one day more am I deified.
>   Who knows but the world may end tonight?

The poem tells a story of uncertain plot: it is possible that we have a monologue by a hedonist who believes in living from moment to moment; we may have a murder by an insane sentimentalist, as in *Porphyria's Lover;* or we may have merely a sentimental view of eternity. As in so many of these poems we have to deduce the plot, and Browning is careful to give a minimum of clues. We thus have to make an "intellectual" effort, and we feel (I suppose) that the poem is intellectual; but it is not—it is a trick by a journalistic fictionist. The language in the stanza just quoted is not interesting at any point nor in the totality of the stanza; the poem is nowhere better than this; and Browning is almost never better than this. *Porphyria's Lover* is more clear, or seems so, but the story is told by a madman and from his point of view, and the murder is made to seem cozy and domestic — so much so, that this fact alone indicates that the narrator must be mad, and we might be wrong about Browning's intention. The third-person narration and explicit moral judgment of Baudelaire in *Une Martyre* are very different. We are made to know the murder and the murderer for what they are, through the mind of Baudelaire, in expository language of great concentration. Browning leaves the judgment of the action to the reader (this was a matter of theory with

Browning as well as of practice) and thus abdicates the most important function of the poet.

All of the poets whom I have been considering in this chapter are associationistic in their procedures, and all of them certainly knew the doctrines of the associationistic psychologists and critics; but few of them, I suspect, thought much about the method as a method — they were simply born into the tradition and they wrote that way. With Browning, however, it is clearly a conscious method: he is not much concerned with associational imagery, or any imagery, except in a few poems; but his method of proceeding from detail to detail is that of association. He tries to characterize a person under stress by the way his mind moves erratically from one thing to another and by his manner of speaking. Consider *Soliloquy of the Spanish Cloister, The Bishop Orders His Tomb,* and *Bishop Blougram's Apology* as random examples. The three speakers are obviously of different moral and intellectual kinds, yet they all speak alike; and all three speak like Robert Browning in *Sordello* and in the opening of *The Ring and the Book.* The method does not characterize the individual speaker, unless we say that it characterizes Browning, and I am sceptical about that. It would seem to be a method deliberately adopted which generated its own mannersims. The method results in confusion, sometimes great and sometimes small, in the communication of the subject; it reduces the poet's judgment (that is, his understanding) to a minimum; it thus makes concentrated phrasing impossible. The one-volume Cambridge edition of Browning runs to 1007 pages in double columns of small print, most of it written in this way; I have read it all. The method becomes a cliché in itself, an insufferable cliché. The style is almost always a matter of excited triviality.

Matthew Arnold exhibits the worst faults of the period most of the time: he is sentimental to the point of being lachrymose; he offers the worst pseudo-poetic diction imaginable; he is capable, although not invariably guilty, of very crude rhythm. He wrote a few excellent lines, most of them contained in two unsuccessful poems, *Philomela* and *Dover Beach.* He is at his worst in *Requiescat,* of which I quote the first two stanzas:

Strew on her roses, roses,
  And never a spray of yew.
In quiet she reposes;
  Ah! would that I did too.

Her mirth the world required:
  She bathed it in smiles of glee.
But her heart was tired, tired,
  And now they let her be.

Repetitions such as those above, and they are not the last, are the
sign of the lazy writer; they are supposed to enhance melancholy,
but they are merely wasted syllables. The inversion in the fifth
line is awkward. The sixth line is one of the worst ever written;
the whole thing is trite; in the background of his easy melancholy
and his jingling meter, one has the uneasy suspicion that there
lurks his curious admiration for Heinrich Heine.

The seventh and eighth lines of *Philomela* are moving and
might have been powerful if supported by a proper context; three
or four of the descriptive lines in the second stanza are passable.
Most of the poem is as bad as the worst of Wordsworth. And one
is puzzled by the presence of Eugenia at the end of the poem:
who is she? where did she come from? and, above all, what is she
supposed to be doing? *Dover Beach* offers more, but only a little.
The description in the first stanza is one of the finest passages in
the century, but the last line of the stanza is an abject cliché. From
here on the poem is bad.

Sophocles long ago
Heard it on the Aegean.

This would do, but then "it brought into his mind" (this phrase
is an awkward introduction to a metaphor) "the turbid ebb and
flow of human misery" (a cliché, or so it seems). Then: "we find
also in the sound a thought." The village poet or orator, the lady
who addresses club meetings, usually "find a thought" in something; the locution is on that level, and no excuses can palliate it.
The poem from here on is merely a morass of bad diction, and it
ends with a solution so weak as to be an evasion of the problem
posed.

Christina Rossetti is for the most part mild, diffuse, and sentimental, but she wrote two remarkable poems: *Rest* and *A Pause of Thought*. The first of these has faults but is less damaged by its faults than are most of the poems of the period. The first quatrain is merely bad. The second quatrain is better, and it culminates in one of the few great lines of the century:

> She hath no questions, she hath no replies,
> > Hushed in and curtain'd with a blessed dearth
> > Of all that irked her from the hour of birth;
> With stillness that is almost Paradise.

The first two lines of the sestet are a little facile; the third line is very fine; the last three lines are good. *A Pause of Thought* is quiet, honest, and moving; it is somewhat softened by some of the milder clichés of Victorian moral reflection, but the poem survives the softening. It is nowhere so great as the best lines of *Rest* and nowhere so weak as the worst. These two poems, unlike most of the poems which I have been discussing, deserve to remain in our literature. A few other poems are interesting for one reason or another. *An End* is almost good; it is honest but lazy. *Dream Land* appears to be the original of Swinburne's *Garden of Proserpine*, and there are other poems which must have influenced Swinburne.

A. C. Swinburne wrote no poems that will endure serious reading. Early in my teaching career most of my students knew him before coming to me, and many admired him greatly; in recent years, few of my graduate students have known more than his name. He has been more parodied than any other poet except Poe. Parody is an indifferent form of humor, but Swinburne lays himself open to it: without realizing the fact he himself parodies the nineteenth century and even parodies himself. The first chorus of *Atalanta* is probably the best poem. After that there is little to choose. A *Leave-Taking* is characteristic. I quote the first two stanzas:

> Let us go hence, my songs; she will not hear.
> Let us go hence together without fear;
> Keep silence now, for singing-time is over
> And over all old things and all things dear.

> She loves not you nor me as all we love her.
> Yea, though we sang as angels in her ear,
> She would not hear.
>
> Let us rise up and part; she will not know.
> Let us go seaward as the great winds go
> Full of blown sand and foam; what help is there?
> There is no help, for all these things are so,
> And all the world is bitter as a tear.
> And how these things are, though ye strove to show,
> She would not know.

The style is consistently controlled; it nowhere lapses from one mode to another. It is resonant and pretentious. The poet has nothing on his mind.

X

THIS ESSAY WILL win me few friends. The readers of poetry and the poets whom I have been discussing have been corrupted by the same ideas and the same models. I understand the nature of this corruption, I think, because my own critical taste was corrupted in the same way; I once admired the *Ode to a Nightingale* and *Dover Beach* as much as anyone — it is odd, when I think back to it. On the other hand, the "reading public" is tired of the styles to which I have been objecting, for, when traces of these styles appear in a poet of our century, the poet is damned. But the poets of the nineteenth century and earlier have become sacred; they are accepted without question; they are not examined with caution; it is sacrilegious to question them. Many readers would justify this situation in terms of historical relativism. But historical relativism is philosophically unsound; and, what is even worse, it is historically unsound. We know perfectly well that there are low periods in the literature of every nation that has ever had a period of distinction and that many nations have produced little or nothing worth reading. If I were to say that there was little or no English poetry of real distinction between Chaucer and Wyatt, few people would be surprised: the text-books tell us the same thing. I am telling my reader now that the eighteenth and nineteenth centuries were low periods in the history of English poetry; the text-books will convey this message to my reader's grandchildren. Bad writing is bad writing wherever it occurs, and no philosophical theory can justify it.

The odd thing about this is that the eighteenth and nineteenth centuries produced far greater prose than we had ever had before, prose that has seldom been equalled since. I know the reason usually given for this — that prose is the more intellectual and sophisticated medium and great minds turn naturally to it once it has become available. But this will not do: we still have to find the work of prose as great as the best poems of Jonson, Greville, Baudelaire, Valéry, Stevens, and others, as great as such poetic dramas as *Macbeth* and *Phèdre,* and the works do not exist.

Then there is another anomaly. The period from Gautier through Valéry was, I am sure, the period of the greatest achievement in the short poem in France; the period from Jones Very to the present, an American period except for the inclusion of Bridges, Hardy, and T. S. Moore, is one of the two greatest periods of poetry in English, and, I think, the greater of the two — I shall discuss aspects of this period in subsequent essays. But these two periods, the one in French and the other in English, were dominated by the same critical and psychological theories which ruined the poetry discussed in this chapter. So far as the modern Americans are concerned there are poets who have not been so dominated, but they are few. What happened? I suspect that it was a feeling of pure horror on the part of a few poets for the styles of their predecessors, a feeling which they could not justify on theoretical grounds. Yeats, Pound, Eliot, Stevens, Frost, Miss Moore, Mina Loy, Williams, Hart Crane, Allen Tate were all dominated by the doctrines which destroyed the poets whom I have just been discussing. And in fact these doctrines destroyed or severely damaged the poets whom I have just named: of this list, Stevens alone wrote a few great poems; for the rest, these are the great eccentrics of our time, but eccentric for eccentric I would rather read the Pound of the early *Cantos* than the Spenser of *The Faerie Queene.* I have written at length about most of these poets and stated that their faults are serious, and I am not now recanting; but these poets are all better than any of the "great" poets to whom I have objected in this essay. The great poems of the modern period in English I shall presently discuss.

A great poet is a writer who has written at least one great poem; great poems are rare, and few men have written more than six or eight, although one finds poets, especially in the Renaissance, who have written an abundance of fine minor poetry. The poet who devotes his life to expounding an indefensible philosophy in bad verse, in the manner of Wordsworth, is not a great poet no mater how great the bulk of his *oeuvre*. He may provide a livelihood for a good many professors, but that is another matter. The trouble with great poems is that they are rare, they are often embedded in a large mass of inferior work, and it takes patience and intelligence to find them, clear away the débris, and exhibit them so that they can be perceived. And there is another problem: few people can perceive them, no matter how hard the critic may try. I hope that the reader will try to bear in mind, however, that the present volume is intended as an act of piety, not as an act of destruction.

I beg the reader to consider carefully the poems on which my standards of judgment have been formed. I discuss most of them in this volume, have discussed some elsewhere. I will name a few of them now: *Down in the depth,* by Fulke Greville; *To Heaven,* by Ben Jonson; *Church Monuments,* by George Herbert; *Low Barometer,* by Robert Bridges; *My spirit will not haunt the mound,* by Thomas Hardy; *Of Heaven Considered as a Tomb* and *The Course of a Particular,* by Wallace Stevens; *Veteran Sirens,* by E. A. Robinson; *The Astronomers* and *Dark Earth and Summer,* by Edgar Bowers; the poems by J. V. Cunningham which I quote in a later essay. Then let us shift for a moment to French: *Les Petites Vieilles, Le Goût du Néant, Le Mort Joyeux,* by Baudelaire; *La Rhapsode Foraine,* by Tristan Corbière; *Le Cimetière Marin, Ébauche d'un Serpent,* by Valéry. These are all mature and civilized poems; the maturity and civilization permeate virtually every line.

It seems to me that the time has come when the facts with which I have dealt in this essay should be clearly stated. The poets to whom I have objected were not good poets, and nearly all of them wrote far too much; we cannot carry this burden forever.

4

The Turn of the Century

THE PRINCIPAL BRITISH poets who began their careers in the late nineteenth century and wrote into the twentieth are Thomas Hardy, Robert Bridges, T. Sturge Moore, and W. B. Yeats. Gerard Manley Hopkins was roughly contemporary with the first two of these but did not live into the twentieth century. Since I have discussed him elsewhere, I will not discuss him here[1].

I

THOMAS HARDY (1840-1928) was, like Emily Dickinson, essentially a naïf, a primitive, but one of remarkable genius. The two differed in certain obvious ways. Emily Dickinson's meters were based mainly on those of the Protestant hymn-books, and were usually (although not always) stiff; Hardy's meters appear to have been based mainly on English folk-songs and ballads, and were usually (although not always) sensitive. Emily Dickinson, in a few poems, probably achieved a greater concentration of meaning than Hardy; but Hardy, in a few, was not greatly inferior. The home-made quality of the work of both is obvious; neither is in any major English tradition.

The simplest and most obvious thing that one can say about Hardy is that he had the best eye for natural detail in all British poetry. Wordsworth is supposed to have been a nature-poet, among other things, but his language is almost always stereotyped and the detail is blurred. Hardy, like Charles Darwin in his *Journal of Researches,* had the seeing eye, and he seldom let any literary nonsense get between the eye and the object. I will il-lustrate the point first with a famous poem: *In Time of "The*

Breaking of Nations." The poem refers to the first world war of the twentieth century:

I

> Only a man harrowing clods
>   In a slow silent walk
> With an old horse that stumbles and nods
>   Half asleep as they stalk.

II

> Only thin smoke without flame
>   From the heaps of couch-grass;
> Yet these will go onward the same
>   Though Dynasties pass.

III

> Yonder a maid and her wight
>   Come whispering by:
> War's annals will cloud into night
>   Ere their story die.

The first six lines are almost purely descriptive. The only word in these lines which seems in the least unusual is *stalk,* and that is not remarkably so. The only figure of speech is in the eleventh line, and that is unpretentious. Yet the landscape, permanent and primitive, is rendered unforgettably in the details of the first six lines; it is rendered by the selection of the details and by their juxtaposition. Each detail reinforces the rest; with a procedure which appears to be that of utter simplicity, Hardy achieves great poetry. *Afterwards* is a poem on a minor subject and the first stanza is not really successful; but it is an honest and moving poem, and the descriptive details show the same extraordinary gift. In the second stanza we have the night-hawk:

> If it be in the dusk when, like an eyelid's soundless blink,
>   The dewfall-hawk comes crossing the shades to alight
> Upon the wind-warped upland thorn . . . .

Here we have two figures, the simile in the first line, and the disguised simile *dewfall* in the second. Both indicate silence and suddenness of appearance; the dew gathers slowly, of course, but

190

one does not see it until it is there. Every detail divests the land-scape of color, but gives it precision; and again every detail reinforces the rest.

There are other poems in which comparable visual imagery is put to the service of Hardy's melodramatic and amateur philosophy: the notion that the world is ruled by a fate or a god, essentially subhuman as regards intelligence, sometimes blind, sometimes ironic, sometimes maleficent. Hardy's ideas in these matters are well known. *The Wind's Prophecy* is an example of this kind of poem: the voice of the wind is the voice of fate; we have mere irony here, but heavy irony, and the result is melodrama. Yet the descriptive details in the first half of each stanza are very fine; these four lines may be the best:

> A distant verge morosely gray
> Appears, while clots of flying foam
> Break from its muddy monochrome,
> And a light blinks up far away.

The method is the same as that which I have already described; the description could hardly be more successful.

There are poems which appear to be very personal. *"My Spirit Will not Haunt the Mound"* is one of the best of these:

> My spirit will not haunt the mound
>   Above my breast,
> But travel, memory-possessed,
> To where my tremulous being found
>   Life largest, best.
>
> My phantom-footed shape will go
>   When nightfall grays
> Hither and thither along the ways
> I and another used to know
>   In backward days.
>
> And there you'll find me, if a jot
>   You still should care
> For me, and for my curious air;
> If otherwise, then I shall not,
>   For you, be there.

"My phantom-footed shape" is a miracle in its way; but the poem reaches its greatest force in the very quiet and very skillful final stanza. There are several poems which appear to refer to his first wife, and two of these, *The Haunter* and *The Voice* are companion pieces. The second has been often quoted; the first is by far the better. *The Haunter* is song, but the refrain is reduced to a minimum. The poem refers to various places, but there is only one really visual image, and it is one of Hardy's best: "Where the shy hares print long paces." The language in general is that of personal sentiment, but the language is not sentimental in the pejorative sense; it is distinguished. *The Shadow on the Stone* appears also to refer to his first wife. There are a few weak phrases, especially in the first stanza: "shifting shadows," and "rhythmic swing," for examples; but there is nothing false or strained. The psychological situation is very subtle, and I find the poem very moving.

The Faded Face is one of a number of songs or of poems resembling old songs and ballads, and is one of the best. The diction in the third and fourth lines of the second stanza is weak, but elsewhere it is close to perfection. I quote the third and last stanza:

> By these blanchings, blooms of old
> And the relics of your voice —
> Leavings rare of rich and choice
> From your early tone and mould —
> Let me mourn, — aye sorrow-wrung,
>   Faded Face,
>   Sorrow-wrung!

During Wind and Rain is another lament over the ravages of time. The descriptive details are of the same kind which I mentioned with regard to *In Time of "The Breaking of Nations"*; they are as unobtrusive as possible, but they are precise and they reinforce each other. The management of stanza, meter, and rhythm is that of a master. *Who's in the Next Room* again suggests the ballad form; the structure, like that of many ballads, is melodramatic; the diction is never bad but is not always as good as it might be. The subject is serious, however, and it seems to me that the poem succeeds; the diction in the second stanza is very great. Another ballad, less successful than the other poems which I have mentioned, is *An Ancient to Ancients*. Most of the diction is stereotyped, and apparently in the interest of irony; but the irony is heavy. The sixth stanza, however, which deals with the passing of the vogue of Tennyson, is effective, and the last three stanzas are moving.

The Darkling Thrush, a relatively early poem, is written in fairly commonplace fourteeners; it does not show Hardy's usual gift for meter and rhythm. As regards the theme, it is serious; in the third stanza the poet seems to be accepting romantic (or Victorian) optimism — in the last stanza he rejects it. The diction and imagery in the first two stanzas are undistinguished except for lines one and two and lines five and six of the second stanza, which are effective, if a trifle melodramatic. The two lines devoted to the thrush, or rather to his physical presence, in the third stanza are Hardy at his best:

> An aged thrush, frail, gaunt, and small,
> In blast-beruffled plume. . .

Hardy was obviously familiar with the bird: the small bird with small bones and loose plumage is there to perfection. *In Tenebris: I* is one of the better poems but not one of the best; the subject is serious, but the statement seems a little baldly dramatic. The *Self-Unseeing* is another serious poem which should have been a great one, but it is nearly ruined by the crude diction of the first three lines of the last and crucial stanza. *Exeunt Omnes* is a memorable poem with no serious flaws, but the theme is the simplest possible version of the passage from grim life to black death, and the language is never quite of Hardy's best. *"I say I'll seek her"* is a minor effort, but it has remained in my mind for over forty years; it verges on folk-song, it suggests colloquial speech; the melancholy of guilt is rendered minutely but firmly.

Hardy is commonly praised for his bad poems; those who dislike the bad are commonly too indolent or too imperceptive to find the good. I beg the reader to consider carefully the poems which I have named.

II

ROBERT BRIDGES (1844-1930) was a poet whose native talent and whose immediate background appear to have been at odds. Theories about what might have happened to a man had his personal situation been different can never be proven and are worth very little except for what they may offer in the way of description of the man's achievement. Bridges was born into the upper classes in England at a time when this fact provided greater material advantages than it might today. He was educated at Eton and Oxford, practiced medicine for a time, then inherited wealth and devoted himself to the writing of poetry. His best poems display a kind of passionate intellectuality, comparable to nothing else in English so much as to the great poems of Fulke Greville, Ben Jonson, and George Herbert; the bulk of his work is corrupted by the facile diction of the nineteenth century. He regarded Shelley as the greatest English poet save Shakespeare, and one of his favorite poems was the piece beginning "Away! the moor is dark beneath the moon." The rhythm of this poem might beguile anyone, but except for three lines it is composed wholly of vulgar stereotypes. Lines nineteen and twenty are excellent in a small way but are hardly worth quoting. Line eight, however, might have been a great line:

> Duty and dereliction guide thee back to solitude.

The line is weighted with feeling which appears to have precise meaning; but the meaning depends upon a precise plot, and there is no plot. We seem to be dealing with a man and two women, or with a man, a woman, and a child; and given Shelley's personal character we could, if we tried, construct a plot. But this will not do; the plot must be written into the poem; the line must be firmly fixed in context.

Bridges was not, apparently, bothered by the bad diction of the poem, and much of his own diction is just as bad and in much the same way. But the line reminds one of his best diction:

> Wherefore to-night so full of care,
> My soul, revolving hopeless strife,
> Pointing at hindrance, and the bare
> Painful escapes of fitful life?

> Shaping the doom that may befall
> By precedent of terror past:
> By love dishonoured, and the call
> Of friendship slighted at the last?

The first two lines display something of the diction to which I have objected; the next six are impressive examples (although there are a few greater) of the quality which I have praised. This poem by Bridges, although it begins with a reference to the state of mind of the poet (the title of the piece is *Dejection*) is not a poem on a plot, whether real or illusory. It is, one might say, an essay on a common human predicament; the language is general, but the generalization is precise with regard to denotation and connotation equally; we know exactly what the poet is talking about and why he feels as he does, and we cannot say this of the poem by Shelley. The second half of the poem deals with the facile way in which the poet feels that he will emerge from his dejection; the tone, though quiet, is ironical and bitter. The whole poem is one of disillusionment. It would be easy to ridicule the poem because of the first two lines; one can, of course, quote them in isolation and make the obvious remarks. But few poems approach perfection, and it is impossible to find a single poem in Wordsworth (to mention only one example) which is not more seriously flawed. Wordsworth's sonnet *Mutability* (one of the *Ecclesiastical Sonnets*) achieves real grandeur in the last two and one-half lines, but the rest of the poem is obviously bad. The poem is commonly accepted in toto, however, as a great poem, by readers who question nothing; and Bridges is commonly brushed aside with equal carelessness. The subject of Bridges' poem is more profound than that of Wordsworth and called for greater mastery.

Why did not Bridges free himself entirely from such diction as Shelley's and Wordsworth's? One can only say that habit is a very powerful force. He must have been taught from his earliest years that these poets were great, and this kind of sentimental language and the pseudo-spirituality of such poets are especially enticing to the adolescent temperament. Had he been forced by circumstances to teach others, he might have been forced to analyze and thus to make distinctions; but his personal life was unperturbed by any kind of pressure from the practical world. Many professors of English, of course, admire these poets still — in fact, most professors of English. But the professors of English lack talent, and one cannot expect much of them. It is remarkable that Bridges managed to achieve as much distinguished poetry as he did; the learned gentlemen who tell us about poetry have little conception of how difficult it is to write a fine poem, even a minor one — the actual writing of the poem is often labor enough, but the antecedent labor that makes the writing possible is the work of years and it is labor of a kind very different from any known to the professor, and far more difficult.

Low Barometer, a very late poem, employs the same stanza, and exhibits a similar diction, but it is more brilliant in every respect: theme, diction, rhythm of line, rhythm of stanza (that is, the management of syntax within the chosen form). The poem deals with an attack on Reason by the "unconscious" mind, which is seen as an inheritance from a remote and savage past. I quote the entire poem:

> The southwind strengthens to a gale,
> Across the moon the clouds fly fast,
> The house is smitten as with a flail,
> The chimney shudders to the blast.
>
> On such a night, when air has loosed
> Its guardian grasp on blood and brain,
> Old terrors then of god or ghost
> Creep from their caves to life again;
>
> And Reason kens he herits in
> A haunted house. Tenants unknown
> Assert their squalid lease of sin
> With earlier title than his own.
>
> Unbodied presences, the pack'd
> Pollution and Remorse of Time,
> Slipped from oblivion reënact
> The horrors of unhouseled crime.

Some men would quell the thing with prayer
Whose sightless footsteps pad the floor,
Whose fearful trespass mounts the stair
Or bursts the lock'd forbidden door.

Some have seen corpses long interr'd
Escape from hallowing control,
Pale charnel forms — nay ev'n have heard
The shrilling of a troubled soul,

That wanders till the dawn hath cross'd
The dolorous dark, or Earth hath wound
Closer her storm-spredd cloke, and thrust
The baleful phantoms underground.

The house is the mind of man; the "tenants unknown" are the forces of what the Christian would call his lower nature, of what the psychologist would call his unconscious mind, of what the anthropologist would call his pre-human memory. It is the last description that Bridges emphasizes, for the tenants have "an earlier title than his own." Bridges sees the humanity of man as something recently acquired and precariously kept. "Air" is figurative, just as the house is figurative: if Bridges were a Christian, one might call it Divine Grace. The non-Christian theist might have a similar concept; Socrates had his daimons; it may be the habit of the civilized man, habit which was created by the will in accord with Reason and which often acts as a saving power when Reason is overcome for the time being. In any of these terms the situation is comprehensible. The poem reaches its most powerful statement in the fourth stanza, but it is powerful throughout; the diction is a miracle of precision; grammar, syntax, and rhythm achieve tightly controlled variation without sacrifice of emphatic driving power. Even more obviously than *Dejection* this poem is an exposition of a predicament common to all men; it does not appear to be a narrative of a particular experience. The language is general in the sense which I have just indicated, but precisely particular in its statement of *this kind* of experience. In my opinion there is nothing greater in English poetry and there is little as great. It may be unfair to praise a poem for advantages which it

197

derives from history, but if we consider two of the greatest poems of the Renaissance, Greville's *Down in the depth* (a very similar poem in some ways) and Jonson's *To Heaven*, they both depend more clearly on the Christianity that Bridges and many moderns cannot accept than Bridges' poem depends, I would judge, on anything unacceptable to the earlier poets. That is, Bridges seems to be more nearly universal, to be less in need of translation. His language seems to me to be fully as great as theirs.

Eros ("Why hast thou nothing"), a poem written a third of the way through his career, some years later than *Dejection*, much earlier than *Low Barometer*, is less interesting in its movement than *Low Barometer*, though one cannot call it faulty in this respect. After a fine first line, we encounter two lines less impressive but not bad; the fourth line is trite and contains an unnecessary inversion. The sixth line is comparable to the second and third; the seventh line seems to contain another "poetical" inversion until we note that Bridges erred in placing a comma at the end, that "so fair" leads directly into the following clause and we have no inversion at all; in line ten there is an unfortunate inversion. The faults are few and relatively mild; they are the kind of thing that the reader accepts without question in the poets of the nineteenth century whom he has been told to admire, but many readers raise great objections when they discover such things in Bridges. In spite of these faults, the poem is a great poem, and great poems are so few that we ought to be willing to consider them.

Eros is the powerful god of antiquity; he is not the Cupid of the Elizabethans. He is naked in every sense; his body is naked of clothing, his face of human meaning; he is pure physical power:

> Surely thy body is thy mind,
> For in thy face is naught to find,
> Only thy soft unchristen'd smile,
> That shadows neither love nor guile,
> But shameless will and power immense
> In secret sensuous innocence.

The characterization of the god is lucid, compact, and marvelous; no word is startling in itself, but every word counts, and every word is a part of a total context that cannot be altered without total ruin.

The Affliction of Richard, a somewhat earlier poem than *Eros,* deals with a theme that one can meet elsewhere in the nineteenth century — the loss of Christian faith; but here a kind of faith is regained, not Christian, not particularly consolatory, but something definite:

> Though thou, I know not why,
> Didst kill my childish trust,
> That breach with toil did I
> Repair, because I must:
>   And spite of frighting schemes,
> With which the fiends of Hell
> Blaspheme thee in my dreams,
> So far I have hoped well.
>
> But what the heavenly key,
> What marvel in me wrought
> Shall quite exculpate thee,
> I have no shadow of thought.
> What am I that complain?
> The love from which began
> My question sad and vain,
> Justifies thee to man.

In the first stanza (which I have not quoted), there are clichés from devotional literature, and the remainder of the poem (which I have quoted) is not free from them. Albert Guérard[2] finds parallel passages in certain poems by George Herbert. The important thing to notice here, if one is capable of noticing it, is that this poem is better than any poem by Herbert save *Church Monuments,* and that it is only slightly damaged by the clichés. The reason for this measure of success is due to the control and variation of tone or total context of feeling; this is what I called "convention" many years ago[3]. Guérard believes that the fiends and their schemes are the medieval theologians and their theological systems; the idea strikes me as gratuitous and as destructive of a great stanza.

The notion of "convention" or total context of feeling is of great interest when one is reading Bridges. His experiments in

199

classical and (so-called) syllabic prosody opened new conventions; a new convention in turn may open the way to new subject-matter or to new aspects of old subject matter. I have difficulty in following the mechanics of his Greek meters; he himself foresaw this and advises the reader to read for the rhythm alone, and in fact the same advice has been given by scholars discussing the ancient Greek poets. But his Greek prosody gives to English verse a new tempo, a new mode of feeling; he does not accomplish much with it, but this epigram is one of the finest poems I know:

> Who goes there? God knows. I'm nobody. How should I answer?
> Can't jump over a gate nor run across the meadow.
> I'm but an old whitebeard of inane identity. Pass on!
> What's left of me today will very soon be nothing.

His experiments in what he called syllabic meter, resulted in something more. Syllabic meter is based on a fixed number of syllables in the line; French meter is syllabic. In French meter there is no problem of stress or accent, for the language has none; but in English there is mechanical stress, and the stressed syllables must be so disposed that they do not recur in a pattern, for if we have a recurring pattern of stresses we do not have syllabic meter but have some variety of standard English meter. Bridges encountered no serious difficulty here, but as a result of his misreading of Milton's intentions in the prosody of *Paradise Lost,* he introduced a theory of elision for the eye alone. That is, in Latin, Italian, or Spanish verse, when two vowels come into juxtaposition, they are reduced to one, and in fact this happens in conversation in the modern languages and probably did in the Latin; but this elision is not natural to English. Bridges decided, however, that this kind of elision was permissible in English if one did not pronounce the language in this way, that is, if one counted twelve syllables to an Alexandrine line but pronounced perhaps fifteen; elision, in brief, was to be seen but not heard. And he apparently permitted himself (when he found it convenient) to refrain from counting a lightly accented syllable interior to a word. This is foolish, for meter is the measure of what we hear in a poem, and if we do not hear it, then it is not there.

The result, in *The Testament of Beauty,* his most ambitious effort in such verse, is an irregular line which usually contains four or five unarguable stresses and an unpredictable number of unstressed syllables in unpredictable places. There is no rhyme. We have verse which is barely verse, but which is nevertheless more regular than prose. It is possible, in this verse, to deal with small details, whether of argument or of description, which could not be handled successfully in standard verse, certainly not in any quantity. The form has something of the inclusiveness of prose without sacrificing entirely the tone and intensity of poetry. I do not mean that it is superior to any other form of verse, for it is not; standard verse in general is more satisfactory. But occasionally it can be made to accomplish something very remarkable, something which would be possible in no other form. I will quote entire the finest passage of the poem, a passage which was famous for some years, but which may come as a surprise to many of my readers. The whole poem, of course, is a long didactic work, in which attention is paid to ancient models. The passage which I have in mind is something on the order of epic ornament; it is the vehicle of a simile, of which the tenor is an attack on Socialism. There is something almost comical about the relationship, but one forgets the comical very quickly as one moves into the main passage. The passage is based on the prose description, and it would seem on the conversation, of C. R. Woolley, the archaeologist who made important discoveries in ancient Sumer, in the Mesopotamian Valley. Woolley's prose is impressive; the poetry is greater, partly because Bridges is able to describe Woolley as narrator. The passage extends from line 270 to 338 of Book IV:

> Thus 'tis that levellers, deeming all ethick one,
> and for being Socialists thinking themselves Teachers,
> can preach class-hatred as the enlighten'd gospel of love;
> but should they look to find firm scientific ground,
> whereon to found their creed in the true history
> of social virtue and of its progress hitherto,
> 'twill be with them in their research, as 'twas with him
> who yesteryear sat down in Mesopotamy
> to dig out Abram's birthplace in the lorn grave-yard
> of Asian monarchies; — and low hummocks of dust

betray where legendary cities lie entomb'd,
Chaldaean Kish and Ur; while for all life today
poor nomads, with their sparse flotilla of swarthy tents
and slow sand-faring camels, cruise listlessly o'erhead,
warreners of the waste: Now this man duly unearth'd
the walls whence Terah flitted, but beneath those walls
more walls, and the elder buildings of a dynasty
of wider rule than Abram knew, a nation extinct
ere he was born: where-thru sinking deeper their shafts
the diggers came yet never on virgin soil, but still
wondering on earlier walls, arches and masonry,
a city and folk undremt of in archaeology,
trodden-under ere any story of man began; and there,
happening on the king's tomb, they shovel'd from the dust
the relics of thatt old monarch's magnificence —
Drinking vessels of beaten silver or of clean gold,
vases of alabaster, obsidian chalices,
cylinder seals of empire and delicat gems
of personal adornment, ear-rings and finger-rings,
craftsmen's tools copper and golden, and for music a harp;
withal in silver miniatur his six-oar'd skiff,
a model in build and trim of such as ply today
Euphrates' flowery marshes: all his earthly toys
gather'd to him in his grave, that he might nothing lack
in the unknown life beyond, but find ready to hand
his jewel'd dice and gaming board and chamber-lamp,
his toilet-box of paints and unguents — Therefore 'twas
the chariot of his pride whereon he still would ride
was buried with him; there lay yet the enamel'd film
of the inlaid perish'd wood, and all the metal gauds
that had emboss'd the rail: animal masks in gold,
wild bulls and lions, and twin-figured on the prow
great panther-heads to glare in silver o'er the course,
impatient of their spring: and one rare master-work
whose grace the old warrior wist not should outliv the name
and fame of all his mighty doings, when he set it up
that little nativ donkey, his mascot on the pole.
    'Twas he who dug told me of these things and how,
finding himself a housebreaker in the home of men
who sixty hundred years afore, when they left life,
had seal'd their tombs from sacrilege and there had lain,
till from the secrecy of their everlasting sleep
he had torn the coverlet — his spirit, dazed awhile
in wonder, suddenly was strick'n with great horror;

for either side the pole, where lay the harness'd bones
of the yoke-mated oxen, there beside their bones
lay the bones of the grooms, and slaughter'd at their post
all the king's body-guard, each liegeman spear in hand,
in sepulchred attention; and whereby lay the harp
the arm-bones of the player, as there she had pluck'd her dirge,
lay mingled with its fragments; and nearby disposed,
two rows of skeletons, her sisterly audience
whose lavish ear-pendants and gold-filleted hair,
the uniform decoration of their young service,
mark'd them for women of the harem, sacrificed
to accompany their lord, the day when he set forth
to enter into the presence of the scepter'd shades
congregated with splendour in the mansions of death.

The meter is not adapted to the didactic method to which Bridges
applied it throughout nearly all of the poem; in fact, it is a poor
meter for a long poem, for its looseness prevents any real variation,
and it becomes monotonous; but in this passage it permits the
accumulation of impressive factual detail and this accumulation
results in a grandeur comparable, perhaps, to the grandeur of the
tomb itself. A new convention results in a new quality of emotion,
which in turn permits new matter to which the emotion is adapted, and we have a new kind of poetry, which, however restricted
its possibilities, is nevertheless an enrichment of our experience.

Of the relatively short poems which I have not yet mentioned,
the best is *Elegy among the Tombs,* a poem roughly contemporary
with *Dejection.* It is longer than any of the short poems I have
mentioned: it is composed of twelve stanzas, each containing six
lines of pentameter. It is flawed in the same way as some of the
other poems which I have mentioned, but there is little in the
British poetry of the nineteenth century which will bear un-
prejudiced comparison with it. Most of the weak lines are in the
first four stanzas; the remaining eight have great cumulative
power. The force of the poem depends in a large measure on the
total argument; the language is quiet, and one cannot quote short
passages to prove its virtues. The epitaph *Askest thou of these
graves* is a fine one. Among the poems which contain fine lines or
short passages are *Elegy: The Summer-House on the Mound,*
and *The birds that sing on autumn eves. Nightingales* and *A*

Passerby, although not remarkable poems, are brilliant and learned metrical exercises; they should be scanned as standard English meter, with many difficult variations.

Two plays (I use the term for lack of another) entitled *The First Part of the History of Nero* and *Nero Part II*, if read as a single work, form one of the most remarkable narrative works that I know. They are not independent works; they are not dramatic in form; they could not be staged. They are a single long narrative in verse, employing the dramatic conventions of acts, scenes, stage-settings, and speakers named in the margin. These conventions make for concentration. The style becomes unfortunately excited on a few occasions, but only on a few. For the most it is compact and effective speech, modulated and clarified by the subtleties of a blank verse which is the work of a master and which is not in any way Elizabethan or Victorian. Nero and Seneca, of course, are the chief characters: Nero is the embodiment of Roman decadence, a decadence scarcely distinguishable in theory and in effect from the decadence of modern Romanticism; Seneca, who pretends to control Nero by reason, becomes his apologist and is corrupted utterly; and we have, through numerous minor characters, a portrait of the corruption of a state. The work was first published late in the nineteenth century, but it seems to have been written with the twentieth century in mind. As far as I am able to judge, it is sound historically. It is far from being a short poem, and so, like *The Testament of Beauty*, is improperly included in this essay; but it is a great work that almost no one has read and so should be mentioned. Any civilized reader will find the critical essays of Bridges to be profitable reading.

III

WE HAVE BEEN told many times that we do not have to take the ideas of W. B. Yeats (1865-1939) seriously in order to appreciate his poetry; but if this is true, Yeats is the first poet of whom it has ever been true. We need to understand the ideas of Donne and Shakespeare in order to appreciate their works, and we have to take their ideas seriously in one sense or another, and it is possible to take their ideas seriously much of the time. A great deal of scholarly work has been done on their ideas, and some of this work has contributed to our appreciation of what they wrote. A great deal of scholarly work has been done on Yeats in recent years; unfortunately, the better one understands him, the harder it is to take him seriously.[*]

I shall refer rather often in this essay to a book by John Unterecker[4]. The book gives a more detailed account than any other which I know of what Yeats was doing or thought he was doing. It accepts without question Yeats's ideas regarding the nature of poetry, ideas which in my opinion are unacceptable. And like almost every other publication on Yeats, it accepts without question the notion that Yeats was a very great poet and it merely substitutes exegesis for criticism. For example, Mr. Unterecker explains the meaning of an early poem, *The Two Trees* (p.47), and I think correctly. Then, with no explanation whatever, he refers to it as "so grand a poem." The poem is obviously a bad poem: it is sentimental and stereotyped at every point. Mr. Unterecker is a split personality: on the one hand he is a careful scholar and on the other hand he is a critic with neither talent nor training. In this he resembles most of the literary scholars with whose work I am acquainted. His book is very helpful notwithstanding.

Mr. Unterecker says (*A Reader's Guide,* p. 23), and I believe correctly so far as Yeats's theory goes: "Because all occult symbols linked ultimately to a universal harmony, any consistent interpretation of one of them was 'right' since it in turn led to that harmony. The only danger, as Yeats frequently pointed out, is that the reader is likely to limit the symbol's meaning and so throw it into the area of allegory." For some readers, this passage may call for brief explanation. In terms of medieval poetry, the word *symbol* refers to an object which has a one-to-one relationship to a meaning: that is, the whale is Satan, and Dante's panther, lion,

---

[*] In this essay I shall discuss a good many of Yeats's poems in detail. It is impractical to quote them in full. After the title of each poem discussed, therefore, I shall give the page number of *The Collected Poems of W.B. Yeats,* The MacMillan Co., New York, 1951.

and wolf, are lust, pride, and avarice. When such symbols occur in the course of a narrative, we have allegory. But Yeats here employs the word *symbol* as we employ it in speaking of French symbolist poetry, and the meaning of the term is reversed. Mallarmé was the great theorist of this kind of thing: his aim was to produce a kind of poetic absolute in which rational meaning would be as far as possible suppressed and suggestions would be isolated. He was not wholly successful in his aim, for many — perhaps most — of his later poems appear to deal, as obscurely as possible, with the theory of this kind of poetry; but he tried. In so far as this kind of effort succeeds, we have, in the very words of the Master, an "aboli bibelot d'inanité sonore." This is what Frank Kermode calls the romantic image[5], that is, the image which is meaningless, inscrutable, the image of which the dancer with the beautiful body and the expressionless face is the perfect type. Kermode disapproves of the method, and he finds it in Yeats, but he is overcome by Yeats (like most professors and literary critics, Kermode is deeply moved by trite language) and considers him a great poet notwithstanding. What Yeats and Unterecker mean by a "universal harmony" it would be hard to say. Mr. Unterecker says elsewhere *(A Reader's Guide,* p. 34):

> Any analogy we can construct for the symbol, any meaning we assign to it, is legitimate so long as we recognize that that meaning is *not* its meaning. Its meaning must be more elusive than any value we can — with words — fix to it. All that the meaning we assign to a symbol can ever be is either part of its meaning or one of its possible meanings. No symbol has a meaning.

And again *(A Reader's Guide,* p. 40) he tells us that the symbol does not give us meaning "but instead the feeling of meaning . . . . an undefined sense of order, or rightness, of congruence at the heart of things." I discussed this theory of the feeling of meaning a good many years ago, in writing of what I called pseudo-reference, and a little later in my essay on Poe. And Mr. Unterecker again: "Yeats allows us to experience . . . . the necessary if momentary illusions of order which give us courage to live." Foolish as these ideas may seem, they are, as nearly as I can make out, very often held by Yeats as well as by Mr. Unterecker, and they are commonly accepted in our time.

Yeats, of course, often deviated from this theory of the symbol and wrote forthright poems; and he often wrote in symbols more nearly akin to medieval symbols than to Mallarméan; and Mr. Unterecker throughout his book writes of particular poems as if their method were medieval; and in fact, if we accept Mr. Unterecker's general theory, there is no justification for his many pages of exegesis. But the theory provides a dark and convenient little corner into which the apologist may retreat rapidly backward whenever he is embarrassed by the meaning.

I will try to summarize the principal ideas which motivate Yeats's poetry. All good comes from the emotions, and even madness is good. *Wisdom* is a pejorative term; *ignorance* is the opposite. In Yeats's later work *lust* and *rage* become increasingly prominent and they represent virtues. Sexual union is equated with the mystical experience or at least participates in the mystical experience in a literal way. This is not the same thing as the analogy of sexual union which is sometimes used by the Christian mystics. The Christian mystics tell us that the mystical experience is absolutely different from any human experience and thus cannot be described in language, but that the experience can be suggested by analogy. This leads, I think, to a more or less fraudulent poetry, for the poet is pretending to deal with an ineffable experience in dealing with something irrelevant to it; but the fraud is, in a sense, an honest one, for the rules of the procedure are known. But for Yeats the two experiences are of the same kind, the only difference being that the sexual experience of living humans is less nearly pure than would be the experience of disembodied spirits: we are given the pure experience in *Ribh at the Tomb of Baile and Ailinn,* in which Ribh reads his book by the pure light given off by the orgasm of the disembodied lovers.

Yeats's concept of what would be the ideal society is also important. Such a society would be essentially agrarian, with as few politicians and tradesmen as possible. The dominant class would be the landed gentry; the peasants would also be important, but would stay in their place; a fair sprinkling of beggars (some of them mad), of drunkards, and of priests would make the country-side more picturesque. The gentlemen should be violent and bitter, patrons of the arts, and the maintainers of order; they should be good horsemen, preferably reckless horsemen (if the two kinds may exist in one); and they should be fond of fishing. The ladies should be beautiful and charming, should be gracious hostesses (although there is a place for more violent ladies — videlicet Mrs. French of *The Tower*), should if possible be musicians, should drive men mad, love, marry, and produce children, should not be interested in ideas, and should ride horseback, preferably to hounds. So far as I can recollect, the ladies are not required to go fishing. What Yeats would have liked would have been a pseudo-18th-century Ireland of his own imagining. He disliked the political and argumentative turmoil of revolutionary Ireland; he would scarcely have thought that the order which has emerged was sufficiently picturesque to produce poetry.

Yeats's cosmological and psychological system has been so fully discussed by others that I shall merely summarize it. He believed that history proceeds through cycles of two thousand years each. Every cycle begins in a state of objectivity (which is evil) and with violence; it proceeds through subjectivity (which is good), through pure subjectivity (which is too much of a good thing), and it then proceeds toward objectivity and ultimate dispersal and a new beginning. The life of every human goes through a similar cycle. Yeats had two diagrams for this process: the diagram of the phases of the moon and the diagram of the interpenetrating cones (gyres, pernes, or spindles). The first of these is a circle with the twenty-eight phases of the moon marked upon it. At the top is the dark of the moon (pure objectivity, where no life is possible); at the bottom is the full moon (pure subjectivity, and at this point in the cycle of the individual man the spirit may leave the body and encounter other spirits); on the opposite sides of the circle are the two half-moons, which complete the division of the circle into quarters. Between the dark and the first half-moon we have a primitive condition of violence and elementary learning, the struggle between the spirit and brutality. Between the first half and the full moon, we approach creativity; and between the full and the second half we depart from creativity. The period of the greatest creativity is on both sides of the full and close to it. Between the second half and the dark we are in the period of wisdom, in which creativity is almost at an end, and are approaching death, in the life of a man, and the end of an era, in terms of the historical cycle. The gyres are most easily represented by Richard Ellmann's diagram of the two isosceles triangles lying on their sides[6]: the short lines of these triangles should be very short in relation to the long lines, and the tip of each triangle should reach to the middle of the short line of the other. This design gives us a cross-section of the interpenetrating cones or gyres. At the point where the long lines intersect, we have the period corresponding to the full moon on the circle. The cones rotate in opposite directions, and one of them is winding the thread of life from the other: this procedure is perning or gyring. At the end of a two-thousand-year cycle there is a sudden and violent reversal and the perning starts in the other direction.

In addition to Yeats's explicit ideas, there are certain consistent attitudes which should be mentioned. In his early work of the Celtic twilight, he relied very heavily for his subjects on the figures of Irish legend: Oisin, Cuchulain, Conchobor, Deirdre, and others, and at this time and later he created a few such characters independently, such as Red Hanrahan, Michael Robartes, and Owen Aherne. But Yeats needed heroes for his work and he came more and more to need contemporary heroes. The result was his attempt to transform himself and his friends into legendary heroes. The most important of the friends were Lady Gregory, Major Robert Gregory, John Synge, Shawe-Taylor, and Hugh Lane; but there were others, among them Douglas Hyde. None of these except Lady Gregory and John Synge would be known outside of Ireland today had Yeats not written about them, and Lady Gregory would be little known. In fact Synge's reputation in the early part of the twentieth century was due at least as much to Yeats as to Synge, and his reputation has shrunken greatly. I can remember the time when Synge was the greatest dramatist in English except Shakespeare. There is no harm in praising one's friends, but when so much hyperbole is expended on people of small importance, the discrepancy between the motive and the emotion becomes increasingly evident with time; there seems to be something ridiculous about it. Maude Gonne was a special case, for Yeats was in love with her; but his equation of Maude Gonne with Deirdre, Helen of Troy, and Cathleen ni Houlihan partakes of his dramatization of himself. His concern with his uninteresting relatives and ancestors would seem to be part of the same dramatization.

I will turn to the principal poems related to the theory of the historical cycles. *Leda and the Swan* describes the rape of Leda by Zeus in the form of a swan, a rape which led to the birth of Helen, the destruction of Troy, and the disintegration of early Greek civilization. The rape introduced the next cycle of Greek civilization, which ended with the collapse of "Platonic tolerance," "Doric discipline," and ultimately the Roman Empire. *Two Songs from a Play* describe the end of the second Greek cycle, and the beginning of the Christian. *The Second Coming* prophesies the imminent end of the Christian cycle. Each of these works deals with violence, for every cycle begins and ends in violence. Yeats admires violence in general and has little use for Platonic tolerance, Doric discipline, or the civilization produced by Christianity. This fact is especially important when we read *The Second Coming*.

The account of the rape in the first eight lines of *Leda and the Swan* (p. 211) is very impressively done, but an account of a rape in itself has very limited possibilities in poetry. The important thing here is this: that the rape is committed on a mortal girl by Zeus. In the significance of this fact will reside the power or weakness of the whole poem. In the first portion of the sestet, we are told that the swan has engendered the fall of Troy and the death of Agamemnon, but there is nothing about the historical cycles: this has to be read in from what we know of Yeats's theories — which are, after all, ridiculous. The greatest difficulties reside in the remainder of the sestet. "Did she put on his knowledge with his power?" The question implies that she *did* put on his power, but in what sense? She was quite simply overpowered or raped. She did not share his power, unless we understand a mystical union in the sexual act, which I think is implied. And what about his knowledge? Was this the knowledge of the fall of Troy and the death of Agamemnon? Was it the knowledge that a new cycle was about to begin (in spite of the fact that there is no reference to the cycles in the poem)? Or was it the omniscience of the god, resulting from the sexual union, a knowledge which would include the two other forms of knowledge? I suspect the last, but I would have difficulty in proving it. Next we have to consider "the brute blood of the air." The swan as such is a brute and flies through the air. Zeus may be thought of as living in the air and descending from the air. But Zeus as such was not a brute in Greek myth, and his animal disguises were disguises; nevertheless he often appeared in brute forms. The brute form may be connected in the mind of Yeats with the identification of sexual union and the mystical experience. Satan, however, was referred to in the middle ages as The Prince of the Air, and he and his demons were said to live "in darkened air." I do not recollect that Yeats has mentioned this fact anywhere, but the fact is easily available, and it seems to me unlikely that Yeats would have overlooked it. Yeats was fascinated with the concept of demonic possession as a form of the mystical experience and with the possibility of obtaining supernatural knowledge through such possession. In *The Gift of Harun al-Rashid* (p. 439), the young wife is possessed by a Djinn, apparently as a result of sexual awakening, and in her sleep she communicates the knowledge which her husband desires. This is a pretty fantasy, I suppose, but one can scarcely take it seriously. But we return to the question: is Zeus a god or a demon, or does it make no difference? I suspect that it made no difference to Yeats, who, as Chesterton said of Blake, appears to have kept bad company in the other world; but it should make a difference if we are to adjust our feelings to the motive, for what is the motive? Then there is the difficulty that the poem ends with a question. A question, if it is really a question, is a weak way in which to end a poem, for it leaves the subject of the poem unjudged. But this question may be, as I suspect it is, a rhetorical question: in this event the answer should be either *yes* or *no.* There is nothing in the poem to help us choose, but, from what I know of Yeats, I think that he expected us to say *yes.* This brings us to the final difficulty: the vehicle of the poem is a Greek myth, and there is no harm in this if the tenor is serious; but the tenor is a myth of Yeats's private making, and it is foolish. That is, if we are to take the high rhetoric of the poem seriously, we must really believe that sexual union is a form of the mystical experience, that history proceeds in cycles of two thousand years each, and that the rape of Leda inaugurated a new cycle; or at least we must believe that many other people have believed these things and that such ideas have seriously affected human thinking and feeling. But no one save Yeats has ever believed these things, and we are not sure that Yeats really believed them. These constitute his private fairy tale, or an important part of it, which he sometimes took seriously and sometimes did not. I see no way to make up one's mind about this poem except to decide that it is one of two things: an "aboli bibelot d'inanté sonore" or an "aboli bibelot de bêtise sonore." I feel sure that it is the latter, but I wish it were the former, for the former would at least be inscrutable and would call for greater skill on the part of the poet. The sonority is real, and I can appreciate it as well as the next man, but it takes more than sonority to make a great poem. Pure sonority eventually comes to seem pompous and empty.

Two Songs from a Play (p. 210) exhibit the same sonorous rhetoric and much of Yeats's private mythology: the difficulties therefore are similar to those in *Leda.* Mr. Unterecker *(A Reader's Guide,* p. 186) gives a page of explanation of the poem. He equates the fierce Virgin and her Star with Virgo and Spica (of the zodiac), with Astraea and the Golden Age, with the staring Virgin (Athena) and the heart of Dionysus; and he tells us that these anticipate respectively Mary and Christ, Mary and the Star of Bethlehem, Mary and the Christian Age, and Mary and Christ's heart. This set of relationships is sufficiently complicated for a poem of sixteen lines in the course of which the relationships are not explained or even suggested, but I suspect that there is one additional complication. In the poem entitled *A Nativity* (p. 332), a poem in which the symbolic method is medieval, we have the line: "Another star has shot an ear"; and of this and other similar figures Yeats tells us: "I had in my memory Byzantine mosaic pictures of the Annunciation, which show a line drawn from a star to the ear of the Virgin. She conceived of the Word, and therefore through the ear a star fell and was born" (*A Reader's Guide*, p. 220). The fierce Virgin at the end of the first song is, of course, Mary; she must be fierce, because each new era begins in violence: we thus substitute Yeats's private myth of the Virgin for the traditional one. Similarly it was the odor of Christ's blood (in the second song) which put an end to Platonic tolerance and Doric discipline; that is, it was the violence of the new religion, the Galilean turbulence of Christ. The Babylonian starlight and the fabulous darkness indicate the same thing: we observe starlight most clearly in the dark of the moon, which is the period of pure objectivity and of the violent reversal of the gyres. The rhetorical force in the poem is close to Yeats's best — but it is purely rhetorical. What he is saying is almost as foolish as what he says in Section III of *The Tower* (p. 195), especially the twelve lines beginning "And I declare my faith." These lines are uttered with a passion which is obviously meant to be convincing, but who can be convinced? The second half of the second song is an excellent elegiac stanza, but it has only a loose connection with what has preceded.

The difficulties are similar in *The Second Coming* (p. 184). In line six, the expression "the ceremony of innocence" is misleading and awkward. By reading *A Prayer for My Daughter*, which follows, one discovers that the phrase means the ceremonious life in which innocence flourishes; but as one comes to it in the poem, it would seem to indicate some kind of ceremony, perhaps baptismal, perhaps sacrificial, perhaps some other. Otherwise the first eight lines are very impressive if one takes them phrase by phrase: the adjective *mere* in the fourth line, for example, is a stroke of genius. But what do the lines mean? One who has lived through the last thirty years or more in adulthood and who has not observed the date of the poem (the volume was published in 1921) may feel that Yeats was writing about the growth of fascism, nazism, or communism:

213

the worst
Are full of passionate intensity.

But the first two are impossible and the third is unlikely. "The best" are the Irish aristocrats; "the worst" are the Irish engaged in politics, who were trying to establish a constitutional democracy and who eventually succeeded. The poem is an attack on civilized government made by a man who felt an intense dislike for democracy and the political activity without which democracy cannot survive — a dislike which was due in part to his native temperament, but largely, I fear, to the fact that Maude Gonne was more interested in politics than in Yeats; by a man who, during much of his later life, was often tempted in the direction of fascism. The first four and a half lines of the second section are an example of Yeats's rhetorical skill, but for their effect they depend upon our belief in his notion of the Spiritus Mundi. From there on we have his description of the beast, which is a fine description. But the account of the beast is not pure description. If we are to take it as seriously as Yeats's language indicates that we should, we must again accept his theory of the gyres as in some way valid. And if we do this, we must face the fact that Yeats's attitude toward the beast is different from ours: we may find the beast terrifying, but Yeats finds him satisfying — he is Yeats's judgment upon all that we regard as civilized. Yeats approves of this kind of brutality. When we consider all of these complications, it becomes very difficult to arrive at an acceptance of the poem, an acceptance both rational and emotional. And what would we mean if we said, in the face of these difficulties, that we accepted the poem emotionally and in no other way? The question seems to mean nothing.

I do not deny that civilization may be coming to an end — there is no way of knowing, although I think that its chances for surviving for a long time are fairly good. But if we are to have a poem dealing with the end of civilization, and one that we can suppose to be great, the poem must be based on something more convincing than a home-made mythology and a loose assortment of untenable social attitudes. We need to invoke the Mallarméan

214

concept of the symbol to save this poem, but we cannot invoke it because the ideas are perfectly clear.

I will consider *Sailing to Byzantium* and *Byzantium*. *Sailing to Byzantium* (p. 191) opens with a very good stanza. The first four lines of the next stanza are unfortunate. In the first two lines we have Yeats's familiar figure of the scarecrow, a melodramatic characterization of his own old age, and one which becomes very tiresome. In the next two lines we have one of his melodramatic renderings of emotion through ridiculous physical action:

> unless
> Soul clap its hands and sing, etc.

The fact that this figure came from Blake does not help it. It is similar to other and earlier passages:

> Until I cried and trembled and rocked to and fro

from *The Cold Heaven* (p. 122), and:

> While up from my heart's root
> So great a sweetness flows
> I shake from head to foot

from *Friends* (p. 122). Both of these poems were published in *Responsibilities*, in 1914, when Yeats was approximately forty-nine years old. The book preceding was published in 1910. These two poems, then, were written between the ages of forty-five and forty-nine, when Yeats ought to have been too old for such immature pseudo-poetics, but actually this kind of thing went on for the rest of his life. The next four lines of the stanza are admirable, and the third stanza is one of the most impressive in Yeats except for the phrase: "perne in a gyre." Yeats is inviting the sages who are now in eternity to return to life (to the gyres) and become his teachers. The phrase, however, is bad in two ways: first it gives us the image of the sages stepping from the wall and then spinning like tops or dervishes; second, it does not really mean this, but is a dead metaphor for the return to life. This is one of many examples of the use of medieval symbolism, which in Yeats amounts to a kind of personal shorthand, of un-

215

realized figures of speech. An unrealized figure of speech, as I use the term, is a figure in which the vehicle or descriptive matter is dead; in such a figure one has to deduce the tenor from the dead vehicle. It would be better to use abstract language precisely. The last stanza is well written but the view here given of the function of the poet (to say nothing of the portrait of God) is distressing; the poet, having achieved immortality, will sing to keep a drowsy emperor awake, and he will sing to lords and ladies who are, presumably, equally drowsy. This is the legendary function of the bard, a function which fascinated Yeats, a function which he seems to have tried to fulfill in the Gregory household. The stanza is no accident. We find much the same idea in an earlier piece, *On Being Asked for a War Poem* (p. 153):

> I think it better that in times like these
> A poet's mouth be silent, for in truth
> We have no gift to set a statesman right;
> He has had enough of meddling who can please
> A young girl in the indolence of her youth,
> Or an old man upon a winter's night.

One cannot object to Yeats's refusing to write a poem to order on war or any subject; but the reason given is feeble and characteristic — it exhibits Yeats's sentimental and anti-intellectual view of the nature of his art. The final words of *Sailing to Byzantium*, "to come," do not in themselves indicate that the poet is in any sense a prophet (there is, of course, no reason why he should be, but this concept might appear to some readers to improve the poem), for he, like the Emperor and the lords and ladies, is now in eternity, and they all know what is to come. What is to come, like what is past or passing, merely provides material for this kind of poetry.

Byzantium (p. 243) has often been regarded as one of the most obscure of the poems, but the meaning is fairly obvious. As most of the commentators say, the poem deals with the poet looking out from eternity on those who are coming in; it thus differs from its companion piece, which deals with the poet's voyage to eternity and his arrival there. Curiously enough, although the city of Byzantium is eternity, it seems to be eternity only by night; by day it is corrupted by fury, mire, and blood — but this difficulty is not really great. The starlit or moonlit dome and the bird of the third stanza have led T. R. Henn (the only commentator, so far as I can recollect, who has risked explaining them) rather far from the Yeatsian system[7]. It seems to me unlikely that the bird is a male symbol and the moon a female. In the first stanza, a starlit dome is a dome in the dark of the moon, in the period of complete objectivity or absolute death; a moonlit dome (on this occasion one is forced to suppose that the moon is full) is a dome in the period of perfect subjectivity, when the spirit leaves the body. Either dome would thus disdain man in his essentially human periods. In the third stanza, the golden bird, like the golden bird of the other poem, is an eternal bird, a bird of absolute death; it is on a starlit golden bough and can crow like the cocks of Hades. The meaning of all this strikes me as perfectly clear, as clear as the meaning of any medieval symbol. Such a bird would be embittered by the moon because the moon marks the stages of human life; the two stanzas support this interpretation in all their details. The second stanza, which is an interruption of the argument conducted in one and three, and which would function more effectively as the third than as the second, gives us the poet's invocation of the dead, his attempt to become one with them. The fourth stanza deals with the purification of the entering spirits, and the fifth with their struggle to enter; as far as the mere logic of the discussion goes, these stanzas ought to be in reverse order. The order probably contributes as much as the esoteric symbols to the difficulty that many readers have found in the poem. The order may have been intentional — may have been an attempt to befuddle the reader into believing that medieval method was Mallarméan method — but after more than forty years of reading Yeats, I believe that the order was accidental. As we have been told, the sea is doubtless a symbol for life, and the dolphins who carry the dead to Byzantium are incidentally phallic symbols: the sea is thus tormented by the phallic symbols and by the gongs which are a call to death. We scarcely have the impenetrable image here (Mallarmé was incomparably more skillful at that); we merely have excitement and carelessness. If we study Yeats's private system, we can discover to a certainty what starlight means: its meaning is as definite as the meaning of Dante's panther. The trouble is that, like Dante's panther, it is merely a short-hand device for an idea. Starlight tells us nothing about death; the panther tells us nothing about lust. In so far as either is described well at the sensory level, it is good decoration — but it is only decoration and does nothing to clarify the subject. Yeats's poem is almost wholly decoration, and the ornaments are from his private myths. The generality of the meaning of the ornament drawn from such myths is essentially of the same kind as the generality of the cliché: it has nothing in common with the precise generalization of abstract terms. Yeats had, in fact, only a vague idea of what he was talking about. He did his talking in terms of sensory details, which everyone believes (in our time) to be essential to poetry. The fact that his sensory details do not embody definite thought (as the sensory details of Stevens and Valéry often do) and the fact that his details are often poorly realized at the sensory level do not disturb his admirers, for his language is violent. We are in search of easy emotion, and we find it in Yeats.

Among School Children (p. 212), like the poems which I have already discussed, is regarded as one of the greatest. The first stanza is quietly and effectively descriptive. The second stanza opens with one of his personal clichés, "a Ledaean body": the body is Ledaean because it is the body of Helen, daughter of Leda — that is to say, the body of Maude Gonne. But none of us have ever seen Leda or Helen, and in a few more years there will be no one who has ever seen Maude Gonne, and the portraits of Maude Gonne which I have seen are not very convincing. This is a somewhat pretentious way of saying "a very beautiful body," but it is not description any more than this phrase of mine would be — it is easy allusion, mechanical association. We have an overtone from the Greek myth and one from the Yeatsian myth, both very thin. Helen destroyed the civilization of her time and was thus heroic. Yeats believed that Maude Gonne was destroying the civilization of her time, and he longed to see it destroyed (although he regretted her personal part in the destruction). Therefore the two women were similar, not merely in their personal beauty but in the consequences of their behavior. But Maude Gonne played a real, though minor, part in establishing a civilized government in Ireland, and her son Sean MacBride played a part also, as his father had done. If Maude Gonne was really heroic (I am not a specialist in Irish history nor an aficionado of the Irish temperament), it was in a way that Yeats was incompetent to understand. Maude Gonne was neither Helen nor Deirdre; she was a vigorous and practical (albeit Irish) woman. She may have had faults and virtues which are irrelevant to this discussion, but Yeats did not understand what she was doing. As Mrs. Yeats is reported to have said, Yeats simply did not understand people. One can find additional testimony to the same effect in the letters of Ezra Pound — letters written when Pound was young and still a pretty shrewd observer. This may seem to be too much talk about a mere phrase: the point is that Yeats regularly employed mere phrases. Other clichés in these lines are: "I dream" and "bent above a sinking fire." In the sixth line the sphere contains the idea in a general way, but not with the precision that would have been possible with abstract language or with a better figure; the egg adds nothing to the significance of the sphere and is comical in itself. The third stanza introduces fewer and less troublesome difficulties; but such phrases as "fit of grief or rage" and "daughters of the swan" are mechanical, and "my heart is driven wild" is stereotyped melodrama of a sort to which I have already objected and shall object again. The fourth stanza is composed almost wholly of similar clichés and concludes with Yeats's favorite, that of the scarecrow. Stanzas five and six are of much the same kind: shoddy diction, carelessly violent diction, and further exploitation of the scarecrow. The two lines about Plato are passable but scarcely profound; the two lines about Aristotle are ridiculous without being witty; the lines about Pythagoras mean nothing and are anachronistic with regard to the history of fiddling. The seventh stanza seems to be the beginning of an important statement, but unfortunately the statement is completed in the final stanza and resolves itself into one

219

which I can understand in terms of the pseudo-mysticism and anti-intellectualism of the past two hundred and fifty years but which I cannot grasp imaginatively — that is, in terms of human life as I know human life. The term *labour* seems to mean fruitful labor or ideal labor, and a labor which costs no effort. But where does this kind of labor exist, except, perhaps, in the life of a tree? The body is always bruised to pleasure soul; wisdom is always born out of midnight oil or out of something comparable. The diction in these lines is abominable: the first two lines are bad enough, but the third and fourth are as bad as Keats's "Here where men sit and hear each other groan." The question addressed to the tree is preposterous: the tree is obviously more than the leaf, the blossom or the bole, but these all exist and can be discussed, and it is because of this fact that we have words for them — the implication of the passage is that the tree is an inscrutable unit, like the Mallarméan poem. The diction of the seventh line is as bad as that of the third and fourth. The last line is similar to the fifth and sixth. When we watch the dancer we may not discriminate, although a choreographer could; but if the dancer and the dance could not be discriminated in fact, the dancer could never have learned the dance. Precisely the same ideas will be found in Emerson's *Blight*, a small affair but somewhat better written.

It may seem to the reader that I am unreasonable in objecting so strongly to trite language, when I have been willing to forgive a certain amount of it in Hardy and Bridges. But in the best of Hardy and Bridges the theme is sound and important; and in Yeats the theme is almost always foolish and ill-defined. In the best of Hardy and Bridges the amount of trite language is small; and in most of Yeats the trite language occupies most of the poem — there are a few poems of which this is not quite true, but there are only a few.

I have had something to say of Yeats's habit of excessive dramatization. I would like to be a little more explicit on this subject and then proceed to a few of his poems on his friends and on his political attitudes. I will quote two of Yeats's less ambitious poems and compare them briefly with two poems by John Synge[8] on the same subjects. First is Yeats's poem *A Coat:* this is the last poem in *Responsibilities* and is his farewell to the style of the Celtic Twilight:

> I made my song a coat
> Covered with embroideries
> Out of old mythologies
> From heel to throat;
> But the fools caught it,
> Wore it in the world's eyes
> As though they'd wrought it,
> Song, let them take it,
> For there's more enterprise
> In walking naked.

As I have tried to show, Yeats never learned to walk naked, although he managed to shed a few of the more obvious ribbons of the eighteen-nineties: but whether naked or bedizened, he never got over his exhibitionism. Here is Synge's poem:

> *The Passing of the Shee*
> After looking at one of A.E.'s pictures
>
> Adieu, sweet Aengus, Meave, and Fand,
> Ye plumed yet skinny Shee,
> That poets played with hand in hand
> To learn their ecstasy.
> We'll stretch in Red Dan Sally's ditch,
> And drink in Tubber Fair,
> Or poach with Red Dan Philly's bitch
> The badger and the hare.

I will now quote Yeats's poem (also from *Responsibilities*) *On Those That Hated 'The Playboy of the Western World':*

> Once when midnight smote the air,
> Eunuchs ran through Hell and met
> On every crowded street to stare
> Upon great Juan riding by:
> Even like these to rail and sweat
> Staring upon his sinewy thigh.

That slow, that meditative man himself wrote as follows:

The Curse

To a sister of an enemy of the authors
who disapproved of 'The Playboy'

Lord, confound this surly sister,
Blight her brow with blotch and blister,
Cramp her larynx, lung, and liver,
In her guts a galling give her.

Let her live to earn her dinners
In Mountjoy with seedy sinners:
Lord, this judgment quickly bring,
And I'm your servant, J. M. Synge.

Yeats's poems are inflated; they are bardic in the worst sense. Synge's poems are witty and unpretentious.

To a Friend Whose Work Has Come to Nothing (p. 107) exhibits the same inflated style and Yeats's predilection for madness. The first ten lines are plain and honest and exhibit a certain moral nobility; the last six, however, recommend madness as a cure for the problem which the poem propounds. We have been told that the poem was addressed to Lady Gregory. Lady Gregory never followed the advice here given, but as she appears in this poem she is merely one in a long series of Yeatsian lunatics.

In Memory of Major Robert Gregory (p. 130) is in praise of Lady Gregory's son, who was killed in the first world war. It is commonly described as one of the greatest poems in our language; I confess that I think it is a very bad poem. The first two stanzas deal with Yeats's recent settling in his new house and with his thoughts about dead friends; the next three stanzas deal with three dead friends in particular: Lionel Johnson, John Synge, and Yeats's uncle George Pollexfen. The next six stanzas deal with Robert Gregory; the final stanza is a conclusion. The first stanza is quiet and acceptable, though undistinguished. The second stanza, undistinguished in general, contains two very awkward details: the third and fourth lines employ a conversational and verbose stereotype to embody simple matter, and the fifth line employs another. The fifth line, however, is bad in other ways: the words *up upon* make a crude combination, and the whole line, "And quarrels are blown up upon that head," gives us, like the two lines preceding, a dead metaphor but this time a mixed metaphor as well. Unless we are imperceptive of the possibilities of language, we visualize something being blown up on top of a head. This kind of thing is common in newspaper writing and in other vulgar writing. I remember a freshman composition from many years ago, in which the student wrote: "This line of study is basic to my field of endeavor." The line by Yeats is the same kind of thing as my freshman's effort, and no apologetic reference to the virtues of colloquialism is an adequate defense. The third stanza, which deals with Lionel Johnson, is stereotyped throughout, but it contains two especially unfortunate details. Johnson is described as "much falling," a sufficiently clumsy phrase in itself, but Pound tells us

> "how Johnson (Lionel) died
> By falling from a high stool in a pub. . ."[9]

It seems likely that Pound's poem was written somewhat after that of Yeats, as nearly as I can judge from the dates at my disposal, and that the passage was intended as a comment on Yeats's phrase. At any rate, it would be a fair enough comment. Immediately below "much falling" we get a very thin reincarnation of Roland's horn. The fourth stanza deals with John Synge. He is described as "that enquiring man," a phrase to which I do not object in itself. But every time Synge appears by name in Yeats's poems, he is described as "that . . . man," and we expect the formula as regularly as we come to expect rock, thorn trees, cold light, shaking and trembling, and scarecrows; furthermore, the unnecessary use of the demonstrative adjective is one of Yeats's most obviously mechanical devices for achieving over-emphasis. The remainder of this stanza is undistinguished, but one should consider these details: in line five, *certain* is used as a pronoun instead of an adjective; in line six we have "a most desolate and stony place"; and in the last we have "Passionate and simple as his heart," a phrase which is not only one of Yeats's common clichés but one which indicates as clearly as many others the anti-intellectual bent of his work. The fifth stanza deals with Yeats's uncle George Pollexfen, who, it seems, had been a vigorous horseman in his youth, but who had devoted himself to astrology in his later years. The diction is dull, but once again there are strange details. For example, if solid men and pure-bred horses are determined by the stars, then why not other men and horses? The limitation could have been clarified by such a word as *even*, but the writing is slovenly; as Pound said long ago, poetry should be at least as well written as prose. The words *sluggish, contemplative,* and *outrageous* indicate that Yeats disapproved of his uncle's later interests because they were, in some sense, intellectual; but Yeats himself was interested, throughout much of his life, in equally pseudo-intellectual studies. Perhaps the stanza is an example of what Cleanth Brooks would call irony; but it is also dull. The sixth stanza is respectably executed except for two details. In the second line, "as it were" says nothing; it may have been used to fill out the line and achieve a rime, or it may have been used in the interests of colloquial style, although it is not colloquial. It seems to be lazy. The next to the last line, "Our Sidney and our perfect man" is exorbitant praise. One might accept it as a mere outburst of grief except for the fact that Yeats devotes the rest of the poem to praising Gregory in these terms: he was a great horseman, scholar, and painter; he had the knowledge to give expert advice in architecture, sculpture, and most of the handicrafts. He may well have been a great horseman, but so is many a jockey; the praise in the other departments, however, appears excessive, for if it were not we should have heard of Gregory's accomplishments from other sources. He appears to have been no Sidney, but a charming and admirable young man who dabbled in the arts. We have familiar stereotypes in the last stanzas: cold rock and thorn, stern color, delicate line, secret discipline, none of them really described or defined; we have the facile commonplaces of the final lines of stanzas eight and nine and the somewhat comical example of misplaced particularity in the final line of stanza eleven. In the twelfth and final stanza, Yeats tells us that he had hoped in this poem to comment on everyone whom he had ever loved or admired but that Gregory's death took all his heart for speech. He had managed to write twelve stanzas of eight lines each, however, before he stopped, but this remark serves as a kind of apology for the loose structure of the poem — a structure which remains loose in spite of the apology.

Coole Park, 1929 (p. 238) is a poem in honor of Lady Gregory and her home, Coole Park, which she had been forced to sell to the Forestry Department, although she was permitted to live there until her death. The poem is a typical meditation on the virtues of old families and on their patronage of the arts, but especially upon Lady Gregory as a force in bringing distinguished men together and guiding their work. The theme is therefore the intellectual force that Lady Gregory exerted upon these men: Douglas Hyde, a negligible poet who became a distinguished Celtic scholar, whose poetry Yeats apparently admired and whose scholarship he regretted; John Synge, whose plays Yeats greatly admired and vastly over-rated; Shawe-Taylor and Hugh Lane, nephews of Lady Gregory and patrons of the arts but scarcely great men; and Yeats himself. Shawe-Taylor and Hugh Lane are described as "those impetuous men." This is a Yeatsian formula to describe distinguished gentlemen, and Synge appears in the usual formula for Synge: "that slow, that meditative man." The unfortunate Hyde is buried in the worst pseudo-poeticism of all, and Yeats employs a prettily apologetic description of himself. The central figure of speech appears in the third stanza. The first two lines of the first stanza place Lady Gregory and a swallow together in what appears to be an accidental juxtaposition, but in the third stanza the men are compared to swallows, and we are told that Lady Gregory could keep a swallow to its first intent, could control the flight of swallows. Obviously, she could do nothing of the sort; we may suppose that she could control talented men in some fashion, but we are not told how. The movement of the swallows is charming; Lady Gregory's influence on the men, presumably an intellectual influence, is never given us. What we have is a fairly good vehicle with almost no tenor, or fairly good decoration of an undefined theme. In the last two lines, however, the third stanza collapses almost completely. Line seven reads: "The intellectual sweetness of those lines." At the level of the vehicle, the lines are those of the swallows' flight; at the level of the tenor we have nothing, for "intellectual sweetness" is merely a sentimental phrase with no conceptual support. The last line of this stanza, "That cut through time or cross it withershins," is especially unclear. As to *withershins* the *Shorter Oxford English Dictionary* gives this account of it:

1. In a direction contrary to the usual; the wrong way — 1721.
2. In a direction contrary to the apparent course of the sun (considered as unlucky or causing disaster) — 1545.

The last line of the first stanza is pseudo-poetic. The third and fourth lines of the last stanza are commonplace, and the sixth and seventh are baffling: why should the mourners stand with backs to the sun and shade alike, and why is the shade sensual? This is verbiage for the sake of verbiage.

The best poem of this kind, I believe, is a late one, *The Municipal Gallery Revisited* (p. 316). There are a good many characteristic defects. In his attempt to achieve a conversational tone (or perhaps out of inadvertence) Yeats wrote a fair number of lines which are awkward in movement. The poem is predominantly iambic pentameter, but if we are to read it in this meter, we encounter problems, some more serious than others. Line four can be read only as three trochees followed by two anapests. In line eight of the same stanza we get this:

> A revolutionary soldier kneeling to be blessed.

That is, we have four syllables in the first foot and either three or four in the second, depending on our pronunciation of *revolutionary*. It is hard to read the first line of the second stanza as anything but an alexandrine. In line three of the second stanza, we have a trochee in the last position if we pronounce *Ireland* correctly, but this is the only line in the poem in which this awkward variation occurs, and we are not prepared for it and are tempted to mispronounce the word for the sake of the rime. Line five in the same stanza is an alexandrine and the first lines of four, five, and six are alexandrines. We have such formulae as "terrible and gay" and "John Synge. . . that rooted man." At the opening of the fourth stanza we have rhetorical exaggeration:

> Mancini's portrait of Augusta Gregory,
> 'Greatest since Rembrandt', according to John Synge;

But this is followed immediately by the almost weary quailification:

> A great ebullient portrait, certainly.

At the opening of the third stanza we have the expression of emotion through physical action:

> Heart-smitten with emotion, I sink down,
> My heart recovering with covered eyes.

But this is an account of an old man looking at the portraits of his dead friends and is understandable in a measure; it seems a somewhat unscrupulous and undignified play for our sympathy, but it has not the empty violence of comparable passages from earlier poems. The transition from five to six is awkward. Yeats apparently thought that the line at the end of five needed a footnote, and I dare say it does; but he puts his footnote in parentheses at the beginning of six, and it is unimpressive as poetry, and it detracts from the unity of six. Except for this defect, six is well enough written, but its effect depends upon Yeats's view of the ideal society, "dream of the noble and the beggarman," a view by which I find myself unmoved. The last stanza over-rates Yeats's friends but is the moving statement of an old man who held them in high esteem and who now reviews them all in the official portraits, all of them being dead. Perhaps the best apology for this poem is to be found in a poem by Robert Bridges, written a good many years earlier, his *Elegy among the Tombs:*

> Read the worn names of the forgotten dead,
> Their pompous legends will no smile awake;
> Even the vainglorious title o'er the head
> Wins its pride pardon for its sorrow's sake;
> And carven Loves scorn not their dusty prize,
> Though fallen so far from tender sympathies.

The best of the political poems, I suspect, is *Easter 1916.* The worst fault in the poem is the refrain, "A terrible beauty is born." One can understand the sentiment, but the diction is pure Yeatsian fustian. In the first stanza I regret the repetition of "polite meaningless words," but the defect is minor. In the line "To please a companion," however, we have an unrhythmical prose if we pronounce *companion* correctly; to save the rhythm, we have to say "companee*un*." In the first seven lines of the next stanza, lines which are passably written, we have Yeats's view of what women should not do. In the next two lines,

> This man had kept a school
> And rode our winged horse,

we have a pseudo-poeticism as bad as Hyde's sword or Roland's horn. A little farther on we have this:

> So sensitive his nature seemed.

The line is written in a rapid tetrameter, and it occurs in a poem which otherwise is written in heavily accented trimeter, and for the moment it ruins the movement. To save the meter, we should have to read *sens'tive*, but the *Shorter Oxford English Dictionary* does not give this pronunciation, and it seems an unlikely one. In the third stanza the stream and the other details of momentary change are the main part of the vehicle; the unchanging stone is the rest. The vehicle, as mere description, is very well handled. The tenor, however, is this: the truly spiritual life consists of momentary change; fixity of purpose turns one to an imperceptive stone. This is familiar romantic doctrine, but I see no reason to take it seriously. In the last stanza, he tells us that the Easter martyrs turned themselves to stone and perhaps in a poor cause, but he praises them for their heroism and laments their deaths. The poem is marred by certain faults of style and by more serious faults of thinking, which we must regard as virtues if we are to be greatly moved.

I will turn now to a few poems which seem to me the most nearly successful.

The Wild Swans at Coole (p. 129) is perhaps the best of these. The line "And now my heart is sore" is unfortunate, but otherwise the poem is excellently written. There are two unobtrusive but brilliant details, the effect of which seems to permeate the entire poem. In the first stanza we are given a quiet but excellent description of the dry autumn at twilight. The fifth line reads: "Upon the brimming water among the stones." The word *brimming* separates the world of water from the world of dryness with an almost absolute precision, and this separation is of the essence of the poem. In the fourth stanza we find a similar detail:

> They paddle in the cold
> Companionable streams. . . .

The cold streams are companionable to the swans but not to the aging human observer. Richard Ellmann gives us an interesting fact about the poem:

> When the poem was first published in *The Little Review* in June 1917, the fifth and fourth stanzas were reversed. By putting the fourth stanza at the end Yeats made it possible to read it symbolically so that his awakening would be his death, a paradox well within his intellectual boundaries. Unfortunately, the word 'but' was now superfluous at the beginning of the last stanza: he nevertheless allowed it to remain[10].

One could employ this incident to illustrate Yeats's carelessness, a carelessness which can easily be documented elsewhere; but the word is not superfluous. In the third line of the fourth stanza the swans are either on the water or in the air, and at the end of the stanza they are in the air. "But now," the last stanza tells us, they are on the water. This seems reasonable. And what is Mr. Ellmann's authority for believing that Yeats's awakening would be his death? If the authority is to be found in Yeats, I have never seen it or a citation of it. The question with which the poem ends would be troublesome if it could not be understood or if it left the final meaning in doubt. Mr. Unterecker (*A Reader's Guide*, p. 132), a disarmingly naïve seeker for richness of ambiguity, has this to say of it:

> This complex question (and many others Yeats will soon be asking) suggests its own mysteries: like that of the swans the pattern of man survives; yet "I", awakening some day (into death?) will find the pattern of immortality "flown away" (and myself immortal?).

Why should the swans be a pattern of immortality? Yeats implies

229

clearly enough that they are an immortal pattern, but that is another matter. As Wordsworth said, "The Form remains, the Function never dies." Alice Meynell made this distinction between the poet (a mortal individual) and the birds (an immortal form):

> Hereditary Song,
>   Illyrian lark and Paduan nightingale,
> Is yours, unchangeable the ages long;
>   Assyria heard your tale.
>
> Therefore you do not die.
>   But single, local, lonely, mortal, new,
> Unlike, and thus like all my race am I,
>   Preluding my adieu.

The idea is easy to grasp, whatever one may think of the style. And why should Yeats's awakening signify his death? Let us remember that the poem was written when Yeats was nearing the age of fifty, and that he saw himself as a man of declining powers. His theories of the phases of the moon and of the gyres were merely a rationalization of opinions which he had long held, and the poem entitled *The Phases of the Moon* appears in the same volume with this poem. Yeats at this time is about to enter upon the fourth period, the period of "wisdom," in which creativity is lost; he is departing from subjectivity, which makes creation possible. The swan, moreover, has been traditionally a symbol for beauty, and in Yeats's system water and water-birds represent subjectivity. I would judge, then, that in this poem Yeats sees in the swans a symbol of his creative power, still present, but soon to be lost. The question then means: "On whom will this talent light when it has left me?" The poem in these terms is clear and a fine poem. The word *companionable*, as I have accounted for it, may seem to offer a difficulty if the talent is understood to be still present; but the talent seems to be on the point of departure, and the water (subjectivity), though companionable to the talent, is about to be uncompanionable to the poet.

I am of Ireland (p. 262) appears to be a dialogue between Cathleen ni Houlihan (Maude Gonne) and W. B. Yeats. The lady seems to be inviting the poet to enter into Irish politics, and he

230

finds the idea little to his liking. The poem is not a great poem, for the subject is too slight, but the movement and diction are masterly. Its chief weakness resides in the fact that it has to be paraphrased so baldly with reference to Yeats's life and prejudices. More information ought to be contained within the poem: more information might have led to a poem of greater intellectual richness or it might have led to a flat didactic poem. It is likely that Yeats chose the best method in the light of his own limitations, but the method is a makeshift.

Long-legged Fly (p. 327) is one of the most interesting poems, but as usual there are difficulties. The first stanza describes Caesar planning a battle to save civilization, and the third gives us Michael Angelo painting the Pope's chapel, that is, creating civilization; but the second stanza describes Helen practicing a tinker's shuffle on the empty streets of Troy. The refrain indicates that all three persons are engaged in deep thought over important action, but Helen is not depicted as thinking — she is depicted as unthinking; and, although Helen brought about the fall of Troy, she did not plan the fall but was merely an accidental cause. Although the detail of the second stanza is exceptionally fine, the theme collapses. Furthermore, in the opening lines of the third stanza, Yeats says that Michael Angelo is painting his Adam in order to provide a sexual awakening for girls at puberty (for documentation of this obsession see *Under Ben Bulben IV*, p. 341) and this strikes me as so trivial (and so wrong) an aim for the painter's work that the poem is badly damaged by it: it is an example of Yeats's pseudo-religious glorification of sexuality. Then there are the two versions of the refrain in the second stanza. In the edition which I am using, the refrain at the end of the second stanza reads "*His* mind." This cannot refer to Helen, and if it is correct, then we have some kind of supernal mind working through all three of the figures; this concept would be very vague, and the first stanza, in this event, would be misleading. The editors of the variorum edition, however, point out that this reading occurs only in my edition, and they give "*Her* mind" as the correct reading. They are almost certainly right, but the bad proofreading in almost all of Yeats's books would seem to indicate at

231

least a possibility that they are wrong. If they are right, then the refrain at the end of the second stanza is meaningless. The descriptive detail throughout the poem and the movement of the lines are about equally beautiful.

I would like to mention a few minor efforts for one reason or another. *For Anne Gregory* (p. 240) is a charming and witty poem. *Crazy Jane Grown Old Looks at the Dancers* (p. 255) is beautifully done as regards diction, syntax, and every aspect of rhythm. One can say, perhaps, that the subject is melodramatic, or, in any event, that it is certainly of small importance. I admire the execution but seldom reread the poem. *Lullaby* (p. 259) is almost equally graceful and is equally slight. *After Long Silence* (p. 260) has often been highly praised. The first six lines are excellent, but at the end we are told that this is "The supreme theme of Art and Song":

> Bodily decrepitude is wisdom; young
> We loved each other and were ignorant.

This is not, of course, the supreme theme of Art and Song, but we ought to consider what the lines mean. Bodily decrepitude and wisdom (a contemptible quality, according to Yeats) are the same thing; both are reached in old age (in the fourth period of the moon). Youth, love, and ignorance are the best things in life, according to the doctrine. Now I shall not speak in favor of bodily decrepitude, for I am beginning to experience it and know what it is; and I have nothing against youth and love, for I observe them about me daily and find them charming. But as a simple matter of fact, wisdom (in the normal sense of the word) is highly desirable and ignorance is not. In the world as we find it, we cannot have everything at once, but we must take things as they come and pay for what we get. However, my interpretation of the sixth line may be wrong. Yeats may have meant that the two friends were discoursing upon the supreme theme for discourse; namely, Art and Song. In this event, the two final lines would mean: *faute de mieux*. Because of the syntax and punctuation, it is impossible to be sure, although the first of my two readings strikes me as the more likely; either way the meaning of the two last lines in themselves remains the same. *The Cat and the Moon* (p. 164) gives us a cat which is beautifully described and a moon which is merely a stage property. *The Gyres* (p. 291) is very badly written: the first stanza in particular is pure Pistol. But the poem is also revealing, for Yeats is welcoming the destruction of civilization with enthusiasm, and is predicting the return of the kind of civilization which he admires and believes once to have existed. The reader of *The Second Coming* should study this poem as a companion-piece. The six poems entitled *Under Ben Bulben* (p. 341) give a clear summary of his ideas and attitudes, and are obviously offered as a final statement. One reads a succinct summary of the social ideas, for example, in the fifth of these, and of Yeats's attitude toward himself in the sixth. Mr. Unterecker believes that the horseman of the epitaph is one of the wild horsemen of the mountains, who descend upon the world in times of disaster; this may be so, but I have always supposed him to be one of Yeats's ideal aristocrats. The wild horsemen appear in the first poem, the mortal horsemen in the fifth (as well as in *The Gyres*).

First of all we should discard the idea that Yeats was in any real sense a Mallarméan symbolist. There is not, so far as my limited knowledge goes, any extensive translation of Mallarmé's criticism. The original prose is extremely difficult, and I do not believe that Yeats ever had sufficient command of French to read it; he certainly had not in the years when he was forming his style. And Mallarmé's verse[11] is more difficult than his prose. The simple fact of the matter is that Yeats (from *Responsibilities* onward, at least, and often before) was usually trying to say something clearly. His obscurity results from his private symbols (which resemble the medieval symbols in their intention), from the confusion of his thought, and from the frequent ineptitude of his style. From *Responsibilities* onward, in fact, he became more and more openly didactic. He quite obviously was deeply moved by his ideas and expected us to be moved by them. But unfortunately his ideas were contemptible. I do not wish to say that I believe that Yeats should be discarded, for there are a few minor poems which are successful, or nearly successful, and there are many fine lines and passages in the more ambitious pieces. But in the long run it is impossible to believe that foolishness is greatness, and Yeats was not a great poet, nor was he by a wide margin the best poet of our time. There are greater poems in Bridges, Hardy, Robinson, and Stevens, to mention no others, and in at least half a dozen later poets as well. His reputation is easly accounted for. In the first place, there is real talent scattered throughout his work; in the second place, our time does not recognize any relationship between motive and emotion, but is looking merely for emotion; in the third place, Yeats's power of self-assertion, his bardic tone, has overwhelmed his readers thus far. The bardic tone is common in romantic poetry: it sometimes occurs in talented (but confused) poets such as Blake and Yeats; more often it appears in poets of little or no talent, such as Shelley, Whitman, and Robinson Jeffers. For most readers the bardic tone is synonymous with greatness, for through this tone the poet asserts that he is great, in the absence of any (or sufficient) supporting intelligence. If the poet asserts his own greatness long enough and in the same tone of voice, the effect is hypnotic; we have seen the same thing on the political platform in the persons of such speakers as Mussolini, Father Coughlin, and Adolf Hitler. But in time the effect wears off, and of course (among poets, anyway) such mountebanks have been following each other in rapid succession and tend to replace each other, whereas the relatively scarce poet of real talent remains, even though under-estimated. While the tone is effective, however, a good deal of damage is done. In our time Yeats has been regarded as the great poet in person, the poet of the impeccable style. He has thus become a standard for critics, with the result that the work of better poets has been obscured or minimized; and he has become a model for imitation, with the result that the work of a good many talented poets has been damaged beyond repair.

IV

T. STURGE MOORE (1870-1944) was the brother of G. E. Moore the

234

philosopher and was the friend and correspondent of Yeats. He was widely acquainted with the distinguished British men of letters of his time, and appears to have known some of the French. He was talented in the graphic arts. And as an item of at least small interest, I should add that he designed the covers and typography for his own books and the covers for certain books by Yeats. He wrote short poems and long, and poems of medium length; he wrote poetic dramas of various kinds, and he wrote a few brief and semi-dramatic pieces which in some ways resemble eclogues, some of which he entitled *Idyllic Monologues;* and he wrote critical prose, dealing with painting and literature. He was influenced by the French Parnassians and Symbolists, to some small extent by Swinburne and the English poets of the nineties, and (unfortunately) by the English nineteenth century; but his work is in a large measure and rather importantly a reaction against these influences. He had a great deal of common-sense in an age which exhibits little; his native talent for poetry was great. But he was an unfinished genius, and is too often disappointing. He seems to have been self-indulgent with regard to the responsibilities imposed by his talent; his writing is successful in only a few works and in a good many passages. But when he is really successful, he is great, and any man who endeavors to understand the influence of the nineties, and of the French poets mentioned, on the poetry and thought of our century will have to study Moore with some attention. I am here concerned primarily with his short poems, but I shall have to mention other works.

In theory, Moore was a counter-romantic, but he was not naïvely so. He was opposed to the pseudo-scientific historical scholarship which was influential during much of his life; he was aware of the unclassifiable act of judgment, both in the composition of the work of art and in the evaluation of the work of art; he was aware of the dangers inherent in the failure to relate this act of judgment to a controlling reason; but he could not write with sufficient precision to clarify the problems which he perceived — his thought too often evaporates into talk about beauty or about circumambient perfumes. Yet he was aware of these problems, far more aware of them than were any of his contemporaries. He was aware also of the necessity of enlightenment from scholarship, but he was aware at the same time that professional scholars were imperceptive blunderers when they attempted critical judgment. It seems not to have occurred to him that the poet and critic might be at the same time a professional scholar, and, by combining all of his activities, improve all of them. In his arguments with Yeats, in their correspondence, he is almost invariably the winner on points, for Yeats was simply foolish and Moore was not foolish; but Moore remains an amateur theorist. Moore's theorizing suffers from a delusion common in his time that it is possible to define an "aesthetic" philosophy that will account for all of the "fine arts." But this is impossible, for any set of statements which one can make that will be true of all the arts, will omit the characteristics which are essential to each. Poetry, music, painting, sculpture, and architecture are radically different in purpose, medium, and nature, in spite of a few superficial resemblances between certain pairs[12].

His thought about human nature and poetry alike appears most clearly in his poems and plays. Briefly, he believed in the development of all of the human faculties; he believed that the cultivation of one potentiality of human nature (and hence of art) at the expense of the rest was an error and might be a tragic error. On the face of it, this notion may not appear very original, but it is true and it has many ramifications, some of them very complex; and the truism is commonly ignored and even held in contempt.

In *Mariamne*, the best of the longer plays, Mariamne errs through pride which makes her demand an inhuman perfection of Herod, and the error leads to her downfall; the idea is simple, the human situation complex. In *Medea*, a very short play, influenced by the Pound-Fenollosa versions of the Noh, Medea sacrifices her humanity (that is, murders her children) in order to achieve the peculiar kind of perfection demanded by Artemis; but Artemis is complex within what seems her simplicity, and her complexity is inhuman — she is "manifold Delia," goddess of several names and natures:

> Orthia, she drinks blood... Hecate... there
> You blench! those names are hers as much
> As Cynthia is. ...

As one commits oneself more and more wholly to this goddess alone (or to her principal adversary, Aphrodite) one commits oneself more and more to despair, and perhaps to self-destruction. Something similar occurs in one of the shorter plays, and I think the greatest, *Daimonassa*[13].

The action of *Daimonassa* is as follows: Kyrkaeus, formerly the tyrant of Orchomenos, has been driven out by his brother, Orcan; he persuades his daughters, Daimonassa and Ferusa, to tempt Orcan's sons to fall in love with them, with the intention of murdering the young men on their wedding night, with the result that Orcan will have no descendants save the grandchildren of Kyrkaeus. The girls fall in love with the young men in the course of the seduction, but Daimonassa carries out her promise to her father notwithstanding. At the last minute Ferusa awakens her bridegroom, tells him of the plot and escapes with him; he is killed by pursuers later in the night, and Ferusa is captured. During the confusion in the castle, Kyrkaeus is killed by Ontaeus, a young musician, who, in turn, is killed by Daimonassa. Daimonassa is in control at the end of the play. It would seem to be an old-fashioned tragedy of blood in a primitive setting, but the central figure is triumphant, not dead, at the end. And yet we can hardly regard her as virtuous or even sympathetic, and this fact has bothered the few people who have commented on the play.

But Daimonassa has destroyed herself spiritually, and in this she is a tragic figure. She has begun by submitting herself to her father's passion for revenge, a revenge born of hatred, and in carrying out the murder she destroys her capacity for love. Ferusa's failure separates the two sisters absolutely, and no further love is possible there. Kyrkaeus is dead, and, at the end of the play, Daimonassa sees herself as a kind of superhuman embodiment of pride and progeniture, her humanity destroyed. Immediately after she has murdered her husband, Daimonassa speaks these words in the course of a long *tirade:*

237

And suddenly now I hear his horrible cry
On realizing that our love was dreamed
And true that knife in his side.
The thing that's done infects the doer's mind.
Who did the deed no longer is who planned it,
But such a stranger to that forward soul
As dreads to look again on what is done.

        o o o o o o

This silence tingles, and a million *ifs*
Fringe the void darkness. . .

Kyrkaeus endeavors to comfort and steady Daimonassa by making her contemplate the permanence of the stars. This is not idle poeticism on Moore's part; he is exhibiting Kyrkaeus as a devotee of the eternally irrelevant, as one who has already renounced his humanity:

Look up; forget what's done. This silence. . . Oh,
The wonder it elicits is divine,
All those suspended points of light impart
Pure peace . . . await attention . . . they have hung
Patient, unheeded o'er flame-gutted cities. . . .

Toward the end of the play, Daimonassa says of herself:

These deep denials of self by self, so rend
The very texture of the stuff we were,
That what remains we are not.

And later she addresses the absent Ferusa:

Ferusa, most unbearably untrue!
I killed my Rhesus to keep faith with thee.
And prove thine equal in our father's aid!
Yet lost thee, lost my husband, lost my father.
And lost the unity of being! . . .

Near the end of the play, Ferusa, now a captive, says:

Courage! . . . my courage dared refuse that crime!
But there! Fact owns no concord with intent!
All mortals mean is mocked in what occurs.
Reality is not related to us.

In speaking these lines, Ferusa is trying to deny complicity because she did not actually commit murder, and is expressing pity

238

for herself; but Moore, in writing the lines, is saying that these people, through choice upon choice, have removed themselves from reality, have lost themselves. The play ends quietly but grimly: Daimonassa sees her future simply as the mother of her father's grandchild, and the guards swear allegiance to her and to the child. The play is short — there is only one act, in fact one scene. There are only a few flaws in the writing, and they are minor: I can think of no other poetic drama in English in which perfection of style is so nearly achieved. The style is adequate to simple situations; nothing is falsified. It rises to great occasions, and in an action so brief and so intense the great occasions dominate the play. I have quoted certain passages to illustrate the theme, but these passages are great poetry. *Daimonassa* is Moore's greatest work and one of the greatest works in English.

In general the plays are sound in conception, and I have been assured by persons more familiar with the stage than myself that most of them could be acted successfully. Half a dozen of them are incomparably superior to any of the plays by Yeats and to any of the poetic dramas written since which have come my way; I do not regard this comparison as high praise, however. Outside of *Daimonassa*, the writing in Moore's plays is uneven. *Mariamne* is probably the best written of the remainder, as it is the best in other ways; beautiful lines and passages can be found in many of the plays, just as they can be found in many of the poems, long and short.

The faults in Moore's style are various: most often one is bothered by the omission of articles and other monosyllabic aids to grammar, the crowding of monosyllables almost evenly stressed and often cluttered with difficult dentals, and downright clichés, most of them from the nineteenth century. It would be possible to illustrate these faults at great length if it were worth the trouble; but Moore has not, like Yeats, been praised for his faults. Moore has not been over-rated, as Yeats has been; he has not even been under-rated — he has been ignored. I will merely quote an example of his style at his worst, therefore — the second of the two sonnets entiled *Silence* — and thereafter will devote my attention to other matters:

239

O where is Silence more alive than dead?
Not where space mutes a myriad furnace suns;
Where time will soon know noise or knew it once,
Corpse-like, she lies on rock- or ocean-bed. . .
Yet as the tender-footed dawn has sped
From east to west, inaudibly she runs
And, while the bird's insensate hymn she shuns,
Yet lark-like climbs within the ecstatic head —
Thought yearns, and hope, surpassed, watches her rise;
While vision's vault distends the aerial dome,
The cage of dreams becomes a permanent home
To house heart's whole content. Then eloquent eyes
Sing Silence, which, if gazing one have heard,
He thenceforth will disdain the uttered word.

Nothing could be worse, but there is a good deal as bad. Yet there are other qualities.

A good many poems exhibit qualities which we think of as those of the nineties or of the first decade of the twentieth century. Hardy and Bridges wrote some of their poems in this period but are not of it, and, in fact, were scarcely noticed. The early Yeats has something in common with the characteristic poets of this school — Symons, Wilde, Lionel Johnson, and Dowson — and he never entirely outgrew them. They provided a literary atmosphere and an audience which facilitated the rapid acceptance of Yeats; they, the Pre-Raphaelites, Swinburne, and the early Yeats were a strong influence on the early work of Pound, and the influence persists even into the latest *Cantos*. Strange as it may seem, it was a few sentences in Pound's early prose which first called my attention to Moore and to Bridges, when I was perhaps seventeen years old. Some of Moore's poems which appear to be of this period may have been written later, for Moore does not arrange his poems in chronological order. The poems in question stand out above nearly everything else that one thinks of as characteristic of the period. I have in mind such poems as these: *Tempio di Venere, To Slow Music, The Vigil, Love's First Communion, A Duet, Shells, A Song of Chiron,* and *The Rowers' Chant.* These poems are all charming and skillful, but they are all dated. *A Duet* is the most successful, and, though slight, is least imprisoned by an insipid mode. It charmed Quiller-Couch and found its way into the *Oxford Book of English Verse*. *The Vigil* is a serious poem, marred by weak diction; it tells us that death is final, and it rejects false consolation. The form in which false consolation appears bears a strong resemblance, amusingly enough, to the realm of the Sidh as we find it in the early Yeats. This is unfortunate, for more than half of the poem is devoted to describing the myth before it is rejected, and the description is in discreetly Yeatsian clichés. *Tempio di Venere* is a graceful exercise suggesting both Heredia and Swinburne. Most of these poems are on themes contrary to the themes characteristic of the poets I have mentioned, but the style belongs to the period, in spite of improvements. These poems would suffice to give Moore a high place in an inferior school of poetry, but they would not place him high among the poets of our language.

Many other poems offer explicit rejections of common romantic ideas and attitudes. *An Aged Beauty's Prayer* is a monologue spoken by an old woman who had been vain of her beauty in youth, a worshipper of the moon (in Moore's terms, a devotee of "pure," or inhuman, discipline), and who almost ruined her life, but came to her senses in time. Her final prayer is to Venus:

> Marvellous Venus, crowned by time
> My locks are white as moon-lit snow,
> My children's chubby children climb
> Up on my knees to sit and crow
> Perched on the ruin of my prime.

> For one thing I petition thee: —
> While generations from these rise,
> Let me ne'er lack heiress, to be
> Like, as maid may, to her whose eyes
> For peril far surpass the sea.

These lines are lovely, and they are especially moving as the conclusion of the narrative; but the poem is too long, and most of it is badly written. The theme, however, is that of *Mariamne*, of *Medea* and of *Daimonassa*, except that in this poem the protagonist saves herself, whereas in the three plays the protagonist fails by sinning against normal love. *On Four Poplars*, which is better written than the two poems which I have just mentioned, deals with the impossibility of trying to infuse one's will into another person, and with the error of attempting to do so. *Plans for a Midnight Picnic* is a poem written for and about children; it is a bad poem, and it may seem unfair to mention it. But it is an explicit rejection of what is often called the pathetic fallacy. No one will be surprised now if we say that it is foolish to read one's human feelings into vegetable nature, but the poem was written early in our century, or perhaps earlier; in any event, it is one more illustration of Moore's anti-romantic bent. One could multiply examples, but these will serve. It may seem strange that a poet so consciously opposed to romantic philosophy should be so corrupted by the style which romantic philosophy had generated, but the essential characteristics of the style had dominated poetry for more than a century and a half when Moore began to write. Habits are formed slowly and are broken more slowly, and communal habits, whether of thought or of feeling, and especially when they have been long established, are especially hard to break. One can observe the same phenomenon in other poets in other traditions. To cope with this problem more than fragmentarily, Moore would have needed the complete literary equipment: he would have had to be a first-rate scholar, a first-rate critic, and a great poet. He was deficient in the first two capacities; it was native poetic gift that enabled him to shake himself clean on a few occasions.

Moore's best short poems are *To Silence*, the first of the two sonnets entitled *Silence*, and *From Titian*. The second and third are better than the first. *To Silence* appears in the fourth volume of *The Poems of T. Sturge Moore*, the others in the first volume. There is another poem, a weak one, about silence, which is entitled *Silence Sings*. In the poems of which the word is a part of the title, the concept resembles Mallarmé's concept of purity, or ideal emptiness (emptiness of meaning). "L'azur," in Mallarmé's vocabulary, signifies spatial emptiness (the sky); "silence," in Moore's vocabulary, signifies temporal emptiness; both spatial and temporal emptiness are in turn symbolic, and signify emptiness of conceptual meaning. Purity, then, is pure connotation, pure suggestion, or (and I think that this again is symbolic, at least for

242

Mallarmé) pure sensation. This filling of emptiness with suggestion or sensation, may seem odd until we recollect that in the romantic tradition reason and concept are the source of all evil, and sensation or emotion or suggestion in itself, "pure" of understanding, empty of meaning, is an absolute good. Mallarmé was in theory almost a "pure" romantic; he regarded "purity" as a good. Moore, on the other hand, was a counter-romantic, although he was sensible of the fascination of the Mallarméan religion, above all as it was embodied in the style of such poets as Mallarmé and Rimbaud. But even Mallarmé was not consistent from beginning to end. In an early poem, entitled *L'Azur* he sees *l'azur* as an evil, the source of ennui and sterility. The language of the poem, like that of other early poems, is very bad Baudelaire. In his later poems he reconciled himself with sterility and made the search for it his subject.

In Moore's terms, surrender to sensation would correspond to surrender to Aphrodite; devotion to pure reason (purity of either kind is impossible, of course, but we can approximate it) or to any "pure" and incompletely human discipline, would correspond to devotion to Artemis. Either procedure would issue in the destruction of human nature, would issue in sterility. Moore's doctrine is simple and obvious, and, except as it is a criticism of romantic doctrine, is not really original. But it is sound, and it is applicable to nearly every aspect of human experience. It is the kind of philosophy which a poet needs, in fact which anyone needs.

To Silence[14] discusses a passive acceptance of pure sensation as something which may be temporary, which may offer spiritual refreshment and return one richer to life, and which is therefore a good; or as something that may tempt or addict one to greater and greater degrees of "silence" or the approach thereto, until one reaches the final Silence, which is death. Death is inevitable, but the search for premature death (suicide) is an evil. We are confronted here with a difficult distinction: that between suicide (perhaps, in a sense, within the limits of physical life) by way of surrender to sensation, emotion, or whim, including, it may be, surrender to drugs or to alcohol, a surrender justified by romantic doctrine and practiced in varying ways and degrees by the romantics, a surrender which leads directly to madness; and, on the other hand, a mysticism which identifies death with surrender to divinity and which therefore finds death desirable. The latter is pagan and somewhat Parnassian, but it bears a haunting resemblance to the experience of St. John of the Cross and even to the Beatific Vision of Aquinas and Dante. I mention this resemblance, not to justify either concept, the Christian or the pagan, for I find both of questionable value, but because there seems to be a similarity and because the pagan version, at any rate, cannot easily be put aside. Both kinds of surrender — to sensation on the one hand and simply to death on the other — draw man away from the full experience of life while that experience is available. Yet many great men have been attracted by the second; for the man whose sense of eternity is real and for whom much, or even most, of life is trivial, the attraction is very strong. Moore's poem *From Titian* deals with the second kind of surrender. Kyrkaeus, in his speech on the stars in *Daimonassa*, is guilty of a corrupt appeal to this attraction, for he invokes the attraction to justify brutal immorality within the limits of what should be the full human life.

As to the first kind of surrender, it may occur in life or in literature or in both. One can see it in much of the life and poetry of Rimbaud, a man of very great natural talent, and one can see it in all of its destructive force in the life and work of Hart Crane, a man of less but real talent. It should be noted that Moore did not at any time surrender himself or his work in this fashion, nor did any other English poet of his generation; but the French Symbolists preceded them, and Moore, at least, understood the Symbolists; the surrender was a part of his tradition, of his immediate background. The simple-minded sentimentalism of most of the poets of the period was a kind of genteel approach to the surrender which was never consummated. Moore knew what the surrender meant. In literature it results in the destruction (as far as possible) of conceptual understanding, in the effort to reach pure connotation. One can never reach this ideal in literature absolutely, for literature is composed of words, and words are first of all conceptual. We are so constituted that even our perceptions are dependant upon our experience with language and can be communicated only in language. It is in language that we live the life of human beings; our language is the great reservoir of communal knowledge and perception, which has been accumulating for thousands of years, on which we can draw in proportion as we have the will and the talent; it is in the fullest command of language that we live most fully. Even Rimbaud and Joyce cannot escape entirely from the conceptual nature of language, but they can reduce the conceptual content greatly, and, no matter how sensitive they may be to the connotative aspect of language, they reduce the total efficiency of language. They are like Moore's swimmer if he refuses to return; they are moving toward dissolution. For connotation itself is diminished in proportion as denotation is diminished; connotation depends for its existence on denotation; a sound which denotes nothing will connote nothing. Yet the exploration of the approach to pure connotation did a good deal to refresh the connotative aspect of language in our tradition, primarily the tradition of poetry in French and English. Moore seems to have been more or less aware of what I have discussed in this paragraph; one can find evidence to this effect in *To Silence* and elsewhere. This awareness should have led him to the kind of poetry which I shall describe in my next essay as post-Symbolist. He approaches this kind of poetry in the first sonnet called *Silence* and in *From Titian*, and at moments in *Daimonassa*, but he might have gone farther. In the latter part of his career he had the late Valéry and the early Stevens (if he had read him) as examples, and in fact Leconte de Lisle on a few occasions went farther in this direction than did Moore.

To Silence is an impressive poem in conception, but the diction does not quite achieve real distinction; it is not bad, but it should have been better. The first of the two sonnets entitled *Silence*, however, is another matter:

> No word, no lie, can cross a carven lip;
> No thought is quick behind a chiseled brow;
> Speech is the cruel flaw in comradeship,
> Whose self-bemusing ease daunts like a blow
> Though unintended, irrevocable!

For wound, a mere quip dealt, no salve is found
Though poet be bled dry of words to tell
Why it was pointed! how it captured sound!
Charmed by mere phrases, we first glean their sense
When we behold our Helen streaming tears.
Give me dry eyes whose gaze but looks intense!
The dimpled lobes of unreceptive ears!
A statue not a heart! Silence so kind,
It answers love with beauty cleansed of mind.

This poem is not really about silence; it deals with a baffling and exasperating incident in a human relationship. In lines four and five, and again in nine and ten, we have an extraordinary perception which has implications beyond the overt theme which I have mentioned: a perception of unintended causation, sudden, inexplicable, as if an electric charge were released without warning. It is this perception which raises a witty poem on an otherwise minor theme to greatness. The way in which Moore runs his sentence past the final rime of the first quatrain into a line which begins the next quatrain but ends the sentence, holding, unrimed for a moment, as if bewildered, is the way of genius. The tone of the poem is both plaintive and ironical: the poem invokes the romantic ideal of silence ironically, as a commentary on a personal blunder and on the poet's helplessness before the motion that he has released. The thoughtless and silent statue was a common representation of romantic purity from Gautier and the Parnassians through the *Cantique des Colonnes*. In fact Valéry's columns do not even have faces. I can find no flaws in Moore's sonnet; the diction is beautiful throughout; in the quality of its execution it is equal to Valéry at his best. In the two passages which I have mentioned he achieves the post-Symbolist imagery if anywhere. The second sonnet under this title is, oddly, on silence and in fact in praise of silence. Silence is described and praised in terms which are romantic in two ways — in their ideas and in the abjectness of their clichés. I have quoted this sonnet earlier as an example of Moore's style at its worst. The two sonnets bear no relationship to each other in theme or in style.

I will quote the whole of *From Titian* (the complete title reads *From Titian's Bacchanal in the Prado at Madrid*):

She naked lies asleep beside the wine
That in a rill wanders through moss and flowers;
Her head thrown, and her hair, back o'er an urn
Whose metal glints from under crimpled gold
Of lately bound-up locks; while her flushed face
Breathes up toward open sky with fast-closed lids,—
As though, half-conscious, her complexion knew
Where stirred the tree-tops, where the blue was vast.
One arm, wrapped in a soft white crumpled vest,
An empty wine-dish guards; her breasts are young;
Young, although massive, torso, loins and thighs,
All hued as clouds are that the morning face.
Beside her foot three shadowed blue flowers glow,
Speedwell, or gentian, or some now lost gem
That then was found in Crete; some gem now lost,
Some precious flower, that then endeared the isles
To hearts of travelling gods and sailor princes.
Though friends of such an one here revel now,
And laugh, carouse and dance, she hears them not;
Brown satyrs, maenads, men, these sing; and hark!
Birds sing, the sea is sighing, and the woods
Do sound as lovers love to hear them:—Sleep,
Sleep, oh! and wake no more; Bacchus has kissed
Thy lips, thine eyes, thy brow; thy joy and his
But lately were as one, therefore sleep on:
Be all past woes forgotten in thy dream!
This noisy crew still haunts thee;— but unheard
They sing, and birds are singing; thou dost sleep:
These dance, carouse, and pledge each other's joy;
Slowly the tree-tops, in the wind's embrace,
Dance too; lush branches and gay vestures float,
Float, wave and rustle, sighing to the wind;
But thou art still; thou sleepest, art divine.
Upon the purple clusters, in his drowse,
The vast Silenus rolls; and through the grass
The red juice trickles, forming rills and streams;
Comes down cascading, prattles past thy couch,
And winds on seaward; thou remainest, thou,
Perfectly still remainest and dost sleep.
These soon will leave thee,— satyr, maenad, faun,
Light-hearted young folk,— these will never stay
Past sundown nor outwatch the pale long eve,
But troop afar with fainter riot and song.
Then, when thou art alone and the wind dropped,

> She then, for ever and for aye, will take thee
> To her deep dwelling and unechoing halls;
> How could she leave thee? she who owns them all —
> Owns all the stars, whose beauty is complete,
> Whose joy is perfect, and whose home is peace;
> While all their duty is to shine for love.

The bacchante has been a part of the Bacchanalian festival, and, as a result of union with the god (Bacchus) through drink or coitus (they might be symbolic of each other in this situation), is asleep. But the sleep is a mystical sleep and will be final; at the end of the poem it is Persephone, not Bacchus, who accepts the devotee. These concepts are comprehensible in terms of what we know of the Greek beliefs involved. In terms of what I have just been saying, we would have the first kind of surrender merging into the second, and this is comprehensible in terms of possible experience. As to the first surrender in the poem (surrender to Bacchus), it is a prelude to death, but death conceived in mystical terms; it is not a surrender to a god who provides a prophetic vision of things to come in time. The reader must be aware that I am not sympathetic with the mysticism of this poem, but the mysticism is not the naïve nonsense of *Leda and the Swan*. It is something that has drawn many men, and in ways that one can understand. The concept is moving.

But the writing also is moving. It proceeds slowly but successfully and is often brilliant. I will mention three phrases in particular which may easily be lost in the reading, for they are very quiet; phrases which seem to me marks of extraordinary genius:

> As though, half-conscious, her complexion knew
> Where stirred the tree-tops. . .
> ● ● ● ● ● ●
>
> travelling gods
> ● ● ● ● ● ●

and, near the end, in describing the realm of Persephone:

> unechoing halls. . .

These may be lost in the context if not mentioned, but they should now be read in the context; they are not "outstanding," but are marvelous moments in a living whole. The repetitions of phrase and rhythm in the ten or twelve lines beginning with the flowers are of a kind that one has encountered before but seldom managed with so much beauty. As the troop leaves her and she moves more surely into the final sleep, the writing achieves remarkable grandeur.

The great achievements are *Daimonassa,* the first sonnet entitled *Silence,* and *From Titian.* This may seem a long essay for the exhibition of so few titles. But these works have been lost and they should be recovered. Many a poet commonly called great has only one or two great poems to his credit, and some have none. And there is more to this poet than these three poems; there are many interesting works of less value; there are many beautiful passages; and there is the remarkable spectacle of his endeavor to understand the tradition into which he was born, and, at one and the same time, to save himself from it and to make something of it.

5

The Post-Symbolist Methods

I USE THE TERM "post-Symbolist" to describe a kind of poetry which develops most commonly and most clearly after the French Symbolists but which sometimes appears before them or independently of them. Logically, it should follow them and should follow from them, but these things happen as they will.

The associationistic doctrines taught that all ideas arise from sensory perceptions, and gradually it came to be thought that all ideas could be expressed in terms of sensory perceptions, but this effort, as in Pound's *Cantos* or in much of Williams ("no ideas but in things"), was doomed to failure. The result is very often a situation in which the poet offers us, or seems to offer us, sense-perceptions for their own sake, and for the sake of whatever vague feelings they may evoke. This dissociation of sense-perception and feeling on the one hand from conceptual understanding on the other finds its chief theorist in Mallarmé, although Rimbaud and Verlaine are also such theorists. These three men are the most distinguished apologists for, and practitioners of, deliberate obscurity. The reader may examine Rimbaud's *Larme* as a remarkably brilliant example of the practice.

The Romantic poets, both English and French, were interested in sensory perception, natural detail, but the interest was for the greater part theoretic; they talk about sensory details, they refer to them, but in stereotyped language, as I have shown—they do not see them or even try to see them. My three Frenchmen see them, hear them, feel them, and sometimes smell them, and with clarity and intensity which is often startling; and they try to isolate them from meaning, and they are surprisingly suc-

251

cessful at it. There is nothing like this in British poetry. There is comparable visual imagery in Hardy, but it is not so employed. This clarity of perception, usually of visual perception, is characteristic of the post-Symbolist poets, but the clear perception is employed in ways different from the Symbolist way and different from Hardy's.

Valéry, in his two great poems, *Ébauche d'un Serpent* and *Le Cimetière Marin*, is the heir to this sensory perception — but these two poems are not poems of hallucination; they are philosophical poems. Both poems contain a good deal of abstract statement, so that there can be no real doubt as to their themes. The sensory details are a part of this statement — they are not ornament or background. The language is often sensory and conceptual at the same time, for example in this line describing the sea: "Masse de calme et visible réserve." The line should be considered carefully. *Calme* and *réserve* are both nouns indicating potency; but both suggest the possibility of immediate act. They are metaphysical abstractions; or to be more precise, they are clearly substitutes for the metaphysical abstraction *potency*, substitutes brought closer to the visual, very close indeed when we remember that the line describes the sea, and substitutes which suggest the abstraction *act*, or *actuality*, but *act* in visible form. *Masse* and *visible* render the perception clearly visible, make it clearly the sea. That is, the sea is rendered as visibly the embodiment of potency on the verge of becoming actual. As a visual image, the line is brilliant; as an intellectual perception it is profound; the visual and the intellectual are simultaneous — they cannot be separated in fact.

There is nothing resembling this line, in the totality of its qualities, in any of the Symbolist predecessors. Nor is there anything comparable in British poetry save, perhaps, for a few lines in Bridges and T. Sturge Moore. The two poems by Valéry are what one might call classical examples of the method, but I have discussed them elsewhere and will not discuss them here[1]. Equally clear examples are *The Cricket*, by F. G. Tuckerman, a poem written about 1870 or shortly before, and without benefit of the French, and *Sunday Morning*, by Wallace Stevens, which was written and the early version of which was published a year or two before the first of the two poems by Valéry (Stevens, of course, knew the French Symbolists quite as well as did Valéry.) To be more precise, I should cite the final sections of the two poems in English as clear examples. These two poems I will presently discuss, and I will discuss others. The poem of the kind which I shall describe is usually but not always put together from beginning to end on the principle of carefully controlled association. We have seen controlled association without imagery in Churchill's *Dedication*. In some of the poems which I shall discuss we have controlled association in conjunction with post-Symbolist imagery; in some we have post-Symbolist imagery with the rational structure of the Renaissance. The controlled association offers the possibility, at least, of greater flexibility and greater inclusiveness of matter (and without confusion) than we can find in the Renaissance structures; the post-Symbolist imagery provides a greater range of thinking and perceiving than we have ever had before. The method, I believe, is potentially the richest method to appear. In fact, I will go farther: I believe that the greatest poems employing this method are the greatest poems that we have, and furthermore that the group of poets whom I shall now discuss are, *as a group,* the most impressive group in English. There is in a few poems by these people a consistent sophistication and profundity of mind, perception, personal character, and style that one can scarcely find in any other group. They are civilized, alive in every way; this is true in her best poems even of Miss Dickinson.

II

F. G. TUCKERMAN (1821-73)* was one of the three most remarkable American poets of the nineteenth century. The others were Jones Very (1813-80) and Emily Dickinson (1830-86). Emerson (1803-82) had talent, which was badly damaged by foolish thinking.

---

* This essay appeared originally as A *Critical Foreword to The Complete Poems of Frederick Goddard Tuckerman* edited by N. Scott Momaday (Oxford University Press, New York, 1965). The present version is slightly revised and enlarged.

253

Bryant (1794-1878) might be described as a fine second-rate poet, better than most of the British poets of the century. Of Poe (1809-49) and Whitman (1819-92) the less said the better[2]. Very was Tuckerman's tutor at Harvard for a brief period, but their connections thereafter appear to have been slight. Tuckerman spent most of his mature life within about eighteen miles of Amherst, but there is no evidence that he and Emily Dickinson ever met or even knew of each other's existence. Miss Dickinson knew Tuckerman's son and probably knew his brother the Amherst botanist, a specialist in lichens, and the distinguished member of the family (a ravine was named after him).

All three of these people lived in isolation from those around them, even it would appear from those in the same house. Critics sometimes wonder about the reason for this, but I am sure that the isolation was caused merely by intense boredom — it could not have been otherwise. They were isolated from each other by their methods and attitudes. Very was a mystical Calvinist who wrote a few fine poems but repeated and diluted himself to almost infinite tedium. Miss Dickinson came from a Calvinistic background, but she appears quite obviously never to have experienced the conversion which she deeply desired: the matter of her best poems is the honest and intelligent appraisal of an impossible situation. She was a country girl, with exasperating mannerisms, but her natural genius was great and she wrote a few great poems. Tuckerman's religious background was Episcopalian, but there are only a few poems which exhibit any explicitly religious interest, the important one being Sonnet XXVIII of the first series ("Not the round natural world").

It is not Tuckerman's relationship to New England poetry which interests me, however; it is his relationship to the romantic and post-romantic poetry in English and in French as we see this poetry in the nineteenth and twentieth centuries. If we confine our attention to the sonnets, we find a chronic melancholy, which, for the most part, appears to have been an indulgence. The death of his wife gave Tuckerman a legitimate cause for melancholy, but the condition seems to have preceded her death, and even after her death it continues, without, except in a few poems, any explicit justification. There is also a consistent interest, not necessarily romantic in itself, but common in romantic poetry, in the description of natural detail. In this description he surpasses the British romantics, except, perhaps, for an occasional line in Wordsworth or Shelley. Wordsworth, the poet of nature, popularized nature but almost never saw it; his descriptions are almost always stereotypes. Tuckerman very often saw it. He used his perceptions of nature in various ways.

Sonnet XVI of the second series describes the deserted house of Gertrude and Gulielma, the deceased sisters who haunt several of the sonnets. The first four lines are excellent, the next three respectable; the eighth again is excellent. The ninth is a sentimental stereotype. In the last five lines, we have one of the most beautiful descriptions in nineteenth-cenutry poetry, but marred again by the second of these lines:

> The wild rain enters, and the sunset wind
> Sighs in the chambers of their loveliness
> Or shakes the pane — and in the silent noons
> The glass falls from the window, part by part,
> And ringeth faintly in the grassy stones.

The faults of the sonnet are those of the nineteenth century; the fine lines are of a kind which the ninetenth-century poets are often thought to exhibit but of which they are seldom capable. Most readers today regard the bad writing of the nineteenth century (as we find it, for example, almost everywhere in Keats and Wordsworth) as great writing; when such writing occurs in later poets, such as Bridges (and we can find a good deal of it in his inferior work), it is regarded as a vice, and it serves to obscure the virtues of such poets. I fear that such lines may obscure the virtues of Tuckerman, for, although he is definitely of the nineteenth century, he has appeared more or less recently in our own century. Bad lines, of course (like bad poems), are always bad, but we should not allow them to obscure the extent to which a poet has emerged from an unfortunate context.

But what is the context? It is certainly that of the nineteenth century, but the sensibility of this sonnet and many others is not that of England or of New England in the nineteenth century. If one seeks an English poet resembling Tuckerman, one will scarcely find him — except in so far as Tuckerman imitates (not too badly) Wordsworth and Tennyson in some of his early, longer, and inferior pieces. If one seeks a New England poet, I can think of no one save Frost in a few short lyrics (*Spring Pools*, perhaps), but Tuckerman had not read Frost, and Frost had almost certainly not read Tuckerman at so early a date. The landscape in the sonnets is that of New England, but the sensibility is that of the gentler French Symbolism, that of Verlaine in particular; yet the French poets had not read Tuckerman, and it is inconceivable that he could have read any of them.

I will quote the first stanza of the fifth poem in Verlaine's *Romances Sans Paroles:*

> Le piano que baise une main frêle
> Luit dans le soir rose et gris vaguement,
> Tandis qu'avec un très léger bruit d'aile
> Un air bien vieux, bien faible et bien charmant,
> Rôde discret, épeuré quasiment,
> Par le boudoir longtemps parfumé d'Elle.

This stanza might serve as a mere expansion of the second line from Tuckerman in the passage which I have quoted. The scene is different, but the theme and the facile sentiment are the same; and in each there is the same sensibility. Verlaine, however, controls this particular tone more successfully throughout his poem, and in this respect his poem is more successful than Tuckerman's. The interesting fact about Tuckerman's line is this: it is inferior to the main body of the poem and so appears defective. Both poems are gentle elegies, and both are minor poems, but the best detail in Tuckerman's poem is better than anything in Verlaine's and the poem is more serious and more moving than Verlaine's.

Sonnet XVIII of the same series is perhaps more nearly uniform in its success, and the last six lines may be the best in the sonnets:

> Here, but a lifetime back, where falls tonight
> Behind the curtained pane a sheltered light
> On buds of rose or vase of violet

> Aloft upon the marble mantel set,
> Here in the forest-heart hung blackening
> The wolfbait on the bush beside the spring.

The poem compares the back-country of the poet's time with the same country sixty or seventy years before; the present scene is dominated by the past; the last two lines are appalling in their darkness and solitude; they take us rather far from Verlaine.

The two sonnets from which I have just quoted belong to a group of six, Sonnets XV through XX of the second series, which form an independent elegy. The procedure is that of controlled association. Sonnet XV introduces the sisters and describes their beauty; the language is not remarkable. The memory of the sisters leads to the description of the deserted house in XVI, which is one of the finest of the sonnets. This in turn leads to a meditation on general change, astronomical, seasonal, and other; the language is not remarkably good in the main, but it is not remarkebly bad; we have a lovely line near the end: "The day is dull and soft, the eavetrough drips." Then comes Sonnet XVIII, which ends with the wolfbait; this sonnet deals with another particularization of change — the first line reads: "And change with hurried hand has swept these scenes." XIX takes us from the wolfbait to other dark scenes of the past, scenes of war with the Hessians, the British, the Indians, and the Shay's men:

> Or from the burning village, through the trees
> I see the smoke in reddening volumes roll,
> The Indian file in shadowy silence pass
> While the last man sets up the trampled grass,
> The Tory priest declaiming, fierce and fat,
> The Shay's man with the green branch in his hat,
> Or silent sagamore, Shaug or Wassahoale.

No phrase here is startling; every phrase is carefully chosen for precision in itself and for its precise relationship to the whole context. The entire sonnet is unforgettable. XX brings us back to the sisters, for whom the elegy was written; it is unmistakably of the nineteenth century, but not offensively so; more lines than the following are for me very beautiful:

257

> What though the forest windflowers fell and died
> And Gertrude sleeps at Gulielma's side?
> They have their tears, nor turn to us their eyes. . .

Next to *The Cricket*, this elegy is Tuckerman's finest poem; the individual sonnets cannot be satisfactorily removed from the group; the force of the whole outweighs particular faults.

Sonnet X of the first series is one of the strangest. It deals with a man of whom we know nothing except that he is obsessed with terror and anguish. The man may be an imaginative projection of the poet or he may be some other man. We know nothing of the reasons for the man's condition; he is as purely romantic as something from Poe, at least when we consider the bare conception of the poem. But Tuckerman's genius emerges in a line as remarkable as this:

> I cannot rid the thought nor hold it close. . .

and in the beautiful descriptive lines below:

> The cricket chides beneath the doorstep stone
> And greener than the season grows the grass.

And then there is the obscure conclusion:

> Nor can I drop my lids nor shade my brows,
> But there he stands beneath the lifted sash:
> And with a swooning of the heart, I think
> Where the black shingles slope to meet the boughs
> And, shattered on the roof like smallest snows,
> The tiny petals of the mountain ash.

There have been a few occasion when I almost thought that I understood the grammar and syntax of this passage, but I do not understand them now. I understand the general intention: somehow the sensory details express the sickness of the man; the tiny details are the items on which he can concentrate; but that is all that we know.

One can observe the same thing in a more vigorous poem, *Larme* by Rimbaud; it is a progression into pure obscurity. The French Symbolists had a theory for this: one finds the theory in the prose and many of the late sonnets of Mallarmé, in *Art Poétique* by Verlaine, and in *Bonheur* by Rimbaud. There is no such theory in Tuckerman; he merely slipped into the practice. The French tradition came out of the practice in the two great poems by Valéry, *Le Cimetière Marin* and *Ébauche d'un Serpent,* written early in our century, and came out of it without benefit of much in the way of theory. Tuckerman, who had slipped into the practice without theory, came out of it without theory in his great poem *The Cricket,* written in his last years.

Briefly, what happened is this: there was an acute sharpening of sensory perception in the romantic movement, mainly in the late nineteenth century in France and in the early twentieth century in the United States, a sharpening taken so seriously as an end in itself that it led to confusion. This sharpening seems to have occurred briefly in the third quarter of the nineteenth century in a village in western Massachusetts, in the work of F. G. Tuckerman. The form of the emergence is as follows: the acute sensory perception remains, but instead of the simple elegiac theme which we get in some of Verlaine, in much of Heredia, and in the first two sonnets from Tuckerman from which I have quoted, instead of the obscurity which we find in Rimbaud, we have a theme of some intellectual scope with enough abstract statement to support the theme; theme and abstract statement charge the imagery with meaning, with the result that the imagery has the force of abstract statement. The imagery is not ornament as it would be in the Renaissance, nor is it merely the pasturage for revery as in much of the poetry of the eighteenth, nineteenth, and twentieth centuries, nor is there anything obscure about its intention. The structure is that of controlled association. The two great poems by Valéry and *Sunday Morning* by Stevens will serve as examples. *The Cricket* is a greater poem than *Sunday Morning* and is almost equal to either poem by Valéry.

The Cricket is composed of five sections; the riming is irregular; the lines vary in length; the meter is iambic. The poem belongs in the tradition of the "great odes," of which *Alexander's Feast* by Dryden is the first well-known example, although *Lycidas* might be regarded as a precursor, for its principles are similar and its influence on later examples is obvious: these poems dealt with what purported to be an important subject, were of some length, and were associational in structure and in the use of imagery (and often loosely associational). Most of the odes of Gray (including the *Elegy*), of Collins, Keats, Wordsworth, Tennyson, and others fall in this category. These poems suggest the structure of *The Cricket*, although the structure of Tuckerman's poem is more controlled than is the structure of most of these. Tuckerman's poem has a background in English poetry of which he must have been conscious. As to its resemblances with later French and American poetry, he was obviously ignorant, and the French and American poets were obviously ignorant of him[3].

The first section is a quiet and affectionate invocation of the cricket merely as a cricket. The adjective *cooing* at the end of this section disturbs some readers. The singular number in this line is collective in effect: we have the confused sound of crickets, not the sharp sound of one. We have the crickets as familiar, almost domestic, creatures; but, in the light of what follows, the gentle and almost sentimental effect of the adjective becomes quietly ironic. In the second section we meet the cricket in multiplicity spread throughout a summer landscape, in which the heat, scent, and sound are hypnotic and stun the sense to slumber; we approach a pantheistic trance; and at the end of the passage the sound of the crickets is compared to the sound of the sea. The sea is a traditional symbol of the changing physical universe from which we arise and to which we return, and it is often in addition a symbol of those elements in human nature which elude understanding and control, and which may be destructive. In the third section we are told that the cricket is dear to the child and is a lover of night, and this carries us farther into the nostalgia for the primitive, the sub-human. The sea recurs in this connection, and, although the lines describing it are the weakest in the poem, they are related to the theme. This brings us to death and the grave and some of the greatest lines in the poem:

> With faces where but now a gap must be,
> Renunciations and partitions deep,
> And perfect tears, and crowning vacancy!

and the two final lines in the section. In the fourth section the cricket and his relatives are projected into primitive antiquity. The procedure has been associational, but the association has been controlled: the cricket has become a symbol for non-human nature and for the primitive and sub-human in human nature and has been used to create a deep longing for these qualities and for death.

The fifth section draws all of these elements together into a final statement and contains the greatest writing in the poem. The poet longs to resemble the old enchanter who employed *evil* drugs to acquire the languages of the lower creatures. He would thus be unwise, would descend through denser stillness, would convert the world to the cricket's wisdom, would gain the low applause of the sub-human world, would possess a great deal, but would yield more. He then recognizes the impossiblity of this choice, and accepts the necessity of living at the human level until the natural end of his life. The conclusion is similar to that of *Le Cimetière Marin*. The philosophic ideas of Valéry are not those of Tuckerman, but the two poems bear a striking resemblance not merely in the conclusions but in the quality of the imagery. The poem resembles Ben Jonson's *To Heaven* in this respect: it is a poem dealing with the sin of despair, of the desire for death. But it is a poem written in a later period, with a different set of ideas and a different sensibility. The sensibility is related to that of Valéry.

The theme has been sufficiently established in conceptual terms; it permeates the imagery. The wilderness with which Tuckerman deals is different from the wilderness at the close of *Sunday Morning*. Stevens' landscape is more vast, but it is a landscape for contemplation and wonder, a French park of cosmic proportions. Tuckerman's landscape is that of the local fields and the bright sunlight; but his wilderness is that of the mind, both conscious and unconscious, and it involves the loss of his love, the despair of his life:

> hearts wild with love and woe,
> Closed eyes, and kisses that would not let go!

Tuckerman was simply aware of more of human life than was

Stevens, aware in the sense that he could really perceive it in his art.

The imagery of the last section, as it occurs, has no need of explanation, and it is not ornamental; the thought of the poem exists in the imagery and develops through it. The imagery is magnificent in its own right:

> Might I but find thy knowledge in thy song!
> That twittering tongue,
> Ancient as light, returning like the years.

There is the marvelous command of cadence, sometimes in the use of the short lines:

> Content to bring thy wisdom to the world;
> Content to gain at last some low applause,
> Now low, now lost. . . .

We continue with the idea of the infinitely numerous but sub-human audience in the realm of temptation and with the sub-human realm of the purely physical, worlds in spite of which the poet must somehow survive:

> For larger would be less indeed, and like
> The ceaseless simmer in the summer grass
> To him who toileth in the windy field,
> Or where the sunbeams strike,
> Naught in innumerable numerousness.
> So might I much possess,
> So much must yield. . . .

The poem proceeds from here to the solution which I have mentioned; and near the end we have one of the greatest passages in our poetry:

> Behold! the autumn goes,
> The shadow grows,
> The moments take hold of eternity.

The Cricket is Tuckerman's greatest poem, and one of his last, perhaps the last. But in the last series of sonnets, one, number XIV, is a kind of leave-taking of the reader:

And me my winter's task is drawing over,
Though night and winter shake the drifted door.
Critic or friend, dispraiser or approver,
I come not now nor fain would offer more.
But when buds break and round the fallen limb
The wild weeds crowd in cluster and corymb,
When twilight rings with the red robin's plaint,
Let me give something — though my heart be faint —
To thee, my more than friend! — believer! lover!
The gust has fallen now, and all is mute —
Save pricking on the pane the sheety showers,
The clock that ticks like a belated foot,
Time's hurrying step, the twanging of the hours:
Wait for those days, my friend, or get thee fresher flowers.

The poem does not employ the kind of imagery which I have just been describing, nor is it associational in structure; it is a traditional poem in every way. It is unlike the earlier sonnets; it seems more aware of death as a reality rather than as a literary perception. It reminds me of Baudelaire.

Tuckerman is marred by the vices of his century, but less marred in many poems than many poets now more famous. *The Cricket,* I feel sure, is the greatest poem in English of the century, and one of the greatest in English, and the amount of unforgettable poetry in the sonnets is large. The most curious fact, so far as I am concerned, is the development through the poetic modes which I have discussed — a development which did not occur in England at all, and which in France required about three generations. In Tuckerman's work it ocurred in the lifetime (not a long one) of one man, in Greenfield, Massachusetts, and without benefit of models.

III

I HAVE WRITTEN OF Emily Dickinson (1830-1886) elsewhere[4]. My previous essay on the poet is an old one, but in general I would still subscribe to it; nevertheless, I have certain new things to say. I was bothered at that time by the crudities in her work; I am more bothered now. But the genius is there, somehow indestructible. In my present essay I shall discuss the aspect of her work which is relevant to my present business, but I shall be forced to depart from this aspect at least briefly.

Let me say a few words about the text. In 1955 Thomas H. Johnson published through the Harvard University Press a variorum edition entitled *The Poems of Emily Dickinson,* expensively printed and bound, in three columns, and boxed. Before this edition we had the poems as edited by Mabel Loomis Todd, the friend and neighbor of the poet, and by Martha Dickinson Bianchi, a niece. And in 1945 we had a volume entitled *Bolts of Melody* (Miss Dickinson seems to have inspired a good deal of bad rhetoric), edited by the daughter of Mrs. Todd, Millicent Todd Bingham. For some years after the Johnson edition, it was assumed that the early editors had tampered excessively with the texts; now we are told that they had tampered very little. I have not seen the manuscripts and cannot judge, but there is no question about one thing: the early versions, especially those of Mrs. Todd, are the best poems, and by a wide margin; furthermore they were a part of our literature for a good many years, and are bound to remain a part, no matter whether they are ultimately described as the works of Miss Dickinson or as works of collaboration. They should be kept in print[5].

What has Johnson done? First he has punctuated the poems with dashes, with the result that they are all but unreadable. Edith Perry Stamm has published an article[6] which purports to explain the origin of the dashes. According to Professor Stamm the dashes are not dashes in the manuscripts but are marks of various kinds intended to indicate the proper intonation for reading aloud; the marks were derived from a few books of elocution in common use at the time and in use at the Amherst Academy while Miss Dickinson was a student there. The marks, as they are described in these texts, are all easily translatable into punctuation marks, and Mrs. Todd would appear to have so translated them without comment. If Professor Stamm is correct, Mr. Johnson translated them all into dashes. Professor Stamm, in turn, has been criticized; but it would seem that Miss Dickinson was not whole-heartedly devoted to dashes, and it is certain that the dashes ruin her poems. Second, Johnson appears to have chosen unfortunate versions of poems wherever they were available. He gives all of the alternative readings for every word in notes, but this leaves the reader with the task of writing out the best version for every poem. Johnson's intention, of course, is to give the poet's final choice for every poem, for he is, bless him, a serious scholar. But how does he know? Even if he can decide to a certainty (and I am skeptical about this) the chronological order of the different versions, there is no reason to believe that the final version would have been the poet's final choice: Miss Dickinson was tinkering with her poems, not preparing an edition. Johnson's experience with editing is more extensive than mine, but his experience with writing poems and with people who write poems is very limited as compared to mine. His method of choosing authoritative versions appears to be naïve; the result has been the destruction of a poet. The only thing one can do in a situation like this is to choose the best versions; this takes talent, and Johnson lacks talent. Mrs. Todd and Mrs. Bianchi have made the best choices by far that we have; in referring to Miss Dickinson's poems, I shall invariably refer to their versions.

I shall try in this essay to describe the "post-Symbolist" tendencies in Miss Dickinson's work. The term is odd in every way in a discussion of this poet, but the tendencies are there. She never heard of the Symbolists. We have no reason to believe that she had even read Tuckerman, who was about nine years her elder and who lived only a few miles away, or that she ever met him; and even Tuckerman had never heard of the Symbolists. We know that she read; she probably read more than we know, for she had nothing to do but read, write, meditate, walk in her garden, and talk with a very few friends and relatives. But there is no mark of her reading on her style. Her meters appear to derive from the Protestant hymn books, although there are variations and sometimes these are brilliant. It would be impossible to show that any poet or school of poets influenced her in the least. She was obviously aware of the romantic ideas then current, ideas about "nature" and other matters, and quite as obviously held them in low esteem. She would have liked to be a Christian, but found this impossible. She seems to have no literary background whatever. In a way, this was an advantage, for she was not tempted to imitate Wordsworth or Tennyson. But it left her un-educated, with no tradition, with nothing but what God gave her. She was almost purely a primitive — not as the American Indians were primitives, but as Grandma Moses was a primitive.

Like Tuckerman, and unlike the British poets of the century, she had a remarkable eye for natural detail:

> The sky is low, the clouds are mean,
> A travelling flake of snow
> Across a barn or through a rut
> Debates if it will go.

Nothing could be more sharp. This is the first stanza; the second and final stanza is weak. Her description of a snake is well known; the poem, *A narrow fellow in the grass,* is damaged irretrievably by her cuteness, but the snake is marvelous:

> The grass divides as with a comb,
> A spotted shaft is seen;
> And then it closes at your feet
> And opens farther on.
> •••••••
> I more than once, at morn,
>
> Have passed, I thought, a whip-lash
> Unbraiding in the sun, —
> When, stooping to secure it,
> It wrinkled and was gone.

One can find many such details. She is often discontented with anything so simply descriptive, however, and the imagery seems to take on meaning which one cannot clearly discern, as in *The wind began to rock the grass:*

> The leaves unhooked themselves from trees
> And started all abroad:
> The dust did scoop itself like hands
> And throw away the road.
>
> The wagons quickened on the streets,
> The thunder hurried slow;
> The lightning showed a yellow beak,
> And then a livid claw.

266

The leaves and dust acquire an inner life of their own; so do the wagons, which appear to move without human aid; all of this is unreasonable, a form of obscurantism, yet it has an ominous quality which is in some way effective. "Hurried slow" is a brilliant phrase where it occurs; I hope that no one will move it into another context. These are the best lines; they are not of her best. There is a similar quality in the imagery of the following poem, but theme and writing are superior here, and the poem, whatever its faults, is a great poem:

> I started early, took my dog,
> And visited the sea;
> The mermaids in the basement
> Came out to look at me,
>
> And frigates in the upper floor
> Extended hempen hands,
> Presuming me to be a mouse
> Aground, upon the sands.
>
> But no man moved me till the tide
> Went past my simple shoe,
> And past my apron and my belt,
> And past my bodice too,
>
> And made as he would eat me up
> As wholly as a dew
> Upon a dandelion's sleeve —
> And then I started too.
>
> And he — he followed close behind;
> I felt his silver heel
> Upon my ankle, — then my shoes
> Would overflow with pearl.
>
> Until we met the solid town,
> No man he seemed to know;
> And bowing with a mighty look
> At me, the sea withdrew.

The sea appears to be the symbol of death, of that which overcomes us and destroys us; it is also a gentleman, apparently bent upon seduction. Death and seduction might seem comparably overpowering to this lady, both to be equally avoided. More generally, the sea embodies the concept of destructive power, physical and psychological, natural and possibly supernatural. The imagery here is animated in the original sense of the adjective; each detail is charged with *anima*. But in the previous poem the imagery merely gave us the illusion of such animation; in this poem we have the real animation, real meaning. The poem illustrates clearly the kind of imagery which I have in mind. The following poem attempts something as ambitious, but does not succeed:

> At half-past three a single bird
> Unto a silent sky
> Propounded but a single term
> Of cautious melody.
>
> At half-past four, experiment
> Had subjugated test,
> And lo! her silver principle
> Supplanted all the rest.
>
> At half-past seven, element
> Nor implement was seen,
> And place was where the presence was,
> Circumference between.

She does not have her eye quite so sharply on the object here; she is being witty with words, rather than perceptive, at a discreet distance. Nevertheless the poem has charm and is clear enough until we reach the last line: *circumference* is an impenetrably obscure word, just as it appeared to me to be thirty years ago, and I think that she chose it with full knowledge of the fact. One can find a good deal of similar obscurity.

I will quote a poem which I quoted in my old essay; I quote it now to illustrate my present thesis:

> 'Twas warm at first like us,
> Until there crept thereon
> A chill, like frost upon a glass,
> Till all the scene be gone.

The forehead copied stone,
The fingers grew too cold
To ache, and like a skater's brook
The busy eyes congealed.

It straightened — that was all.
It crowded cold to cold —
It multiplied indifference
As Pride were all it could.

And even when with cords
'Twas lowered like a freight,
It made no signal, nor demurred,
But dropped like adamant.

The poem is one of a number that define the absolute cleavage between life and death, between the living and the dead. The pronoun is neither masculine nor feminine, but neuter: *it;* we are not talking about a person. The dead body is something, but we do not know what; it is beyond our experience; it is not human. We watch the body change from living to dead. The change is physical, because we can see or imagine the physical — the unimaginable is implied. Or, rather, the reality of the unimaginable is implied. Lines eight, nine, ten, and eleven are the center of the poem: in eight and nine the living becomes dead; in ten and eleven there is no life, but rigor mortis occurs cell by cell; in eleven *indifference* indicates the new and unimaginable state. Line twelve is doubly unfortunate: the grammar is unpardonable and it exaggerates and sentimentalizes what has been accomplished in eleven. The last stanza is a satisfactory summary.

The grammar in twelve is barbarous, and in four we have an unduly forced subjunctive, but for whatever the fact may be worth this is a different kind of bad grammar from what we may find in Collins or Blake. It is not loose and wandering, as in Collins; it is not obscurely incomplete, in the manner of Blake's dread hand and feet; the lines are grammatical, and the meaning is clear, but the grammar is bad. And it is not the bad grammar of colloquial speech nor yet of ignorance. It appears to come from a kind of nervous impatience and from the eccentric and sentimental self-indulgence of a lonely woman.

The point which I wish to make is this: in the best lines sense-perception and concept are simultaneous; there is neither ornament nor explanation, and neither is needed. This is the new kind of imagery which I am trying to demonstrate in this chapter. In the progress from stanza to stanza there is no trace of associationism, controlled or other, and this is true of most of her poems. We usually have, as here, a straight narrative order or a simple expository order. The poem is crude, but at its best moments very great; in comparison, the poems which I treated in my third chapter are trivial, even the best of them. Miss Dickinson often writes badly, but she sometimes writes perfectly, as in a few lines in this poem and throughout a few poems. Most of the poets whom I treated in my third chapter never suspected the nature of good writing.

I could illustrate the quality shown here with other poems, but I prefer now to quote a poem which seems successful as a whole, which is dominated by abstract statement rather than by imagery, in which the imagery, though present and of the same kind, has retreated into a condition closer to pure abstraction:

> The Moon upon her fluent route
> Defiant of a road,
> The stars Etruscan argument,
> Substantiate a God.
> If Aims impel these Astral Ones,
> The Ones allowed to know,
> Know that which makes them as forgot
> As Dawn forgets them now.

This is Mrs. Todd's version, at least as printed. I take it that *stars* is possessive; or perhaps it should be followed by a comma, but this I doubt. The comma at the end of line six raises questions; with the comma line six is in apposition with five, without the comma it is not. If we retain the comma, we have no subject for *Know;* but on the other hand Dawn forgets the astral ones, the stars and moon, not a collection of unidentified entities. Therefore we must keep the comma, and *The Ones allowed to know* functions in both ways: it is in apposition with *Astral Ones,* and it is the subject of *Know* in line seven. I would hesitate to use such a

270

contraction myself, but it works reasonably well here. And this form had been used before; the Greeks had a name for it, *apo koinou,* a name which the reader may find in the second edition of *Webster's Unabridged Dictionary*[1]. The Greeks who first used the form were doubtless as ignorant of its name as was Miss Dickinson.

In this poem, as in the last, we have phrases which contain image and idea simultaneously: "fluent route defiant of a road"; "Etruscan" at the level of idea (that is, modifying "argument") implies remote antiquity and its consequent authority and perhaps implies obscurity as well, and at the level of visual image (that is of the "stars") implies remote antiquity and the visual obscurity of the stars now fading into dawn. The second quatrain is a very condensed comment upon the first: the *if* is important, for it reduces the statement of the first quatrain from certainty to possibility, it puts the knowledge in doubt but does not deny the possibility of the knowledge. "The Ones allowed to know": the nature of this phrase places the knowers far from us and from our understanding. The poem is as compact as possible, and, after due examination, clear. The diction is the diction of genius; the poem is very great.

In the following poem, sensory detail has retreated even farther into the general, but it is still there; the poem does not illustrate my thesis, but is so fine a poem that it should be quoted:

> I read my sentence steadily,
> Reviewed it with my eyes,
> To see that I made no mistake
> In its extremest clause, —
>
> The date, and manner of the shame;
> And then the pious form
> That "God have mercy" on the soul
> The jury voted him.
>
> I made my soul familiar
> With her extremity,
> That at the last it should not be
> A novel agony,

> But she and Death, acquainted,
> Meet tranquilly as friends,
> Salute and pass without a hint —
> And there the matter ends.

ne second stanza is Miss Dickinson at her worst, and the sex of the soul changes from the second to the third stanza. But if the reader will be sufficiently charitable to strike out the second stanza, he will then have the poem which Miss Dickinson ought to have given us; it is unfortunate that Miss Dickinson did not have, as most poets have had, a literate friend or two to look at her poems and advise. The following poem, like the one just quoted, is traditional in its method, but is one of her best:

> The difference between despair
> And fear, is like the one
> Between the instant of a wreck
> And when the wreck has been.
>
> The mind is smooth — no motion —
> Contented as the eye
> Upon the forehead of a Bust
> That knows it cannot see.

I have quoted some of the great poems. Among those which I have not quoted are these: *Our journey had advanced, The last night that she lived, A light exists in spring, As imperceptibly as grief,* and *There's a certain slant of light.* Perhaps I should add *Farther in summer than the birds;* this ought to have been one of the best and is certainly one of the most fascinating, but it is seriously marred. The theme of the poem is in some measure similar to the theme of *The Cricket.* And perhaps I should warn the young reader that the word *antiquest* in the third stanza is the superlative form of the adjective *antique;* I have been acquainted with generation upon generation of students, both undergraduate and graduate, who have read the word as *anti-quest.*

IV

WALLACE STEVENS (1879-1955) is central to my discussion of post-

Symbolist method, but by now it should be possible for me to indicate his contribution briefly. I have discussed him at greater length elsewhere[8]. *Sunday Morning* is one of the earliest of his poems, and states his central theme: that there is no life after death, that man is isolated in time and space but in a universe of magnificent beauty, that man should cultivate his senses and his emotions to the utmost for only thus can he fulfill the destiny allotted him. Stevens is a hedonistic nominalist. The hedonism, as I have pointed out in my early essay, led to boredom, romantic ennui; and to alleviate the boredom the poet was moved to greater and greater indulgence in stylistic excess. The nominalism was the source of another difficulty: Stevens desired order in his universe, but his philosophy could not provide it. He sought this order in a concept of the Imagination, borrowed from Coleridge, but modified. For Coleridge, the Imagination was a link to trans-cendent reality; for Stevens there was no transcendent reality, but only the reality of the nominalist, a universe of discrete particu-lars. By means of the Imagination, however, and the Imagination not responsible to any transcendent truth, the poet could create Order. The trouble with this order was that it was imaginary, not real; reality remained what it had always been. The clearest statement of the doctrine, or defense of it, can be found in *The Idea of Order at Key West;* "She," the singer, is the Imagination; the sea is reality. The doctrine could not of its very nature be satisfactory to him, and in a late poem, *The Course of a Par-ticular,* he seems to renounce it. This poem is a mournful and ironic commentary on the ideas he had been propounding for many years, and places him, "in the absence of fantasía," in the pure desolation of reality:

> The leaves cry. It is not a cry of divine attention,
> Nor the smoke-drift of puffed-out heroes, nor human cry.
> It is the cry of leaves that do not transcend themselves,
>
> In the absence of fantasía, without meaning more
> Than they are in the final finding of the ear, in the thing
> Itself, until, at last, the cry concerns no one at all.

The puffed-out heroes are the characters of his mythology, created to expound his theory. *Fantasía* is the Greek word for Imagination, but it is the source of *fancy, fantastic, fantasy,* and *phantasm.* The primary meaning is essential here; the other meanings surround it as ironic and embittered phantasmagoria. The poem is a great one, perhaps his greatest; but to understand it one must be familiar with the years of bootless effort and bad writing. The poem is a very clear example of post-Symbolist imagery, and of controlled association[9].

Stevens' doctrine of the Imagination, like the doctrines of the Imagination that preceded it in the eighteenth and nineteenth centuries, is a psychological doctrine purely and simply; it does not deal with language or the proper use of language, and it offers no guidance to the writer in his writing. In Stevens, as in his predecessors, it generated a bad style. Yet Stevens is different from his predecessors in an important respect: he was born with a talent for great writing; the talent appears in the poem from which I have just quoted and in a few others. Stevens, in his best poems and passages, is a master of the resources of meter and syntax, and of the resources of rhythm that can result from meter and syntax; and he is a master of diction. These facts are well known, and I shall waste no time on them; but I would like to add that in my opinion he is, in these respects, fully the equal of Ben Jonson and the superior of Donne, Sidney, or the Shakespeare of the sonnets. I will now turn to the use of imagery in *Sunday Morning.*

In the first stanza the protagonist

> . . .feels the dark
> Encroachment of that old catastrophe,
> As a calm darkens among water lights.

The catastrophe I take to be death in general and the death of Jesus in particular. If one has ever seen a calm darken among water lights on a large bay or lake, the image is unforgettable[10]. A few lines farther on, "The day is like wide water without sound," and the water-image is extended. In the next six stanzas, the religious and ethical problems are discussed. In the second stanza, Stevens offers us a simple-minded romantic doctrine, that of emotions for their own sake as the only "divinity" of which we are capable; the ideas are feeble and are couched in feeble style — this is an embarrassing passage. The third stanza deals with Jove and his movements on earth, commingling his blood with ours, and the consequent acquisition by humans of a measure of divinity; at the end, the stanza reiterates that the earth must be our paradise. The fourth and fifth stanzas give us the dialogue between the poet and the woman on the subject of paradise; the sixth describes the paradise of traditional belief as unchanging and therefore a generator of ennui. The seventh stanza offers a hint of pantheistic solution. With the eighth and final stanza I shall presently deal. The second stanza is bad; the third and sixth are merely passable; the other stanzas are beautifully written. Yet the total argument (with the possible exception of what we get in the second stanza) seems necessary; the last stanza depends for its success on what has preceded.

In the final stanza we return to the water, which by now has become more real than figurative:

> She hears upon that water without sound
> A voice that cries, "The tomb in Palestine
> Is not the porch of spirits lingering.
> It is the grave of Jesus, where he lay."

That is, Jesus was not the Saviour; he was a man who died. And the poet draws his conclusions:

> We live in an old chaos of the sun,
> Or old dependency of day and night,
> Or island solitude, unsponsored, free,
> Of that wide water, inescapable.

In the first water-image, death encroached as a calm darkens among water lights; then the day was like water; then infinite space is water — bright, beautiful, inscrutable, the home of life and death — and earth is a floating island. Every phrase in this passage is beautiful at the descriptive level, but the descriptive and the philosophical cannot be separated: *chaos, solitude, unsponsored, free, inescapable* work at both levels. The sensory

275

detail is not ornament; it is a part of the essential theme. In the next three lines there is a measure of separation:

> Deer walk upon our mountains, and the quail
> Whistle about us their spontaneous cries;
> Sweet berries ripen in the wilderness.

Out of context this is merely description, but fine description; in context it is a part of what precedes and what follows. Two words make the philosophical connection: *spontaneous* and *wilderness*. The quail are non-human, free, spontaneous; they can be admired but not understood; they are a part of the wilderness. The last lines are similar, except that the number of charged words is greater:

> And, in the isolation of the sky,
> At evening, casual flocks of pigeons make
> Ambiguous undulations as they sink
> Downward to darkness on extended wings.

Out of context these lines are fine description but minor poetry; in context they are great poetry, and the words responsible are: *isolation, casual, ambiguous,* and *darkness.* If the passage could be considered out of context, these words would not be suspected, I imagine, of carrying any real meaning beyond the descriptive meaning. Their significance has been prepared by the total poem, and they sum the poem up.

These pigeons are different from Shakespeare's lark in Sonnet XXIX. The lark was merely a lark, with the author's personal sentimentality imposed upon it arbitrarily. The pigeons embody an idea as well as a feeling, and the idea motivates the feeling. The pigeons cannot be separated from the idea: they are a part of the universe which the poet is trying to understand, and at this point they are an efficiently representative part. The rational soul and the sensible soul are united: we do not have the purely rational soul of Jonson nor the purely sensible soul of Pound; and there is no decoration. The universe which Stevens describes is ambiguous in its ultimate meanings. But there is nothing ambiguous in the style; ambiguity is rendered with the greatest of precision. And the universe is one which we can recognize as our own, even if we disagree with Stevens' philosophy. The physical details are not ingenious set pieces; we know where we are.

Sunday Morning and *The Course of a Particular* are two of the greatest of Stevens' poems. These are the others: *Domination of Black, The Snow Man, On the Manner of Addressing Clouds, Of Heaven Considered as a Tomb,* and *The Death of a Soldier.* All of these exhibit the kind of poetry which I am discussing, some more clearly than others. There are many other poems in Stevens that cannot be spared, most of them in *Harmonium.* There is little after *Harmonium* which I could not do without; but in addition to *The Course of a Particular,* there is a small affair in *Opus Posthumous* entitled *A Letter From* (the first of *Two Letters*) which I would like to preserve.

If we eliminate the poems on the Imagination and the miscellaneous exercises in foolishness, Stevens appears to have one central theme: the situation of the isolated man in a meaningless universe. In the great poems this is almost his single theme. In *Sunday Morning* the universe, though meaningless, is beautiful; there is mitigation by hedonism. In *Of the Manner of Addressing Clouds,* the universe is still beautiful but is appalling; the only mitigation comes from speech, poetry:

> These
> Are the music of meet resignation; these
> The responsive, still sustaining pomps for you
> To magnify, if in that drifting waste
> You are to be accompanied by more
> Than mute bare splendors of the sun and moon.

The Death of a Soldier gives us the same universe with no mitigation. In *The Snow Man* the universe has turned to ice; in *Domination of Black* and *Of Heaven Considered as a Tomb,* it has gone to black night. I do not object to Stevens' refusing to offer any consolation to the reader; I myself can offer none. But the confrontation of this universe, the almost pure confrontation, confrontation without human complications, is a very limited theme; there is more to be said about life even in Stevens' universe than Stevens has suspected. Stevens is a man who understood very little, but that little is of great importance, and his understanding, his language, is one of the marvels of our literature.

V

OF ALL OF THE POETS whom I consider in this chapter, Louise Bogan (1897-   ) may seem to be the least properly included, not because of any lack of excellence in her work but because her work may seem of another kind. The difficulty is this: all five of the other poets, even Miss Dickinson, seem to have had a certain familiar acquaintance with ideas, whether good or bad; all are philosophical poets. Miss Bogan does not think, or thinks as little as possible; she has never even thought about her art, and for this reason has been a very poor critic. Her perceptions are not related to ideas as are those of Stevens, or not as clearly so. This results in a certain limitation of her themes. Yet within limits she thinks about what she says, for she uses language with distinction and thought is thus inevitable. I will try to indicate the difficulty and justify my including her as I proceed.

All of her best poems employ the rational structure of the Renaissance; none is associational. Nearly all of the best include a large measure of generalized statement. It is the quality of her imagery which will justify or fail to justify her inclusion. And let me say first of all that her imagery has one important quality in common with that of the other poets now under consideration: it is luminously clear. There is nothing of the nineteenth century in Miss Bogan's imagery or in her poetry generally.

I will begin with an early sonnet, first published in the summer of 1926 in *The New Republic*. It is called *Simple Autumnal:*

> The measured blood beats out the year's delay.
> The tearless eyes and heart, forbidden grief,
> Watch the burned, restless, but abiding leaf,
> The brighter branches arming the bright day.
>
> The cone, the curving fruit should fall away,
> The vine stem crumble, ripe grain know its sheaf.
> Bonded to time, fires should have done, be brief,
> But, serfs to sleep, they glitter and they stay.

278

Because not last nor first, grief in its prime
Wakes in the day, and hears of life's intent.
Sorrow would break the seal set over time
And set the baskets where the bough is bent.

Full season's come, yet filled trees keep the sky
And never scent the ground where they must lie.

The poem deals with a longing for the death which will not come.
The young woman who wrote the poem had her reasons for this
longing, but she does not disclose them in detail. The reason given
is grief in general, grief which feels itself cut off from life's intent;
this is comprehensible. Lines two and three and again seven and
eight are the passages which I have especially in mind. One
could brush these off as examples of the pathetic fallacy, but
they are not that: it is the eyes and the heart that are "forbidden
grief," that are restrained spiritually; they watch their physical
counterpart, the leaf that is literally burned, restless, but abiding.
The fires are similar to the leaf. The leaf and the fires are real,
they are not falsified; their resemblance to the human observer
is limited, and there is no pretense that it is otherwise, but it is
real, and the human observer sees this reality in language that
seems to move on the page. The poem is admirably written
throughout, but these are the great moments.

Miss Bogan's greatest poem, I am sure, is *Exhortation*:

Give over seeking bastard joy
Nor cast for fortune's side-long look.
Indifference can be your toy;
The bitter heart can be your book.
(Its lesson torment never shook.)

In the cold heart, as on a page
Spell out the gentle syllable
That puts short limit to your rage
And curdles the straight fire of hell,
Compassing all, so all is well.

Read how, though passion sets in storm
And grief's a comfort, and the young
Touch at the flint when it is warm,
It is the dead we live among,
The dead given motion, and a tongue.

The dead, long trained to cruel sport
And the crude gossip of the grave;
The dead, who pass in motley sort,
Whom sun nor sufferance can save.
Face them. They sneer. Do not be brave.

Know once for all: their snare is set
Even now; be sure their trap is laid;
And you will see your lifetime yet
Come to their terms, your plans unmade, —
And be belied, and be betrayed.

The poem tells us to give over the search for joy. Indifference can be our toy — it could not be more than a toy in this stoical condition, nor could anything else. The disillusioned heart will be a book in which we can read; this reading puts us at a remove from our immediate experience just as a book does, and gives us the understanding of the experience instead of the meaningless suffering; the tone of all this is bitterly ironic, but at the same time the advice is seriously meant. The most important thing that we shall learn from this reading is the fact that, in spite of the minor consolations offered in lines eleven, twelve, and thirteen, we live among the dead, but "the dead given motion and a tongue." These are the dead living, who constitute the vast majority of the population, the dead living, who, according to their own natures, hate the small number of the living on sight and with intensity; the description of their physical presence and moral natures in the fourth stanza is the greatest moment in a great poem, and it is the passage which illustrates my thesis. It was these dead living who generated in the poet the bitterness of the first stanza and the rage of the second. But the poet is outnumbered and will be destroyed. It is a poem of hatred for those who hate, and at the same time a poem of fear and desperation.

It is possible that I misread the poem, that when she speaks of the dead she is speaking of the dead and gone, who in some metaphorical manner have returned to haunt her, that this is a poem telling us that we shall be overcome in the end by death; but I think not. This interpretation would leave the first two stanzas and the first three lines of the third unexplained; that is, the bitterness and rage would be merely a chronic condition of the poet, without a cause in the poem, and the clause introduced by *though* would have no purpose. And it would not account for the intense activity of the dead in lines twenty through twenty-five, lines in which moral concept permeates physical appearance, as metaphysical concept permeates landscape detail in the last section of *Sunday Morning*.

It may come as a surprise to my gentle reader that he and his friends can appear in this light to a distinguished poet; but so they often do, and with excellent reason, and this is not the only poem on the subject[11]. The distinguished poet is a member of the smallest of all "minority groups," and during most of his life and often for all of it, is regarded as everyone's inferior and as a fair object of contempt.

The fourth stanza is the climax, but everything is precisely to the purpose in its place; consider the deadly efficacy of "Spell out the gentle syllable" and of "curdles the straight fire of hell." The first three lines of the third stanza are mild clichés which are used ironically. In general I dislike the use of the cliché even in this fashion, but the passage is brief and the irony is intense and is a necessary part of the poem. This passage is introduced by *though:* although all this foolish comfort has been given us, yet. . . . The main clause, and, in fact, the rest of the poem, discuss the main problem.

In *Kept* there is imagery which resembles that of the fourth stanza of *Exhortation* but does not equal it in power, remarkable as it is. The poem deals ostensibly with the putting away of the toys of childhood, dolls and the like; but these toys are really the memories of the most-loved experiences of youth and perhaps later, which have to be laid aside as we proceed, and laid aside with pain because they have become a part of us:

> But we must keep such things
> Till we at length begin
> To feel our nerves their strings,
> Their dust, our blood within.

> The dreadful painted bisque
> Becomes our very cheek.
> A doll's heart, faint at risk,
> Within our breast grows weak.
>
> Our hand the doll's, our tongue. . . .

They have become a part of us, have possessed us, are destroying us, and so must be destroyed, with whatever pain.

Song for a Lyre is a love song for the dead love. It does not offer quite the same kind of imagery which I have been discussing, but something, perhaps, which is very close. It opens with a quiet description of an autumn landscape in which the poet is moving into sleep, and in the second stanza into dream. The stream of the second stanza and the return to the dead love in sleep, in the third, are marvelously rendered.

No other poem by Miss Bogan illustrates the procedure which I have been discussing, at least so far as I can perceive, but these are not her only fine poems. *Medusa* is a vision of death seen as an eternally arrested present, a vision which seems to come from a dream or a moment of madness, remembered later. The poem is almost all imagery: there is no real explanation except the title, and that might be figurative. The successive images, as static images, merely illustrate the general subject; but they are different from each other in detail, and the differences encourage interpretation, and there has been a good deal; but interpretation is not controlled by the text as it is in the other poems which I have been discussing. The poem is therefore obscure, and the tone is violent; the poem is a bit melodramatic. *The Mark* is a poem in which shadow is compared (by implication) to death. Little is said about death except that it is inevitable; the shadow-imagery becomes very intricate and is hard to follow — I cannot see that the imagery is justified in terms of the subject, but it is interesting. *Come, break with Time* is a song on the approach of death; it is simpler, as it should be for the simple subject; it is better written in every way. *Henceforth from the Mind* is almost as fine a poem as *Exhortation;* it deals with the retreat of life from flesh into mind as age advances. The imagery of the third and fourth stanzas comes closer to traditional simile and metaphor than does the imagery which I have been discussing; yet it is not ornament but is an effective part of the theme. The language of the second stanza is a bit commonplace.

VI

EDGAR BOWERS (1924-   ) was born and raised in northern Georgia; he comes of Presbyterian stock. For some years he has lived in California. He served in the Second World War in counter-intelligence, and, after the fall of Germany, he remained for some time with the forces of occupation, engaged in the work which was popularly known as "de-Nazification." Most of these facts are important for the understanding of some of his poems. Bowers has the temperament of the mystical Calvinist, but he has too good a mind to accept the Calvinistic faith or any other. The temptation to believe what one desires to believe, the temptation to deceive oneself, whether the desire is for religious faith or for something else, is a theme which occurs in several poems, and words such as *deceit* and *guile* are recurrent[12].

The following poem is called *Dark Earth and Summer;* it is written in three-beat accentual verse:

> Earth is dark where you rest
> Though a little winter grass
> Glistens in icy furrows.
> There, cautious, as I pass,
>
> Squirrels run, leaving stains
> Of their nervous, minute feet
> Over the tombs, and near them
> Birds grey and gravely sweet.
>
> I have come warm of breath,
> To sustain unbodied cold,
> Removed from life and seeking
> Darkness where flesh is old,

Flesh old and summer waxing,
Quick eye in the sunny lime,
Sweet apricots in silence
Falling — precious in time,

All radiant as a voice, deep
As their oblivion. Only as I may,
I come, remember, wait,
Ignorant in grief, yet stay.

What you are will outlast
The warm variety of risk,
Caught in the wide, implacable,
Clear gaze of the basilisk.

This in its general form is an example of very closely controlled association. The poem describes a landscape in two seasons, as if the seasons were simultaneous; the seasons are both symbolic, and exist simultaneously in the mind of the speaker. We have, first, late winter or early spring, with the icy furrows and the winter grass that had grown under the snow; this is the season of the graves. And we have the season of early summer, of life, of "the warm variety of risk," from which the poet has come. The sensory detail in the first two stanzas is very fine in itself, but it seems almost purely descriptive on first reading; its significance emerges as we come to the third stanza. Then the vision of summer appears suddenly, but this is not a simple vision: it is eternal summer, "all radiant as a voice, deep as their oblivion," and this vision returns him to the grave, but the final image, that of the basilisk, is one of immobile light. This is a poem about death as death, and it offers no solace. But it is also a vision of the eternal, a vision of the magnificent emptiness of the eternal, a vision which offers no solace. This is the vision of the modern mystic who is also an intellectual man; it is not so different from the mystical vision of earlier Christianity as some readers may think, but it is more clear-sighted, is without hint of subterfuge. The basilisk is one of the most magnificent images in our poetry, but the entire poem is magnificent and is without any flaw that I can discern.

The Astronomers of Mont Blanc appears to be related to the last poem:

Who are you there that, from your icy tower,
Explore the colder distances, the far
Escape of your whole universe to night;
That watch the moon's blue craters, shadowy crust,
And blunted mountains mildly drift and glare,
Ballooned in ghostly earnest on your sight;
Who are you, and what hope persuades your trust?

It is your hope that you will know the end
And compass of our ignorant restraint
There in lost time, where what was done is done
Forever as a havoc overhead.
Aging, you search to master in the faint
Persistent fortune which you gaze upon
The perfect order trusted to the dead.

In its structure the poem is as rational as any poem of the Renaissance; it consists of a question and answer. The first two lines suggest for a moment the opening of Stevens' *Of Heaven Considered as a Tomb:*

What word have you, interpreters, of men
Who in the tomb of heaven walk by night,
The darkened ghosts of our old comedy?

But the poems are very different; the questions are very different; the astronomers are more definite than the interpreters; and Bowers' heaven is far more vivid and more terrifying than that of Stevens. *Of Heaven,* like most of Stevens' poems, contains a slight mockery of the poet's own seriousness; the gentle seriousness of Bowers in the face of an overpowering perception is more effective. Bowers moves into sensory perception at once, and sensory perception and its significance are simultaneous. In the third line we have the appalling vision of the expanding universe disappearing into infinite space, and then the vision of absolute death in the image of the moon. The moon is the real basilisk; not the basilisk of archaic myth but the basilisk of the modern telescope or space-photograph; it is the basilisk in itself, cut off from everything pertaining to the warm variety of risk. It is the absolute vision. The generalized comment arrives at the very end, and it is no less powerful than that which precedes, but we

285

are at no loss to understand the meaning of the imagery as we come to it. This is a perfect example of the kind of imagery which I am trying to illustrate. I can find no flaws in the poem. The very gentleness of the diction — "mildly drift and glare, Ballooned in ghostly earnest" — and the gentle but complex rhythms fix our attention on the vision, they do not distract. It makes the poem by Stevens appear a little fussy for the occasion.

The two poems which I have quoted are two of the three best which Bowers has written; the third is *Adam's Song to Heaven* — I will discuss it briefly. *Heaven* and *God* appear to be interchangeable concepts here. The poem is rational in structure, although explicitly rational connectives are suppressed, so that the structure is not obtrusive. The first two stanzas address the infinite deity; but in the third stanza there begins the source of the poet's problem, the uncertainty whether the deity is real or a projection from his own mind:

> And all your progeny time holds
> In timeless birth and death. But, when, for bliss,
> Loneliness would possess its like,
> Mine is the visage yours leans down to kiss.
>
> Beautiful you are, fair deceit!
> Knowledge is joy where your unseeing eyes
> Shine with the tears that I have wept
> To be the sum of all your thoughts devise.
> ••••••
> What are you then! Delirium
> Receives the image I despair to keep.
> And knowledge in your somber depth
> Embraces your perfection and your sleep.

The deity is inscrutable; its perfection seems to be identical with sleep. It is very close to the basilisk and the moon. If Bowers had lived in the seventeenth century, he would have been a great devotional poet. He lives in a more difficult and more sophisticated period; he is still a great devotional poet, but of a sort that George Herbert would not have understood. He makes the devotional poets of the seventeenth century appear very innocent and far away.

I have discussed his greatest poems, but there is great poetry elsewhere, and in addition to this there is distinguished poetry which is less ambitious. In the two volumes which Bowers has thus far published, there are fifty-three poems, none of them really long. Most of the poems are worth keeping for one reason or another. The bulk is small, but the poems are dense and require careful reading.

The Stoic is a clear example of the post-Symbolist procedure in both its aspects. It deals with the bombing of Germany as witnessed by an unidentified observer, "the stoic." The poem opens with the sound of distant cannon and the moonlight bombing of Munich:

> All winter long you listened for the boom
> Of distant cannon wheeled into their place.
> Sometimes outside beneath a bomber's moon
> You stood alone to watch the searchlights trace
>
> Their careful webs against a boding sky.
> While miles away on Munich's vacant square
> The bombs lunged down with an unruly cry
> Whose blast you saw yet could but faintly hear.

This gives us the setting: enormous violence in a moonlit distance. The observer meditates on the eternal Alps and their winter landscape, and then on

> Eternal Venice sinking by degrees
> Into the very water that she lights.

There is the vast panorama of Europe, changeless or changing slowly, with violent change here and there. The observer remembers the new Berlin, now being destroyed, and an incident which was reported even in the American newspapers:

> Where just short weeks before, a bomb unaimed
> Had freed a raging lion from its cage,
> Which in the mottled dark that trees enflamed
> Killed one who hurried homeward from the raid. . .

We remember the "unruly cry" of the bombs in the second stanza; the bombs become random agents for releasing random violence of a kind unsuspected. And the poem goes on to the end:

287

And by yourself there standing in the chill
You must, with so much known, have been afraid
And chosen such a mind of constant will,

Which, though all time corrode with constant hurt,
Remains until it occupies no space,
That which it is, and passionless, inert,
Becomes at last no meaning and no place.

It is the greatest poem in English dealing with war; this may be a small distinction, but, in any event, it is a great poem.

Of the remaining poems in the first book, I would suspect that the best are *The Prince* (although it could be cut), *Three Thousand Years from Troy, The Virgin Mary,* and *From William Tyndale to John Frith.* As to *The Prince,* I should warn the reader that the dedication seems to be irrelevant to the poem; the Latin epigraph may be directed to the prince or to the recipient of the dedication. The poem is a monologue spoken by a German prince to an American officer of the occupation, a prince who had hated the Nazis, whose son had hated them; whose son, however, had eventually been overcome by his German patriotism, had served as a spy, had been captured and shot. The last paragraph of this poem, especially, is very great.

The second book is perplexed, almost tortured, by a subject which seems to be stated clearly in *A Song for Rising* — clearly in spite of the somewhat Dickinsonian grammar of the last line: it is the conflict, quite simply, between what the poet is and what he should be. It seems simple enough, so stated, but it verges on something like hallucination more than once, an experience somewhat schizophrenic, somewhat solipsistic. The trouble with the term *solipsistic* is that even *solus ipse* appears sometimes to be in doubt. One can find the subject in *The Mirror, In a Darkness, An Answer, The Dream,* and in the sequence *Autumn Shade. An Answer* and *Autumn Shade* strike me as less successful than the others. The poems in *Autumn Shade* argue through references to sensory detail which are not sharp at the sensory level and not clear at the intellectual; we have the kind of associationism to which I have objected in the eighteenth and nineteenth centuries.

VII

N. SCOTT MOMADAY (1934-   ) may seem too young for inclusion in a discussion of this kind, but I would remind the reader of my definition of a great poet: a poet who has written at least one great poem. In my opinion Momaday has written the poem, as well as a few fine lesser poems, and his work is very much to my purpose[13].

I will quote a poem called *The Bear*. The poem owes something to Faulkner, but it is essentially Momaday's. It is written in syllabic verse. The first and third lines of each stanza contain five syllables apiece, the second and fourth contain seven; as in all syllabic verse, the accented syllables must vary sufficiently in number and position that they do not form a pattern (a pattern would give us standard meter) but must still contribute to the rhythm:

> What ruse of vision,
> escarping the wall of leaves,
> rending incision
> into countless surfaces,
>
> would cull and color
> his somnolence, whose old age
> has outworn valor,
> all but the fact of courage?
>
> Seen, he does not come,
> move, but seems forever there,
> dimensionless, dumb,
> in the windless noon's hot glare.
>
> More scarred than others
> these years since the trap maimed him,
> pain slants his withers,
> drawing up the crooked limb.
>
> Then he is gone, whole,
> without urgency, from sight,
> as buzzards control,
> imperceptibly, their flight.

The poem is more descriptive than anything else, yet in the third and last stanzas the details are more than physical and indicate something of the essential wilderness. The sensory perception is very acute, very quiet, as if the observer himself were almost as much at home in the wilderness as the bear. The language is at every point very quiet and could as well be the language of distinguished prose. The poem is poetry by virtue of the careful selection of details and the careful juxtaposition of these details, selection and juxtaposition which result in concentration of meaning, and by virtue of its rhythm, which is the rhythm of verse, but very subtle. Of all the poets of the past decade or so who have experimented with syllabic verse, Momaday is the only one to use it with real success.

My next poem, *Buteo Regalis*, describes a hawk at the moment of attack. The lines of this poem are of ten syllables each; lines two, four, five, and six are in iambic pentameter, and the others are syllabic — Momaday controls this change of movement with perfect success:

> His frailty discrete, the rodent turns, looks.
> What sense first warns? The winging is unheard,
> Unseen but as distant motion made whole,
> Singular, slow, unbroken in its glide.
> It veers, and veering, tilts broad-surfaced wings.
> Aligned, the span bends to begin the dive
> And falls, alternately white and russet,
> Angle and curve, gathering momentum.

This seems to be more purely descriptive than *The Bear*. The language could be that of prose, except for the rhythm, but of absolutely distinguished prose, free of all cliché, not of journalistic prose. Yet the language deserves more attention. We are given a *rodent*, not a rabbit, or a prairie dog, or a kangaroo rat. His frailty is *discrete*, that is, considered separately, just as his purely rodent nature is considered separately, in the defensive turn. It is the abstract movement of the abstract rodent, which we might get in a line-drawing of two or three strokes. The first and third lines, in their syllabic rhythm suggest the sudden hesitation; the four pentameter lines suggest the smooth motion of the soaring hawk; the last two lines in their syllabic rhythm and fragmented phrasing, suggest the rapid and confusing descent. This is done with absolute economy, quietly, yet with uncanny perception. Perception of what, however? Is it only the perception of physical objects observed? It seems rather perception of the "discrete" wilderness, the essential wilderness. It is this quality in both of these poems which brings them within the limits of my present subject.

Both of the poems just quoted, though remarkably fine, are minor poems. The next poem is Momaday's most impressive achievement. It is in standard meter throughout; the general method is that of controlled association:

Before an Old Painting of the Crucifixion
The Mission Carmel
June 1960

I ponder how He died, despairing once.
I've heard the cry subside in vacant skies,
In clearings where no other was. Despair,
Which, in the vibrant wake of utterance,
Resides in desolate calm, preoccupies,
Though it is still. There is no solace there.

That calm inhabits wilderness, the sea,
And where no peace inheres but solitude;
Near death it most impends. It was for Him,
Absurd and public in His agony,
Inscrutably itself, nor misconstrued,
Nor metaphrased in art or pseudonym:

A vague contagion. Old, the mural fades. . .
Reminded of the fainter sea I scanned,
I recollect: How mute in constancy!
I could not leave the wall of palisades
Till cormorants returned my eyes on land.
The mural but implies eternity:

Not death, but silence after death is change.
Judean hills, the endless afternoon,
The farther groves and arbors seasonless
But fix the mind within the moment's range.

291

Where evening would obscure our sorrow soon,
There shines too much a sterile loveliness.

No imprecisions of commingled shade,
No shimmering deceptions of the sun,
Herein no semblances remark the cold
Unhindered swell of time, for time is stayed.
The Passion wanes into oblivion,
And time and timelessness confuse, I'm told.
These centuries removed from either fact

Have lain upon the critical expanse
And been of little consequence. The void
Is calendared in stone; the human act,
Outrageous, is in vain. The hours advance
Like flecks of foam borne landward and destroyed.

The first two stanzas deal with the experience of the Crucified, as it was suggested in the mural. They bring up the idea which will recur in the fourth stanza, the desolate calm following any tragic event, a calm the nature of which we may sense in the wilderness, near the sea, especially near death; and in the latter part of the second stanza we have a statement of the uniqueness of this experience for the Crucified. These lines are worth our attention: to say that the experience was unique and then try to describe it would be a contradiction, a falsification; Momaday does not try to render the unique experience but instead gives us a statement of the nature of uniqueness, in relation to the inner experience of Christ, after the line on his outer and public appearance. These lines are as powerful as any I know; they illustrate a way in which abstract statement can be utilized effectively. In the third stanza he recollects that this is, after all, a mural, old and disintegrating; the scene of the mural, mute in constancy, is not real. The sea is real, but in the distance it also is mute in constancy; he remembers how the view of the sea had held him till his eyes had drifted back after the cormorants. And then the mural comes back to mind. The third stanza may seem obscure on first reading if we do not keep in mind the position of the observer, in the old mission near the ocean, his mind moving back and forth between the two objects.

"The mural *but implies* eternity." I have italicized two important words. The mural does not render eternity, nor explain it; Momaday is too cautious an observer of his experience to suspect anything so foolish. It merely implies eternity but it does imply it, and it implies nothing else. The line ends with a colon, which indicates that the implication will be explored. The first line of the fourth stanza may bother the reader for a moment, for, in the usual sense, death, like any other occurrence, is change; but this is not what Momaday is talking about. Death itself is a process, a part of life; but in the silence after death we have a different state entirely, an essentially inscrutable state, which is implied by the immobile mural. The remainder of the fourth stanza describes the mural, with reference to the details which imply eternity, details which resemble our experience but suggest a state removed from it, details which are neither the one thing nor the other, which are sterile though beautiful.

The fifth stanza is a commentary on the fourth but refers back to the third as well: it tells us that in the mural there are none of the movements which indicate the presence of time, nothing to

> remark the cold
> Unhindered swell of time,

a phrase in which we are reminded of the ocean swell outside, now as if it were at hand and powerful, but in which the swell appears to be stayed even before the fact is stated in the next few words. Time is stayed; we are in eternity in the mural; but for the moment we are in eternity this side of the mural as well. On this side of the mural the Passion wanes into oblivion; time and timelessness seem to become one. The phrase "I'm told" is not something inserted for a final foot and a rime, as one of my young friends once suggested; it is there for a clear purpose. It is a weary confession that we are dealing with a mystery, about which we cannot know as much as some people claim.

In the first two lines of the fifth stanza we have a quick light rhythm as we see the little movements which indicate life in time; this is slowed somewhat in the third line, which summarizes and begins to move into the magnificent image of time; this sentence is compact but complex in syntax and rhythm alike. The rhythm of the fifth line is slow and pensive, and that of the sixth is similar. The command of rhythm, whether linear, syntactic, or in some other way stanzaic, is that of a master; but the reader who has learned to read poetry aloud can find this command throughout.

The last stanza is a commentary on what has preceded, a summing up and a final judgment. The phrase *either fact* indicates two facts: the real crucifixion and the crucifixion depicted in the mural. The *expanse* has been *critical* in two senses: it has been a test of the centuries following the Crucifixion; it should have been a period of crisis, of great change. But nothing really to the purpose has occurred; there was a moral void; time was geological, not human; the extreme sacrifice was in vain. The indications of time before us are as trivial as flecks of foam moving in to disappear in the beachsand.

I have tried to explain this poem in great detail, because the poem, although not obscure, is difficult and requires careful reading. I myself did not understand it for a long time, and I know other readers, and very intelligent readers, who do not understand it yet. The poem is worth understanding. Every word, every mark of punctuation, every cadence, every detail of grammar and syntax is a precise and essential part of an act of profound understanding.

The poem displays both of the post-Symbolist methods which I have been discussing. First we have controlled association: this is seen most clearly in the third stanza and in the movement back and forth thereafter between the mural and the ocean, but it occurs throughout the poem. Second, we have post-Symbolist imagery, imagery weighted with intellectual content; the fifth stanza is the most obvious example, in "the cold unhindered swell of time," but we can find it elsewhere. And there is purely abstract statement on occasion, and very powerful abstract statement.

VIII

THE SIX POETS WHOM I have discussed in this chapter are spread over a century in time and a continent in space, and their backgrounds are as varied. Frederick Goddard Tuckerman (1821-73) was born in Boston and spent most of his mature life at Greenfield, a village about eighteen miles from Amherst, in western Massachusetts. He was educated in private schools before entering Harvard, which he was soon forced to leave because of trouble with his eyes. But then he entered the law school and graduated in 1842. His entire education after secondary school appears to have occurred in less than two years. He tried the practice of law but dropped it; his father left him enough money so that he could live on his income; he lived as a recluse, for the most part, an amateur student of astronomy and botany, and a poet. Emily Dickinson (1830-86) was born in Amherst of a moderately wealthy family, was educated at Amherst Academy and for one year at Mount Holyoke Female Seminary. Otherwise she spent her entire life in the family home, as completely secluded from human company as possible. Wallace Stevens (1879-1955) was born in Reading, Pennsylvania, attended Harvard for three years, and then studied law at the New York Law School. He received his degree in 1903 and for a time practiced in New York City. In 1916 he was employed by the Hartford Accident and Insurance Company, of which he became vice-president in 1934. He appears to have been a man of a good deal of wealth and one who enjoyed the pleasures which wealth provides; at the same time, if rumor is to be trusted, he avoided literary company as an unpleasant nuisance. Louise Bogan (1897-   ) was born in Maine of Irish stock; her formal education, I believe, extended little if at all beyond high school; she has earned her living in various ways but for a good many years has been a teacher in various colleges and universities. She has lived in New York City during most of her life. Edgar Bowers (1924-   ) was born and raised in northern Georgia, near Atlanta, where his father was a nurseryman. After his military service in the Second World War, he came to Stanford University as a graduate student in English;

after completing his doctorate, he taught in the east for a few years and then came to the University of California at Santa Barbara, where he has been established for some years. N. Scott Momaday (1934-   ) is a Kiowa Indian. He was born at Lawton, Oklahoma, not far from Anadarko, the Kiowa Agency. His parents have been teachers at Indian schools throughout their adult lives and for many years have taught in a school at a pueblo in northern New Mexico; it was here that Momaday spent his later childhood. His father is a painter, his mother a writer of stories for children. After graduating from the University of New Mexico, Momaday taught for a year at Dulce, a small town in northern New Mexico and on the reservation of the Jicarilla Apaches. He entered Stanford University in the fall of 1959 as a graduate student in English and completed his doctorate in the spring of 1963. Since that time he has been a member of the English faculty at the University of California at Santa Barbara, a colleague of Bowers. He is the editor of *The Complete Poems of Frederick Goddard Tuckerman* (Oxford University Press, New York, 1965).

For the past three years Bowers and Momaday have been well acquainted; otherwise, no two of these poets have known each other personally. Tuckerman, because of the nature of his publication, could have influenced none of the others; even Momaday, when he was writing the poems herein discussed, had only a slight acquaintance with him. Miss Dickinson was known to all four of the subsequent poets, but it would be hard to prove an influence. It would be easier to make a case for the influence of Stevens on the poets who followed him, but this influence, if there was one, was of the most general sort. The influence of Valéry on Bowers would be easier to prove, but it is not obvious. These poets have in common with each other and with Valéry the modes of writing which I have discussed, and all write with the greatest of distinction in their best poems, but otherwise there is no marked resemblance among them; no perceptive critic would mistake an unidentified poem by one of them as the work of one of the others. They are all obviously of fairly modern times as regards their subjects and styles, but subject, style, emotional tone, personal character vary from poet to poet. They mark a new kind of poetry, however; there is nothing like it elsewhere in English, except perhaps for a few poems by Bridges and T. Sturge Moore; there is little if anything like it in French except in Valéry and perhaps in a few poems by Leconte de Lisle. This poetry, as a method, is more inclusive, more perceptive, than anything we have had before; these poets illustrate and justify the method. They deserve very careful attention.

6

The Plain Style Reborn

J. V. CUNNINGHAM (1911-   ) seems to me the most consistently distinguished poet writing in English today, and one of the finest in the language; to make myself clear, however, I shall have to begin with a few reservations.

Some years ago Cunningham did a very rash thing; he published an essay on his own poems[1]. I wish he had never written it, but it is interesting, it is in print, and one has to use it. One must look at Cunningham's doctrine of Haecceity. I will begin with a few of his own words:

> "All choice is error." For choice implies exclusion, rejection, restriction, limitation. To choose *this* is not only to prefer one thing to something else. . . . Any realized particular, anything which is this and not that and that, is by the very fact evil. For to be this is to exclude not only any other alternative but to exclude all else in the universe. Perfection is in possibility, in the idea, but that which is realized, specific, determined, has no possibilities. It is precisely this and nothing else at all. It is lacking in all the being in the universe other than its own particularity. The more realized a thing is the greater its defect of being; hence any particular choice is as such evil though morally it may be the best choice.

The poem which embodies this doctrine most clearly is one which is not mentioned in *The Quest of the Opal,* for it was written later than the poems there discussed. It is called *Agnosco Veteris Vestigia Flammae*[2]:

> I have been here. Dispersed in meditation,
> I sense the traces of the old surmise —
> Passion dense as fatigue, faithful as pain,
> As joy foreboding. O my void, my being

> In the suspended sources of experience,
> Massive in promise, unhistorical
> Being of unbeing, of all futures full,
> Unrealized in none, how love betrays you,
> Turns you to process and a fluid fact
> Whose future specifies its past, whose past
> Precedes it, and whose history is its being.

The poem is beautifully written, and it would be very moving if
one could imagine the experience. But what we have here is a
kind of mysticism of pure passivity (which would be unconscious-
ness), of retreat to the womb. The mysticism in question has no
religious sanction, and its only philosophical sanction is a handful of assertions by Cunningham. Superficially, it may seem to
resemble the doctrine of Valéry's Serpent, for the Serpent sees
himself as evil because a creature (and therefore a sufferer of
privation); but the Serpent seeks to increase his being by the
mastery of more knowledge — that is, by further choice; and this,
of course, is what Cunningham has done in fact. I have known
Cunningham for more than thirty years; during these years, he
has tried, as he tells us, to realize various choices in poetic form
as precisely as possible. Yet his being (his intelligence) has increased, not diminished, from choice to choice. Cunningham is
fully aware that he is more intelligent now than he was fifty
years ago. Fortunately the doctrine affects only a few of Cunningham's poems.

The Quest of the Opal is troublesome in other ways. I will
quote Cunningham's poem *To the Reader*, which is one of his
finest:

> Time will assuage.
> Time's verses bury
> Margin and page
> In commentary.
>
> For gloss demands
> A gloss annexed
> Till busy hands
> Blot out the text,

300

And all's coherent.
Search in this gloss
No text inherent:
The text was loss.

The gain is gloss.

Cunningham is a textual scholar by profession, and at the level
of the vehicle this is an ironic comment on textual scholarship. At
the level of the tenor, however, it describes Cunningham's usual
way of writing poetry; that is, he draws abstractions from the
experience and discards the experience itself. The "text" is the
experience; the "gloss" is the poem. If the poem is ironic at the
level of the vehicle, it is deeply bitter at the level of the tenor, for
the loss is real, and the word *loss* refers not merely to the discarded material but to the personal suffering involved, just as the word
gloss refers to the wisdom gained from the suffering. The double
meanings of these words are not a whimsical imposition of my
own; they are clearly evident in the poem, and they are largely
responsible for the extraordinary concentration and force of the
poem. But in *The Quest of the Opal*, it seems to me, he violates
his own principle, for on many occasions he tries to read the text
(the experience) back into the gloss (the poem). In the case of
Poets Survive in Fame, the effort is mildly irritating but no worse,
for the poem is perfectly clear in itself. In *The Beacon* and *Un-
romantic Love* the problem, I think, is more serious. Neither of
these poems is clear without notes. The first appears to be more
or less Platonic, but if we try to read it in Platonic terms there
are difficulties; the second poem, as it stands on the page, has
always seemed to me wholly obscure, although the details of
phrasing and rhythm are remarkable. When we turn to the notes
in *The Quest*, however, I cannot understand the notes, much less
read them into the poems. This doubtless indicates a defect of my
understanding.

Reason and Nature presents another and perhaps related
difficulty. "The pool in a pure frame," says Cunningham in *The
Quest,*

301

is the perfection of reason in which reason can see only its own construction, and one's notion of his identity in such a construction. The unchanging, unalterable pool, therefore, is a fiction, a device of method. But what we call the real pool, the pool of sensation and experience where we may find a willow or two, is not unrippled. Though the alterations of its surface be as minute as the slight waves caused by skimming flies, these results of chaos and change will exemplify no given rule, will be the realization of no definable method. Nor will any isolatable part of change be a microcosm containing implicitly the whole, nor will it be a calculable curve from which the whole may be inferred. Our experience does not validate induction, just as our postulates have as such no reference.

The poem is shorter than the explanation:

> The pool in a pure frame,
> This mirror of the vision of my name,
>   Is a fiction
> On the rippled surface of reflection.
>
> I see a rippled pool
> Where the flies skim. Its angles have no rule.
>   In no facet
> Is the full vision imaged or implicit.
>
> I've heard, in such a place
> Narcissus sought the vision of his face.
>   If the water
> Concealed it, could he, drowning, see it better?
>
> I know both what I see
> And what I think, to alter and to be,
>   And the vision
> Of this informs that vision of confusion.

One can find the explanation in the poem with a little labor. What bothers me most about the poem is the method. A great part of the poem is devoted to the pool, yet the pool as such is unrealized, is a dead pool; the details are stereotyped. The pool, however, is the occasion for the sermon, the argument, and the argument is all but crowded out of the poem by the uninteresting remarks about the pool. The argument could have been handled more effectively in Cunningham's more characteristic method. The pool

302

and the argument do not fuse into a single successful being as do the vision of the moon and the argument in *The Astronomers,* by Bowers. Cunningham is seldom perceptive of the physical universe around him; he does not know what to do with it. Pool and argument are brought together by force and each is beaten with a club. Furthermore, as far as my limited understanding goes, the explanation eliminates any justification for Cunningham's poetry or for any other poetry. I confess that I retain a kind of bucolic distrust of all theories which seem to be in obvious conflict with the facts of life.

There is another aspect of Cunningham's early poetry which bothers me. *The Metaphysical Amorist* is precisely and gracefully written. It has real virtues. But it remains an exercise in wit, interesting for one or two readings but no more. *The Chase* is similar in these respects but offers yet another difficulty. The hunted rabbit is compared to a young lady pursued by lovers:

> For when the dogs retreated, fought,
> And circled the embarrassed doe,
> The doe moved only to be caught,
> Quite pleased to be encircled so. . . .

The rabbit behaves like a young lady, but not like a rabbit, and I have never seen dogs retreat and fight before closing in on a rabbit. At that point in a hunt the dogs have only one idea, and their concentration on it is really extraordinary. The scream of the dying rabbit is unforgettable. The comparison will not stand, and the poem is false.

Except for *Agnosco...,* the poems to which I have objected were written between the ages of twenty and twenty-nine. It is not surprising that the weaker poems of any poet should be early. There are, however, certain suprising facts with regard to the early work. Even the poems to which I have objected are in many ways distinguished; they are better than most of the poetry which has been published in the last thirty years or in any other comparable period. Furthermore, three of Cunningham's great poems were written within this period: *Poets survive in fame* and *The Phoenix* (both of these were written at the age of about twenty-one); and Epigram 8 of *The Judge is Fury.* And some of the finest minor poems belong to the same period: *The Symposium, Fancy, The Helmsman, Timor Dei, Choice,* and perhaps others.

It was shortly after these early poems, however, that Cunningham's style hardened into what is perhaps the most consistently successful style of our time. *To the Reader,* which I have quoted, is a good example. Another is *Meditation on Statistical Method:*

> Plato, despair!
> We prove by norms
> How numbers bear
> Empiric forms,
>
> How random wrong
> Will average right
> If time be long
> And error slight,
>
> But in our hearts
> Hyperbole
> Curves and departs
> To infinity.
>
> Error is boundless.
> Nor hope nor doubt,
> Though both be groundless,
> Will average out.

The opening lines contrast Plato's theory of numbers as absolute forms with a modern theory of numbers as statistical and relativistic devices; but this contrast is merely the vehicle — the poem deals with theories of the understanding of human experience. In the tenth line we have the word *hyperbole,* the name of a figure of speech, exaggeration. But the word *hyperbola* is the name of a mathematical curve which never returns to intersect itself. One can call this a pun in the grand manner of the Renaissance or a condensed metaphor, as one prefers. The poem is witty in the best sense, but it is more than that: it is a statement about the irreducibility of human passion. *On the Calculus* is another poem which employs a vehicle from mathematics:

> From almost all to almost naught I flee,
> And *almost* has almost confounded me,
> Zero my limit, and infinity.

The poem is based on a passage in Pascal but improves on the passage and adds to it. The *Meditation* deals with a moral problem, *On the Calculus* with a metaphysical; Epigram 43 of this collection deals with a problem which is moral, metaphysical, and theological:

> In whose will is our peace? Thou happiness,
> Thou ghostly promise, to thee I confess
> Neither in thine nor love's nor in that form
> Disquiet hints at have I yet been warm;
> And if I rest not till I rest in thee
> Cold as thy grace, whose hand shall comfort me?

All three of these poems define truths which cannot be avoided, but they offer no solace unless clear understanding — that is, rational comprehension combined with propriety of feeling — be solace.

There is another kind of matter, not wholly unrelated to this last, which may give the reader trouble unless he can consider it dispassionately. This is the matter related to the doctrine of hatred or anger. The doctrine, briefly, and as nearly as I can understand it, is that hatred is the only cleansing emotion and the most moral of emotions. Baldly put, the doctrine is not beguiling and may even seem shocking, but it is not without a justification in experience. During the Romantic movement a great deal of sentimental nonsense was written about the isolation of the artist, and the nonsense usually verges on self-pity; there is a trace of sentimental self-pity in Cunningham's poems *Envoi* and *Forgiveness*. The fact remains, however, that the artist, if he is really an artist, is really isolated, and his personal life in this respect is a hard one. There are few people with whom he can converse freely without giving offense or becoming angry. It is no accident that so many great writers have sooner or later retreated from society: they retreat because they are excluded. A first-rate poet differs from his contemporaries (and I include those who think of themselves as literary contemporaries) not in being eccentric or less human, but in being more central, more human, more intelligent. But the difference in this respect between, let us say, a great poet and most distinguished scholars is very great, and few scholars are distinguished; and the scholar cannot recognize the difference and is scarcely prepared to admit the possiblity of the difference, for he regards himself as a professional man of letters. To the scholar in question, the poet is wrong-headed and eccentric, and the scholar will usually tell him so. This is bad manners on the part of the scholar, but the scholar considers it good manners. If the poet, after some years of such experiences, loses his temper occasionally, he is immediately convicted of bad manners. The scholar often hates him (I am not exaggerating), or comes close to hating him; but if the poet returns hatred with hatred (and surely this is understandable), he is labeled as a vicious character, for, after all, he is a member of a very small minority group. The poet may become neurotic under such pressure; there is no comparable pressure on the scholar, and he usually remains normal. Cunningham deals with this problem in an unusually gentle way in Epigram 35 from *The Judge is Fury*:

Hang up your weaponed wit
Who were destroyed by it.
If silence fails, then grace
Your speech with commonplace
And studiously amaze
Your audience with his phrase.
He will commend your wit
When you abandon it.

Gentle as the poem may seem, it depicts an incident in Hell. Epigram 25 of the same group deals with the same theme more bitterly:

Dark thoughts are my companions. I have wined
With lewdness and with crudeness, and I find
Love is my enemy, dispassionate hate
Is my redemption though it come too late —
Though I come to it with a broken head
In the cat-house of the dishevelled dead.

Hatred sometimes gives one a very clear view of ugliness of other kinds. This is called *Ars Amoris:*

306

Speak to her heart!
That manic force
When wits depart
Forbids remorse.

Dream with her dreaming
Until her lust
Seems to her seeming
An act of trust.

Do without doing!
Love's willful potion
Veils the ensuing
And brief commotion.

If the reader should fail to understand the intention of this poem, there are other poems which will serve as footnotes. This is Epigram 9:

Within this mindless vault
Lie *Tristan* and *Isolt*
Tranced in each other's beauties.
They had no other duties.

This, from the same group, is called *History of Ideas:*

God is love. Then by conversion
Love is God, and sex conversion.

These lines give us a succinct summary of a major transition: they take us from the New Testament to W. B. Yeats.

There is also the attitude of indifference; it amounts almost to a doctrine, perhaps a more resigned and more mature form of the doctrine of hatred. It appears in an early poem, Epigram 8 of *The Judge is Fury,* as a common-sense objection to

Those fools who would solicit terror,
Obsessed with being unobsessed,
Professionals of experience
Who have disasters to withstand them
As if fear never had unmanned them. . . .

In the later poems it becomes a more and more consistent attitude; it may be related to the determinism which Cunningham defends in *The Quest.* I cannot understand this determinism as a doctrine[3], but I can understand it as an attitude related to his very clear view of the ugliness of most experience: we cannot control the accidents of life or the attacks of other persons, and these may seem to overwhelm us and deprive us of our own powers. Some of Cunningham's best poems have come from this stoicism. This is Epigram 8 of *Doctor Drink:*

> On a cold night I came through the cold rain
> And false snow to the wind shrill on your pane
> With no hope and no anger and no fear:
> Who are you? and with whom do you sleep here?

And this is entitled *New York: 8 March 1957*:

> Lady, of anonymous flesh and face
> In the half-light, in the rising embrace
> Of my losses, in the dark dress and booth,
> The stripper of the gawking of my youth,
> Lady, I see not, care not, what you are.
> I sit with beer and bourbon at this bar.

What are the sources of Cunningham's style? The mature style is what we would call the plain style if we met it in the Renaissance. It is free of ornament, almost without sensory detail, and compact. But it is a highly sophisticated version of the plain style, and is very complex without loss of clarity. It comes closer, perhaps, to Ben Jonson and a few of his immediate contemporaries than to anyone else. Cunningham has long admired Jonson and has studied him carefully. The resemblance of Cunningham's minor epigrams to the minor epigrams of Jonson may seem very close until one examines the tradition of the epigram throughout Europe in the Renaissance and in the Latin literature preceding: then it becomes evident that we merely have two men working in a common and widespread tradition. As Cunningham tells us, his mature style tends toward the epigrammatic, and this whole tradition is behind it. As to Jonson, many of his best poems are farther from the epigram than are Cunningham's, but he grows out of an English tradition which is semi-epigrammatic and out of a Latin tradition which Cunningham also has studied.

And yet it is hard to estimate the formative influence of this body of poetry, although it has certainly supported Cunningham in his convictions. Cunningham's family were victims of the Great Depression, and when Cunningham was in his late teens he went on the road as a wandering writer for trade journals; during this time he struck up a correspondence with me and sent me two or three poems; he came to Stanford when he was twenty years of age, nearing twenty-one. He had acquired a fair amount of scholarship for anyone of his age before he had been forced into his wandering life; but he was young, and the life was a hard one and was scarcely conducive to concentrated study. My memory is often faulty, but I believe that at least two of the poems which he has retained were written before he came to Stanford: *Experience* and *Noon*. One can see the traces of the later style in these poems. The following poem, in which the mature style is fully established, was written when he had been at Stanford for perhaps a year:

> Poets survive in fame,
> But how can substance trade
> The body for a name
> Wherewith no soul's arrayed?
>
> No form inspires the clay
> Now breathless of what was
> Save the imputed sway
> Of some Pythagoras,
>
> Some man so deftly mad
> His metamorphosed shade,
> Leaving the flesh it had,
> Breathes on the words they made.

The poem is somewhat dense in terms which are philosophical or theological, yet the terms are familiar and should give no serious trouble: *substance, form, soul* (anima), *breath* (anima), and *imputed*. And Pythagoras is supposed to have taught a doctrine of reincarnation. The poem tells us that the poem lives only in the mind of the intelligent reader, not on the page; it gives us Cunningham's concept of true scholarship, and he knows that this kind of scholarship is very rare. I know that Cunningham had been reading Renaissance and Latin poetry when he wrote

309

this poem, but he had not been at it long. It would be impossible, I think, to name any particular poet as the model for this poem. It is a poem written within a major tradition, and, I am sure, a great poem. *The Phoenix,* written at about the same time, is also a great poem, but it is off the main line of Cunningham's development; to see the difference, one should compare it to Epigram 43 of *The Judge is Fury,* which is on the same subject. In one of Cunningham's later poems he reverts to his concept of scholarship, with, I suppose, memories of his own youth. The poem is entitled *For a College Yearbook:*

> Somewhere on these bare rocks in some bare hall,
> Perhaps unrecognized, wisdom and learning
> Flash like a beacon on a sleeper's wall,
> Ever distant and dark, ever returning.

Cunningham's style is in no sense the personal style of some one else, nor is it an archaic style. If a poet of our time were to attempt the ornate style of Sidney or of Spenser, he would fail, even if he did not use archaic language or old matter. The ornate style is ineffective, and was obsolescent even when Sidney and Spenser were using it. The plain style, however, if mastered, as it was by Jonson, is unmannered; it is free of the eccentricities of the time, the place, and the man; it is perennially useful. Cunningham's matter is not that of Jonson or of any other poet of the Renaissance. Some of his epigrams are in the early manner, but few could have been written by an early poet. His work deals with his own matter, matter which would not have been conceivable in the Renaissance. And he deals with his own matter as effectively as Jonson deals with the matter of Jonson. Jonson's character was a Christian character, a character which I think is no longer possible for an intelligent man. Cunningham's spiritual situation is much more difficult, and by that measure his achievement has been more difficult. Just as the styles of Sidney and Spenser are dated today, the styles of pseudo-mythic hypertension which we find in most of Yeats and Crane, and of aimless associationism which we find in most of Pound and his disciples, will be dated tomorrow. But the style of Cunningham, on the one hand, and the style of the best of Valéry on the other, will not be dated. The styles and the matter are firm.

II

CATHERINE DAVIS (1924-   ) has learned a great deal from Cunningham. She has sometimes departed farther from the epigram than Cunningham has ever done, but she has not been notably successful in these⁴ longer efforts. In her best epigrams, she is quite as successful as Cunningham; her best poems are fewer in number; the range of her successful work is much narrower than his; she is a lesser poet. But she is no more his imitator than he is Jonson's; her matter is her own and so is her management of the epigram. I quote three epigrams from a group of seven called *Insights:*

> 2. *To the Spirit of Baudelaire*
> *Wind of the wing of madness!* What is this?
> O you that shuddered then, what mantic bird?
> What travesty, dark spirit, of the Word?
> What last cold exhalation of your bliss?
> What passage to what end? Speechless abyss.

> 5.
> Pity, Catullus, these late revellers
> Who celebrate their passing with a shout,
> These idle, disabused malingerers
> Who wait defeat, as in a barbarous rout
> Amid a wreck of cities, empires lost:
> They are as faggots in a holocaust.
> Pity, among the rest, this sparrow verse.

> 7. Guercino's *Et in Arcadia ego*
> Even in Arcady, the mouse, the fly,
> And death agape confront the passerby.

These poems hardly require explication; the matter is serious; the style is impeccable.

7

Conclusions

THE PRESENT BOOK rounds out my career as a critic, at least as nearly as this kind of thing can happen without a preconceived plan such as no one is likely to have when he begins. The present chapter, unfortunately, will have to be fragmentary: I shall have to summarize, make brief additions, and make suggestions for future study.

I

MY FIRST BOOK OF criticism, *Primitivism and Decadence* (1937) bore the subtitle "A Study of American Experimental Poetry," and that is what it was in the main. The book dealt with the ways in which poems have been constructed in various periods, but with especial reference to the American poetry of the early twentieth century. If I were writing the book today, I think that I could write it more efficiently and with a less elaborate terminology; but I did the best that I could at the time, and I think that the book is essentially sound. My second book was *Maule's Curse, Seven Studies in the History of American Obscurantism* (1938); this book contained essays on Hawthorne, Cooper, Melville, Poe, Very and Emerson, Emily Dickinson, and Henry James, essays which endeavored to evaluate these writers and at the same time to trace in them some of the ideas and procedures which had led to the forms of decadence which I had described in my preceding volume. This book contained also a selection of the poems of Jones Very, in an appendix. The poems in this appendix, taken together with the poems quoted in my essay, should be of some interest. Very is not a great poet, but at his best he is a fine minor poet, and these are his best poems, gath-

313

ered from a bulky mass of repetitious work which has long been out of print. *The Anatomy of Nonsense* (1943) contained essays on Henry Adams, Wallace Stevens, T. S. Eliot, and John Crowe Ransom. These three books were reissued in a single volume, *In Defense of Reason* (1947), along with a new essay in introduction and a new essay on Hart Crane. Shortly before the publication of this collection, I had published *Edwin Arlington Robinson* (1946), through New Directions[1]. And in 1957 I published *The Function of Criticism: Problems and Exercises*. This book contains: an essay called *Problems for the Modern Critic of Literature*, in which I compared the various literary *genres*, and tried to evaluate them with reference to each other, concluding that the short poem is the most civilized, that is to say the greatest; an essay called *The Audible Reading of Poetry*, which, along with the essay entiled *The Influence of Meter on Poetic Convention* in my first volume, is of the utmost importance in connection with my present work; essays on Hopkins and Frost; and an essay called *English Literature in the Sixteenth Century*. If the reader will consider the essays mentioned, he will see that I have discussed in my earlier work most of the important poets not discussed in the present volume; and if he will consult the index of *In Defense of Reason*, he will see that I discuss others besides.

I should mention another matter. In the *Hound and Horn* for July-September, 1933, I published a review of the *Oxford Book of Sixteenth Century Verse*; this was later expanded into an essay of some length entitled *The 16th Century Lyric in England*, which appeared in three issues of *Poetry* in 1939, those of February, March, and April. This essay was revised some two or three times to serve as lecture notes at Stanford; the final revision, along with additional matter on the seventeenth century, was written during the academic year of 1961-62, to serve as the first chapter of this book. The 1939 version of this essay seems to have acquired a wide but quiet reputation in academic circles. It has influenced a good many books and articles which have given it at most but passing acknowledgment[2].

II

WHEN I WAS WRITING THE first of the books which I have mentioned, I was greatly concerned with what seemed then (and still seems) the grave defects in the methods of most of the really talented poets who had written in this century. I had been influenced by these poets and by the French Symoblists in my own poetry, and late in 1927 or early in 1928 I decided to abandon the methods which I had been employing and undertake methods which seemed more sound; this was, in brief, a serious matter for me — it was not merely academic. For some years I examined these poets and their backgrounds, with distress that writers of such remarkable talents could submit themselves to ideas and procedures so damaging. I believe that my analyses of these writers were sound; but the ideas which did the damage were merely ideas inherited from the eighteenth and nineteenth centuries and then carried to their logical conclusions by writers of real talent.

There are differences between the ideas of Wordsworth and of Robert Frost, for example, but the central ideas are the same. Wordsworth wrote a few short passages worth remembering for the present, but no good poem. Frost wrote a few fine minor poems: *The Most of It* and *Spring Pools* are probably the best; in my essay on Frost I discuss these and a few others. In writing of Hart Crane some twenty years ago, I pointed out that the ideas which destroyed Crane's talent were the same ideas which one can find in Whitman, but that they seem less destructive in Whitman, or seem so to many readers, because Whitman is utterly lacking in literary talent, so that the effect of the ideas never becomes clear. Crane's gift for language often gives us living detail, such as we never find in Whitman; one is then forced to concentrate on what the detail is doing or failing to do. Crane's *Repose of Rivers* is a monologue spoken by a river, presumably a tributary of the Mississippi, then the Mississippi, on its way to the Gulf; the details of the river itself, "that seething steady, leveling of the marshes," the mammoth turtles, and others are marvelous at the descriptive level. But these details imply human expe-

315

riences symbolized, and the human experiences can only be vaguely guessed, and the mystical union with the Gulf is vaguer still. And this is the clearest of his poems and the best organized. The details force us to notice the defects; it is hard to notice anything in Whitman.

So with the rest of these poets. The two greatest influences on Pound were Swinburne and Browning: Swinburne in the texture of his style and Browning in the extreme associationism of structure (if that is the proper term). The influence of Swinburne and of his disciples of the nineties is plain in the poems of *Provença* and earlier. *Salve Pontifex (A.C.S.)* was written in praise of Swinburne three years before Swinburne's death; Pound reprints it in *Lustra* (Knopf: 1917), with the note: "Balderdash but let it stay for rhythm." It is written in undistinguished free verse, in a language which is simultaneously that of Pound and that of Swinburne, and unmistakably so. *The Cantos* have gone through a good many forms, but the first *Three Cantos* appeared in *Poetry* in June, July, and August of 1917 and then in a somewhat modified form in *Lustra;* it is the second version which I have before me. The first *Canto* opens thus:

> Hang it all, there can be but the one "Sordello,"
> But say I want to, say I take your whole bag of tricks,
> Let in your quirks and tweeks, and say the thing's an art-form,
> Your "Sordello," and that "the modern world"
> Needs such a rag-bag to stuff all its thought in . . . . .

And it continues. It is a frank confession of indebtedness, and the style here and in much of the rest of the *Canto* is strongly marked by Browning. As Pound went on, the associational procedure became even more extreme, probably because Pound's subjects were far more tenuous than Browning's; but in the best of the *Cantos* the details are far more interesting than those of the master. It is in the details, however, that the Swinburnian pseudo-poeticism shows itself — less crudely than in Swinburne, of course, but unmistakably. *Canto IV* is probably of more consistent interest than any of the others, although a few other early *Cantos* are close rivals. We have a long passage beginning with *Ityn!* and taking us through Actaeon, in which the fragments are

316

connected with each other by virtue of the fact that each deals with a tale of cannibalism or of transformation, and a few with both; the whole *Canto* appears to deal with marriage in the most general sense, and the fragments range over many periods and many countries; among the countries are Provence, Greece, China, Japan, and Persia[3]. There seems to be nothing else in the theme. The detail in this *Canto* is remarkable throughout, but is heavily inlaid with poetical mannerism:

> Bathing the body of nymphs, of nymphs, and Diana,
> Nymphs, white-gathered about her, and the air, air,
> Shaking, air alight with the goddess. . . . etc.

This kind of thing reaches its most comical moment in the first line of *Homage to Sextus Propertius VI:*

> When, when, and whenever death closes our eyelids. . .

This poem itself may be the best in Pound, but it is heavily mannered.

These are the faults: there is almost no subject-matter, and what little one can disentangle is foolish; there is no structure, unless rhythmical revery is structure; the mannerisms are extreme and incessant. One would call the style verbose, except that by definition verbosity is the use of words in excess of the occasion, and there seems to be no occasion. Pound is a man who is deeply moved by the sound of his own voice. Yet the details and the cadences in some of the early *Cantos* are very lovely; I think that they will remain when the poets whom I have discussed in Chapter III have been long forgotten. In the very nature of the case, however, most of Pound will disappear. The sheer bulk is enormous; all save a little of the writing is insufferably dull; there is something pathetic about Pound's slogan: "Make it new." A few of the *Cantos* (the first seven, perhaps), a few of the early satirical notes (*The Faun* and *Pompes Funèbres II,* especially), and the best of the translations (if that is the proper term) should live for a long time. But it is not great poetry; it is superior Swinburne. As Crane makes us more acutely aware of the defects of Whitman, so Pound makes us more acutely aware of the defects of his predecessors. In both poets there is something which is admirable, and this sharpens our sense of the defects.

William Carlos Williams (1883-1963), in his view of life and of poetry, was an uncompromising romantic. It is surprising, in the light of this fact, that he appears to have been a devoted husband, father, and physician, eminently virtuous and practical in these capacities, and often naively shocked by the behavior of some of his bohemian acquaintances who held the same ideas but acted upon them. He was a thorough bore in print except on a few occasions. He believed in the surrender to emotion and to instinct as the only way to wisdom and to art: *The Trees* is one of his many explicit statements of this notion. He believed that art is the product of a character which is "automatically first-rate" (*Blues*, for May 1929); this is a version of Rousseau's doctrine of the "beautiful soul," which Irving Babbitt discusses at length in *Rousseau and Romanticism* and which Jane Austen parodies in her first work of fiction, *Love and Friendship*. Williams, of course, believed that the doctrines originated with himself. Williams' artist would have no need for ideas and no awareness of them; in fact, he would display no signs of consciousness whatever. Williams distrusted all ideas and sought value as far as possible in the concrete; in an early poem called *Paterson* he reiterates the phrase "no ideas but in things" (this idea, like Pound's imagism, is an end-product of eighteenth-century associationism); and he distrusted the entire range of emotion which is motivated by ideas, for he was in no position to distinguish good ideas from bad, and hence, in this realm, sound emotion from false. In *A Poem for Norman McLeod* he writes: "The revolution/ is accomplished/ noble has been/ changed to no bull." Any emotion arising from the contemplation of an idea, whether moral, metaphysical, or religious, appears to him merely sentimental. He distrusts traditional form, as a kind of restraint or inhibition: since he fails to grasp its meaning and uses, it appears to him another mechanical sentimentalism; and he desires that the theme create its own form, like other believers in organic or imitative form from the eighteenth century onward, and like these believers he offers animal and vegetable comparisons — a poem moves as a crab moves or grows as a cabbage grows. But in this desire he was often frustrated by his congenital talent, for in his best poems he has made of free verse a complex accentual meter, very difficult to control and creating very binding conventions of feeling.

His poetry, therefore, concentrates on the concrete; the only ideas which it occasionally expresses are those which I have outlined, and since the ideas are bad, the poetry which deals with them is bad. At his best, Williams offers merely sharp impressions of objects observed, either in isolation or in accidental sequence, or forced by a purely rhetorical violence, as in *Romance Modern*, into some kind of formal unit. In such a poem as this last — and there are many such — the form, or emotion, which enacts the violence is unmotivated, and the whole effect, in spite of any interesting details, is one of excited over-statement. Sometimes the sharp impression of the object observed, however, may have an intrinsic meaning, and when it is offered in isolation, in a single poem, the poem may have power: *Complaint* and *The Great Figure* from *Sour Grapes* (1921) are such poems; they are not great, but they are far better than the poem about the red wheelbarrow. *Pink confused with white* from *Spring and All* (1923) is another such poem. *By the road to the contagious hospital* from *Spring and All* is his best poem: it deals with the force of vegetable nature and the season behind it coming to life in the spring; it could have been sentimentalized, but is not. *To Waken an Old Lady* from *Sour Grapes* and *To a Dead Journalist* (*Recent Verse*, 1938) complete the list of his best pieces. All are very fine work, but are very small; they are more serious and are better executed than anything by Pound or Miss Moore. But it is foolish to think of Williams as a great poet; the bulk of his work is not even readable. He is not even an anti-intellectual poet in any intelligible sense of the term, for did not know what the intellect is. He was a foolish and ignorant man, but at moments a fine stylist.

Marianne Moore (1887-   ) employs precisely the same general method of constructing her poems as does Pound in his *Cantos* or Williams in his longer efforts; that is, there is essentially

319

no governing theme, and the movement from detail to detail is purely associational. There is almost always, it is true, a brief moral attached at the end of the poem and sometimes at the beginning, but it is almost always trivial and not seriously relevant. Like the *Cantos*, her poems derive what value they have from the details. The details, unlike those of the *Cantos*, are almost invariably realistic (sometimes in an exaggerated way) rather than hyper-poetical; the tone is likely to be ironical or sometimes self-righteously didactic rather than bardic. The details are often, especially in the earlier poems, genuinely entertaining: see *Poetry*, for example, or *The Monkeys* (its original title, *My Apish Cousins*, may have come to strike the author as ambiguous), or *England* or *A Grave*. The details are often laboriously forced, as in *The Fish*. Sometimes they are the details of good, plain descriptive prose, as in *The Steeple-Jack*. The rhythms may be elaborately brilliant as in the free verse of *The Grave*, but the elaboration is far in excess of the occasion, like the elaboration of syntax and grammar in all of her poems. The rhythm is usually violently monotonous. I remember a good many descriptive details and epigrams from a few early poems, but I can no longer read her with any feeling more kindly than boredom. The wit is a bird-wit; she reminds me too strongly of her own parakeet:

> trivial and humdrum on examination, destroying
> bark and portions of the food it could not eat.

Mina Loy (ca. 1883-   )[4] proceeds in much the same associational manner in many of her poems, but in her best, *Der Blinde Junge* and *Apology of Genius,* we have an organized treatment of serious subjects. Her habit of continuous alliteration and fragmented rhythm are troublesome mannerisms. She has nowhere written a poem as sucessful as the best of Williams, but she has attempted more in the two poems just mentioned and she is successful to a remarkable degree. She is the most serious of the poets whom I have just been discussing. She had an unusually good mind, but it remained uneducated, and it exhausted its materials rather early; at least she knew when to stop.

T. S. Eliot (1888-1965) I have discussed at length in an

earlier essay. I wish to add merely a few remarks to relate him to my present group. Except for the poems in quatrains in his second collection, his method has been associational, for the most part, and rather loosely so. Pound seems to have been the chief influence, but there are important differences. Both men borrow compulsively from earlier poets: Pound seems to borrow these passages merely because he likes them and cannot get them out of his head; in Eliot they are usually employed ironically, but almost always, so far as one can judge, because of some sort of thematic relevance — the relevance is likely to be far-fetched, however, and the exegetes make very amusing reading, Mr. Brooks in particular. The texture of Pound's detail is very poetical, laid on with very thick oil; Eliot seems to be looking for the prosaic, the matter-of-fact.

Everything that I have said of Eliot so far seems to be to his advantage in comparison with Pound, yet he is inferior to Pound. Pound has a much better ear. Eliot's quatrains move heavily; even Donne can manage the tetrameter line with greater skill. Eliot's free verse is comparably monotonous; the monotony of the movement, combined with the journalistic detail, achieves an effect which appears to pass as profound, or perhaps merely as ominous. Let the reader consider the opening of the first section of *Burnt Norton*. I will not quote. The first ten lines deal somewhat expansively with what might fairly be described as simple-minded profundities; then we come to the sad little clichés about the rose-garden, the rose-leaves, and the door never opened. This is the method. The tone of voice is low; the rhythms are dull and seem close to prose, but they are not the rhythms of good prose; the language is that of discreet journalistic cliché and sentimentality. But it is quiet; it appears to be understatement; it must be profound. Sometimes the theme deserves serious treatment, but the treatment is nowhere serious; the treatment is lazy and diffuse. At its worst, the style degenerates into mere reportage of casual detail, depressing detail. The method is that of Dyer or Collins in the eighteenth century: a typical item is mentioned — a gothic pile in Collins, a pile of rubbish in Eliot — and we are supposed to have the typical, that is the "correct," reaction or

321

association, and to have it automatically and with great force. And many of us do, and will be angered by these remarks, but this kind of writing has no life of its own and ultimately becomes very tiresome. Eliot is the least interesting of the poets whom in this book I have called the eccentrics, whom in my first book I called the decadents. He has inspired generations of imitators because he is easy to imitate.

Allen Tate (1899-   ) is a poet who has promised a great deal throughout his career but has never produced it; he is a poet of a dozen or fifteen fine short passages, a few of them superb, and no successful poem. *The Cross* is his most impressive poem and is characteristic. In the first eight lines we are told that the Christian revelation burst like a flame from a pit, blinding forever those who, having once recognized it, turned away from it. The poem then says that divine love so hates our human condition that it curses us with mortal strife — I presume the strife between good and evil — until such time as we taste of salvation and then taste no more of death. But the lines here are curious; we have the young wolves:

> Until beside the blinding rood
> Within that world-destroying pit
> Like young wolves that have tasted blood,
> Of death, men taste no more of it.

The reader will doubtless recollect the old myth to the effect that once young wolves have tasted blood, they will no longer take their mother's milk. The comparison of the soul who has tasted of conversion to the young wolf who has tasted blood and so become a killer is sufficiently curious, but the grammar of the last line is even more remarkable. The line means: "Men taste no more of death." Perhaps Tate intended an example of *apo koinou* to be interpreted thus: "Like young wolves who have tasted the blood of Christ's death, men taste no more of death but taste only Christ's blood." But this is too confused to be impressive. Then follows the fine conclusion, beginning with Tate's most magnificent line: "So blind, in so severe a place." But who is so blind? Not the men who have just tasted of the divine blood in the preceding line and so will taste no more of death. This line has to be referred back to "those, once seeing, turning back," the damned, in line eight. Eight lines on the saved intervene; there is no clue to the reference. My mind is a slow one, but my intentions are better than those of most readers; it took me five or six years of occasional but careful readings to clear up these obscurities. And now that I understand the poem, I still do not like it; I find it clumsy, and I do not believe that clumsiness is a virtue. One finds comparable difficulties throughout Tate, and an inflated and redundant rhetoric.

The poets whom I have discussed in this section of this chapter, along with Yeats and Hopkins, and along with Stevens most of the time, might be described as the great eccentrics of the modern period. By this I do not mean that they are great poets, for they are not: the great poets are Bridges, Hardy, Robinson, Moore, Cunningham, and the six poets whom I discussed in Chapter V. But any man who writes a few great poems — no man writes many — will write lesser work: some of it may be fine minor work, some of it may be bad, some of it may be eccentric in a way that is interesting at least for a time. And a fine minor poet may also be bad much of the time, or eccentric, and in fact is likely to be. Stevens is one of my great poets; he is also a fine minor poet; but most of the time he is one of the eccentrics. Frost and Williams each wrote a few fine minor poems. The eccentrics, as such, are all motivated by the same ideas about poetry and human nature which destroyed the poetry of the eighteenth and nineteenth centuries: they are nominalists, relativists, associationists, sentimentalists, and denigrators of the rational mind. It may appear that one or another of these terms may not apply to one or another of the poets, but I think that a close examination will show that all apply to all. Like the earlier poets they have lost control of poetic structure; that is, of language, of their mode of understanding, of their own being. This defect is more obvious in their work than in the work of their predecessors because the violence has been carried farther and because they have more talent than their predecessors and so bring life to the details which they cannot control or unite. Their virtues, in combination with their defects, seem to have generated an unfortunate charac-

323

teristic which is common to all of them: a pretentiousness of style of one kind or another. Stevens and Miss Moore in their respective ways are fussy to the point, very often, of being foolish; Pound and Tate, in somewhat different ways, are resoundingly pompous. Most of these poets are most often obscure, and the obscurity seems due to the mannerism; but one suspects that the mannerism in turn is due to the fact that the poets have very little to say, are not really sure that the little is worth saying, and so prefer obscurity to candor. A poet may be difficult because of concentrated statement of profound matter, or because he has developed a vocabulary of his own, or for both reasons, and this is sometimes true of Stevens, but in general one will find little of this kind of difficulty in these poets.

Some of these poets and some of my great poets carry over from the nineteenth century a delusion which I have not mentioned, the delusion that greatness is shown in extreme productivity. One of my most distinguished colleagues at Stanford is reported to have remarked in a conversation at which I was not present that he had always thought that a great poet was a poet who wrote a great deal of poetry. This notion provides the professor (or other critic) with an easy standard; he can recognize the great poets with neither taste nor effort. And one or two of the great poets so recognized will provide him with enough busy-work to make him an eminent man in his profession. But as bulky poet is added to bulky poet, the patience even of the professors will wear thin. And the taste which enables a reader to recognize a good poem among fifteen hundred or more pages of bad is very rare, and the really valuable poems, if there are any, in the work of such poets are likely to be lost. I cannot help feeling that if Bridges, let us say, had written a great deal less and studied the nature and history of his art a great deal more, he might have produced perhaps a dozen poems as great as *Low Barometer* and they would be easier to find. As things stand, if Bridges survives, he will have my talent to thank as well as his own, and I might never have been born.

III

THIS BUSINESS OF survival is far more precarious than the reader may think. The arts are not in the least democratic, and poetry is the most difficult of the arts. In any major American university at the present time, there are more men who can discuss with each other the latest and most abstruse theories of physics and mathematics and discuss them intelligibly than there are men in the entire nation who have the combined talent and education to read and discuss poetry with competence; the number will never be large, for talent is scarce, but the number might be increased by better education. Good poems, to put it briefly, do not survive automatically.

Let me illustrate with a poem from *The Oxford Book of English Verse,* a poem by Mark Alexander Boyd (1563-1601):

> Fra bank to bank, fra wood to wood I rin,
>   Ourhailit with my feeble fantasie,
>   Like til a leaf that fallis from a tree,
> Or til a reed ourblawin with the win.
>
> Twa gods guides me: the ane of them is blin,
>   Yea and a bairn brocht up in vanitie;
>   The next a wife ingenrit of the sea,
> And lichter nor a dauphin with her fin.
>
> Unhappy is the man for evermair
> That tills the sand and sawis in the air;
>   But twice unhappier is he, I lairn,
> That feidis in his hairt a mad desire,
> And follows on a woman throw the fire,
>   Led by a blind and teachit by a bairn.

The poem is a minor poem: that is, the subject is a formulary subject of the period, and the subject, though important, is not of the greatest; we have the familiar mythology of the subject. The figures employed in lines three and four and in most of the sestet are familiar. The poem seems damned, and if one sees no more than what I have mentioned, so it is. But there it is, one of the most extraordinary poems in our language. The formulary organization common to the period, that of careful and rational

325

exposition, is an initial virtue of great importance; it will not, of itself, make a good poem, but it will make a good poem possible. The structure of the sentences is vigorous throughout, and the statement in the first two lines, though not great, is a vigorous introduction to the subject. The rhythms throughout are nervous and expert. It is the second quatrain that brings the poem up from the commonplace, that charges the entire poem with the full potential of the qualities which I have been describing. The first foot is a spondee, which makes the initial and passionate movement pause and waver, as if in meditation; the second is a slow and heavily accented trochee, which reinforces this effect; these feet fix our attention on what follows. The characterization of Cupid in the second line of the quatrain is a fine one, and the characterizing description of Venus in the next two lines is one of the greatest moments in our poetry. The sestet handles familiar ideas with vigor, and the last line is especially fine. The poem is one of the best poems of the sixteenth century; I would call it unforgettable except that few people notice it.

Who was Boyd? And how did he reach us? I have never seen another of his English poems, nor have I ever read anything about him, except for Pound's comment on this sonnet in *The ABC of Reading* (1934): "I suppose this is the most beautiful sonnet in the language, at any rate it has one nomination." The Stanford University library, an unpredictable and far from compendious collection, contains the following: *Delitiae Poetarum scotorum hujius aevi illustrium*, Amsterdam, 1637, in four volumes (very small), edited by Arthur Johnston. This contains Latin verse by eminent Scots of the period preceding, including M. A. Boyd's *Epistolae Heroidum et Hymni*, an epigram on the death of Boyd ("Poeta Suavissimus") by John Johnston, and poems by a Robert Boyd.

I discovered the poem in *The Oxford Book of English Verse* many years ago. But where and how did Quiller-Couch discover it? Quiller-Couch was a man of very small talent; his anthology is a poor one, and it is especially poor in the Renaissance. But we are greatly in his debt for this poem. I placed the poem on the reading list for my course in the English lyric perhaps thirty years ago, and I always called it to the attention of my students. In recent years it has found its way into two or three anthologies, which, I fear, will not long survive. I have never mentioned it before in print, and it is not in Professor Williams' anthology[4]. It would be interesting to know if Boyd did anything else of value; perhaps the gentlemen of the Scottish Text Society or of the University of Edinburgh could help us. It would be interesting to know how many readers have admired the poem in *The Oxford Book of English Verse*. I suspect that the number is small. The anthology might easily disappear from print, for it is now obsolete, and the poem with it. Yet the poem should be preserved as long as our language is read.

IV

EDWIN ARLINGTON ROBINSON (1869-1935) is the only great poet, according to my calculations, of whom I have thus far written nothing in this volume. I have published a book about him, as I have said, but I would like to say a little here. His best short poems are *The Wandering Jew, Veteran Sirens,* and *Eros Turannos,* with *Luke Havergal* as a fourth. There are other fine poems, which I listed in my book and most of which I described, but these are the best. Robinson uses less sensory detail than do most modern poets, sometimes almost none; in a way, his style tends toward the plain style, but there are differences.

As Hoyt H. Hudson pointed out in an essay to which I refer in my book, Robinson seems to have been strongly influenced by W. M. Praed, a nineteenth-century writer of light verse. Praed's verse at its best is fairly quick and witty, but sentimentally witty; it lacks concentration; it is graceful in a somewhat mechanical way; it is journalistic. Browning, as I have tried to show earlier, writes a very similar verse, but of course he is a good deal better than Praed; Browning also influenced Robinson, sometimes more, sometimes less. The aspect of Browning's style which most influenced Robinson was this journalistic superficiality of statement; the associational method, although it appears in Robinson in certain poems, never took the same hold on Robinson that it

327

did on Pound. Robinson had far more native talent than either Browning or Praed.

The result, as I have said, is a style that approaches the plain style, but from the wrong models; even at his best, Robinson never exhibits the sophistication of style that one can find in Jonson or Cunningham. And Robinson's ear is dead, a fact which may account for a part of the difficulty.

But his subjects are often impressive, and his style often rises so close to the occasion that he must be ranked as one of the great, as in these stanzas portraying the aging prostitutes in *Veteran Sirens:*

> The burning hope, the worn expectancy,
> The martyred humor, and the maimed allure,
> Cry out for time to end his levity,
> And age to soften its investiture;
>
> But they, though others fade and are still fair,
> Defy their fairness and are unsubdued;
> Although they suffer, they may not forswear
> The patient ardor of the unpursued.
>
> Poor flesh, to fight the calendar so long;
> Poor vanity, so quaint and yet so brave;
> Poor folly, so deceived and yet so strong,
> So far from Ninon and so near the grave.

The defects of the style are visible, but only barely. The statement of the particular pathos is concentrated and true.

V

I WISH TO SAY a very little of two minor poets of great distinction, both women, and very different from each other: Adelaide Crapsey (1878-1914) and Janet Lewis (1899-   ).

Adelaide Crapsey died of tuberculosis, and a good many of her poems seem to be written with imminent death in mind; her health began to fail in 1908, her illness became acute in 1913. In the early part of this century tuberculosis provided a very different experience from that which most recent sufferers have known; the drugs which are now used to treat the disease had not been discovered. I know nothing of Miss Crapsey's medical history, but I know a great deal of my own, less than a decade later. The patient was often allowed, or even encouraged, to exercise; the only known cure, and this was known to only a few physicians, was absolute rest, often immobilized rest. The disease filled the body with a fatigue so heavy that it was an acute pain, pervasive and poisonous. Miss Crapsey must have known this fatigue, and most of her best work was written during the years of increasing illness. She had been heavily influenced by the poetry of the 'nineties, but learned skill, not mannerism; she admired Landor and addressed a quatrain to him, but her own diction is more perceptive than his, not stereotyped; she seems to have known something of Japanese poetry, probably by way of the French, before it was made popular in this country by Pound. She was a single lady, of delicate sensibility.

The resulting poetry is hypersensitive, sometimes to the point of sentimentality; it is extremely personal, most of it concerned with her immediate predicament. She was famous for some years after her death; I have three editions of her poems on my shelves, the last published in 1938 (*Verse*, published by Knopf). By now she is almost forgotten; one could assign various reasons for this fact, but I think that the main reason is the anthologists, who have an infallible taste for the weakest work of any poet whom they consider.

She is often at her best in poems which are impersonally descriptive but which suggest a scene more comprehensive than that described:

> Look up. . .
> From bleakening hills
> Blows down the light, first breath
> Of wintry wind. . . look up, and scent
> The snow.

It is cleaner, less sentimental, than most Japanese poems as we have known them in translation; it achieves more effectively than did almost any of the work of the Imagists the aims of Imagism. *Roma Aeterna* is similar, but the subject is more impressive and the poem has more power:

329

> The sun
> Is warm to-day,
> O Romulus, and on
> Thine olden Palatine the birds
> Still sing.

The next is more personal; it deals with a sudden and almost hallucinatory realization that she is leaving life; it is her finest poem:

> I know
> Not these my hands
> And yet I think there was
> A woman like me once had hands
> Like these.

The next is probably the best of the poems in other forms:

> *To Man Who Goes Seeking*
> *Immortality, Bidding Him*
> *Look Nearer Home*
> Too far afield thy search. Nay, turn. Nay, turn.
> At thine own elbow potent Memory stands,
> Thy double, and eternity is cupped
> In the pale hollow of those ghostly hands.

The following is a very poor poem; it is one of her last; it is worth quoting because it indicates the experience from which the poems come:

> Pain ebbs,
> And like cool balm,
> An opiate weariness
> Settles on eyelids, on relaxed
> Pale wrists.

This is not melodrama; she is writing of what she knew; but she is too near death, too feeble, to write well.

If the experience sometimes overpowered her literary tact, we should nevertheless try to be patient, for there are enough fine poems to justify our patience: *Snow, Anguish, Moon-Shadows, Night-Winds, Roma Aeterna, Amaze, Niagara, For Lucas Cranach's Eve, Dirge, Song, Angélique, Chimes, To Man Who Goes Seeking Immortality*. It is a formidable list. A good many are slight, but all are distinguished, all are in their way honest and acutely perceptive. They are the work of a lady who was obsessed with the necessity of writing well; we should not let them disappear.

Janet Lewis[6] has devoted most of her work to fiction, in which, if I may be forgiven for saying so, I think that she is one of the relatively small number of distinguished professionals of our time. By comparison, she has been an occasional poet; her *Poems 1924-1944* contains only forty-eight pieces, and of these six or seven are negligible. Her themes are for the most part domestic, but the domestic theme can be as good as any other. She is a stylist of remarkable native gift and possesses an unusual knowledge of song and ballad stanzas and rhythms; she has as fine an ear for poetic movement as one can easily find in English. Her weakness is domestic sentiment, which sometimes goes all the way to sentimentality. It appears not in her subjects, but in her diction and only fragmentarily; it ruins few poems, probably none, and her book as a whole is far more distinguished than most, but it weakens a good many poems and often her most ambitious. These are the poems which succeed most fully: *Girl Help, Love Poem, The Manger, Remembered Morning, Going Home from the Party, The Clock, For Elizabeth Madox Roberts, In the Egyptian Museum, Lines with a Gift of Herbs,* and *Old Love.* All of these save the last four and *Love Poem* are very slight; none, I suppose, is a great poem; but most of them are masterly.

I will quote one of the earliest and slightest, and then a later poem which I think the best. The following is called *Girl Help:*

> Mild and slow and young,
> She moves about the room,
> And stirs the summer dust
> With her wide broom.
>
> In the warm, lofted air,
> Soft lips together pressed,
> Soft wispy hair,
> She stops to rest,

And stops to breathe,
Amid the summer hum,
The great white lilac bloom
Scented with days to come.

There is almost nothing to it, really, except the rich characterization of a young girl with her life before her and the description of a scene which implies an entire way of life. The meter is curious; one is tempted to call it irregular three-beat accentual, but it seems to be irregular iambic trimeter. On the second basis, the first line starts with a monosyllabic foot, and the fourth line has two feet, both iambic. But *wide* and *broom* are almost evenly accented, and both are long; if one is moved by this to choose the accentual theory, *her* is too lightly accented to count, although it would count as the accented syllable of an iambic foot. There are a few other such problems later in the poem. But there is no problem with the rhythm; the fourth line virtually gives us the movement of the broom, and the seventh and eighth give us the movement of the girl; the movement of the poem is that of indolent summer in a time and place now gone; the diction, like the rhythm, is infallible.

In *Lines with a Gift of Herbs* the domestic theme is generalized into a greater theme:

The summer's residue
In aromatic leaf,
Shrunken and dry, yet true
In fragrance, their belief,

These from the hard earth drew
Essence of rosemary,
Lavender, faintly blue,
While unconfused nearby

From the same earth distilled
Grey sage and savory,
Each one distinctly willed, —
Stoic morality.

332

The Emperor said, "Though all
Conspire to break thy will,
Clear stone, thou emerald, shall
Be ever emerald still.

And these, small, unobserved,
Through summer chemistry,
Have all their might conserved
In treasure, finally.

The herbs and the gift of herbs are a charming but small matter;
the manner in which each herb preserves its identity, while drawing on the same sources of nourishment, is familiar — but odd
when one pauses over it. But it is more than this: it is one of the
permanent and reassuring beauties of the world immediately
around us. The language is precise, I would say perfect, at every
point. The fourth stanza, with its momentary suggestion of
rhetorical irrelevance, as it actually moves into the moral, with its
sudden citation of the imperial Stoic as an authority for the
moral, raises the poem to something very near greatness.

VI

THERE ARE A GOOD MANY minor poets in the twentieth century
who should be mentioned now and studied later by the historian
of the century when he arrives. I cannot claim to have found all
of them, but I suspect that I have found most. I will give as short
an account as possible of those who strike me as most interesting
for one reason or another.

Walter Conrad Arensberg (1876-1954)[6] was a wealthy man
who was a pioneer and brilliant collector of modern painting and
sculpture, mostly European. He collected pre-Columbian American arts as well, and found some excellent specimens; but there
are better collections. Both collections are now housed in the
Philadelphia Museum of Art. He was a friend of Alfred Kreym-
borg, the founder of *Others*, and he doubtless helped to finance
that magazine; he was a friend and admirer of Wallace Stevens
and Mina Loy. As a poet, he was a frail and discreetly sentimental, yet skillful, disciple of the 'nineties, sometimes in free verse,

sometimes in rimed. His most remarkable achievement is a very fine translation of a very difficult poem: Mallarmé's *L'Après-Midi d'un Faune.*

Donald Evans (1884-1921)[7] was another friend of Stevens, a better poet than Arensberg, a man who was probably influenced in a measure by Robinson, who probably influenced the early Stevens and was influenced by him. His best work obviously develops from the nineties, both in its wit and in his moral attitudes. He is expert, brilliant, and somewhat brittle. He should be recovered and preserved, at least for the present.

Agnes Lee (1868-1939)[8] was a Chicagoan, unacquainted with Arensberg or Evans, but deeply interested in the French poetry of the nineteenth century. Her best poems are *A Statue in a Garden,* as fine a piece of Parnassianism as one will find, but essentially a literary exercise; *Her Going,* solid in conception but damaged throughout by a measure of cliché; *Black Flowers and White;* and a small but very beautifully executed piece called *The Sweeper,* of which Charles Gullans has written a very inferior imitation. In general, her poems are poor. She translated Gautier's *Émaux et Camées* and a collection by Fernand Gregh, but the translations are not successful.

John Crowe Ransom (1888-   )[9] is known primarily as a critic, and I have discussed him at length elsewhere. His best poems are *Bells for John Whiteside's Daughter, Dead Boy,* and (perhaps) *Piazza Piece.* My essay on his criticism indicates the sources of the weaknesses of his poems; a foreign acquaintance once said to me that his poems and prose alike are too full of the sentimental Southern irony which characterized the fiction of James Branch Cabell and Ellen Glasgow, and I believe that this is true; Ransom is dated, in his style and in his ideas. But the poems mentioned above have a real charm.

S. Forster Damon (1893-   ) has been a professor English at Brown University and a well-known scholar for many years[10]. His best poems are *Family Portrait* from his second collection, *The Mad Huntsman,* and whatever one can find in *Nightmare Cemetery. Nightmare Cemetery* as a whole is more interesting than any poem it contains. This remark is not intended as praise;

the writing is awkward and somewhat stereotyped throughout, and no single poem really survives. But the book is extremely witty with a kind of desperate wit; titles, paintings, designs which accompany the text are a part of the wit. After the last poem, and on the opposite page, there is a print, perhaps a linoleum print, of a design that seems to be at once a bat and a skeleton, wearing a top-hat; in the middle of the bat there is the word *Finis,* with a question mark under it. Above is the printed inscription: In-scrutable to the Last *(or so He thought);* below: *(Nonnulla desunt).* The description sounds silly, and there is an element of silliness in it, but the entire page, in its own right, and in its place, offers something more. The book is a kind of abbreviated *Confidence Man* in verse; not an imitation, not as great, probably more readable. Two hundred copies were printed; the very nature of the book will make it impossible to reproduce.

Stanley J. Kunitz (1905-   )[11] is the author of three poems that should be kept in mind for some years to come: *For the Word is Flesh, The Words of the Preacher,* and *Ambergris.* These were written in the days (the late nineteen-twenties) when a good deal of attention was being paid to the Metaphysical School; these poems show the influence of this interest and are somewhat literary in tone (that is, are literary exercises, in a sense); but they are distinguished poems. This poet's work has deteriorated steadily, as a result of his submitting himself to worse influences.

R. P. Blackmur (1904-65)[12], like Ransom, was known primarily as a critic. Blackmur's verse was sensitive but loose; he had little gift for structure or for precision of thought. His best poems, as far as I know his work, are *Sea Island Miscellany* II and VI and the fine sonnet entitled *Phasellus Ille.* But these are extraordinary poems. Blackmur is the best of the poets whom I have discussed in this section of this chapter.

VII

THERE ARE A FEW other poets whom I would like to discuss, most of them certainly minor poets; since my association with them at one time or another was more or less close, I would like to treat them together. First I will name a few poets who were members of the Poetry Club of the University of Chicago.

The Poetry Club was founded in 1916; among the founders were Robert Redfield, later to become a well-known anthropologist, and Donald Peattie, later to become a popular writer on "nature." In 1917 Elizabeth Madox Roberts (1881-1941), Glenway Wescott (1901-   ), and I were elected to membership; another new member was James Vincent Sheehan, later known as Vincent Sheehan when he became a popular journalist; and still another was Maurine Smith, who died in 1919 at the age of twenty-three. Janet Lewis (1899-   ), later to become my wife, and whom I have already discussed, was elected a year later. The founding fathers disappeared almost immediately and left the club to the new members.

Miss Roberts later became a very famous novelist; her work, which was translated into several languages and was quite as famous abroad as at home, is now almost forgotten. She had been a good deal of an invalid throughout her life, was an introvert and temperamentally, at least, a solipsist. She was fascinated by subtle perceptions and by psychological oddities, and she cultivated mannerisms of style in prose and in verse. We all came together when Harriet Monroe and the New Poetry were the dominant principles in American poetry, or at any rate in Chicago. Miss Monroe wanted an absolutely independent American poetry, using native American speech, and we got Carl Sandburg. Yeats was the most popular lecturer before ladies' clubs in the country; his reputation was enormous; and he made the reputation of Synge. Synge was overrated, but he had solid virtues; unfortunately, he used a poetical variety of Irish speech which, I am assured, was never spoken by an Irishman, and he became an example of what the "native" writer should be, and a model. Miss Roberts was a Kentuckian and was obsessed by Kentucky folk speech and materials. Her first novel, *The Time of Man* (1926), employs the folk speech in the mouths of her characters, where it should be; but in this novel the same speech is infiltrating her own prose, and this infiltration continues rapidly until she is almost unreadable. And yet the later books, especially the second, *My Heart and My Flesh* (1927), are sometimes more interesting in certain passages: the accounts of the psychological eccentricities and agonies of female children who feel themselves isolated, and of women who resemble the children, are often very moving.

Her most ambitious effort in verse was a collection of poems about children, perhaps for children, perhaps not, entitled *Under the Tree* (Huebsch, 1922; Viking, 1930). The book is perceptive and witty; the protagonist is a child like the children of the novels; the meter is a bit mechanical, and this is curious, for in Miss Roberts' other verse there is usually a better ear. The book invites comparison with *A Child's Garden of Verses*; Miss Roberts is more entertaining than Stevenson in her observations of slightly eccentric children, but Stevenson is the better poet and should outlast her. In 1940 she published *Song in the Meadow* (Viking), which includes all of her other verse which she intended, it would seem, to preserve. The protagonist here is the protagonist of *Under the Tree* and of the novels, especially of the first two novels. There is the interest of folk poetry and folk speech, driven back into childhood and personal eccentricity. None of it is first-rate; some of it is bad; much of it is fascinating; this may in the end prove to be her most interesting book in any medium. Many of these poems are extremely derivative: from Janet Lewis, from Emily Dickinson, from Hopkins, from others. Many are not. Many are close to folk-song. In spite of the best of intentions, I cannot find a poem which I wish to quote; but the poems are interesting[18].

Maurine Smith was another invalid, whose life was short and racked by extreme pain; she was a finer sylist than Miss Roberts or than Glenway Wescott; her style was born in her—she was far ahead of all of us at the time. It is an amazing style for anyone so young, so handicapped, and of so limited an education. But her youth and her illness restricted her matter; the poems are very slight. They are better, however, than many that have been famous in our time.

Glenway Wescott published his first collection of poems, *The*

Bitterns, in 1920; his second, a small book called *Natives of Rock,* in 1925.[14] During the next two or three years he published a few poems, and his best, in magazines, mainly *Poetry* and *The Dial;* these poems deserve reexamination. His poems have little substance, however; they are rich in overblown imagery; but in their way they are very skillful. He abandoned poetry for fiction, and his early fiction is overloaded with adjectives and other descriptive rhetoric, imitative of Lawrence. His style became cleaner in time; *Apartment in Athens* is admirable, and the short novel called *The Pilgrim Hawk* is one of the fine works of fiction of our time.

These three poets are minor poets, but people of remarkable talent. The student who wishes to study them in detail will find their books and pamphlets and the complete manuscripts of Maurine Smith in the Poetry Club collection at the University of Chicago—kept, I believe, with the Harriet Monroe Collection of modern poetry.

VIII

Second, I will name a few poets who have been my associates or students at Stanford University since 1927. I have already discussed five of these: Edgar Bowers, N. Scott Momaday, J. V. Cunningham, Catherine Davis, and my wife, Janet Lewis. There are others who should be mentioned, most of them minor poets but some of them very fine poets and some distinguished in other ways; these people, who are not a group, but a series, or a series of groups, are far more impressive than the group which gathered at the University of Chicago for a few years.

Howard Baker (1905-   )[15] appeared at Stanford in 1927 as a first-year graduate student; this was my first year there as a graduate student; we met quite by accident. He remained at Stanford for a year, then went to the University of California at Berkeley, where he took his doctorate. He then taught for three years at Harvard, and then abandoned teaching in favor of raising oranges and olives in the southern San Joaquín valley. In recent years he has done a little teaching at the University of California at Berkeley and at Davis. He has written very few poems, none for some years; his best poems are very early: *Dr. Johnson* and *Pont Neuf* in particular. In general, Baker's style is very unsteady and his ear is bad, and he indulges in irresponsible associational procedures *(Ode to the Sea* is one of the worst examples: the sea is life, and anything on its shores gets into the poem). But the poems which I have mentioned are solid poems and a few others are good: *The Quiet Folk, Violation of Logic,* and perhaps *Psyche.*

Don Stanford (1913-   ),[16] now Donald E. Stanford, professor of English at Louisiana State University, is not to be confused with a Don Stanford who published commercial fiction in the nineteen-forties and fifties. Stanford is the editor of Edward Taylor, the colonial American poet, and is one of the co-editors of *The Southern Review,* New Series. Stanford's poems are few in number and very small, but the best of them are excellent: *The Cartesian Lawnmower, The Bee, The Meadowlark, Summer Scene,* and *The Thrush.*

Ann Stanford (1917-   )[17] has published four books of verse; the first three are derivative and for the most part dull. In the fourth she has developed a new style, in a few poems, which seems her own. It is not the kind of style which I most admire, but it is real. It is a free verse which is not really verse, in one of the best poems, *The Riders,* but rather a kind of casual but perceptive prose; which is a combination of such verse and of occasional blank verse in the other poem, *Union Station.* This kind of thing has been common in recent years, but has never, I think, been quite so well done. The matter is personal and domestic and could become sentimental but does not; the poems are honest and charming. Neither the matter nor the method, I suspect, can be carried much farther without repetition and ultimately self-destruction.

Alan Stephens (1926-   )[18] is a member of the English faculty at the University of California at Santa Barbara, a colleague of Bowers and of Momaday. His best poem is the first in his second book, and I suspect the first written of the poems in that book; it is called *Prologue: moments in a glade:*

Abiding snake:

        At thirty-four
By unset spirit driven here
I watch the season. Warily
My private senses start to alter,
Emerging at no sign from me
In the stone colors of my matter.

You that I met in a dim path,
Exact responder with a wrath
Wise in conditions, long secure.
Settled expertly for the kill
You keep a dull exterior
Over quick fiber holding still. . .

Rocking a little, in a coarse
Glitter beneath fine, vacant space,
The hillside scrub oak interlocked
Where year by year, and unattended,
And by abrasive forcings raked
Against itself, it had ascended.

And yet below me sixty feet
A well of air stood dark and sweet
Over clean boulders and a spring.
And I descended through a ripple
Of upper leaves, till noticing
That a rock pattern had grown supple,

And whirred. I quietly backed off.
I have considered you enough.
The rattle stopped; the rigid coil,
Rustling, began to flow; the head,
Still watching me, swayed down to crawl,
Tilting dead leaves on either side.

You in the adventitious there,
Passion, but passion making sure,
Attending singly what it chose
And so condemned to lie in wait
Stilled in variety — to doze
Or wake as seasons fluctuate,

Eyes open always, the warm prey
At best but happening your way.
And I too slowly found a stone
To break your spine; and I have known
That what I will have surely spoken
Abides thus — may be yet thus broken.

The landscape is that of the dry hills of Southern California, on the seaward side, in this case near Santa Barbara. I spent my childhood in similar country farther south; Stephens describes it with a kind of absolute precision, and he describes the snake with an absolute precision. The description is fascinating, all but miraculous. But what is the poem about? In the first stanza Stephens seems to identify himself with the snake; then in stanzas two through five he describes himself and the snake as separate beings, hostile, watching each other; in stanza six and in the first two lines of seven the snake is watching for his prey, and I think the poet (identified with the snake again) is watching for his subject—the snake's eyes are always open because he literally has no eyelids, the poet's because of his spiritual nature. And then the poet, separate and hostile again, reaches for a stone. *Too slowly:* did he kill the snake or not? We are not told, and the fact is troublesome. And yet ultimately it may not matter, for, either way, the poet finds himself in the same uncertain predicament as the snake at the end. The poem is very fine in every way: diction, rhythm, syntax, symbolism. It is doubtless an example of what I have called the post-Symbolist method and should perhaps be called a great poem. It is Stephens' best and one of the best of our time.

It gives us a very strange self-portrait: the poet is watching himself watching; he is also watching himself watching himself. He seems to be withdrawn from all other human concerns. One finds an approach to this condition in the earlier poems, certainly in the best of them: A *Walk in the Void, The Daimon's Advice, Anniversary Sequence* (in this especially), *Written from a Grove* (in this the least, if at all), and *The Sum.* These are all good poems, the work of an interesting mind; in most, the style falls just short of distinction, most often because of a poor ear. Except for the poem which I have quoted, the second book is inferior to the first: the dead ear shows itself throughout, especially in some portraits, perhaps symbolical, perhaps not, of insects, in toneless free verse, and in the experiments in syllabic meter which I will describe separately. But the poem which I have quoted has in a high degree the virtues which the other poems lack.

Helen Pinkerton (1927-   ) has published only one book and that a very small one which has had almost no circulation: *Error Pursued* (The Cummington Press and the Stone Wall Press, Iowa City, MCMLIX); the book contains thirteen poems, all of them short; of these, four, I think, would not be missed if omitted, although they are very well written. The remaining poems are very fine. Helen Pinkerton is strictly a devotional poet; she appears to live in a tightly closed world, to be unaware of most that is going on around her. Yet within these limits, she is a master of poetic style and of her material. No poet in English writes with more authority.

Wesley Trimpi (1928-   ) is an associate professor of English at Stanford, a specialist in the Renaissance.[19] He is the author of the best book that we have on Ben Jonson's poetry, and this, in turn, is the best book that we have on the poetry of the English Renaissance. His early collection of poems is the work of a talented undergraduate; the few later poems that he has published are distinguished, but he appears to have abandoned poetry for scholarship.

Charles Gullans (1929-   ) is another distinguished scholar —in the Renaissance and in the field of modern poetry and criticism. He is the editor of the poetry of Sir Robert Ayton (Scottish Text Society), and is an associate professor of English at the University of California at Los Angeles. He has published only one book of verse, *Arrivals and Departures* (University of Minnesota Press, 1962). The aspect of his work which most bothers me is his habit of borrowing phrases, entire passages, and subjects from the work of other people. This sort of thing has been done before: it was common among the classical poets; a good deal of it went on in the Renaissance all over Europe; Ben Jonson recommended it; *Lycidas* is virtually a mosaic of borrowed passages, and there are many borrowed passages in *Paradise Lost*. In our time Pound seems to have borrowed every passage that he could remember; he seems unable to distinguish between what has happened to him personally and what has happened in historical or legendary times and what he has read in his favorite poets and politicians. Eliot borrows quite as heavily, but with a little more of deliberate intention. But Gullans borrows more heavily than is customary and frequently because this seems to be his only source of inspiration. In *The Southern Review* for the spring of 1966 he publishes a poem on a painting by Poussin which is modeled closely on T. Sturge Moore's poem on a painting by Titian. The imitation is unmistakable; Gullans' poem is a different poem in detail and theme; it may be meant as a commentary on Moore's poem; it may be better, though I think it inferior. If it were a lone example, it would not bother me. He often borrows phrases, sometimes successfully, often disastrously. It seems to me that one of the most impressive aspects of the best poetry of this century has been its originality, its exploration of new themes and new methods; this originality, and the large measure of success in this originality, set it above the poetry of the Renaissance, or so I believe. And I think that Gullans often becomes a parasite upon original men and fails to make the same effort that they have made in writing their own poems. Yet he himself has written fine poems in which the borrowings or accidental echoes are no more serious than in the work of other men. His best poems, I think, are *Autumn Burial: A Meditation*, and *St. John's, Hampstead;* very close to these are *Daimon I, Daimon II, After Analysis* (he is not referring to psychoanalysis), *Autumn: an Ode,* and *First Death.* The style is hard and compact, often close to the plain style of the high Renaissance; the thought is original and often profound; there is a considerable variety of subject.

Thom Gunn (1929-   )[20] has published more than most of these people, and he is better known than most. Currently he is an associate professor of English at the University of California at Berkeley; he came to Stanford from England in 1954, and has lived in California since, except for a brief stay in Texas. His first book is negligible; his best work is in his second and third. The number of interesting poems is too large for a list here; I will name only a few: *Autumn Chapter in a Novel, The Corridor, Vox Humana, In Santa Maria del Popolo, The Annihilation of Nothing, From the Highest Camp.* The best of these is probably *In Santa Maria del Popolo,* which I quote entire:

> Waiting for when the sun an hour or less
> Conveniently oblique makes visible
> The painting on one wall of this recess
> By Caravaggio, of the Roman School,
> I see how shadow in the painting brims
> With a real shadow, drowning all shapes out
> But a dim horse's haunch and various limbs,
> Until the very subject is in doubt.
>
> But evening gives the act, beneath the horse
> And one indifferent groom, I see him sprawl,
> Foreshortened from the head, with hidden face,
> Where he has fallen, Saul becoming Paul.
> O wily painter, limiting the scene
> From a cacophany of dusty forms
> To the one convulsion, what is it you mean
> In that wide gesture of the lifting arms?
>
> No Ananias croons a mystery yet,
> Casting the pain out under name of sin.
> The painter saw what was, an alternate
> Candor and secrecy inside the skin.
> He painted, elsewhere, that firm insolent
> Young whore in Venus' clothes, those pudgy cheats,
> Those sharpers; and was strangled, as things went,
> For money, by one such picked off the streets.
>
> I turn, hardly enlightened, from the chapel
> To the dim interior of the church instead,
> In which there kneel already several people,
> Mostly old women: each head closeted
> In tiny fists holds comfort as it can.
> Their poor arms are too tired for more than this
> —For the large gesture of solitary man,
> Resisting, by embracing nothingness.

The poem is remarkably vigorous; it is far better than anything by half a dozen poets of this century who are commonly called great. The fragmentary but vivid description of Saul beneath the horse, and the rhetorical effectiveness of the explanation in line twelve and the four lines following; the unpleasant or pathetic people in the third and fourth stanzas; these things are effective. The command of grammar and syntax is admirable; the rhythm is vigorous without being very subtle. Gunn, as a rule, has a dead ear, and the fact makes much of his work either mechanical or lax in its movement, but here the movement is excellent. But like Donne at his best, Gunn seems merely to make his peace with the meter; the meter is not a medium in which he lives. Gunn has a better mind and a wider range of interests than Alan Stephens, and he has written a larger number of readable poems than Stephens; but in the poem by Stephens which I have quoted there is something which Gunn lacks—lacks here and in all of his poems. It is an intensity of vision, monomaniac, if you wish, for the moment, which renders the subject—total and in all its details —a living thing, moving on the page. I am driven to metaphor, but the quality is real. Bowers has it in a number of poems; Momaday in a few; Cunningham renders his abstractions in this fashion. Gunn's subject strikes me as potentially better than the subject of Stephens' poem, but his poem is not as good. Yet it is a distinguished poem, and misses being a great poem by very little. Like many of Gunn's poems, it exists on the narrow line between great writing and skillful journalism. Gunn's poems seem to come just a shade too easily.

Ellen Kay (1930-   ) has published only one book, *A Local Habitation* (Alan Swallow, 1958). She has abandoned poetry and the world to enter an Anglican nunnery. She tends to dramatize herself and her subjects to excess, and is frequently given to indulgence in unnecessary ornament. There are two poems which are worth keeping in mind: *The Reply of Pluto to Ceres* and *De Casibus Virorum Illustrium*. Both are serious and are very well executed, although the second employs an awkward kind of syllabic meter.

Some of my former students are derivative of me, although

345

few of those whom I have mentioned here, and those very little; some are derivative occasionally of some one else. But most poets have their antecedents. These poets resemble all other poets in this: they should be judged on their best poems. These are all very intelligent people. It has been a common practice for years for casual critics to ridicule my students in a parenthesis; this has been an easy way to ridicule me. And the sneer is the easiest of all weapons to employ; it costs the user no labor, no understanding, and I should judge that it raises him in his own estimation. But I think that the time has come when my faithful reader may as well face certain facts, no matter how painful the experience: namely, that I know a great deal about the art of poetry, theoretically, historically, and practically; that a great many talented people have come to Stanford to work with me; that I have been an excellent teacher; that six or seven of my former students are among the best poets of this century; that some of these and a few others are distinguished scholars.

If the student of the future, however, wishes to make a professional study of these people, he will find at Stanford no collection of materials similar to that of the Poetry Club at the University of Chicago; nor will he find any collection of modern poetry such as he will find at the University of Chicago, at Brown University, or at a few other institutions. Twenty or twenty-five years ago, a new head librarian at Stanford asked me to make a list of the books of modern verse in the Stanford library which should be preserved in a special collection. The number was not large, but I had managed to get a certain number of books into the library for my teaching. I devoted my free time for perhaps two weeks to making the list. Nothing was done with the list. Such of the books as have not been lost, destroyed, or stolen are still on the open stacks in very bad condition. I listed volumes, many first editions, by poets now the most famous of our time. On a few subsequent occasions I suggested to the more eminent members of my department the importance of such a collection; but I was given to understand that the materials were unimportant, that I, after all, was scarcely competent to deal with the problem, and that I seemed to be making an effort to magnify my importance in the department.

IX

IN DISCUSSING BRIDGES, I wrote of his theory of syllabic verse which is not really syllabic and of how it issued in the slow, irregular, more or less accentual verse of *The Testament of Beauty,* a verse which, in spite of its somewhat archaic diction and unfamiliar spelling, achieves an effect much closer to that of very good prose than one will find in most poetry, and occasionally with admirable results. Bridges' daughter, Mrs. Elizabeth Daryush, saw the error in her father's theory of elision for the eye alone and experimented for some years with a truly syllabic verse.[21] Mrs. Daryush is a very minor poet but at her best a fine one. She is a "literary" poet much of the time, as Landor is a "literary" poet. At her best she is a good deal better than Landor. Her technical virtuosity within very short poems is sometimes brilliant. I have been ridiculed for praising her by various people who have never read her, among them Mr. Thom Gunn, who has never learned to spell her name. She is just a good as I have claimed, no better; but better than any other poet produced in England between T. Sturge Moore and Thom Gunn. England has not given us much notable poetry in the past two hundred and fifty years; let us face the fact and cherish what there is.

I will quote a poem of four stanzas entitled *November.* She employs a line of five syllables in this piece, and rimes alternately. The principles of the measure are these: there must be a fixed number of syllables to the line—this is the measure; the number and position of the accented syllables must vary from line to line; unaccented syllables may rime with each other or with accented:

> Faithless familiars,
>   summer friends untrue,
> once-dear beguilers,
>   now wave ye adieu:

    swift warmth and beauty
        who awhile had won
    my glad company,
        I see you pass on.

    Now the still hearth-fire
        intently gloweth,
    now weary desire
        her dwelling knoweth,

    now a newly-lit
        lamp afar shall burn,
    the roving spirit
        stay her and return.

The poem is a very small one, but the subject is real; the diction
is skillful, sometimes a skillful controlling of familiar counters;
the rhythm is remarkably beautiful—it is the rhythm that renders
the other aspects of the diction manageable. The poem ought to
remain among the permanent minor poems of the language, but
I dare say that no one will read it with sufficient attention to save
it from dissolution. At present, however, we have it on the page
before us. I beg the reader to notice at least the rhythm; the
rhythm is a verse-rhythm, the poem moves and lives, and we can
hear it.

Marianne Moore began her career with a few short poems in
verse both regular and rimed, poems which have always reminded
me of certain poems by Barnabe Googe and George Turbervile;
she proceeded very shortly to free verse, and before long to her
own variety of syllabic verse. Everyone is familiar with her
versification by now: she employs stanzas, sometimes short and
sometimes long, with lines of different lengths but in recurring
patterns; the rime is usually regular; the rimes may fall on weak
syllables, on articles, on prepositions, or in mid-word; the rhythm,
if you can so name it, is merely a vigorous and continuous mechanical movement. My own chest-capacity does not always provide
me with sufficient breath to reach the end of her sentences. I
have come to find this kind of versification meaningless, uninteresting.

As a teacher of poetry at Stanford, especially of the writing of poetry, I explained these experiments in syllabic verse, the methods of writing "free" verse, the various forms of rimed accentual verse, and, of course, standard verse; I tried to explain the potentialities of these forms and their limitations. One or two students tried to emulate Mrs. Daryush a good many years ago, but little came of the effort. In the academic year of 1953-4, however, Donald Hall, now of the English faculty of the University of Michigan, was a member of my writing class, and toward the end of the year he began to experiment with his own variety of syllabics. I quote an example written later[22]:

> Charlotte, "the angel of assas-
> ination," is unrelaxed.
> She is not deep but she is tall.
>
> Charlotte is upright inches
> in front of the rest. Her skin
> advances while Marat's recedes.
>
> Marat goes rushing nearly
> away from the painting. (He
> must lift her for the guillotine.)
>
> Death is emotion. Charlotte
> is stiffened with will, and she
> will never move or make a sound.

In this poem, the first two lines of each stanza contain seven syllables each, the third eight, but with one exception—the first line of the poem contains eight. I am pretty sure of this, because I have tried to count the syllables; but I cannot hear the measure, nor can I hear any rhythm. The poem is dull in other respects; there is really nothing there. But my point at present is that the sound is dull; this is not verse, nor is it even respectable prose. Now Donald Hall is a charming man and possesses a good deal of learning, but he has no talent for poetry, and if this were the end of the story, I might better have omitted him altogether.

In the autumn of 1954 Thom Gunn came over from England and joined the class; Hall moved on to Harvard to become a Junior Fellow. Hall and Gunn had been acquainted in England previously. Gunn was at Stanford for about four years, except for a year of teaching in Texas. While at Stanford, he wrote his first poem in syllabic verse, *Vox Humana,* in lines of seven syllables each, with imperfect rimes in a regular pattern; this poem is the last in Gunn's second volume. The second section of his third book is composed entirely of syllabics, and his last book is entirely in syllabics. In spite of Gunn's rimes, I can detect no pattern that I can recognize as that of verse; the poems move like dead prose. During the year 1956-7, Alan Stephens was a member of my class, and Miss Ellen Kay was a member during all of these years. Miss Kay was one of the earliest experimenters with this kind of verse. Stephens was irritated by all of these experiments and wrote a poem entitled *The Vanishing Act,* a parody of the method, which appeared in his first book with the dedication: *syllabics for T. G.* It is worth quoting:

> After he concluded that
> he did not wish to raise his
> voice when he spoke of such mat-
> ters as the collapse of the

> Something Empire, or of things
> the folk suffer from, he sim-
> ply set in words such meanings
> as were there, and then, when he

> finished the final verse, van-
> ished in the blank below it:
> he'll reappear only on
> the next page (not written yet).

But Stephens changed his mind. His second book contained a group called *Sevens:* each line contains seven syllables, each stanza contains seven lines, and each poem contains seven stanzas. But unfortunately there are only four poems; up to this point there had been something almost Irish about it. I personally would have taken a sort of ritualistic satisfaction in reaching the seventh line of the seventh stanza of the seventh poem. I cannot understand why he did not go through with it; there was absolutely nothing to stop him. I quote the first stanza of the first poem:

> My wife and I stand watching
> our three small sons veer and skid
> in dust scattered with mica,
> points of light zigzag with them
> down the fragrant trough of air
> the road makes in the trees — road
> and roadside store are quiet.

The group continues like this to the end. One has to count, line by line, to be sure that the poet is obeying the rules; but the worst of it is that one does count, for there is nothing else to do.

In 1962 or 1963, J. V. Cunningham, a professor of English at Brandeis University and already past fifty years of age, taught as a visitor for a semester at the University of California at Santa Barbara, and Stephens seems to have converted him; for in a pamphlet entitled *To what strangers, what welcome,* a pamphlet containing fifteen poems which purport somewhat ineffectively to be a sequence, eight are in syllabics although not all are in sevens. The sequence does nothing for the individual poems and they do not constitute a convincing or interesting sequence; there is no harm, therefore, in naming the best poems, numbers 10 and 15, nor in quoting the second of these:

> Identity, that spectator
> Of what he calls himself, that net
> And aggregate of energies
> In transient combination — some
> So marginal are they mine? Or is
> There mine? I sit in the last warmth
> Of a New England fall, and I?
> A premise of identity
> Where the lost hurries to be lost,
> Both in its own best interests
> And in the interests of life.

This is the best poem thus far written in an unfortunate mode. Cunningham has two advantages over the other practitioners of the mode: he has more talent to begin with, more to be broken down and thrown away; and his poems are shorter. It is a good poem in a mild way, but it represents a somewhat melancholy decline for Cunningham. During the past few years, poems in this mode have appeared on both sides of the Atlantic, by men whose names are strange to me and whose poems I cannot remember.

These poets apparently try to achieve what they consider the quiet and honest monotone of prose; their effort is similar to that in much of the free verse of Eliot, Auden, and Robert Lowell. But, like these three poets, they seem to have forgotten that prose should be at least as well written as poetry; they mistake the casual diction of journalism for the diction of whatever it is they seek, and their poems are dull.

The poem by Mrs. Daryush which I quoted early in these remarks is a very small poem, but it is a real poem; the two syllabic poems by Momaday which I quoted at the end of Chapter V are also real poems, though minor. The medium is *used* in these three poems, it is doing something; the poems live. The medium has serious limitations, limitations which I discussed in my first volume of criticism, *Primitivism and Decadence;* but if one insists on experimenting with it, one should do something interesting.

X

WE HAVE BEEN TOLD that this has been a century of great translators. To what extent this is true is a question, but there has been some fine translation; it is scattered, unlisted, undescribed, uncollected; it should be studied, and I can give only a brief indication of what should be done.

There are two kinds of translation which are valuable: (1) the kind which gives us a fine poem in English, even though it may not give a good account of the original; (2) the non-literary translation which is accurate in a basic and lexicographical sense and which may help the reader with a limited knowledge of the language in question to read the original—or which may, with the addition of intelligent and scholarly description, assist the reader to a general idea of the nature of the original literature. The two kinds are distinct and should not be confused, and both are valuable. Nevertheless one may find an occasional poem which seems to belong to both classes, and many people have endeavored to give us poems supposedly of one class or of both which are very bad. The literary critic—and I mean the competent literary critic—is the only man who can evaluate poems of the first class; the specialized scholar is the only man who can evaluate translations of the second. The critic, of course, may very well be, and in fact should be, a competent scholar in two or three languages other than his own. The mere scholar, however, should be careful to stay in his place; he should not say that Pound is a bad poet because he misunderstood certain phrases in *The Seafarer* or Propertius. Scholars find it very difficult to stay in their place. The scholar could give us useful information, however, about poems of the first class.

Although Pound is not the first modern translator of distinction, he is the man who gave the modern movement in translation its first great impetus, and any study should begin with him. His version of *The Seafarer* and his *Homage to Sextus Propertius*, especially VI of this group, are his best, but *Cathay* and some of the Provençal versions, especially the early *Alba Innominata*, are very fine. From *The Seafarer* Pound omits the "Christian passage" in order to restore, I suppose, what he considers a pagan poem, and he has to make a small and plausible change just before the omission; he seems to have misunderstood seven or eight words which are easily available in the standard dictionaries; toward the end he inserts a line of his own, which is the best in the poem; he improves on the original and gives us a fine poem. The whole business of Propertius, in the original text and in Pound's versions, is much more complicated and should be left to an intelligent specialist. The translations from the Chinese were based upon the literal but unfinished translations of Ernest Fenollosa; but the scholars tell us that his literal versions contain errors. Pound sought assistance from Japanese scholars rather than Chinese. The style, though a little soft, is distinguished; from what I can learn, Pound's style does not resemble the Chinese in the least.

Pound's *Cathay* created an enormous interest in Chinese and

Japanese poetry. His translations of the Japanese Noh (via Fenollosa) created an interest in this form. The influence of these Japanese dance-dramas on the plays of Yeats is well-known; Pound was Yeats's secretary while he was writing them; there is a reverse influence, however, which I have never seen mentioned —from time to time in the beautifully cadenced prose of Pound's Japanese dancers there occurs a discreetly Irish locution. For years it was almost impossible to open a literary or semi-literary periodical without encountering an essay on Japanese or Chinese poetry, or translations, or at the very least imitations. The influence of *Cathay* on much of Williams strikes me as obvious, and it is, I think, a softening influence.

One great professional scholar emerged in the course of all this: the Englishman, Arthur Waley. His knowledge of Chinese and Japanese is said to be impeccable; his translations are said to be accurate, although if we consider what later scholars have told us about Japanese poetry, about double-meanings, for example, accurate translation of many poems is probably impossible. The style of his Chinese poems is modeled on the style of Pound's, but is less distinguished; Waley gave us excellent versions of the Noh, again less distinguished than Pound's. Waley surpasses all competition, however, in his translations from the Japanese Uta (short poems, longer than the hokku). This poem by Onakatomi Yoshinobu is the finest English poem which we have from the Japanese:

> The deer which lives
> On the evergreen mountain
> Where there are no autumn leaves
> Can know the coming of autumn
> Only by its own cry.

Yone Noguchi made some excellent translations into his quaint but often effective English. There were other translators in the 'twenties and earlier who deserve reexamination. Since about 1947 there has been a rapid growth of inerest in Chinese and Japanese in the universities; there are some distinguished scholars; some of the young men have written very informatively about Japanese

354

poetry and have translated extensively, but their translations are not literature.

The interest in Chinese and Japanese poetry was, of course, closely related to the interest in Imagism, and this interest inspired for a shorter time a widespread interest in the poetry of the American Indian, and many modern poets tried to imitate Indian poetry. Nearly all of the translations, however, antedated the modern movement in poetry, some of them having been made well back in the nineteenth century. The translations from the *Bulletins* of the Bureau of American Ethnology. We have already an excellent book on these translations: *The Sky Clears*[23] by A. Grove Day, published in 1951 by Macmillan and later in paper covers by Bison Books, the University of Nebraska Press. Day's book quotes more poems complete than one will find in any of the anthologies and his selections are better; the poems are embedded in his own text, which draws upon the work of the anthropologists to explain the poems. The book provides complete bibliographies.

From the time of Washington Matthews, the great translator from the Navaho, onward, the anthropologists seem to have tried for a precise rendering in the diction of good prose, but in a rhythm (unrimed) resembling the rhythm of the original. The best of these versions are models for all translators. These are a few translations from the Chippewa (Ojibway) by Frances Densmore:

> The sound is fading away
> It is of five sounds
>   freedom
> The sound is fading away
> It is of five sounds
> ••••••

> *Song of the Trees*
>   The wind
>   only
>   I am afraid of.
> ••••••

> Across the river
>   they speak of me
>   as being.

355

As my eyes
  search
    the prairie
      I feel the summer in the spring.
●●●●●●

It will resound finely
    the sky
      when I come making a noise.
●●●●●●

Whenever I pause
    the noise
      of the village.

This is Frank Russell translating from the Pima:

Many people have gathered together
And I am ready to start in the race,
And the swallow with beating wings
Cools me in readiness for the word.

Far in the west stands the Black Mountain
Around which our racers ran at noon.
Who is this man running with me,
The shadow of whose hands I see?

There are other translators and many poems. The poems are
sometimes as simple as they look, but they have marvelous precision. Sometimes they have meaning, religious, magical, ritualistic, or locally humorous, and these sometimes complicate the
poem profitably as a poem and sometimes unprofitably. Brinton's
translations from the Nahuatl, unfortunately, are somewhat rich
in nineteenth-century poeticism, but the great poem on death by
Nezahualcoyotl somehow survives the ordeal.

There have been many translations in our time from the
Greek. I have no Greek and so come to these translations as I
come to those from the Japanese or the Nahuatl. But the translators will find few readers as careful, as interested, or as ready
to be convinced. Yet the translations from Greek lyric poetry
leave me unimpressed. I have not read all, but I have read many.
The translations from Homer and from the tragic dramatists by
Richmond Lattimore, Francis Fergusson, and Robert Fitzgerald
are convincing at all times and are often magnificent; but the

translations from the lyric poetry, whether by the translators from early in the century—H.D., Richard Aldington, and Edward Storer—or by the more recent translators, such as Lattimore (again) and Dudley Fitts, leave me wondering whether Greek lyric poetry deserves its reputation. And the many translations that have appeared in *Arion: A Quarterly Journal of Classical Culture* leave me no more convinced. The Ojibways are more impressive.

The following translation is from Anyte of Tegea, by Richard Aldington:[24]

> Myro, a girl, letting fall a child's tears, raised
> this little tomb for the locust that sang in the seed-land
>   And for the oak-dwelling cicada; implacable Haides holds
> their double song.

This is one of the best that I can find. The version is given us in prose and seems to represent a real effort at accuracy. The subject is a small one and could scarcely result in a great poem, but it might be a fine poem in the original. As it stands, it is merely touching in a small way and is less effective than Yone Noguchi's version of Chiyo's lament for her dead child:

> The hunter of drangonflies!
> Today how far away
> May he have gone.

The poems translated by Dudley Fitts and Richmond Lattimore seem for the most part more trivial than this poem by Anyte, and so do most of the poems of Anyte translated by Aldington. I have never seen a translation of Sappho or of Pindar that made either poet appear interesting, although, as a reader of *Arion,* I have, heaven knows, seen many translations of both. I do not know whether the trouble lies in the poems or in the translators, but I strongly suspect the poems. Surely, Greek is not a more difficult language than Japanese or Chippewa; and the versions of Homer and the tragic dramatists are impressive. I have never seen an English version of a Greek lyric or epigram which came even near to equaling an imitation by Bridges, which I have quoted in my essay on Bridges: "Who goes there?" The poem makes me think that Bridges must have found poems in the Greek to admire.

In concluding, let me remind the reader of Arensberg's brilliant translation of *L'Après-Midi d'un Faune*. It should not be forgotten.

XI

THE TWO GREAT PERIODS in the poetry of our language are the period from Wyatt to Dryden, inclusive, and the period from Jones Very to the present, and the second period does not seem to have come to an end. In the second period there are only a few poets from the British Isles of any importance: Hardy, Bridges, and T. Sturge Moore in particular; and, in their various ways, Hopkins, Yeats, Elizabeth Daryush, and Thom Gunn. The rest are American, and many of the Americans are very great, and there are among the Americans some minor poets as distinguished as the best of the Renaissance.

Before my retirement I taught both periods for many years, and, as a result of almost endless reconsideration of the materials in both periods, I have come to the conclusion that the second is certainly the greater. The subjects of the Renaissance are in the main sound and important, but they are few and formulary; the methods employed are sound but simple and formulary; in spite of one's admiration for the best work, one comes to feel a deadly monotony in the period. The moderns to whom I have referred in this voulme ás the eccentrics have their own monotony; each of these concentrates on a personal mannersism, on what the modern politician would call a particular public image; their ideas are few, unoriginal, and unsound; but they are experimenting with their styles and in different directions and they have their interesting moments. And of course a few of them escaped from their mannerisms on a few occasions into fine achievements.

The great poets of the second period, however, and the best of the minor as well, have in their successful poems dealt with matter more original than that of the Renaissance and quite as important, and they have developed richer methods, and the best of them have been more expert. They have had to overcome

358

greater problems; they have had to think their way, as best they have been able, through a multiplicity of disturbing possibilities; the problem of adjusting their emotional lives to their intellectual lives has thus been greater; they have had to find their respective ways among a greater confusion of possibilities in the matter of poetic style. The poets who have managed at times to surmount these difficulties have achieved in the process a greater knowledge, a greater sophistication, a greater dignity, than one can find in any earlier period. They are more fully alive, more fully realized as human beings.

I have had neither the time nor the inclination in this book or previously to write at length of the poets who have temporarily, from decade to decade, had great reputations, some of whom may still have them: John Masefield, Alfred Noyes, Edgar Lee Masters, Carl Sandburg, Vachel Lindsay, Amy Lowell, Elinor Wylie, Edna St. Vincent Millay, E. E. Cummings, Archibald MacLeish, Dylan Thomas, W. H. Auden, Robert Lowell, Richard Wilbur. I name them lest the reader think that I do not know about them. The learned scholar who wishes to devote a history to these poets has my blessing.

I have not been able to write a satisfactory account of the minor poetry of this century, nor of the translators. I am an old man, near the end of my strength, and this book must be brought to a close; much of this chapter has had to be superficial. Many of the best poets now writing are much younger than I am, and the final evaluation of their work will have to be done at a later date and by later men.

Certain particular things should be done in the near future, however. We need a more exhaustive study of the minor poetry of this century and of the translators. It is urgent that we have editions of Mina Loy and Donald Evans and R. P. Blackmur, and these editions should be prepared by men of professional competence, not by young men recommended merely by a few local professors. When I say professional competence, I mean the inclination to careful scholarship combined with scholarly training (this is becoming increasingly rare in our universities) and with the critical intelligence which seems to be found only in men with at least a little poetic talent. Such men will find other things that need doing. Such men should be encouraged in our departments of English, if this is not too much to ask, instead of discouraged or driven out.

Finally, let us beware of saying that the best poets of our time deal with the subjects which are most important to our time. This would be a rash thing to say of the poets of any period, but it is infinitely rash in speaking of the poets of our own. This fallacy will mean in practice that we shall praise the poets who write of those subjects which seem most important to us, in our ignorance and stupidity: Anglicanism, Whitmanism, Agrarianism, Rosicrucianism, Communism, or something else. It will be easy to be moved by the poet who writes badly of our own emotions; in fact this facility has generated most of the criticism of our time. Five hundred years from now the subjects which will appear to have been most important to our time will be the subjects treated by the surviving poets who have written the most intelligently. The best poets have the best minds; ultimately they are the standard. When that time comes, my distinguished reader, his favorite poets, his favorite subjects, and all of the members of his élite group will have turned to dust.

Notes to Chapters

INTRODUCTION

[1] I trust that the aesthetic philosopher who is reading me will notice my adjective. The adjective is commonly and properly applied to fine Airedales, dachshunds, and greyhounds, to mention no more; but these breeds have different purposes and so differ widely from each other in their proportions. The proportions of the beautiful dog of any breed, however, are always pleasing to the expert.

[2] I have discussed the subject stated in this sentence in a good many places. See especially *Preliminary Problems* and the essay on John Crowe Ransom in my volume *In Defense of Reason*.

[3] For detailed discussion of rhythm and meter see my essay entitled *The Influence of Meter on Poetic Convention* in the volume *In Defense of Reason,* and my essay *The Audible Reading of Poetry* in the volume *The Function of Criticism.*

CHAPTER ONE

[1] The portions of this essay which deal with the sixteenth century are now in their third published version. The first was a review of *The Oxford Book of Sixteenth Century Verse* (1932), which appeared in The Hound and Horn, Vol. VI, No. 2. The second was an essay greatly enlarged from the review, which appeared in Poetry (Chicago) in February, March, and April of 1939. These speculations therefore go back for more than thirty years. Some of the remarks about current critical opinion may now seem out of date, but they were true enough twenty years ago, and I have let them stand.

[2] For a discussion of the essentially logical structure of sixteenth-century poetry, and something of the background of this structure, see *Logic and Lyric,* by J. V. Cunningham, Modern Philology, August 1953. This essay is republished in Cunningham's volume *Tradition and Poetic Structure* (Alan Swallow, Denver, 1960).

³ In a review of my own poems published in 1953, Professor Austin Warren expresses resentment at my naming poems in this fashion. He seems to find it insulting. It is not intended to be so. I do this regularly in the interests of clarity. It is pointless to praise or blame a poet without offering evidence. Furthermore, many intelligent people, especially young people, have not read all of these poems, and a few may be grateful for the lists. And I do not believe that Professor Warren has read the poems often enough.

⁴ The most remarkable achievements of the school are to be found in Sir Thomas Wyatt (1503-1542), George Gascoigne (1542-1577), and in the much later Sir Walter Raleigh (1552-1618), but it left a strong mark on greater poets, Greville and Jonson especially. Thomas Nashe (1657-1601) made two of the best contributions, and others were made by Barnabe Googe (1540-1594), whose only volume appeared in 1563, and by George Turbervile (1540-1610).

⁵ *Poems by Alexander Scott,* from a manuscript written in the year MDLXVIII, Printed in Edinburgh by Balfour and Clarke, MDCCCXXI, edited by David Laing. My copy of this collection is bound into a single volume with *The Poetic Remains of some of the Scotish Kings,* published by John Murray, Albermarle Street, London, 1824, and edited by George Chalmers, Esq.

⁶ The poulter's measure is composed of couplets, the first line having twelve syllables, the second fourteen; this is sometimes broken down to a four-line stanza of six, six, eight, and six. The only explanation of the name that I know is to the effect that the London poulters gave two extra eggs to the customer who bought two dozen.

⁷ My choices would be: Wyatt, Gascoigne, Sidney, Greville, Raleigh, Nashe, Shakespeare, Donne, and Jonson. Of these I feel sure that Greville and Jonson are the greatest.

⁸ This poem is a lullaby for the poet's youth and youthful vigor. The fifth stanza is addressed to the poet's penis. I mention this fact because several learned Renaissance scholars of my acquaintance have not understood the stanza. Quiller-Couch understood it and omitted the stanza from the *Oxford Book of English Verse.*

⁹ Published by Houghton Mifflin Co., Boston and New York, 1929.

¹⁰ *Logic and Lyric,* contained in *Tradition and Poetic Structure* by J. V. Cunningham (Alan Swallow, Denver, 1960). Cunningham argues persuasively in this essay that the line "Brightness falls from the air" should read *hair* for *air,* and at this writing two anthologies have adopted this reading. The reading appears to be incorrect. See *The Practice of Historical Interpretation and Nashe's "Brightness falls from the ayre,"* by Wesley Trimpi, scheduled to appear in *Journal of English and Germanic Philology* (JEGP) in 1967.

¹¹ *The Works of Thomas Nashe,* edited by Ronald B. McKerrow, with

362

corrections and supplementary notes by F. P. Wilson. Basil Blackwell, Oxford, 1958. See Vol. IV, page 416 and following.

[12] Some of the best poems in Fellowes' *English Madrigal Verse*, exclusive of poems by Campion and of poems usually attributed to him, are the following:—Alison:*What if a day;* Bateson: *I heard a noise;* Byrd: *I joy not, My mind to me, Where fancy fond, O you that hear this voice, When younglings first, Is love a boy;* Gibbons: *The silver swan, Lais now old;* Morley: *Now is the gentle season, Round, around, In nets of golden wires, Now is the month of maying, Sing we and chant it, No, no Nigella, Thus saith my Galatea, Fire! fire! my heart, Damon and Phyllis squared, Ladies, you see time flieth;* Mundy: *Were I a king, In midst of woods or pleasant grove;* Peerson: *Can a maid, The spring of joy is dry;* Pilkington: *Pour fourth, mine eyes, Stay nymph, the ground, Have I found her;* Vautor: *Sweet Suffolk owl, Weep, weep, mine eyes, Dainty Sweet bird;* Ward: *Sweet pity, wake;* Weelkes: *Welcome sweet pleasure, Death hath deprived me;* Attey: *Vain hope, adieu;* Barley: *Short is my rest;* Cooper: *Oft thou hast;* Sorbine: *Some can flatter, Sweet Cupid;* John Dowland: *Dear, if you change, Sleep, wayward thoughts, His golden locks, Fine knacks for ladies, Behold a wonder here, Flow not so fast, ye fountains, Stay time awhile thy flying, Go nightly cares;* Jones: *Once did I love, Shall I look, O thread of life, How many new years;* Pilkington: *Whither so fast;* Porter: *Love in thy youth.*

[13] The poem has been variously ascribed to Greville, Dyer, and Spenser. The virtues and the faults of the poem equally exclude Spenser, in my opinion. Dyer is possible. Greville seems probable.

[14] Perhaps I should comment briefly on the diction of the poem. "I did hope for your promotion" means "I hoped that you would promote me—to succes in love." "Succession" means "progeny." "Spectacles" is the word that our grandmothers used for the ear-hooked eyeglasses that most of us wear to improve our sight.

[15] M. W. Croll: *The Works of Fulke Greville, a Thesis.* University of Pennsylvania, 1901.

[16] John Crowe Ransom antedates me by many years in this heresy. See his essay *Shakespeare at Sonnets* in *The World's Body* (1938). Ransom's objections and my own are similar in some respects and different in others. My own tardiness in seeing Shakespeare's weakness is evidence (a) of the effect of established habit on critical judgment and (b) of the curious way in which a shifting mixture of the good and the bad can produce a result which it is difficult to judge objectively.

[17] *Shakespeare's Sonnets Dated, and other essays,* by Leslie Hotson, London, 1949.

[18] *The Well-Wrought Urn,* by Cleanth Brooks.

[19] Mr. Brooks commonly employs the same kind of defense in dealing with passages in other poems which he recognizes as badly written: for

example, in dealing with the epitaph in Gray's *Elegy* and with a passage in Wordsworth's *Intimations*. That is, he invokes as a respectable principle what I have called elsewhere the fallacy of imitative form.

[20] The poem was originally published, I believe, without stanza-breaks, but the poem is rimed in stanzas and the typographical separation into stanzas clarifies the structure.

[21] See *Marvell's Horatian Ode*, by John M. Wallace, PMLA, March 1962, Vol. LXXVII, Number 1.

[22] In the volume entitled *Tradition and Poetic Structure* (Alan Swallow, Denver), and in the essay entitled *Logic and Lyric*.

[23] *The Argument of Marvell's Garden*, Essays in Criticism, 11-3, July 1952.

[24] The *Daily Meditations* of Philip Pain were first printed in Cambridge, Mass. in 1668. The only other edition which I know is a photolithic copy of the original issued by the Huntington Library in 1936, with an introduction by Leon Howard. As to Edward Taylor, see *The Poems of Edward Taylor*, edited by Donald E. Stanford, with an introduction by Louis L. Martz, Yale University Press, 1960. Reissued in paper by Yale in 1963, with a new introduction by Stanford and none by Martz.

[25] These poems were discovered by Charles Gullans, who has done a scholarly edition of Ayton, published by the Scottish Text Society.

[26] One of Rochester's poems is an interesting curiosity: *Why dost thou shade thy lovely face?* This is a love poem which can be found in the *Oxford Book of English Verse*. It is a revision of a devotional poem by Francis Quarles, which begins with the same line and can be found in the *Oxford Book of Seventeenth Century Verse*. Rochester's revisions are not extensive, but they are interesting. The two versions indicate the close relationship between devotional and erotic poetry in the period. The poem by Quarles is almost as erotic as the poem by Rochester; the poem by Rochester is almost as devotional as the poem by Quarles. Rochester had the greater talent, and, as Quiller-Couch says in a footnote, he improved his original.

[27] The most comical aspect of this weakness occurs in the invocation to the Ninth Book of *Paradise Lost*. I have always suspected that some day some one would write an essay on Milton entitled *Easy, my unpremeditated verse!* The Ninth Book, incidentally, should be compared with *Ebauche d'un Serpent*, by Valéry. Valéry's serpent is a profoundly intellectual creature; Milton's is not.

CHAPTER THREE

[1] For a historical discussion of these ideas as they appear in literary criticism, see *The Mirror and the Lamp*, by M. H. Abrams, Oxford University Press, 1953. For a brief but lucid account of the associational doc-

trine in the eighteenth century, see *John Keats' Fancy*, by James Ralston Caldwell, Cornell University Press, 1945, especially Chapter Two, "The Rationale of Sensation," and more especially pp. 51-68. Neither Abrams nor Caldwell appears to understand the disastrous consequences of these ideas, but their historical accounts are of great value. This note does not pretend to be a complete bibliography; it is a suggestion for the young.

[2] See *Verb Tense in Blake's "The Tyger,"* by Fred C. Robinson, PMLA for Dec. 1964 (LXXIX-5). Robinson leaves no doubt.

[3] *Blake, Prophet against Empire,* by David V. Erdman, Princeton University Press, 1954. See pages 178-9 especially.

[4] Longman's Green and Co., 1950.

CHAPTER FOUR

[1] *The Poetry of Gerard Manley Hopkins,* contained in *The Function of Criticism,* by Yvor Winters (Alan Swallow, Denver, 1957).

[2] *Robert Bridges,* by Albert Guérard Jr., Harvard University Press, 1942.

[3] *In Defense of Reason,* Alan Swallow, Denver, pp. 75-89.

[4] *A Reader's Guide to William Butler Yeats,* by John Unterecker, the Noonday Press, New York, 1950.

[5] *Romantic Image,* by Frank Kermode, The MacMillan Co., New York, 1957.

[6] *Yeats: The Man and the Masks,* by Richard Ellmann. The Macmillan Co., 1948. P. 228.

[7] *The Lonely Tower,* by T. R. Henn, Methuen and Co. Ltd., London, 1950. p. 220.

[8] *Poems and Translations,* by J. M. Synge, John W. Luce and Company, Boston, 1911.

[9] "Siena Mi Fe'; Disfecemi Maremma" from *Hugh Selwyn Mauberly.*

[10] *The Identity of Yeats,* by Richard Ellmann, Oxford University Press, 1954, p. 253.

[11] For an example, let me refer the reader to "literal" translations of *Tout Orgueil* by Fry and Fowlie respectively. Both men knew French thoroughly and Fry was working with a French collaborator. Both men were intelligent and were conscientious students of the poet. The two versions of the sestet are essentially the same, but both are ungrammatical, and this fact ought to have put the translators on their guard, for Mallarmé is one of the most grammatical of poets, even though his syntax is seldom French. What we really have in the sestet is a suspended sentence, of which "le sépulcre" is the subject; this fact, plus the fact that the antecedent of "elle" follows the pronoun instead of preceding it, has thrown the translators off. The translation should go as follows (I translate the first three lines in reverse order for the purpose of clarifying the grammar): The sepulcher of disavowal/ gripping as if with claws/ the inevitable agonies of the past/

(this sepulcher) under a heavy marble (slab) which it (i.e., the console) isolates/ is lit with no other fire/ than the glittering console. The console is not a table, but is an ornamental bracket, presumably one of a pair, supporting a marble mantel-piece. The fireplace is the sepulchre of disavowal because letters (I suppose) have been burned in it: it contains a claw-footed grate or claw-footed andirons. The poem describes a room in a deserted house, a house which offers us only the dead rhetoric of a once-living grandeur. "The heir," if he should chance to come down the corridor, would doubtless bear a strong family resemblance to Nerval's "Prince d'Aquitaine, à la tour abolie." Ultimately, this is one of many poems on ideal emptiness, or pure poetry. This kind of thing is as remote from Yeats's talent as it would have been from his understanding. Any obscurity in Yeats is simple-minded obscurity.

[12] I have referred in this paragraph to *Correggio*, by T. Sturge Moore, London: Duckworth and Co.; New York: Charles Scribner's Sons, 1906; to *Armour for Aphrodite*, by T. Sturge Moore, Grant Richards and Humphrey Toulmin, at the Cayme Press Ltd., XXI Soho Square, London, MCXXIX; and to *W. B. Yeats and T. Sturge Moore, Their Correspondence 1901-1937*, edited by Ursula Bridge, Routledge and Kegan Paul Ltd., London, 1953. I shall have occasion also to refer to *The Poems of T. Sturge Moore, Collected Edition*, in four volumes, MacMillan and Co. Ltd., St. Martin's Street, London, 1931, 1932, and 1933.

[13] My account of this play is mainly a summary of a complete discussion written by Robert Wilburn Canzoneri in *The Plays of T. Sturge Moore*, a doctoral dissertation submitted at Stanford University in 1965. The dissertation deals with all the plays and relates their themes; it is in the plays that we get the best account of Moore's moral concepts. The moral concepts are closely related to the ideas about poetry which we can find in the prose and in some of the shorter poems, ideas which I have discussed a few times over a good many years. Canzoneri's book should be published.

[14] I discussed this poem in terms similar to the terms I employ here in an essay entitled *Primitivism and Decadence*, which was contained in a book of the same title, a book which is now a part of my volume *In Defense of Reason*. My first discussion of Moore appeared in The Hound and Horn VI-3, April-June 1933, pp. 534-45.

CHAPTER FIVE

[1] See my volume *The Function of Criticism*, the first essay, pp. 68-78.

[2] For better or worse, I have said something of them elsewhere, however: See my volume *In Defense of Reason*. There is an essay on Poe in this volume, and an essay on Very and Emerson. The reader may consult the index for fairly detailed remarks on Bryant, Whitman, and Emerson.

³ *The Cricket*, in an imperfect version, was first published by The Cummington Press in 1950.

⁴ *In Defense of Reason*, by Yvor Winters (Alan Swallow, 1947), *Emily Dickinson and the Limits of Judgment*. This essay was first published in 1938.

⁵ Any volume of selections of the early versions should contain the following poems as an irreducible minimum: *Drowning is not so pitiful, At half-past three a single bird, I started early, A narrow fellow in the grass, There came a wind like a bugle, The wind began to rock the grass, Farther in summer than the birds, As imperceptibly as grief, A light exists in spring, There's a certain slant of light, The sky is low, What mystery pervades a well, Safe in their alabaster chambers, The last night that she lived, Because I could not stop for Death, I read my sentence steadily, Our journey had advanced, It was not death, Great streets of silence, After a hundred years, I felt a funeral in my brain, Adventure most unto itself, The difference between despair, She died at play, I think that the root of the wind is water, The long sigh of a frog, The moon upon her fluent route, The feet of people walking home, To this apartment deep, "Heavenly father," The stars are old, I did not reach thee.* Some of these are great poems, most are not; and of those in the second classification some are worse than others. But all contain passages or qualities which make them essential. I may have overlooked a few poems, but I am right about these—these poems *must* be preserved, and preserved in the pre-Johnson forms.

⁶ *Emily Dickinson: Poetry and Punctuation*, by Edith Perry Stamm, The Saturday Review XLVI (March 30, 1963).

⁷ Actually, I employed this form once many years ago in some lines describing a mockingbird in a poem entitled *See Los Angeles First*, but this was not a very serious poem. About as many years ago, my colleague, Herbert Dean Meritt, wrote a doctoral dissertation at Princeton entitled "The Construction *apo koinou* in the Germanic Languages."

⁸ *Wallace Stevens, or the Hedonist's Progress*, in my volume *In Defense of Reason*. This is an old essay, but, with the footnote added in a later printing, covers the essential problems, I believe, of Stevens' best work. A good deal has been published since which I find of little value; within recent years there have been two Stanford dissertations on Stevens, however, which throw a great deal of light on Stevens' intentions: one by Grosvenor E. Powell, the other by Margaret W. Peterson. Mrs. Peterson uncovers a great deal of information about Stevens' reading and shows its relevance to an understanding of his work. But no scholarship can alter the fact that Stevens' work after *Harmonium* is repetitious, verbose, unnecessarily obscure, and, ultimately, a source of labor for the reader with which the reader can profitably dispense.

⁹ I have quoted these lines as they appeared originally in *The Hudson Review* for the Spring of 1951. In *Opus Posthumous* we find *air* instead

of *ear;* this destroys the precision of the argument and weakens the poem immeasurably. This may have been an error on the part of the printer or the editor. Or it may be a casual improvisation on the part of Stevens. Grosvenor E. Powell has checked Stevens' recorded readings against the printed texts available, and has found Stevens reading versions which have never been published, as if he were improvising on the spot.

[10] One can observe this, for example, on any of the Great Lakes on a quiet day in winter. A light wind whips the surface of the water and creates small ripples which glitter; in the distance, a calm settles in the midst of the wind, and the glitter disappears and we have instead something resembling shadow, and this calm may move swiftly or slowly in almost any direction. I mention this because so few people in our time have observed this kind of thing. I have met students who thought that Stevens was talking about artificial lights on water at night. The image is a marvelous perception, but the reader must share the perception, not invent another and inferior perception.

[11] See *Several Voices out of a Cloud,* by the same poet. This is a far less successful poem, but it supports my interpretation of *Exhortation.* See also *Apology of Genius,* by Mina Loy; and *Epigrams: A Journal* No. 23, and perhaps a few other poems by J. V. Cunningham; and, if curiosity persists, see *Two Old-Fashioned Songs,* by myself. And there are others.

[12] Bowers has published two books: *The Form of Loss* (1956) and *The Astronomers* (1965), both issued by Alan Swallow, Denver.

[13] Aside from a few early poems which may be neglected, Momaday has published these poems: *The Bear, Buteo Regalis,* and *Pit Viper,* in the New Mexico Quarterly for the Spring of 1961; and *Before an Old Painting of the Crucifixion* and *Angle of Geese* in the Southern Review for the Spring of 1965. To my regret, Momaday has devoted most of his energy to prose in the past three or four years; there is solace in the fact that the prose is distinguished.

CHAPTER SIX

[1] *The Quest of the Opal, A Commentary on "The Helmsman",* by J.V. Cunningham (Alan Swallow, 1950). This pamphlet deals not only with the poems included in *The Helmsman,* Cunningham's first book of verse, but with such poems in the next volume as were written during the same period. The dates were 1931 to 1941 inclusive. The poems were written between the ages of about twenty years and thirty years. *The Quest* was republished in *The Journal of John Cardan, together with The Quest of the Opal and the Problem of Form* (Alan Swallow, 1964). Cunningham has published another book of prose: *Tradition and Poetic Structure* (this includes the earlier *Woe or Wonder*) (Alan Swallow, 1960), and a pamphlet which is relevant to this essay: *An Essay on True and Apparent Beauty in* . . . .

Epigrams, by Pierre Nicole, translated by J.V. Cunningham (The Augustan Reprint Society, Publication No. 24, Series IV No. 5, Los Angeles, William Andrews Clark Memorial Library, University of California, 1950). His principal collection of poetry is *The Exclusions of a Rhyme* (Alan Swallow, 1960). More recently he has published a pamphlet, *To What Strangers, What Welcome* (Alan Swallow, 1964).

[2] The title is a phrase which occurs in line 23 of Book IV of the *Aeneid*. I have been told that the poem expresses Dido's sentiments, not Cunningham's but this is pure nonsense. The passage in the *Aeneid* is a part of Dido's dialogue with her sister Anna, in which she confesses that she is beginning to feel toward Aeneas as she had once felt toward her dead husband Sychaeus: "I feel the traces of an old flame." Dido tries to suppress the new love out of loyalty to the old, but Anna persuades her to give up the attempt. Dido's speech is a kind of Racinian tirade on this subject. Cunningham borrows a few phrases, modifies them to his own purpose, and writes a poem which is pure Cunningham, which really has nothing to do with Dido and which is not at all Vergilian.

[3] The crux of the matter is that if we guide ourselves to a choice by reason, the reason determines our choice. I can see how a Calvinist might argue that God determines our reason, or how a materialist might argue that our power of reason (its scope and quality) might be determined by inheritance or something else. But this is not what Cunningham means: he uses the word *determines* just as the Calvinist might use it; but the reason, not God, is the determiner. What we have is the use of a single word, or rather a single sound, in two opposed meanings. In so far as we have the power of reason, it is the one thing that frees us in some measure from determination.

[4] Miss Davis is a difficult poet in a way which I find irritating. It is unnecessarily difficult to get hold of her work, and this is her fault. She has published two beautifully printed pamphlets: *The Leaves*, by Catherine Davis (Bembo Press, MCMIX); *Second Beginnings*, by Catherine Davis (The King's Quair Press: mcmlxi). She herself printed both of these pamphlets on her own handpress. She has published a few things elsewhere, notably a group of epigrams called *Insights* in *The New Poets of England and America*, edited by Hall, Pack, and Simpson (Meridian Books 1957), and nine poems in The Southern Review for Winter 1965 (I-1, N.S.). I find this last group of little interest. The second pamphlet contains her best work, and I quote from a group therein called *Insights;* this is not the same group as that by the same title in the anthology.

CHAPTER SEVEN

[1] This is the only volume of my criticism still in the hands of any pub-

lisher other than Alan Swallow. And this is the only one I have ever written on assignment. James Laughlin IV, then a young man and one of our nation's most eminent skiers, told me to write a book quoting extensively and analyzing the quotations, so that the book would serve as a good introduction for the reader unfamiliar with the poet. I did so. Laughlin then discovered that MacMillan would charge more for the quotations than he could afford — or would afford. He asked me to rewrite the book; I declined. He then asked me to omit all save the most fragmentary quotations and to give references to page and line for all the rest. I changed the copy in this way. Mr. Laughlin then went off to an international ski meet in New Zealand and left the book in the hands of one of his recently acquired understrappers, some kind of poet. I received no proof sheets whatever. In due time I received six copies of a finished book. There are many errors, among them many errors in reference to page and line, and many of these so serious that no reader can possibly find his way to the passages discussed.

[2] The most interesting case occurred in 1963, with the publication through Anchor Books (Doubleday) of *English Renaissance Poetry, a Collection of Shorter Poems from Skelton to Jonson,* edited by John Williams. From Wyatt through Jonson Professor Williams' selections are almost nine-tenths my own, as I listed them in 1939, and his introduction follows my 1939 essay very closely much of the time, sometimes almost verbatim. This might seem less remarkable were it not for the fact that my selection of poems and my treatment of the century were largely new, almost revolutionary. At my request, the publishers asked Professor Williams to write a note of acknowledgement; it was written and inserted as a loose sheet in the front of the book. It does not give a precise statement of the debt, but it will do. In the first chapter of the present book, I also follow my old essay in a general way, and sometimes use it verbatim, and I repeat the old reading list. I mention Professor Williams, because I do not wish to give the impression that I am borrowing a large part of my book from him. His anthology will be useful to the students reading this book, for many of the poems to which I refer are hard to find; unfortunately, he often uses inferior versions — his version of Wyatt's *Tagus Farewell* is all but unintelligible, and he uses an inferior version of *The Lie,* by Raleigh. *The Oxford Book of Sixteenth Century Verse* will serve as a corrective for some of these errors; it offers the best texts but too seldom the best poems.

[3] Few of my readers, I am sure, will have difficulty in recognizing Pound's allusions and quotations and grasping the local significance; but the reader whose education has been deficient should consult: *Annotated Index to the Cantos of Ezra Pound, Cantos I-LXXXIV,* by John Hamilton Edwards and William W. Vasse, with the assistance of John J. Espey and Frederic Peachy, University of California Press, Berkeley and Los Angeles, 1957, 325 pages.

⁴ See my detailed discussion of this poem, *In Defense of Reason*, pp. 75-82.

⁴ Kenneth Fields has written an essay on Mina Loy, with bibliography appended; it is scheduled for publication in *The Southern Review*.

⁴ See note 2 above.

⁵ Janet Lewis has published four collections of poems: *Poems of Janet Lewis*, Manikin Number One, Monroe Wheeler, Bonn, Germany, undated; *The Wheel in Midsummer*, The Lone Gull, Lynn, 1927; *The Earth-Bound*, The Wells College Press, Aurora, 1946; *Poems 1924-1944*, Alan Swallow, Denver, 1950. The second and third volumes omit a good deal of early work from the first two; the fourth contains one poem added to the preceding volume. Her best novels are the four historical novels now published by Alan Swallow: *The Invasion, The Wife of Martin Guerre, The Trial of Sören Qvist, The Ghost of Monsieur Scarron;* Gollancz has published the third and fourth of these in England, and Rapp and Carroll the second. There is another novel, *Against a Darkening Sky*, Doubleday, Doran and Company, Inc., Garden City, N.Y., 1943; and a collection of short stories, *Good-bye, Son*, Doubleday and Company, Inc., Garden City, N.Y., 1946.

⁶ Arensberg published two books of verse, through Houghton Mifflin Company, The Riverside Press, 1914 and 1916: *Poems*, and *Idols*.

⁷ Donald Evans published: *Discords*, Philadelphia, Brown Brothers, 1912; *Two Deaths in the Bronx*, Philadelphia, Nicholas L. Brown, 1916; *Nine Poems from a Veletudinarium* (sic), Philadelphia, Nicholas L. Brown, 1916; *Sonnets from the Patagonian*, Nicholas L. Brown, 1918; *Ironica*, New York, Nicholas L. Brown, 1919. *The Poetry of Donald Evans* by Cornwall Hollis (a pseudonym for Donald Evans), a pamphlet for which I have no date or other information.

⁸ Agnes Lee's books were: *The Legend of a Thought and Other Verses*, published under the name of Martha Agnes Lee, in Chicago, 1889; *The Round Rabbit And Other Child Verses*, Small Maynard and Co., Boston, 1901; *The Border of the Lake*, Sherman, French and Company, Boston, 1910; *The Sharing*, Sherman, French and Co., 1914; *Faces and Open Doors*, Ralph Fletcher Seymour, Chicago, 1922; *New Lyrics and a Few old Ones*, same, 1931; *Under One Roof*, Ralph Fletcher Seymour, Chicago. The last two books appear to be without copyright; the last, which appeared shortly after her death and is dedicated to me, is undated. In *Poetry* for Sept. 1939 I published an obituary essay on Agnes Lee: I did not mention the last book, because I did not then know of its existence.

⁹ Ransom's two most important books of verse are both called *Selected Poems*, the first published in 1945, the second (A revised and enlarged edition) in 1964. These and all of his earlier collections are published by Knopf.

¹⁰ S. Foster Damon has published three books of verse: *Astrolabe, Infinitudes and Hypocrisies* (Harper and Brothers, 1927, New York and Lon-

don); *Tilted Moons* (Harper and Brothers, 1929, New York and London); *Nightmare Cemetery, A Hallowe'en Frolic*, by Samuel Nomad (published, or printed, in Providence, Rhode Island, in 1964) — *Samuel* is Damon's first name, and *Nomad* is *Damon* spelled backward. Damon's best single poem, *The Mad Huntsman*, appeared in a very small magazine called *Smoke*, published in Providence, Rhode Island, in May of 1931; this has been republished in *Two Centuries of Brown Verse*, on pp. 221-22 (Providence, Rhode Island, Bicentennial Publications Committee, 1965). Another and longer poem, unsuccessful, I think, but interesting, called *Seelig's Confession*, appeared in *Smoke* for December of 1933.

[11] Books by Stanley Kunitz are: *Intellectual Things* (Doubleday, Doran 1930); *Passport to the War* (Henry Holt, 1944); *Selected Poems 1928-1958* (Little Brown and Co., 1958). The poems which I have named appear in all three volumes.

[12] This footnote will have to be completed by posterity, for I do not have all the data that I need. In 1937, Blackmur published through Arrow Editions, New York, a collection called *From Jordan's Delight*. I have this book before me, and I believe that it contains most of his best work. Fourteen or fifteen years later he published another collection which I have seen, but with regard to which I do not have the usual information. The book is doubtless at Princeton. It was printed by Victor Hammer, a remarkable genius in the field of cryptographic typography, in a type which Hammer himself designed. The letters in this type resemble Mayan glyphs and are essentially inscrutable. The book is a fine example of printing for printing's sake — and the poetry be damned.

[13] See *Elizabeth Madox Roberts*, by Frederick P. W. McDowell, Twayne Publishers, Inc., New York, 1963. This book contains a good deal of useful information, bibliographical and other, and a fair amount of misinformation.

[14] *The Bitterns*, by Glenway Wescott, like *The Keen Edge*, by Maurine Smith, was published by Monroe Wheeler, Evanston, Ill. *The Keen Edge*, which is undated, contains *A Foreword*, one short page in length, by myself; *Natives of Rock*, by Glenway Wescott, was published by Francesco Bianco, New York, with decorations by Pamela Bianco.

[15] Howard Baker has published two collections of verse: *A Letter from the Country* (New Directions, The Poet of the Month Series, 1941); *Ode to the Sea and Other Poems* (Alan Swallow, 1966). Other books: *Induction to Tragedy, A Study in the Development of Form in Gorboduc, The Spanish Tragedy and Titus Andronicus* (Louisiana State University Press, 1939); *Orange Valley*, a novel (Coward McCann, Inc. 1931).

[16] Stanford has published two very small collections of verse, *New England Earth and Other Poems* (The Colt Press, San Francisco, mcmxli); and *The Traveler* (The Cummington Press, Rome, Mass., mlmv). He is the editor of *The Poems of Edward Taylor* (Yale University Press, 1960, with a foreword by Louis L. Martz); in 1963 this book was reissued in paper

covers with a new introduction by Stanford and with no introduction by Martz.

[17] Ann Stanford is a remote cousin of Don Stanford; both are remote relatives of Senator Stanford, who founded Stanford University. Neither ever met the Senator or any of his close relatives; they had not met each other until they found themselves together at Stanford University a good many years ago. Ann Stanford's one important book is *The Weathercock* (The Viking Press, New York, 1966). She is a professor of English at San Fernando State College, California.

[18] Alan Stephens has published two books of verse, both through Alan Swallow: *The Sum*, 1958; *Between Matter and Principle*, 1963.

[19] Trimpi has published one book of poems through Alan Swallow: *The Glass of Perseus*, 1953. His best poems are: *Oedipus to the Oracle*, a poem of some length in blank verse, which appeared first in the *Paris Review*, Spring-Summer 1957, and later in *The New Poets of England and America*, edited by Donald Hall, Robert Pack, and Louis Simpson, Meridian Books, 1957; and *On the Dedication of My First Book*, which appears in *Laurel, Archaic, Rude* a collection of twenty-six poems published privately by the Department of English at Stanford on the occasion of my retirement in 1966. Through the Stanford University Press in 1962 he published *Ben Jonson's Poems: A Study of the Plain Style*. He has published a number of papers on the Renaissance in the learned journals.

[20] Thom Gunn has published: *Fighting Terms* (Fantasy Press, Oxford, England, 1954, and later published in the United States in a somewhat revised version which I have not at hand); *The Sense of Movement* (Faber and Faber, London, mcmlvii and in the United States by The University of Chicago Press, 1957), *My Sad Captains* (the same two publishers, 1961); and *A Geography* (The Stone Wall Press, Iowa City, 1966).

[21] The poems of Mrs. Daryush were published by the Oxford Press (London) in small volumes spread over a good many years. In 1948 I published a small book of her work, *Selected Poems*, with a critical introduction, through the Swallow Press and William Morrow and Company (New York); this book is now distributed by Alan Swallow (Denver). The poems in this book are her best; my introduction gives an acocunt of them which I will not here repeat.

[22] From *The Dark Houses*, by Donald Hall, Viking Press, New York, 1958.

[23] Day, a man of almost my own age, took his doctorate at Stanford early in the nineteen-forties, and for many years was head of the department of English at the University of Hawaii. I believe that he has now retired. This book was originally a doctoral dissertation, done under my direction, the first, or one of the first, that I directed. It is vanity that impels me to mention the fact. Day has written many other books.

[24] *The Poems of Anyte of Tegea*, translated by Richard Aldington, with *Poems and Fragments of Sappho*, translated by Edward Storer. London, The Egoist Ltd., 1919.

Index of Poets & Critics

376

COLOPHON

Typefaces used in this book are Linotype Caledonia, 11-point leaded 2 points, with display handset in Perpetua 18 and 24 point. Printed by letterpress on 60-lb. Warren's 66 Antique. The binding is Columbia's Bayside linen. The book was edited and designed by Gus Blaisdell.

Many problems of design were solved by Frank Mahood, Art Director of the University of New Mexico Press, who gave willingly of his free time and whose advice was invaluable. For this author and editor express their thanks.